Computer Communications and Networks

For further volumes:
http://www.springer.com/series/4198

The **Computer Communications and Networks** series is a range of textbooks, monographs and handbooks. It sets out to provide students, researchers and non-specialists alike with a sure grounding in current knowledge, together with comprehensible access to the latest developments in computer communications and networking.

Emphasis is placed on clear and explanatory styles that support a tutorial approach, so that even the most complex of topics is presented in a lucid and intelligible manner.

Nikolaos P. Preve

Editor

Grid Computing

Towards a Global Interconnected
Infrastructure

 Springer

Editor
Nikolaos P. Preve
School of Electrical and Computer Eng.
Iroon Polytechniou str. 9
National Technical University of Athens
157 80 Athens
Greece
nikpreb@mail.ntua.gr

Series Editor
A.J. Sammes
Centre for Forensic Computing
Cranfield University, DCMT, Shrivenham
Swindon SN6 8LA
UK

ISBN 978-0-85729-675-7   e-ISBN 978-0-85729-676-4
DOI 10.1007/978-0-85729-676-4
Springer London Dordrecht Heidelberg New York

Library of Congress Control Number: 2011930257

British Library Cataloguing in Publication Data
A catalogue record for this book is available from the British Library

Printed on acid-free paper

Springer is part of Springer Science+Business Media (www.springer.com)

Smile, Smile my little soul,
and the world will be a better place...

Preface

Grid Computing was a vision of using and sharing computers and data in the early 1990s. The integration, coordination, and sharing of computer resources which are geographically disperse among different physical domains and organizations became an every day reality. This emerging infrastructure aims to provide a mechanism for sharing and coordinating the use of heterogeneous computing resources.

The term "Grid" is used as an analogy with the electric power grid, which provides pervasive access to electricity. Grid Computing has its roots in e-Science and has evolved from parallel, distributed, and high-performance computing. Grid Computing is a dominating technology that has undoubtedly changed the landscape of computer science. During these years, Grid Computing achieved to overcome every obstacle and challenge, and comprised an incontrovertible paradigm for future computer networks.

Up to now, this new evolving technology achieved to provide to its users the ability to utilize at maximum the existing resources across a network. Grid Computing takes collective advantage of the vast improvements that have occurred over the last few years, in microprocessor speeds, optical communications, storage capacity, the World Wide Web, and the Internet. A set of standards and protocols are being developed that completely disaggregate current compute platforms and distribute them across a network as resources that can be called into action by any eligible user or machine at any time.

The continuous progress in scientific research demanded for computational power leading to more and more powerful computer platforms in order to be able to solve high-resource demanding scientific problems. Many research projects and varied applications such as astrophysics, biology, chemistry, drug discovery, ecological modeling, mathematics, operations research, physics, and complex simulations are now driven by Grid Computing.

The explosive growth of computer science influenced the Information Technologies (IT) departments which have a vital role in shaping and conducting businesses orientation. The organizations focused on a more efficient utilization of their IT resources leveraging competition through a flexible and cost-effective infrastructure that fosters innovation and collaboration.

Consequently, tremendous capabilities and capacities that Grid Computing offers attracted the interest of academics, researchers, scientific communities, and computer industry around the world. Nevertheless, the question for the grid technology still remains. Grid Computing will become something like the Electric Grid of the twenty-first century.

The book structure brings together many of the major projects that aim to an emerging global Grid infrastructure. The present book aims to explore practical advantages and emphasize on developed applications for Grid Computing.

The contents of this book have purposely been selected and compiled with a reader focus in mind, in order to provide a comprehensible and useful knowledge for different readers with different needs. Through the presented practical approaches containing loads of information which came from real cases, this book aims to enable the reader an in-depth study of Grid technology. Thus, the primary target group of this book is academics, researchers, and graduates. Our purpose is to provide them with insights that can serve as a basis for further research on Grid Computing.

As a secondary target audience, the book focuses on industry and potential buyers of Grid solutions. Another aim of the book is to provide industries and IT department heads with a thorough understanding of how businesses can benefit from Grid Computing in order to motivate them to adopt Grid solutions in their enterprises. Also, system designers, programmers, and IT policy makers will learn about new applications and the book may serve them as a useful reference book. Also, systems designers, programmers, and IT policy makers will learn about new applications finding in the book a useful reference guide.

Thus, this book has a wide-ranging scope while it appeals to people with various computer abilities. It is written for readers with an extensive computing background, providing them an easy-to-follow path through extensive analysis and paradigms about the various Grid systems that are available today. Therefore, it will be a useful tool for researchers and professionals as it aims to help them understand and use Grid systems for scientific and commercial purposes.

The book received 153 chapter submissions and each chapter submission was peer-reviewed by at least two experts and independent reviewers. As a result, 27 chapter submissions were accepted, with an acceptance rate 17.6%. In this book 12 chapters out of 27 are contained which are divided into four parts: (I) E-Science, Applications, and Optimization; (II) Resource Management, Allocation, and Monitoring; (III) Grid Services and Middleware; and (IV) Grid Computing for Scientific Problems.

I hope that the reader will share my excitement and will find this book informative and useful in motivating him to get involved in this magnificent scientific field.

School of Electrical and Computer Engineering,   Nikolaos P. Preve
National Technical University of Athens,
Athens, Greece

Acknowledgments

Many people deserve my sincere appreciation for their contribution to this book by their willingness. Authors spent countless hours for the completion of their chapters contributing to this project. I would like to give them my special thanks and express to them my appreciation for their patience, hard work, and excellent contributions in their area of expertise. Without them this book would not be a reality. The contributing authors have done a remarkable work providing exquisite chapters and meeting the tight timeline.

I would like to express my special thanks to Mr. Wayne Wheeler, Senior Editor, for his interest from the initial phase of this book. Special thanks also to Mr. Simon Rees, Senior Editorial Assistant, for his assistance and to the Springer editorial team for their efforts and support. Furthermore, I would like to thank Ms. Lakshmi Praba, Project Manager at SPi Global, and her team for their great care in the book producing an excellent outcome.

Finally, I want to thank my family for their support throughout this project, and my institution for creating the necessary environment for this project.

Contents

Part III   Grid Services and Middleware

Part IV   Grid Computing and Scientific Problems

Contributors

Ján Astaloš Institute of Informatics, Slovak Academy of Sciences, Bratislava, Slovakia

Roberto Barbera Division of Catania, Italian National Institute of Nuclear Physics, Via Santa Sofia 64, Catania 95123, Italy

Department of Physics and Astronomy, University of Catania, Catania, Italy

Francisco Brasileiro Department of Systems and Computing, Universidade Federal de Campina Grande, Campina Grande, Brazil

Paul Brenner University of Notre Dame, Notre Dame, IN, USA

Riccardo Bruno Division of Catania, Italian National Institute of Nuclear Physics, Via Santa Sofia 64, Catania 95123, Italy

Santanu Chatterjee University of Notre Dame, Notre Dame, IN, USA

Alexey Cheptsov High Performance Computing Center Stuttgart (HLRS), Universtitat Stuttgart, 70550 Stuttgart, Germany

Christos Chrysoulas Technological Educational Institute of Patras, Notara 92 Street, Patras 26442, Greece

Leandro Ciuffo Division of Catania, Italian National Institute of Nuclear Physics, Via Santa Sofia 64, Catania 95123, Italy

Brian Coghlan Department of Computer Science, Trinity College Dublin, Ireland

Yuri Demchenko University of Amsterdam (UvA), Leuvenstraat 92, Amsterdam 1066HC, The Netherlands

Ciprian Dobre Computer Science Department, Faculty of Automatic Controls and Computers, University Politehnica of Bucharest, Office EG303, Spl. Independentei, 313, Sect. 6, Bucharest 060042, Romania

Piotr A. Dybczyński Astronomical Observatory, A. Mickiewicz University, Słoneczna 36, 60-286 Poznań, Poland

Mary Grammatikou Network Management and Optimal Design Laboratory (NETMODE), School of Electrical and Computer Engineering (ECE), National Technical University of Athens (NTUA), 9 Iroon Polytechneiou Str., GR 157 80, Zografou, Athens, Greece

Yi Gu Department of Computer Science, University of Memphis, Memphis, TN 38152, USA

Raul Isea Fundación IDEA, Caracas, Venezuela

Jesús Izaguirre University of Notre Dame, Notre Dame, IN, USA

Marián Jakubík Astronomical Institute, Slovak Academy of Sciences, Tatranská Lomnica 05960, Slovakia

Eamonn Kenny Department of Computer Science, Trinity College Dublin, Ireland

Roland Kübert High Performance Computing Center Stuttgart (HLRS), Nobelstraße 19, Hochstleistungsrechenzentrum, Stuttgart 70569, Germany

Giuseppe Leto INAF-Osservatorio Astrofisico di Catania, Via Santa Sofia 78, Catania I-95123, Italy

Aggelos Liapis Research & Development Department, European Dynamics SA, 209, Kifissias Av. & Arkadiou Str, Maroussi, 151 24, Athens, Greece

Diego R. Lopez RedIRIS, Spain

Constantinos Marinos Network Management and Optimal Design Laboratory (NETMODE), School of Electrical and Computer Engineering (ECE), National Technical University of Athens (NTUA), 9 Iroon Polytechneiou Str., GR 157 80, Zografou, Athens, Greece

Rafael Mayo Centro de Investigaciones Energeticas Medioambientales y Tecnologicas (CIEMAT), Avda. Complutense, 22, 28040 Madrid, Spain

Nasos Mixas European Dynamics SA, 209, Kifissias Av. & Arkadiou Str, Maroussi, 151 24, Athens, Greece

Esther Montes Centro de Investigaciones Energeticas Medioambientales y Tecnologicas (CIEMAT), Avda. Complutense, 22, 28040 Madrid, Spain

Luboš Neslušan Astronomical Institute, Slovak Academy of Sciences, Tatranská Lomnica 05960, Slovakia

Gabriele Pierantoni Department of Computer Science, Trinity College Dublin, Ireland

Vassiliki Pouli Network Management and Optimal Design Laboratory (NETMODE), School of Electrical and Computer Engineering (ECE), National Technical University of Athens (NTUA), 9 Iroon Polytechneiou Str., GR 157 80, Zografou, Athens, Greece

Antonio Juan Rubio-Montero Centro de Investigaciones Energeticas Medio-ambientales y Tecnologicas (CIEMAT), Avda. Complutense, 22, 28040 Madrid, Spain

Diego Scardaci Division of Catania, Italian National Institute of Nuclear Physics, Via Santa Sofia 64, Catania 95123, Italy

Nicolas Sklavos Informatics & MM Department, Technological Educational Institute of Patras, Notara 92 Street, Patras 26442, Greece

Aaron Striegel University of Notre Dame, Notre Dame, IN, USA

Douglas Thain University of Notre Dame, Notre Dame, IN, USA

Nikitas Tsopelas European Dynamics SA, 209, Kifissias Av. & Arkadiou Str, Maroussi, 151 24, Athens, Greece

Justin M. Wozniak Argonne National Laboratory, 9700 S. Cass Avenue, Argonne, IL 60439, USA

Qishi Wu Department of Computer Science, University of Memphis, Memphis, TN 38152, USA

Part I
E-Science, Applications, and Optimization

Chapter 1
Leveraging the Grid for e-Science: The Remote Instrumentation Infrastructure

Alexey Cheptsov

Abstract The grid technology provides great support for diverse scientific applications, offering them access to a virtually unlimited computing and storage resource pool. In the main application areas of the modern grid, much interest has recently arisen around operational support of instruments, sensors, and laboratory equipment in general. The complex of activities related to this topic can be summarized under the interdisciplinary subject remote instrumentation, where the term instrumentation includes any kind of experimental equipment and a general framework for remote accessing that equipment. However, efficient adoption of the grid by a concrete scientific domain requires considerable adaptation and integration efforts to be performed on different levels of middleware, networking, infrastructure resources, etc. The chapter summarizes the main steps and activities towards the establishment of a Remote Instrumentation Infrastructure, a grid-based environment that covers all of those issues which arise while enabling the remote instrumentation for e-Science on practice.

1.1 Introduction

Over a number of recent years, the grid has become the most progressive information technology (IT) trend that has enabled high-performance computing (HPC) for a number of scientific communities. Large-scale infrastructures such as EGEE (Enabling Grids for E-science) and DEISA (Distributed European Infrastructure for Supercomputing Applications) in the European Research Area, OSG (Science Grid)

A. Cheptsov (✉)
High Performance Computing Center Stuttgart (HLRS), Universitat Stuttgart,
70550 Stuttgart, Germany
e-mail: cheptsov@hlrs.de

N.P. Preve (ed.), *Grid Computing: Towards a Global Interconnected Infrastructure*, 3
Computer Communications and Networks, DOI 10.1007/978-0-85729-676-4_1,
© Springer-Verlag London Limited 2011

in USA, or NAREGI (National Research Grid Initiative) in Japan served as a test bed for performing challenging experiments, often involving results acquired from complex technical and laboratory equipment. However, as the grid technology has matured, the main interest is currently shifted toward the real sources of the processed data which are diverse instruments and sensor devices, many of them might greatly benefit from distributed computing and grid technology in general.

Remote instrumentation, which means providing control on distributed scientific instruments from within scientific applications, offers a promising way of how the modern grid technology can enhance the level of scientific applications usability, allowing them to have shared access to unique and/or distributed scientific facilities (including data, instruments, computing, and communications), regardless of their type and geographical location. The recent attempts outcome of such projects, as RinGrid (Remote Instrumentation in Next-Generation Grids), GridCC (Grid-enabled Remote Instrumentation with Distributed Control and Computation), CIMA(Common Instrument Middleware Architecture) which strive to design a service-oriented grid infrastructure for management, maintenance, and exploitation of heterogeneous instrumentation and acquisition devices, in conjunction with computation and storage grid resources, resulted in a Remote Instrumentation Infrastructure, which has been set up in the frame of the EU-funded DORII (Deployment of the Remote Instrumentation Infrastructure) project. Leveraging facilities of the traditional grid, the e-Infrastructure [5] should allow scientific applications to provide a full-service operational support of the experimental and laboratory equipment on the grid (Fig. 1.1).

The goal of this chapter is to address main objectives of the Remote Instrumentation Infrastructure deployment and introduce state-of-the-art solutions for hardware, middleware, and networking enhancement of the traditional grid that should enable integration of remote instrumentation applications and services within high-performance computing environments.

We will first present the main application areas and highlight some typical usage scenarios of the remote instrumentation coming from different e-Science domains; in particular, earthquake community, environmental science, and experimental science. Focusing on the identified use cases, we will try to generalize how the standard computation and storage grid technology can be beneficial for operational support of the remote instrumentation resources and in the context of the so-called Internet of Things. Then we will provide an overview of the work done in the European Research Area on remote instrumentation support on the grid and show the way how the available solutions can be beneficially consolidated in the Remote Instrumentation Infrastructure.

We will also introduce advanced middleware architecture which is outcome of the DORII project and allows users and their applications to get an easy and secure access to various remote instrumentation resources and benefit from the high-performance computing and storage facilities of the traditional grid. Introducing the main components of the architecture, we will present how the EGEE gLite middleware that glues together all the grid resources and is used in the big majority of the resource centers can be enhanced and adapted for use with the applications providing and utilizing remote instrumentation devices. We also highlight

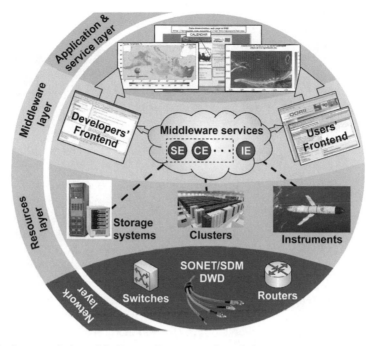

Fig. 1.1 Conceptual view of the Remote Instrumentation e-Infrastructure

the performance analysis aspect for the parallel MPI (Message-Passing Interface) applications integrated in the e-Infrastructure. Finally, we will address the production infrastructure fabric and networking layer of the Remote Instrumentation Infrastructure. Materials collected in the chapter rely heavily on results and experience of the DORII project, the authors are involved in.

1.2 Related Work

1.2.1 Remote Instrumentation in the e-Science

Instruments and sensors which produce, collect, and acquire large volumes of data are widely used in science and technology (Fig. 1.2). Remote instrumentation, which means a method of providing data acquisition and control of scientific instruments from remote locations [15], facilitates control and interaction operations with instruments. Remote instrumentation is an interdisciplinary task. Remote instrumentation allows users to get easy and secure access to complex and often expensive laboratory equipment from outside of their labs, as well as share them, enabling therefore lots of the collaboration perspectives.

Development and spread of the remote instrumentation technology opens new opportunities for many scientific communities. A great variety of instruments may

Fig. 1.2 Examples of remote instruments: (**a**) glider, (**b**) car sensor network, (**c**) synchrotron

benefit from the remote instrumentation, among them are such large-scale data facilities as a synchrotron (Fig. 1.2c) or even micro devices which, however, are often comprised in sensor networks (Fig. 1.2b) and therefore produce huge amount of data.

Below we present some typical examples of instruments operated in different e-Science domains, in particular environmental science, earthquake, and experimental physics applications.

1.2.2 Environmental Science

Environmental domain spans a significant range of e-Science and offers a number of instruments, such as Glider (Fig. 1.2a), which is an oceanographic device performing long-term and long-distance measurement missions. Glider is a typical device [6] used in operational oceanography (environmental science domain). Operational oceanography is a branch of oceanography devoted to monitor, analyze, and predict state of marine resources as well as sustainable development of coastal areas.

Measurements of physical, chemical, and biological parameters are the basis for research and development in oceanography [13]. Decades ago, it was still necessary to venture with ships to the location of interest and perform the measurements manually. This was costly in time, personnel, and funds. The first instruments which automate registration of the necessary information were deployed in ocean moorings since the 1950s. They can conduct measurements for periods up to 3 years. The measured data become available to the scientists only after the recovery of the instruments. In the 1970s, satellites caused another jump in observation systems. Large parts of the world's oceans could be covered in a short time and the data became available to oceanographers only minutes or hours after the measurement. Unfortunately, not all interesting parameters can be observed from a satellite. Especially data from the interior of the oceans is inaccessible to satellites. In the past decade, satellite phones, energy-saving microelectronics, and new materials lead to a new generation of instruments. These instruments are basically autonomous; some of them drift with ocean currents or move along predetermined courses and transmit their data in regular intervals via satellite to the scientist on land. Glider is the youngest member in the family of oceanographic instruments. This is an autonomously diving and slowly moving platform for measurements. Glider can travel for several months over distances of several 1,000 km and continuously perform measurements along their characteristic zigzag dive path [7].

A whole network of oceanographic scientific instruments, including a set of Gliders, is currently deployed in the Mediterranean Basin in the frame of MERSEA project [11]. In particular, they are used for near real-time observations at the sea surface and in the water column, producing such important characteristics, as temperature, salinity, and pressure profiles, etc. This task is facilitated by means of special numerical simulation models, such as OPATM-BFM, developed by an oceanographic institute from Trieste (Istituto Nazionale di Oceanografia e di Geofisica Sperimentale, OGS) [8]. OPATM-BFM is a parallel, coupled physical–biogeochemical model that produces short-term forecasts of some key biogeochemical variables (e.g., chlorophyll) for the Mediterranean Sea [8]. Physical forcing fields (i.e., current velocity), used by OPATM-BFM, are indirectly coming from Float measurements.

Each of the described parts of the oceanographic scenario (collecting the data by instruments and performing complex simulation on those data by applications) poses several challenging scenarios for integration with European as well as worldwide grid infrastructures. Moreover, a great challenge would be to compose the above-mentioned analysis phases in a common operation chain, a workflow which links the remote measurement with the computational outputs, including all the steps of the data downloading, treatment, and post-processing, as well as running simulation model and results evaluation.

1.2.3 Experimental Physics Utilizing Large Synchrotron Facilities

Experimental stations in facilities like Synchrotrons and Free Electron Lasers of ELETTRA (Elettra Synchrotron Light Source) produce huge quantities of data [1]. These data need to be analyzed online, which requires considerable computing power and often teamwork. The problem is even more difficult considering the increased efficiency of the light sources and detectors. Complex calculations are required to take diffraction images and convert them into a 3D protein structure. Similarly, complex calculations are required to produce tomograms and then perform an analysis of the results.

The results of these analyses often need to be visualized by a distributed team and used to modify interactively the data collection strategy. Data from instruments and sensors are saved in distributed repositories, computational models are executed, and an interactive data mining process is eventually used to extract useful knowledge.

This kind of application requires both the support of a standard grid computing environment, i.e., a Virtual Organization (VO), a set of distributed storage and computing resources and some resource brokering mechanism, a workflow definition and execution environment, and the capability to integrate instruments (the detectors) and interactively collaborate in the data analysis process. A Quality-of-Service (QoS) handling mechanism is necessary to use the available network structure effectively. This poses a great challenge to efficient use of the application using facilitates provided by the traditional grid.

1.2.4 Earthquake Simulation Using Sensor Networks

Sensor networks are used in many industrial and civilian application areas, including industrial process monitoring and control, detection of and response to natural disasters, and many others. For example, EUCENTRE (European Centre for Training and Research in Earthquake Engineering) has developed a number of applications which perform pseudo-dynamic simulations using substructuring. This means that a part of the building being simulated is a virtual structure, while another part is a physical specimen placed in a laboratory and equipped with actuators (to apply forces or displacements) and sensors (to measure reactions). The simulation server collects the data provided by the sensors and the calculated response of the virtual building components, putting all together in order to represent this set as a unique structure. All the applications require both the support of a standard grid computing environment, which is a virtual organization, a set of distributed storage and computing resources and some resource brokering mechanism, a workflow definition and execution environment, and the capability to integrate instruments (the detectors) and interactively collaborate in the data analysis process.

Such systems also take advantage of remote instrumentation in terms of access to computational capabilities for speeding up the calculation of shake maps. In particular, fast shake maps are very useful for damage assessment in a post-seismic scenario, when it is necessary to coordinate in a safe and quick way rescue team operations. A network of seismic sensors should be deployed and connected by means of a wireless connection to a grid infrastructure. In the presence of an earthquake, all the typical seismic parameters (epicenter, magnitude, ground acceleration, etc.) are estimated and then used to build fragility curves. In the easiest implementation, the application has only to perform an interpolation accessing a database of use cases already calculated (with a nontrivial computing effort, simplified by the grid), in order to fit the current situation. In the other case, the map is calculated immediately after the earthquake parameters are recorded.

The materials collected above present only some of many examples of scientific instruments which are utilized in e-Science and might greatly benefit from remote instrumentation. Summarizing requirements coming from the mentioned domains, e-Science generally lacks a stable and reliable infrastructure to support complex experiments based on remote instrumentation.

Over a number of the last years, the European as well as worldwide grid infrastructure have grown substantially, providing significant computing and storage resources to various research and development communities. Efficiency of the remote instrumentation might also be largely achieved by integration with the existing infrastructures, like grids. However, due to complexity of adaptation and integration efforts needed, the traditional infrastructures haven't been successfully applied for most of those domains so far.

1.2.5   Toward an Advanced e-Infrastructure for Remote Instrumentation

In recent years, the progress of high-performance computing and networking has enabled deployment of large-scale infrastructures, like those promoted by the OSG and TeraGrid projects in USA, NAREGI in Japan, or EGEE and DEISA in the European Research Area. These infrastructures provide powerful distributed computing environments with thousands of CPU cores and petabytes of storage space available for complex application. However, grid can also greatly support remote instrumentation, offering Remote Instrumentation Services which go far beyond facilitating networked access to remote instrument resources. Providing Remote Instrumentation Services should establish a way of fully integrating instruments (including laboratory equipment, large-scale experimental facilities, and sensor networks) in a service-oriented architecture (SOA), where users can view and operate them in the same fashion with computing and storage resources offered by the traditional grid.

Initiatives that strive to address issues of remote accessing and operating diverse remote instruments and experimental equipment has been particularly studied and developed in the frame of several European projects, such as RinGRID and GRIDCC, or CIMA in USA. The first evaluation of the synergy of remote instrumentation with next-generation high-speed communication networks and grid infrastructure that allows for better usage of the existing, often underutilized research instrumentation, as well as of the networking and computation aspects for providing instrumentation as a service was done in the frame of the RinGRID project. First recommendations concerning the usage of scientific instrumentation in a grid environment, build on the Open Grid Services Architecture (OSGA), were collected by RinGrid. The requirements that are implied or directly suggested by the users, like security and policies, instrument virtualization, monitoring and accounting, workflow and execution management, but even presence of a local collaborator, were elaborated on at this point as well. Moreover, RinGrid worked out the development guidelines for the Remote Instrumentation Service interfaces that should be provided within a grid environment.

A practical attempt to implement the solutions proposed by RinGrid was exemplarily performed within the GRIDCC project. The main outcome of the project was the development of the first prototype of Instrument Element, a special middleware for interconnecting an instrument/service with a grid infrastructure, based on current grid implementation standards (mainly adopted by EGEE, the largest European grid infrastructure for e-Science). Similar attempts, but for the Globus-based grids, were performed within the CIMA project.

However, irrespective of a concrete infrastructure, the extension of one with the complex of activities for providing Remote Instrumentation Services is not trivial and straightforward, and requires addressing a number of issues in middleware and network architecture design, application development, and instrumentation and measurement-related aspects.

The Deployment of Remote Instrumentation Infrastructure (DORII) project aims to establish a so-called e-Infrastructure, an ICT-based research environment, in which all researchers – whether working in the context of their home institutions or national or multinational scientific initiatives – have shared access to unique or distributed scientific facilities including data, instruments, computing, and communications, regardless of their type and location in the world [10].

DORII aims at promoting the e-Infrastructure among those e-Science domains with experimental equipment where the ICT technology is still not presented at the appropriate level and instrumentation is not integrated in any infrastructure. The DORII e-Infrastructure is thus intended to close the gap between the grid and scientific domains, providing and utilizing Remote Instrumentation Services, in particular in the communities presented above (environmental science, earthquake, and experimental physics).

Among the requirements collected in RinGRID, the DORII e-Infrastructure focus especially on the following:

- To provide a set of standard capabilities to support remote instrumentation in a grid environment, including a suitable abstraction of the remote instrumentation, in order to make it visible as a manageable grid resource
- To design a service-oriented grid architecture that enables to integrate instruments as a service
- To set up a flexible, problem-oriented middleware architecture, which not only provides users with services for remote instrumentation, but also enables full-fledged user-level tools for promoting the e-Infrastructure to the end user and application developers, hiding the complexity of the underlying grid technology

The following strategic goals and objectives were recognized for the Remote Instrumentation Infrastructure [10]:

- Integration of instrumentation and remote instrumentation applications with the e-Infrastructure and maintenance on the production level
- Adaptation of the e-Infrastructure functionality across selected areas of science and engineering

- Deployment and management of the persistent, production quality, distributed instrumentation integrated with the e-Infrastructure
- Promotion of the e-Infrastructure services in the integrated environments of scientific and engineering instrumentation, networking, visualization, and computational infrastructures
- Generalization and deployment of a framework environment that can be used for fast prototyping in other application environments

The Remote Instrumentation Infrastructure offers a promising vision how the modern grid computing technology can support and enhance the level of managing, maintaining, and exploiting heterogeneous instruments and acquisition devices for the e-Science. In the next section, the basic aspects of the Remote Instrumentation Infrastructure deployment and further use are presented, with focus on the know-hows in the middleware architecture, infrastructure as well as networking management solutions.

1.3 Remote Instrumentation Infrastructure for e-Science

1.3.1 Middleware Architecture

Middleware composes an important layer of the Remote Instrumentation Infrastructure. The middleware architecture is intended to promote the e-Infrastructure to various users (application providers, end users in the industrial cycle, etc.) and their applications, hiding the complexity of the grid technology and offering along with diverse Remote Instrumentation Services also rich featured user-level clients for efficient accessing, controlling, and utilization of those services [3].

The application requests, in particular presented in the previous section, cover the following main components to be included into the architecture:

- A set of flexible grid services for interconnection of instrumentation with the infrastructure
- A full-featured GUI toolkit (analog of the control room) that enables easy access and discovering of grid resources and services and serves a rich user collaborative suite
- A workflow management and monitoring system for setting up and management of complex scientific experiments performed on the infrastructure
- An integrated application development environment, with enhanced "on-grid" debugging and deployment features
- A visualization and analysis back end for the data produced by applications in the infrastructure
- Parallel application implementation libraries, with integrated performance analysis possibilities and back ends for visualization of performance characteristics

By setting up the middleware architecture, conforming to the requests collected above, the Remote Instrumentation Infrastructure has greatly reused the sustainable

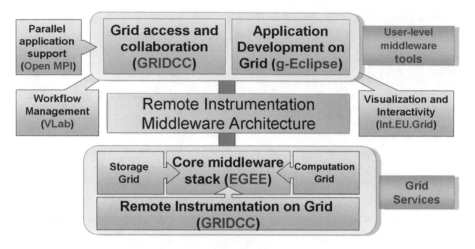

Fig. 1.3 Middleware architecture for the Remote Instrumentation Infrastructure

outcomes of several projects performed in the European Research Area, instead of the development from the scratch (Fig. 1.3).

The tools and services which are outcome of those projects and proved their usability for an e-Infrastructure in practice make up a core of the middleware architecture for the Remote Instrumentation Infrastructure. Adoption of those tools from the existing releases as well as necessary improvement and adaptation to the requirements to the Remote Instrumentation Infrastructure has been performed within the DORII project, ensuring that the full potential of the grid technology is enabled for e-Science.

The architecture (Fig. 1.4) relies heavily on EGEE project's outcome, which has set up the world's largest grid infrastructure with significant computing and storage resources as well as developed middleware (gLite) for interconnecting those resources. The basic gLite computing and storage services are extended in the architecture by the Instrument Services for interactively control and monitoring of the remote instruments, that are outcome of the GRIDCC and DORII projects.

The core of the Instrument Services is the Instrument Element (IE) middleware that represents a virtualization of diverse data sources and provides the traditional grid with an abstraction of a real instrument/sensor, and a grid user with an interactive interface to remotely control an instrument. Instrument Element greatly extends the functionality of the e-Infrastructure to interactively control and monitor the remote instruments both by the users and from within the applications.

In addition to the basic grid services, including the Instrument Element, the architecture consolidates a selection of the user-level tools that are although not considered as a part of the infrastructure as the users can glue them to the applications on demand but they facilitate fulfillment of the extra requirements of the applications to the e-Infrastructure, such as easy accessing the grid services and resources, workflow management, interactivity, and control of the simulation as well as data and result visualization. Below we provide a high-level description of those

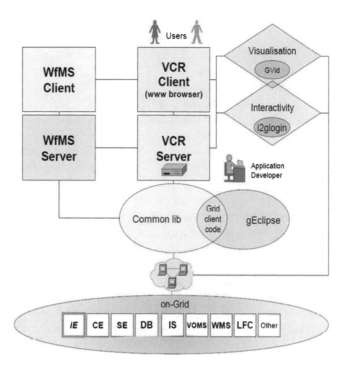

Fig. 1.4 Middleware architecture main tools and services

middleware architecture components as well as adopted remote instrumentation specific grid services.

1.3.2   Basic Grid Services

The middleware architecture relies on gLite – the EGEE middleware redistribution that glues together the resource centers included to the Remote Instrumentation Infrastructure. The gLite middleware consists of services divided into four groups: information system, job management system, data management system, and security-related services.

The information system provides detailed information about the services as well as available resources of the infrastructure. This information includes, for example, type and amount of computational, storage and instrument resources, location of services that is necessary in order to access those resources, etc. The information system is used in various tasks such as resource matching and job brokering regarding the specific user requirements. Monitoring and accounting services rely on the information system as well. Information system's services used for the purposes of the Remote Instrumentation Infrastructure are: the Berkeley Database Information Index (BDII) and the R-GMA that provides accounting information.

The job management system provides access to the e-Infrastructure's computational resources. The basic services of the job management system include the Computing Element (CE) and Workload Management System (WMS). CE is a generic interface to a computing resource (grid site) consisting of a number of the Worker Nodes, CPU cores, the user application is executing on. CE supports various local queue management systems (including PBS, Torq, and other common) for starting user jobs on the site's Worker Nodes. The Workload Management System (WMS) is a high-level service that arranges the execution of user jobs on the available CE (among ones assigned to the user's virtual organization). The assignment of a CE for the concrete user job performs is based on the resource availability at time of submitting the job as well as characteristics of the grid sites, acquired from the information system.

The data management system consists of three major components: data storage, data catalogue, data scheduling, and metadata services. The Storage Element (SE) is a grid service that allows the users to store and manage data files in the file space assigned to their virtual organization. Data is stored on disk pool servers and can be accessed via different data access protocols (e.g., gsiftp). The LCG File Catalogue (LFC) provides a central registration service for data files distributed amongst the various SEs, offering the users to index their data files in a unix-like namespace, irrespective of the location on a concrete SE.

The security services provided by gLite are mainly presented by the Virtual Organization Membership Service (VOMS). VOMS is a system for managing authorization data within virtual organizations. VOMS provides a database of user roles and capabilities and a set of tools for accessing and manipulating the database and using the database contents to generate grid credentials for users when needed. Another useful service might be provided by the Remote Instrumentation Infrastructure is the proxy renewal (MyProxy) service, which supports longtime running jobs and applications that need a valid proxy certificate throughout their lifetime.

1.3.3 Instrument Services

Further to gLite, the instrument services which are developed within the DORII project and provide remote access to the instruments integrated to the e-Infrastructure, are included to the architecture.

The Instrument Element (IE) middleware represents a virtualization of data sources in a grid environment. Instrument Element also adds a possibility to include such devices as scientific instruments and sensors in the data elaboration process [3]. The main goal of the Instrument Element is to provide users with a simple way of attaching their scientific instrumentation to basic grid services. The IE framework offers a common interface for accessing instrumentation and provides support for secure access control, concurrency control, simple grid storage access, and JMS publishing (Fig. 1.5).

Instruments and sensors are interfaced via Instrument Managers that permits connections to physical devices or more precisely, their control systems. Instrument Managers consist mainly of the Java client code for the instrumentation and should run inside the IE installation (Tomcat servlet container).

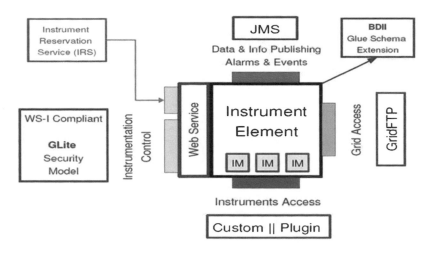

Fig. 1.5 The instrument element architecture

1.3.4 Virtual Control Room (VCR)

VCR is a rich featured, single sign-on web portal that serves a central front-end to the e-Infrastructure with an intuitive and user-friendly interface (Fig. 1.6). VCR was originally developed during the GRIDCC project and the development is pursued within the DORII projects. VCR serves a complete desktop environment for the e-Infrastructure's end users [3].

VCR allows users to get easy access to the e-Infrastructure services (CE, SE, and IE). Upon the user registration, short-term (usually 12 h) proxy certificates are created. Such certificates are used then for authentication at computing and storage resources belonging to the user's virtual organization. While the proxy is valid, the users can discover the grid resources and services (including instrumentation services), browse the SE content (including LFC), as well as create and submit JDL jobs to the WMS. Moreover, VCR also serves a complete user collaborative environment, offering a set of groupware tools for support of scientific teamwork that includes an e-logbook, integrated chat, wiki-like help system and people and resource browsers.

1.3.5 Workflow Management System (WfMS)

The traditional batch processing of grid jobs and workflow execution based on file exchange between the components is not suitable in most of the remote instrumentation scenarios. For support of the applications that perform complex experiments described through workflows, the architecture includes a Workflow Management System (WfMS). The main goal of the WfMS is to support users in definition, management and monitoring of the measurement scenarios [3]. The first prototype

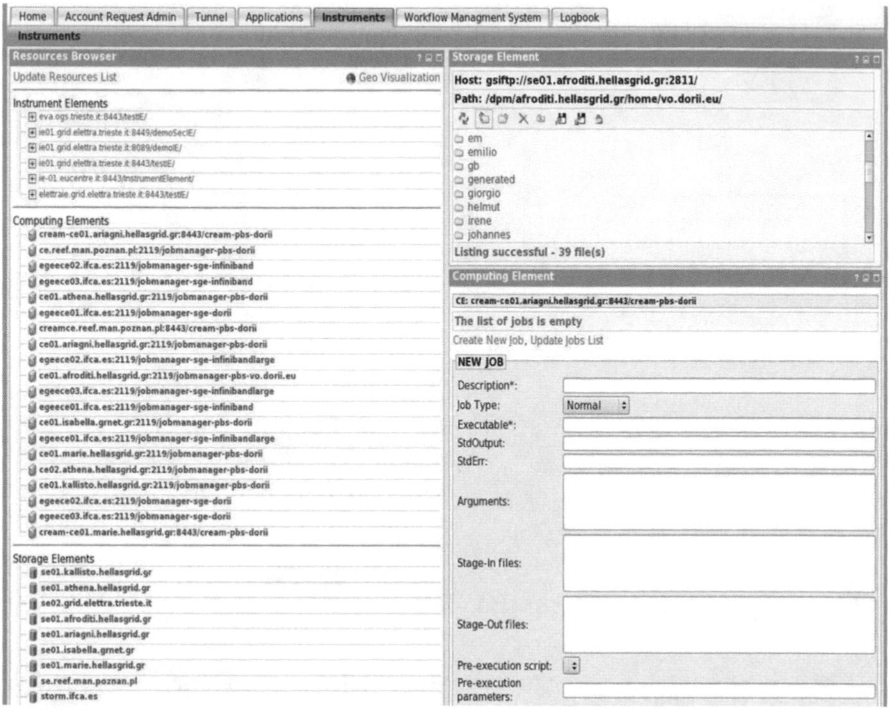

Fig. 1.6 Virtual control room, the e-Infrastructure front-end

of the workflow management system, oriented on the instrumentation tasks, was developed for nuclear magnetic resonance spectroscopy (within the VLab project) and used by scientist to design and manage their experiment scenarios. During the DORII project, WfMS was extended to support the remote instrumentation tasks.

In the frame of the Remote Instrumentation Infrastructure, WfMS facilitates interconnection of computational and experimental job scenarios in a single execution graph (Fig. 1.7). In the workflow graph, the nodes correspond to storage (data and operations on them, both for input and output actions), computing (execution of a computing grid job), and instrumentation (interaction with physical device integrated with the infrastructure through the Instrument Element interface) tasks/blocks, whereas edges (connection links) presents the dependencies among those tasks.

The WfMS is a client–server system consisting of two main parts – the Workflow Editor and Manager. The Editor is a lightweight graphical interface (Fig. 1.8) to the WfMS, intended for the end users. The main functions of the Editor are as follows:

- To enable VO-based access to e-Infrastructure services (CE, SE, and IE)
- To support the users by creation, construction, editing, customization, and sub-mission of the workflow for the execution as well as monitoring of the workflow execution status

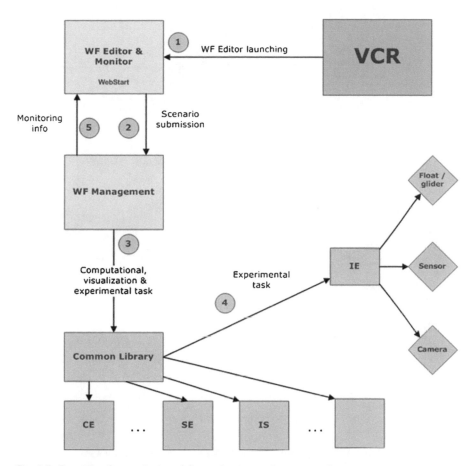

Fig. 1.7 Example of a standard workflow using remote instrumentation

The workflow actions and user requests specified through the Editor are handled by the Workflow Manager, a server part of the WfMS. Being deployed on the infrastructure resources and connected to the Editor through the web service mechanism, the Manager hides the complexity of using the e-Infrastructure services from the end users.

1.3.6 Application Development Environment for the e-Infrastructure

To support the application development activities, including tracing and remote debugging tasks, the middleware architecture adopts g-Eclipse; an integrated user desktop development environment. g-Eclipse extends [3] the basic Eclipse IDE functionality and visual interfaces by the special grid-enabling plug-ins to provide specific functionality to access the e-Infrastructure resources and services, and develop grid applications.

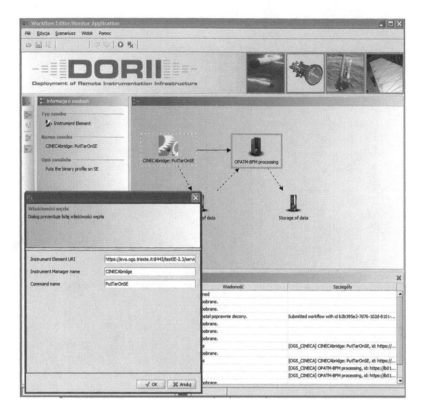

Fig. 1.8 Example of the workflow editor interface

The native Eclipse IDE is extended by the following perspectives:

- User perspective aims to allow the users to execute an application on the e-Infrastructure, monitor the progress of the application execution, and manage their data files on the storage resources.
- Operator perspective provides an interface to manage the local as well as e-Infrastructure resources, including CE, SE, and IE, assigned to the Virtual Organization to which the user belongs.
- Developer perspective aims to provide application developers with the appropriate tools for program development (e.g., via Eclipse Java/C/other programming languages Development Toolkits), debugging, and deployment.

The development perspective (Fig. 1.9) is of especial interest for the Remote Instrumentation Infrastructure's development community as it considerably accelerates the application development and deployment cycle and reduces the time needed to bring their applications to the production level [14].

The development of any application is a continuous process of coding, debugging and testing, executing, monitoring, and maintaining. This process is even more complicated in case of the grid applications, since they are actually executed on the remote e-Infrastructure resources, that obviously affects all phases of the development.

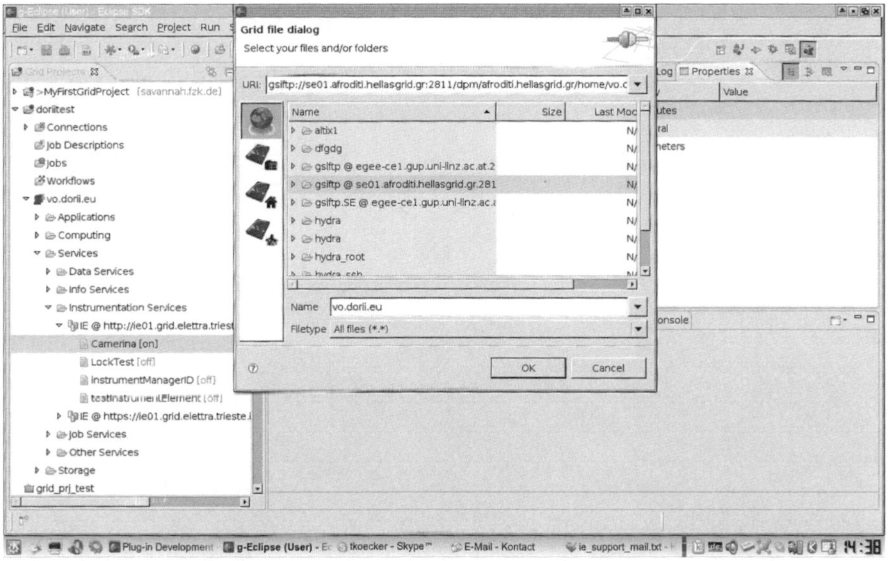

Fig. 1.9   Remote debugging of a MPI parallel application of the e-Infrastructure

g-Eclipse offers the e-Infrastructure users a mechanism to interface the existing development and debugging tools, usually applied for their applications, to locally operate the grid applications and jobs. This is achieved by creating a special application-transparent interactive communication channel for interfacing the application binaries that are built and deployed remotely on the e-Infrastructure. The users hence develop the application code on the local machine, whereas the code instance is automatically deployed and executed on-grid. g-Eclipse provides support for several kinds of the grid middleware, including gLite which makes up the core of the Remote Instrumentation Infrastructure's services.

1.3.7   MPI-Parallel Application Support

Over the last decades, the Message-Passing Interface (MPI) has become a standard in the area of distributed memory parallel computing. MPI is an industry standard API specification designed for high-performance computing on multiprocessor machines and clusters. Parallel applications implemented by means of MPI [3] are although not the main focus of the Remote Instrumentation Infrastructure, but they are widely used to improve the efficiency of computation-intensive post-processing and simulation algorithms performed on the data acquired from instruments (Fig. 1.10). Therefore, providing a MPI implementation by the CEs is a mandatory requirement to any e-Infrastructure.

Among the available MPI implementations, Open MPI was chosen as it has proved practical usability for applications from several European grid projects, including EGEE. Open MPI is the full MPI-2.1 implementation for improved running parallel

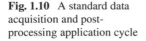 **Fig. 1.10** A standard data acquisition and post-processing application cycle

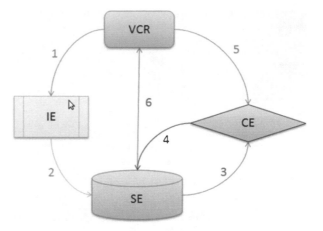

applications in high-performance and grid environments. Open MPI is production quality middleware, portable and maintainable, serves a complete run-time environment for improved running parallel applications. Among the Open MPI features, the following are of especial interest for the Remote Instrumentation Infrastructure: Full MPI-2.1 standards conformance, thread safety and concurrency, dynamic process spawning, network and process fault tolerance, support network heterogeneity, run-time performance measurement and instrumentation, and high performance on the most platforms.

Another considerable feature of Open MPI concerns integrated performance analysis. While the MPI standard is easy to use and implement, it is extremely difficult to develop parallel programs in an efficient way. In many cases, the application performance can heavily suffer from various communication-related issues when running on the e-Infrastructure heterogeneous computing resources. Performance analysis can greatly support application developers in the identification of the main bottlenecks and performance [4] degradation issues in the implemented algorithms. For this purpose, the famous VampirTrace tool was integrated to Open MPI. VampirTrace is a program tracing package that collects a very fine-grained event trace of a sequential or parallel program.

In particular, being applied for parallel applications, the trace provides comprehensive details on the communication events that occurred in the application instances/processes. This information can be visualized by any backend supporting the Open Trace Format, for example, Vampir (Fig. 1.11) or g-Eclipse. The parallel applications implemented with Open MPI benefit from the integration with VampirTrace greatly, as can be analyzed on every grid site which provides Open MPI support.

Open MPI is a stable and high-performance solution for implementation of parallel applications. Nevertheless, other popular MPI libraries as MPICH are also supposed to be supported by the Remote Instrumentation Infrastructure. However, irregardless of the MPI library used for implementation, launching of a MPI application in a grid environment is awkward and sophisticated by the

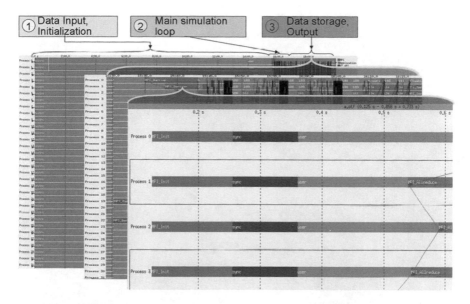

Fig. 1.11 Example of the communication profile visualization for a parallel MPI application

heterogeneous nature of the grid sites, the computing elements of those deploy various job schedulers, worker node interconnect, and file systems. In order to provide a necessary abstraction level for the MPI jobs from the characteristics of a concrete grid site, the MPI-Start tool is included to the architecture.

MPI-Start is a tool for improved running MPI applications specially designed for the e-Infrastructure to enable MPI applications to abstract from different MPI libraries, file systems, and job managers of the grid site. MPI-Start is a set of shell scripts intended to close the gap between the Workload Management System and configuration of the Computing Elements. Different CE schedulers are supported by MPI-Start, including SGE, Torque/PBS, and LSF. Along with Open MPI, MPI-Start supports LAM, MPICH, and PACX MPI implementations. MPI-Start support is straightforward for running MPI-parallel applications on the e-Infrastructure.

1.3.8 Remote Visualization of Scientific Data – GVid

The data acquired from the e-Infrastructure's instruments as well as obtained during the post-processing and simulation might be analyzed by the users at the end of each work cycle. The e-Infrastructure can greatly support the data analysis phase by allowing the users to perform the interactive visualization of the data without necessity of replicating those data to the user local machine. Especially important is the remote visualization when handling unprecedented amounts of data becomes a crucial part of performing scientific experiments. To address the user particular need of the remote visualization, the middleware architecture

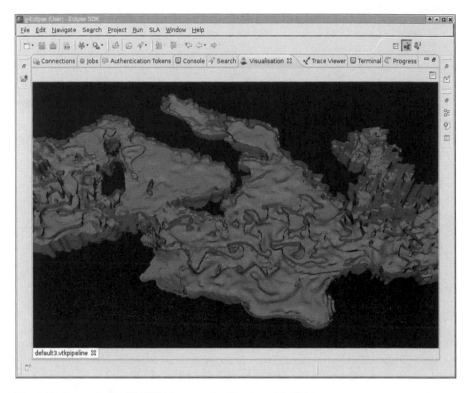

Fig. 1.12 Example of a NetCDF data set visualization with GVid

adopts GVid – a middleware extension for interactive video streaming of the visualization content [12]. By combining standard video streaming technology with scientific visualization functionality and performing the combination of both within a grid infrastructure, novel functionality for exploration of (large-scale) data is enabled for the end users by the Remote Instrumentation Infrastructure. The users should hence greatly benefit from the e-Infrastructure also for processing, transporting, and rendering the scientific visualization for better understanding of the scientific problem at hand.

The GVid architecture follows the client–server approach. The server component enables to run and render applications on remote sites, and encodes their graphical output into a video stream. The client application, which is implemented as a Java applet (Fig. 1.12), not only displays the video stream, but also permits the user to interact with the remotely running application. For this purpose, input events on the client side are sent to the server where they are passed to the visualization application. This application can react accordingly and its graphical response is streamed back to the client. As a transport layer provider between the infrastructure and user local machine, GVid utilizes glogin to transport the video stream and input events [3]. This enables the user to submit visualization jobs to the grid, which eliminates the need to transport whole data sets to the local machine. Instead, data located in the grid can be analyzed using a local web browser. The functionality provided by GVid can be summarized in the following:

- The server component allows to grab the graphical output of an application and to encode it into a video stream.
- The client (GVid applet) can access the stream produced by the server, display the video in a browser window, and forward user input back to the remotely running application.
- GVid supports Visualization Toolkit (VTK), OpenGL Utility Toolkit (Glut), and arbitrary X Window System (X11) applications.

1.3.9   Integration Aspect

The above-presented components are the outcome of several big projects such as GRIDCC, VLab, Int.EU.Grid, and others serving various strategic goals and objectives. However, integration of those tools and services within the common middleware architecture, performed in DORII, has enabled setting up a highly con-figurable user-centric middleware environment which enhances the e-Infrastructure to fulfill the remote instrumentation requirements. Thereby, considerable develop-ment, adaptation, and integration effort was performed during DORII in order to achieve this goal. In particular, VCR should provide the users with a launch mechanism for Workflow Editor, visualization should be integrated with both VCR and WfMS, the GVid transport layer provider – glogin – might greatly extend the VCR functionality to support interactive applications and many others [3].

Moreover, there was a strong need from the user-level middleware compo-nents to access underlying grid services (gLite and Instrument Services) of the e-Infrastructure in a seamless way. For this purpose, the middleware architecture adopts DORII Common Library – a solution developed in DORII which provides a single access point for the user-level middleware tools to the infrastructure's grid services. Common Library is designed in a way that ensures the component interoperability within the architecture and simplifies the installation of the user-level middleware build on top of it.

1.3.10   Test Bed Infrastructure Resources

First attempts to deploy and operate persistent, production quality, and distributed instrumentation integrated with an e-Infrastructure have been successfully performed during the DORII project. Based on expertise and demands coming from the pilot applications, described briefly in the following paragraphs, DORII builds and oper-ates a sustainable infrastructural test bed that addresses different areas of e-Science and can be used for fast prototyping of other collaborative remote instrumentation applications and services.

The following pilot applications [9] are the main focus of the DORII infrastructure activities:

1. Earthquake community with applications focusing on simulation and laboratory tests as well as monitoring of earthquake activity.

   (a) Network-Centric Seismic Simulations (NCSS) permit usage of actuators and strain gauges instead of a building simulator.
   (b) Earthquake Early Warning System (EEWS) aims at recording seismic data acquired from sensors, possibly in real time, and while processing them in order to extract time history for ground velocity, ground acceleration, and displacements.

2. Environmental community applications aiming at monitoring and collecting observations at geographically distributed places, transmitting the data for processing in near real time, and finally, comparing the experimental results with several models

   (a) Oceanographic and coastal observation and modeling Mediterranean Ocean Observing Network (OCON-MOON) utilizes specific oceanographic instruments that perform near real-time observation of the Mediterranean basin as well as simulation application (OPATM-BFM) for short- and long-time prediction for the future periods.
   (b) Oceanographic and coastal observation and modeling using imaging (Horus-Bench) uses digital cameras located along the north coast of Spain for monitoring of the sea coasts and river surface (beachgoers, intertidal profile, etc.) and their postmortem analysis (e.g., using SWAN, a see wave simulation model).

3. Experiment science community with experimental stations in facilities like Synchrotrons and Free Electron Lasers

   (a) Small Angle X-ray Scattering (SAXS) beam line is mainly intended for time-resolved studies on fast structural transitions in the sub-millisecond time region in solutions and partly ordered systems with a SAXS resolution of 1–140 nm in real space
   (b) SYnchrotron Radiation for MEdical Physics (SYRMEP) beam line has been designed by Sincrotrone Trieste, in cooperation with the University of Trieste and the INFN, for research in medical diagnostic radiology using monochromatic and laminar-shaped beams.

The pilot application set described above covers typical scenarios of the e-Infrastructure usage as well as several use cases which put especial requirements to the e-Infrastructure's storage and computing resources. In order to facilitate the use of the Remote Instrumentation Infrastructure for a wide variety of applications, including those specified by European Strategy Forum on Research Infrastructure (ESFRI), the requirements have been carefully analyzed and taken into account by setting up the test bed infrastructure. A short summary of the resource requirements specified by the Remote Instrumentation Infrastructure's pilot applications is collected in the Table 1.1.

Table 1.1 Summary of pilot application resource requirements

Application	Infrastructure requirements			Security
	CPU	Storage	Software	
NCSS	1 job per run, duration (0.5–2 h), 2–3 times/week	10–20 GB	Static compilation C/C++ code and libraries	Not strict, VO users
EEWS	1 job per run, duration up to 2 days, depending on earthquake occurrence	1–10 GB	Static compilation C/C++ code and libraries	Not strict, VO users
OCOM-MOON	1 job per run for floats and glider data, 1×32 CPU MPI job for OPATM-BFM, duration less than 7 h	Several MBs for floats and glider data, 80 GB for 1 operational run (17 days) for OPATM-BFM	C/C++ Code, OpenMPI v1.3 installed in the infrastructure	Not strict, VO users
Horus Bench	1 job per run	10–20 GB	Static compilation C/C++ code and libraries	Not strict, VO users
SAXS	1 job per run with duration several minutes and frequency of 1/2 Hz during experiment	1–5 GB per run	Static compilation of C/C++ code and libraries	In some cases, data access is restricted to specific researchers
SYRMEP	1 job per run with duration of 2 h and frequency of 1/2 Hz during experiment	3–10 GB per run	Static compilation of C/C++ code and libraries	In some cases, data access is restricted to specific researchers

Table 1.2 The remote instrumentation infrastructure resources

Country	Partner	Site	CPUs (Cores)	Storage (TB)
Poland	PSNC	PSNC	2128	4
Spain	CSIC	IFCA-CSIC	1680	230
		IFCA-I2G	1680	230
Italy	ELETTRA	ELETTRA	160	20
		SISSA-Trieste	24	0.5
		INFN-Trieste	276	0
Greece	GRNET	HG-01-GRNET	64	4.78
		HG-02-IASA	118	3.14
		HG-03-AUTH	120	3.13
		HG-04-CTI-CEID	114	2.87
		HG-05-FORTH	120	2.33
		HG-06-EKT	628	7.76
		TOTALS	5432	278.51

Following the strategy to reuse existing resources instead of setting up a new infrastructure, the Remote Instrumentation Infrastructure relies on computational and storage resources of the National Grid Initiatives (NGIs) of the countries that participate in creating the Infrastructure, such as Germany, Greece, Italy, Poland, and Spain. Those NGI resources were already available as part of the EGEE infrastructure. Moreover, the infrastructure also comprises newly contributed resources which didn't belong to any available e-Infrastructure before. A dedicated Virtual Organization (vo.dorii.eu) was created for sharing the Remote Instrumentation Infrastructure resource with the user applications.

In total, there are 11 sites currently providing a total number of 5,432 CPUs while the total storage available on those sites is around 278 TB for the Remote Instrumentation Infrastructure (Table 1.2). Moreover, there has been a substantial increase of the contributed resources observed during the DORII project duration, as, for example, a node with GPU capabilities installed on the PSNC site.

All the necessary high-level grid services for the Remote Instrumentation Infrastructure have been set up by DORII, including WMS, top BDII, VOMS, MyProxy, and LFC. In order to efficiently manage the e-Infrastructure resources included from EGEE or contributed additionally as well as to provide an easy way for integration of new instrumentation resources, DORII also provides dedicated operations and user support management architecture for the e-Infrastructure (Fig. 1.13).

The registration point for all resources and services in the DORII infrastructure is the Hierarchical Grid Site Management system (HGSM). HGSM provides the list of the site BDIIs for the e-Infrastructure, and top-level BDIIs to be populated. Monitoring and operational support of the sites relies on EGEE management structures and monitoring tools for production quality resources. Deployment of the middleware presented in the previous section is done according to the procedures that are followed in EGEE after evaluation of the applicability of new middleware releases.

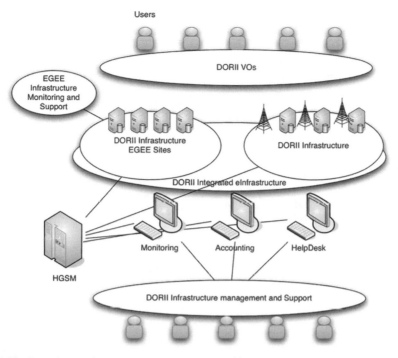

Fig. 1.13 Operations and user support management architecture

1.3.11   Networking Resources and Monitoring Aspect

Since the typical remote instrumentation scenarios span over a wide range of various instrumentation devices, different physical quantities need to be measured and converted into a signal, so as to be read by an observer or by an instrument. The type of access network is strictly dependent on the location and area extent where sensors are scattered. Adami [2] has collected the following technologies which are used for the above-presented infrastructure test bed:

- WLAN, sensors, and IEs located in the same laboratory
- WLAN/WiMax, geographically distributed sensors
- Satellite Link, geographically distributed sensors over a very large area, for example, sea, ocean, regional or national area
- Cellular Networks, sensors located in isolated areas without other telecommunication network coverage
- DSL, sensors located in areas where telecommunications carriers offer such network services

In the most cases, data is acquired through more than one sensor and in some cases, a Wireless Sensor Network (WSN) must be deployed. The Table 1.3 summarizes exemplary networking characteristics of the above-discussed applications.

Table 1.3 Sensor network characteristics of the pilot applications

Application	Sensor type	Sensor location	Connection type
NCSS	Actuators Seismic sensors	Lab	Wired LAN
EEWS	Seismic sensors	Wide area	WSN + WiFi/ WiMax
OCOM-MOON (FLOAT)	CTD (conductivity, temperature, and depth) sensors	Wide area (Mediterranean Sea)	Argos satellite system + Internet
OCOM-MOON (GLIDER)	CTD sensors Turbidity sensors Oxygen sensors	Wide area (Mediterranean Sea)	Iridium Satellite Link
HORUS	Digital cameras, temperature sensors, pressure sensors	Wide area	WiFi + DSL/ UMTS/GPRS
SAXS	Detectors Others sensors	Local	Wired LAN
SYRMEP	Detectors Others sensors	Local	Wired LAN

As in case of the computational and storage resources, a substantial amount of heterogeneous instruments and sensors also requires a special monitoring system, the e-Infrastructure needs to be equipped with. For this purpose, an advanced network monitoring architecture is implemented in the Remote Instrumentation Infrastructure's network. The architecture allows system analysts to identify end-to-end connectivity problems, service interruptions and bottlenecks, and is able to monitor if the given Quality-of-Service (QoS) performance metrics by the specific application requirements are within acceptable limits. Since each site is connected to its national research and education network (NREN) and interconnected with other sites through the GÉANT network, end-to-end traffic is monitored and network statistics are collected by means of the architecture tools.

Special attention has been given to the distributed nature of the e-Infrastructure's network, since it contains: (1) the local area networks of the participating institutions, including highly heterogeneous data collection parts (sensor networks, satellite links, ADSL, high-speed data transfer), (2) the corresponding NRENs providing access to each national research network and to the Internet, (3) GÉANT, as the backbone interconnecting NRENs, and (4) the Remote Instrumentation Infrastructure network is IPv6 enabled.

To cover all those aspects, the network monitoring architecture includes the following multi-domain traffic monitoring tools:

- Smokeping, for network latency measurement (Fig. 1.14)
- Pathload, for the estimation of the available bandwidth along a network path
- SNMP-based Web applications, for monitoring network interface utilization

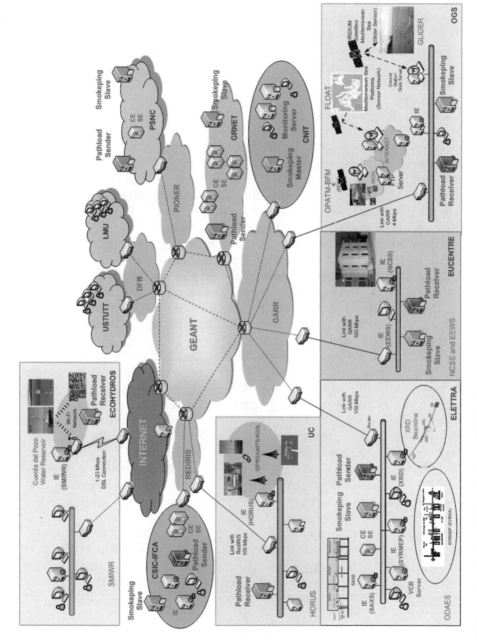

Fig. 1.14 Network monitoring with Smokeping and Pathload tools

1.4 Future Research Directions and Issues

The pilot version of the Remote Instrumentation Infrastructure has been successfully set up during the DORII project. The DORII research and developments made a step forward for leveraging the traditional e-Infrastructure's resources to fully support the Remote Instrumentation Services. The enhanced e-Infrastructure was deployed and tested on different remote instrumentation communities, also aiming to a great range of other applications. However, the efforts performed within DORII can be greatly extended in the future.

Analyzing the current state in remote instrumentation systems, it can be noted that a big effort must be put forth to adapt the existing systems to new users and community requirements. Based on current experiences in DORII and its predecessors, a new definition might be proposed for commonly available grid objects, like computing and storage elements. This will be done by extending the distributed computing environments, in the same matter as in case as was made for the EGEE-based e-Infrastructure, with an innovative additional abstract layer, based on the Instrument Element presented in this chapter. Refinement and empowering of Instrument Element functionalities toward integration of heterogeneous instrumentation, aiming at the complete definition of an architectural element that can become a standardized middleware component, is an important research direction in further extending the Remote Instrumentation Infrastructure's level of service. This implies the DORII Common Library design heavily, as it is supposed to be the main infrastructure service provider for a wide range of the user-level middleware components.

On the other hand, improvement of the currently available limitation in possibilities to, trouble-free, incorporate new instruments is also an important improvement direction for the Remote Instrumentation Infrastructure in the future. Usually, this process needs significant effort from system developers. The current limitation in the domain-specific integration of the remote instrumentation should be overcome by offering new, flexible, and innovative way of providing service-oriented instrumentation, such as advanced instrument reservation, for example, It will increase better e-Infrastructure resource (including the remote instrumentation) utilization, especially when interactive access is required. Human interaction introduces new limitations which must be taken into consideration (in particular to be addressed in the workflow solutions).

Accounting of scientific instruments is also a very important functionality which the current edition of the Remote Instrumentation Infrastructure is currently lacking. It should provide information about resource utilization (again, including the remote instrumentation), in particular allowing for the phases of the application life cycle (e.g., preparation, parameters tuning, and actual execution), which next could be accounted with different rates.

Another innovation concerns the advanced monitoring which will be used to provide up-to-date information about instruments and running experiments. It will extend standard mechanisms and incorporate added value, like proactive monitoring in order to facilitate fast problem resolution.

This strategy is inline with a complex of activities performed currently in the European Research Area toward creating a Virtual Research Environment, a dynamic and temporally isolated environment which allows users to proceed with the complex experiment, whereby the remote instrumentation tasks might be greatly supported as well.

1.5 Conclusion

There are numerous areas of science and technology that require broad international collaboration for their success. A number of problems may be addressed by using complex equipment and top-level expertise, which is often locally unavailable for most of the institutions. Remote instrumentation is a new branch of the ICT domain oriented at the integration of scientific instruments into e-Infrastructure and empowering possibilities in conducting experiments. The possibility of having shared access to complex scientific and even industrial equipment independently of their physical location, in a way as grid technology has enabled for computation and storage facilities worldwide, is a great step forward toward designing next-generation Remote Instrumentation Services (RIS). An e-Infrastructure capable of providing RIS creates absolutely new spectrum of opportunities for a number of research projects, some examples of which were collected in this chapter.

Combining RIS with the traditional grid computation and storage services, enabled by large-scale sustainable e-Infrastructures within a single VO, the RII presented in the chapter materials allows scientist to expose, share, and federate, within a common application workflow, various instrumental resources, performed by means of universal abstractions that apply to diverse e-Science domains. Moreover, in perspective, the Remote Instrumentation Infrastructure may well become a significant component of the future distributed computing infrastructure.

The goal of the chapter was twofold. The major purpose was to present how the functional components of the current e-Infrastructures can be extended and refined for enabling virtualization and effective management of real remote instrumentation on various levels such as middleware, networking, and resources. On the other hand, with this chapter, the authors would like to encourage the direct involvement of a wider set of user communities to bring their operational experience in the experimental activities to be carried out on the Remote Instrumentation Infrastructure.

Acknowledgments We kindly acknowledge to the consortium of the EU project "DORII" for the provided materials and the European Commission which funded the DORII project (under contract no. 213110).

References

1. Adami, D., Cheptsov, A., Davoli, F., Liabotis, I., Pugliese, R., Zafeiropoulos, A.: The DORII project test bed: distributed eScience applications at work. In: Proceedings of the 5th International Conference on Testbeds and Research Infrastructures for the Development of Networks & Communities and Workshops TridentCom, Washington, DC. ISBN: 978-1-4244-2846-5. doi 10.1109/TRIDENTCOM.2009.4976247 (2009)
2. Adami, D.: Final design of the distributed infrastructure over the GEANT Network. DORII DSA1.3 Deliverable. Retrieved from http://www.dorii.eu/resources:network:deliverables (2009)
3. Cheptsov, A.: First prototype of integrated products from previous projects. DORII DJRA3 Deliveralbe. Retrieved from http://www.dorii.eu/resources:adaptation:deliverables (2009)
4. Cheptsov, A., Dichev, K., Keller, R., Lazzari, P., Salon, S.: Porting the OPATM-BFM application to a grid e-Infrastructure – optimization of communication and I/O patterns. Comput. Meth. Sci. Technol. 15(1), 9–19 (2009)
5. Cheptsov, A., Keller, R., Pugliese, R., Prica, M., Del Linz, A., Plociennik, M., Lawenda, M., Meyer, N.: Towards deployment of the remote instrumentation e-Infrastructure. Comput. Meth. Sci. Technol. 15(1), 65–74 (2009)
6. Flemming, N., Vallerga, S., Pinardi, N., Behrens, H., Manzella, G., Prandle, D., Stel, J. (eds.): Operational Oceanography – Implementation at the European and Regional Scales. Elsevier oceanography, vol. 66. Elsevier, Amsterdam (2002)
7. IFM-GEOMAR: Glider cruising the ocean. Retrieved from http://www.ifm-geomar.de/index.php?id=1241&L=1 (2008)
8. Lazzari, P.: Coupling of transport and biogeochemical models in the Mediterranean Sea. PhD thesis in Environmental Science, University of Trieste, Trieste (2008)
9. Liabotis, I.: Final description of the deployed management infrastructure. DORII DSA2.4 Deliverable. Retrieved from http://www.dorii.eu/resources:deployment:deliverables (2009)
10. Meyer, N.: Integrating e-Infrastructure and scientific instrumentation. British Publishers. Retrieved from http://viewer.zmags.com/publication/116913e6#/116913e6/22 (2009)
11. Pinardi, N., Nittis, K., Drago, A., Crise, A., Poulain, P., Cardin, V., Manzella, G., Reseghetti, Alvarez, E., Cruzado, A., Tintore, J., Zodiatis, G., Hayes, D.: Operational oceanography observing system developments in the Mediterranean Sea in support of the MFSD implementation. Retrieved from http://www.moon-oceanforecasting.eu/files/medgoos_moonreport-updatejune2009.v9.pdf (2009)
12. Polak, M., Kranzlmüller, D.: Interactive videostreaming visualization on grids. Future Generation Comput. Syst. 24(1), 39–45 (2008)
13. Salon, S., Poulain, P.M., Mauri, E., Gerin, R., Adami, D., Davoli, F.: Remote oceanographic instrumentation integrated in a GRID environment. J. Comput. Meth. Sci. Technol. 15(1), 49–55 (2009)
14. Wolniewicz, P., Meyer, N., Stroiński, M., Stuempert, M., Kornmayer, H., Polak, M., Gjermundröd, H.: Accessing grid computing resources with g-eclipse platform. J. Comput. Meth. Sci. Technol. 13(2), 131–141 (2007)
15. Wunnava, S.V., Hoo, P.: Remote Instrumentation Access and Control (RIAC) through internetworking. In: Proceedings of the IEEE Conference Southeastcon, Lexington, pp. 116–121 (1999)

Chapter 2
Supporting e-Science Applications on e-Infrastructures: Some Use Cases from Latin America

Roberto Barbera, Francisco Brasileiro, Riccardo Bruno, Leandro Ciuffo, and Diego Scardaci

Abstract In this chapter, we describe a successful methodology to support e-Science applications on e-Infrastructures put in practice in the EELA-2 project co-funded by the European Commission and involving European and Latin American countries. The heterogeneous requirements of the e-Science applications, coming from several scientific fields, makes difficult to provide them with a support able to satisfy all the different needs. Usually, the grid middleware adopted, gLite in the case of EELA-2, provides applications with general tools not able to meet specific requirements. For this reason, a really powerful e-Infrastructure has to offer some additional services to complete and integrate the functionalities of the grid middleware. These services have to both increase the set of functionalities offered by the e-Infrastructure and make easier the tasks of developing and deploying new applications. Following this methodology, EELA-2 deployed 53 e-Science applications out of the 61 supported in total, in its enriched e-Infrastructure during its life.

R. Barbera
Division of Catania, Italian National Institute of Nuclear Physics,
Via Santa Sofia 64, Catania 95123, Italy

Department of Physics and Astronomy, University of Catania, Catania, Italy

F. Brasileiro
Department of Systems and Computing, Universidade Federal de Campina Grande,
Campina Grande, Brazil

R. Bruno • L. Ciuffo • D. Scardaci (✉)
Division of Catania, Italian National Institute of Nuclear Physics, Via Santa Sofia 64,
Catania 95123, Italy
e-mail: diego.scardaci@ct.infn.it

N.P. Preve (ed.), *Grid Computing: Towards a Global Interconnected Infrastructure*,
Computer Communications and Networks, DOI 10.1007/978-0-85729-676-4_2,
© Springer-Verlag London Limited 2011

2.1 Introduction

In this chapter, we describe a successful methodology to support e-Science applications on e-Infrastructure starting from the experience of the EELA-2 project [9] co-funded by the European Commission and involving European and Latin American countries. In order to satisfy all heterogeneous applications requirements and to simplify the access to the grid infrastructure, a set of special services has been developed to enhance the functionality of the gLite middleware [12] and provide users with a richer platform.

The middleware services developed have widened the number of potential applications taking benefit of the grid e-Infrastructure and, moreover, have speeded up the porting of applications to run in the grid. It can be considered general and applied in other similar contexts.

This chapter is organized in the following way. Section 2.1 introduces e-Science in Latin America. Section 2.3 describes the main characteristics of applications involved in the EELA-2 project. Section 2.4 presents the additional services developed, according to applications requirements, to enhance gLite functionalities. Section 2.5 describes how these services have been adopted by the EELA-2 applications. Future perspectives and conclusion are then drawn in the last two sections (Sects. 2.6 and 2.7, respectively).

2.2 Related Work

Latin America has been one of the regions supported by the European Commission through the Information and Communications Technology (ICT) scheme. Grid computing has been funded through the EELA [8], and EELA-2 projects with a noticeable success.

The EELA-2 project (E-Science Grid facility for Europe and Latin America) is EELA's second phase. It aims at building and operating a production grid infrastructure, which provides computing and storage resources from selected partners across Europe and Latin America. During its first phase, a collaborative human network was established by means of several advances in the grid infrastructure setup, deployment of new certification authorities, support of pilot applications, and organization of many workshops and training events that made the Latin American research community aware of what grid could do.

The current EELA-2 production infrastructure operates middleware Core Services located in both Europe and Latin America [11], and works with grid sites that have demonstrated to have an adequate maturity level in par with what is expected from a production environment. It also maintains virtual organization services, with one main Virtual Organization (VO) – named "prod.vo.eu-eela.eu" – gathering the infrastructure services. It is also worth mentioning that EELA-2 adopts both the gLite middleware and the OurGrid [6, 16] middleware; the former powers its service infrastructure, while the latter is used to set up a complementary opportunistic infrastructure.

2.3   Supporting e-Science Applications in Latin America

It is well known that the development of grid computing was initially driven by the requirements of efficient processing of the huge amounts of data generated by High Energy Physics experiments such as those running at the CERN Large Hadron Collider (LHC) [5]. However, investments to promote grid computing within new scientific communities in several regions of the world have been attracting new research groups interested in investigating the potential benefits that grid computing can bring for their academic pursuits. Indeed, grid has proven to be a very effective way of tackling intensive computing needs such as those found in climate simulations and drug discovery.

Based on our experience supporting 61 applications in the framework of the EELA-2 project, we have noticed that grid users may be broadly divided into three groups:

- Those participating in collaborative experiments which require High-Throughput Computing (HTC) across many computing and storage clusters.
- Those that have computational and storage demands that cannot be handled by their local resources in a reasonable time – these users require to access extra resources belonging to others only for the purpose of attending the excess in their workload.
- Those with modest computational needs that could be easily handled by a local cluster or storage server; in this case, the affiliation of these groups with a large grid project might allow them to overcome the digital divide just by granting access to extra computing resources.

Such a diversity of users is one of the consequences of the grid expansion across many institutions/countries facing different maturity levels of Information Technology (IT) infrastructures, network connections, and e-science awareness. This is also reflected on the application's profile. On one hand, EELA-2 supports applications that run thousands of parallel jobs per week which last for many hours and handle gigabytes of data, but on the other hand, there is also bag-of-task application that runs one single job on an occasional basis and consumes relatively much less computing resources. Figure 2.1 shows the current distribution of the 61 EELA-2 applications per scientific domain.

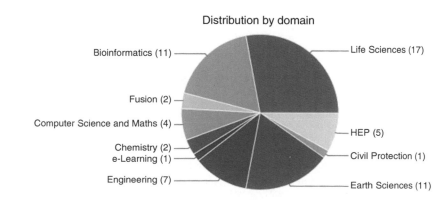

Fig. 2.1 Distribution of EELA-2 applications per scientific domain

2.4   Developing e-Infrastructure Services for e-Science Applications

To cope with all heterogeneous aspects presented above and to meet the requirements of the applications, a set of special services has been developed. These services enhance the functionality of both the gLite and the OurGrid middleware giving the EELA-2 users access to richer middleware, reducing the amount of application development, and generally accelerating the adoption of grid technologies.

The identification and the development of these services has been conducted with the goal of increasing the reach and the usability of e-Infrastructure by assembling/reengineering existing technologies and developing new ones that could facilitate the installation, management, and use of the grid infrastructure. By increased reach, we mean more sites belonging to the grid infrastructure, with more resources being shared, more users being served, and a more diverse range of applications being supported. By increased usability, we mean the addition of services that can ease the tasks of developing and deploying new applications, as well as installing, managing, and deploying the core infrastructure. Therefore, the development of these additional services has focused mainly on the design, implementation, and deployment of new infrastructure-oriented and application-oriented grid services.

The infrastructure-oriented services have been developed to provide alternatives to ease the installation, management, and use of the e-Infrastructure. To this end, the following services have been built:

• A gateway between gLite and Ourgrid [2, 16], a simpler peer-to-peer (P2P) technology, to provide alternative ways to make resources available to the grid infrastructure and to simplify the access to the infrastructure for new users and applications
• The porting of the gLite User Interface and Computing Element to the Microsoft Windows platform [17] to facilitate the access to the infrastructure to Windows users and to allow Windows Applications to use the infrastructure
• The Storage Accounting for Grid Environments (SAGE) [19], a system to measure the usage of storage resources in a gLite based on grid infrastructure whose main task is to collect information from physical devices and make this data available to system administrator to account the storage at higher levels

The application-oriented services have been developed according to the feedback of the users and site administrators:

• The Grid Storage Access Framework (GSAF) [20], an object-oriented framework designed to access and manage Data Grid via APIs. It provides developers with a development tool to write application that adopts grid as Digital Repository hiding the fragmentation and the complexity of the Data Grid Services. GSAF also provides a basic transaction layer for multiservice operation (i.e., synchronization of data operations).

- The Secure Storage [18] is a service for the gLite middleware which provides the users with a set of tools in order to store confidential data in a secure way and in an encrypted format (e.g., medical or financial data) on the grid storage elements. The data stored through provided tools is accessible and readable by authorized users only, preventing also the administrators of the storage elements to access the confidential data in a clear format (e.g., insider abuse problem).
- OPeNDAP Meta-Finder, a tool for searching geographical information data sets available at the Web through OPeNDAP servers. By filling a form, the user can search for data sets containing some wanted attributes and variables such as spatial coverage, temporal coverage, atmosphere temperature, precipitation, etc. To make queries easier, tag clouds are shown with some suggestions of tags to classify published data sets.
- The Watchdog [3] is a tool that allows users to watch the status of a running job when it runs on a working node tracing the evolution of produced files.
- The lcg-rec-* tools allow users to perform recursive Grid File Operations such as copies and deletion.
- DIRAC is an alternative to overcome an infrastructure limitation of not having many Computing Elements able to support MPICH2 jobs.

In the following sections, we describe in detail the additional services that caused a major impact in terms of increasing the reach and the usability of the EELA-2 e-Infrastructure.

2.4.1 A Gateway Between gLite and OurGrid

The gateway technology we use is the 3G-bridge proposed in the context of the EDGeS project [4]. Jobs originated in one system run in the other in a completely transparent way, using the standard gLite user interface and the OurGrid broker. Nevertheless, jobs may carry additional requirements to force their execution cross-platforms.

A middleware-specific adaptor is responsible for converting the jobs from their particular native format to a canonical format defined by the 3G-bridge; the translated jobs are stored in the gateway database to be later dispatched to the appropriate grid. The gateway software constantly inspects the gateway's database looking for jobs that need to be dispatched. For each grid to which the gateway interfaces, there is an instance of a middleware-specific plug-in that implements a job management API defined by the 3G-bridge. Upon detecting that a job needs to be dispatched, the gateway identifies to which grid the job should be submitted and calls the appropriate functions in the correspondent plug-in instance. The plug-in is responsible for creating a new job in the appropriate format and submitting it to the grid to which it is associated. When the job is completed, the database is updated and, eventually, the user interface is notified.

We have developed a Java implementation of the 3G-bridge and plug-ins for both gLite and OurGrid. The OurGrid plug-in is implemented by a modified version of the OurGrid Broker that implements the 3G-bridge API; a peer representing the gateway is instantiated to serve this Broker, and jobs are submitted to the OurGrid system through the Broker as if they had been submitted by the user. The gLite plug-in uses a standard gLite User Interface to submit jobs to the gLite back end.

Suitable adaptors have been developed to map OurGrid and gLite jobs sent to the gateway into jobs described in the canonical format and stored in the 3G-bridge database. The adaptor that allows OurGrid jobs to be stored in the gateway's database for execution in the gLite system is implemented by a modified version of the OurGrid Worker.

This new Worker is called a Front-End Worker, since it does not manage a resource, but simply provides access to resources managed by other components. The Broker sees the Front-End Worker as a normal Worker and dispatches jobs to it in the same way it does for other Workers. The fact that the task is actually executed in a gLite grid is completely transparent from the Broker's perspective. For gLite, we have implemented a modified version of the CREAM (Computing Resource Execution and Management) Computing Element [7] that is able to store gLite jobs in the 3G-bridge database.

The common syntax for the jobs was obtained by the definition of a MySQL database schema [15] that allows the storage of jobs in a canonical format. Regarding the availability of extension points, it could be reached by the development of a plug-in framework that uses a common interface, called GridHandler, allowing the implementation of middleware-specific plug-ins. So, each deployed plug-in implements a different strategy of job execution management on the destination grid back end. The software was written in Java [13] and fully deployed as an Apache Tomcat [1] application.

2.4.2   Porting gLite to the Microsoft Windows Platform

We rebuilt parts of both the Globus Toolkit and the gLite middleware to allow the execution of the gLite middleware on Microsoft Windows operating systems. This work allowed us to provide a gLite Windows User interface, facilitating the access to the infrastructure to Windows users and, moreover, a gLite Windows Grid Site, allowing Windows Applications to use the infrastructure.

The Grid2Win GUI is a Graphical User Interface running on both Windows and Linux operating systems. We designed the Grid2Win GUI to operate in cross-platform style. We used the wxWidget cross-platform library that gives us the certainty to build on Windows, Linux, MacOS, and other operating systems (provided that a gLite command line user interface exists for such operating system). Figure 2.2 illustrates the elements involved in the execution of gLite UI over different operating systems using Grid2Win.

This GUI (Graphical User Interface) gives the possibility to use the grid in a easy way, like any other windows program, allowing to download/upload files with just one mouse click, submitting a job, wizard-driven authentication process,

Fig. 2.2 Grid2Win GUI on
Linux and Windows

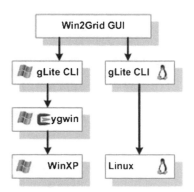

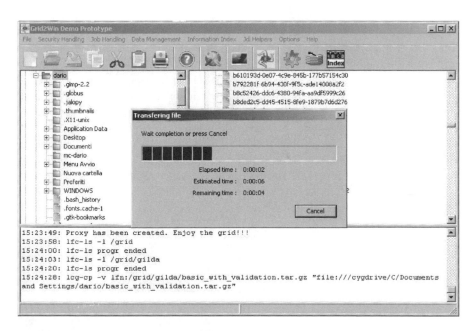

Fig. 2.3 A snapshot of the Grid2Win GUI

wizard-driven Job Description Language (JDL) creation, etc. Since this GUI is not linked to the underlying UI, it works even if the command line programs change (provided that their correspondent binaries still exist and the interfaces are still the same which is likely to be the case). Figure 2.3 shows a snapshot of the interface.

The deployment of a gLite grid site on Microsoft Windows allowed computational nodes to run Windows-based applications. To achieve this goal, our first approach to Microsoft Windows computing farms was based on the Torque/MAUI scheduler, a free version of PBS (Fig. 2.4). The farm is composed of a unique central node with Linux operating system in which the Gatekeeper and the Torque/MAUI head node are running (a gLite Computing Element) and a set of Worker Nodes with our rebuilt version of the gLite WN package.

Fig. 2.4 Computing element
with Microsoft Windows
Worker Nodes

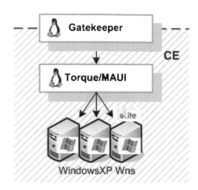

2.4.3   Grid Storage Access Framework

Grid Storage Access Framework (GSAF) is a tool developed to access and to manage
Data Grid via APIs that solves several common design problems of the applications
providing developers with a tool to write application that adopts grid as Digital
Repository hiding the fragmentation and the complexity of the Data Grid Services.

Within a grid infrastructure, files are stored inside Storage Elements (SE); the
grid services that take care of data persistency). They can be replicated on several
SEs for ubiquity, security, and sharing purposes. Relationships between locations of
files, replicas, and their logical names are kept within a specific File Catalogue
Service. For each file, it is possible to associate some descriptive attributes (metadata schema), and values (schema instance) can be assigned to them, modified,
quantified, and queried through a specific Metadata Catalogue Service.

Since Data Grid Services (File Catalogue, Metadata Catalogue, and Storage
Elements) are independent from each other and work in a "stand-alone" mode,
applications that want to adopt them must implement specialized and decoupled
software components according to a vertical architecture (Fig. 2.5).

This fragmentation leads to the following problem: for each application, developers
must always write the same code in order to include data services capabilities and
take care about the atomicity, coherence, and the synchronization of data manipulation. Furthermore, there are neither tools nor services that help clients (both end user
and software modules) to maintain semantic coherence and integrity consistency
among files stored on the SEs and their entries inside the File Catalogue and the
Metadata Catalogue. These are considered big limitations of the Grid Storage System
and our effort has been in the direction of addressing them via a software layer that
can solve both problems. We can say that GSAF implements a kind of Software
Engineering Pattern for grid applications, offering a standard solution for a common
problem according to the principle of write once and use everywhere.

The analysis of the architecture of a generic enterprise application emphasizes
the problem of the fragmentation described above. Typically, this kind of application
follows the three-layer architecture model, derived from the MCV (Model, Control,
View) design pattern (Fig. 2.6).

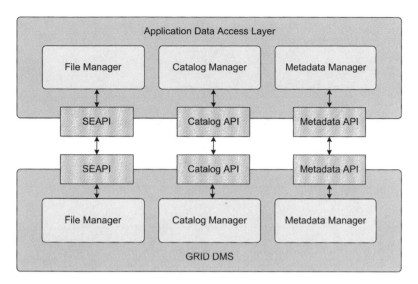

Fig. 2.5 Grid data services integration schema

Fig. 2.6 Grid data services integration schema

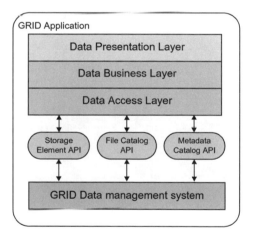

As shown in Fig. 2.7, the Data Presentation Layer consists of the graphical interfaces that make the user able to interact with the application. The Data Business Layer collects all software components that implement the behavior of the given application. The Data Access Layer is made of software components that allow the application to manage data and metadata, typically ASCII files, XML files, digital objects, SQL data, etc. It is evident how developing enterprise applications over grid means to replace the traditional Data Access Layer with an appropriate interface that allows business components to manage data stored on the Data Management System (DMS) and presentation objects to search and retrieve data from it.

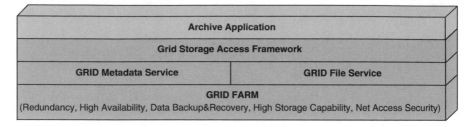

Fig. 2.7 Layered architecture view of GSAF

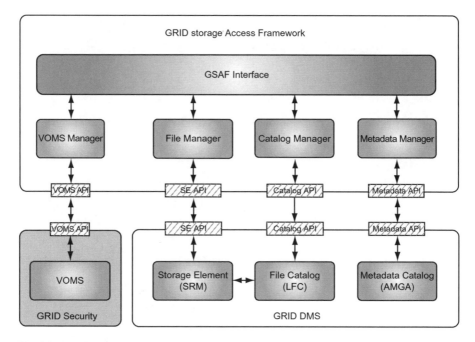

Fig. 2.8 Architectural framework view of GSAF

GSAF represents this interface (Fig. 2.7). It is an object-oriented framework built on top of the gLite Metadata Service and gLite File Services that exposes classes and related methods. These, in turn, hide the complexity and the fragmentation of the several underlying Application Programming Interfaces (APIs) for applications located above it.

GSAF wraps each gLite Data Services through a corresponding software module built on top of the related API. Figure 2.8 shows the architecture of the framework. The File Manager provides functions to interact with the Storage Element allowing the upload/download of files to/from the SE. The Catalogue Manager is related to the File Catalogue Service and provides functions to register and de-register files. It also allows browsing and managing virtual directories. The Metadata Manager interfaces the Metadata Catalogue Service wrapping all metadata-related functions.

The Virtual Organization Membership Service (VOMS) Manager is responsible to get a valid proxy from the VOMS server. Finally, the main module, the GSAF Interface, works as a dispatcher for the application requests and as a coordinator of the underlying components. It provides a unique interface and takes care of both data atomicity and coherence including the transaction capability.

2.4.4   The Secure Storage Service

The Secure Storage Service (SSS) for the gLite middleware provides users with a set of tools to store in a secure way and in an encrypted format confidential data, for example, medical or financial data, on the grid storage elements. The data stored through the provided tools is accessible and readable only by authorized users. One of the important contributions of this service is that it solves the insider abuse problem, as well as it prevents the administrators of the storage elements to access the confidential data in a clear format.

The Secure Storage Service has been designed to be integrated into the gLite middleware. It consists of the following components (Fig. 2.9):

- Command Line Applications: Commands integrated into the gLite User Interface to encrypt and upload, as well as download and decrypt files on the storage elements.

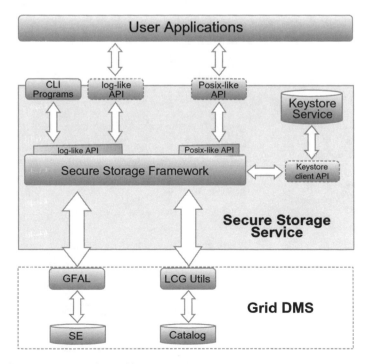

Fig. 2.9 Secure storage service architecture

- An Application Program Interface: The API allows the developer to write programs able to manage confidential data using the Secure Storage Service.
- The Keystore: A new grid element used to store and retrieve users' keys in a secure way.
- The Secure Storage Framework: A component of the service, internally used by the other components. It provides encryption/decryption functions and other utility functions. It takes care of the interaction with the Grid Data Management System.

Advanced Encryption Standard (AES) algorithm is the default encryption algorithm used in the Secure Storage Service with a 256-bit long key. However, the service is able to support new symmetric algorithms, thanks to its modular architecture.

This service provides a set of new Command Line Applications on the gLite User Interface. These applications allow users to manage confidential data in a secure way. The Command Line Applications of the Service used to upload/download data to/from storage elements are described in the following:

- *lcg-scr*: the input parameters of this command are a local file, a storage element, a Logical File Name (LFN), and a list of users authorized to access the file. The command generates an encryption key, encrypts the input file, and uploads it on the storage element, registering its LFN in an LFC (LCG File Catalogue) file catalogue. Moreover, it stores the key generated and used to encrypt the file in the keystore. An ACL will be created and associated to the encryption key on the keystore. This ACL will contain all users authorized to access the file, represented by a list composed by pairs of Distinguished Name (DN), and Fully Qualified Attributes Name (FQAN). Figure 2.10 depicts the steps involved in the execution of this command.

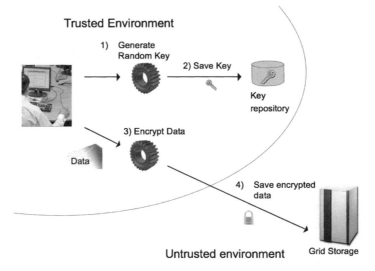

Fig. 2.10 lcg-scr command: (1) A new random secret key is generated, (2) the key and the ACL are saved on the keystore, (3) the input file is encrypted inside user-trusted environment, (4) the encrypted file is uploaded on the grid storage element

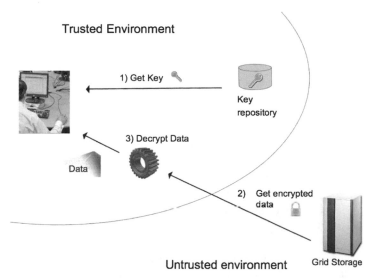

Fig. 2.11 lcg-scp command: (1) Get the secret key from the keystore; this operation fails if the user is not authorized, (2) download the encrypted file on the local machine, (3) decrypt the file and save it on the local file system

- *lcg-scp*: the input parameter of this command is an LFN. It downloads the encrypted file identified by the input LFN, gets the key to decrypt the file from the keystore, decrypts the file, and then stores it on the local file system. This command successfully returns only if the user is an authorized user (the authorization procedure is described later on in this document. Figure 2.11 shows the steps involved in the execution of the lcg-scp command.

2.4.5 The Watchdog

The Watchdog is a tool that allows grid users to control and monitor the execution of their own jobs. The need to monitoring and control the job execution while the grid application runs on the Worker Nodes is one of the primary needs of grid developers since they can easily interact with the running jobs.

Monitor and control grid jobs are not only useful during the early development phases of grid applications, but they are also useful to aid the application users when exploiting the production infrastructure. Thanks to a Job monitoring and control tool, grid jobs may produce real-time results or even let the application be piloted by the user. It is also possible to stop unnecessary computations avoiding costly waste of time for both users and infrastructure resources.

The early design of the Watchdog has been developed to assist all grid applications requesting long computation time. The idea behind the Watchdog was to inspect the execution of a grid job monitoring, timely, a set of files produced by the grid job while it is running on the Worker Node. Soon this simple idea has been enriched with different features and capabilities, creating a very flexible and powerful tool to monitor and also control the job execution.

The EELA-2 grid infrastructure currently relies on the gLite middleware version 3.1 and this release of the middleware does not provide any flexible way to monitor and control the grid job execution. The gLite 3.1 only offers a basic and native support for the job monitoring named the Job Perusal mechanism. The Workload Management System (WMS) handles directly the Job Perusal monitoring system, and its behavior is directly piloted by a set of specific statements of the Job Description Language (JDL). Exactly like the Watchdog, the Job Perusal mechanism allows to check periodically the content of files produced by the jobs while they are running on the WN. Although the Job Perusal mechanism provides a standard way to monitor grid job files, it cannot be considered as flexible as the Watchdog is. Moreover, the Job Perusal mechanism has been introduced since gLite v3.1 and few grid developers feel confident with this newly introduced middleware capability while very few tests have been made so far. In the EELA-2 community, there are no applications that are currently adopting the Job Perusal.

The Watchdog consists of few bash script files; this decision has been taken to help grid application developers to easily customize the Watchdog behavior accordingly to their personal needs. The grid application user has just to set up a configuration file and include the Watchdog files into the Job Input Sandbox.

The Watchdog does not need any special installation to be done by the grid site administrators and it has been built only on top of existing gLite services, this implies that the use of the Watchdog does not compromise the grid security or the Job execution performances.

The way the Watchdog uses to monitor and control the job execution consists of mainly two possibilities: Timely, keep track of Job files content (log files, output streams, etc.) and allow the execution of commands or scripts sent by the user while the grid job runs. In the Watchdog terminology, the monitor files are called "file snapshots" and these files may report the whole content of the file or just the last changes happened during the last time interval. The list of files and the kind of snapshots can be changed anytime. It is also possible to change the time interval and stop/resume/end the monitoring while the job runs.

The Watchdog interaction between the monitored jobs and the user can be done in three different fashions:

• Using an LFC file catalog
• Using an AMGA server
• Using a mounted Network File System (NFS) accessible from the WN; if one is foreseen by the site administrators (AFS, NFS, etc.)

Recent efforts have been made to improve the quality of the user interface developing a command line interface as helper tool in order to easily get file snapshots from monitored files and submit commands to be executed on the Worker Node by the Watchdog on the user behalf.

2.5 Exploit the Additional Grid Services

In this section, we describe how the additional grid services have been adopted by the applications.

2.5.1 Application Porting and Final Balance at the End of the EELA-2 Project

At the end of the project on March 2010, 53 applications out of the 61 supported in total were successfully deployed and interfaced with the grid middleware (Table 2.1). It is worth mentioning that some EELA-2 resource centers also support the Virtual Organization (VOs) from well-known High-Energy Physics (HEP) experiments such as ALICE, ATLAS, LHCb, CMS, and Pierre Auger.

Several applications use the additional grid services developed by the project. These services helped to speed up the application porting on the grid infrastructure and sometimes made possible the gridification of some applications.

The complete list of applications supported by EELA-2, as well as its descriptions and references, can be retrieved from the URL http://applications.eu-eela.eu.

2.5.2 Increasing the Reach of e-Infrastructure

The EELA-2 infrastructure has profited from the additional services developed in many ways. The services that provide with a major benefit in raising the reach of e-Infrastructure are, first, the adoption of the OurGrid middleware, that has increased the portfolio of middleware supported by the EELA-2 infrastructure and, second, the porting of the gLite to the Microsoft Windows platform that allows Windows Applications to use the infrastructure.

The adoption of OurGrid allowed non-dedicated resources to be added to the infrastructure. Moreover, it allowed resources, dedicated or not, to be added to the infrastructure without the need to change their operating system. The seamless integration of these resources was made available thanks to the work carried out in the EELA-2 project that enhanced the OurGrid middleware to use the same kind of certificates that are used by gLite and other established grid middleware. Figure 2.12 shows a snapshot of the monitoring page for the opportunistic part of the EELA-2 infrastructure. As it can be seen, around 300 cores are available in this part of the infrastructure and the tendency is that this number will substantially increase.

Figure 2.13 shows the availability of cores in the opportunistic grid during the last quarter of 2009. As it can be seen, the total number of cores that can potentially be available to the grid kept over 300 during the whole period shown. From these, a little less than 50% are normally available.

Table 2.1 Applications deployed on EELA-2 infrastructure

Application	Scientific domain	Country
AERMOD	Earth Sciences	Cuba
AeroVANT	Engineering	Argentina
Aiuri	Computer Science and Mathematics	Brazil
BiG (Blast)	Bioinformatics/Genomics	Spain
BioMD	Life Sciences	Brazil
bioNMF	Bioinformatics/Genomics	Spain
BRAMS	Earth Sciences	Brazil
C/CATT-BRAMS	Earth Sciences	Chile/Brazil
CAM	Earth Sciences	Spain
CardioGrid Portal	Life Sciences	Argentina
CATIVIC	Life Sciences (Chemistry)	Venezuela
Cinefilia	Computer Science and Mathematics	Italy/Brazil
CIS – Classification of Satellite Images with neural networks	Earth Sciences	Ecuador
CROSS-Fire	Civil Protection	Portugal
DicomGrid	Life Sciences	Brazil
Dist-SOM-PORTRAIT	Bioinformatics/Genomics	Brazil
DistBlast	Bioinformatics/Genomics	Brazil
DKEsG	Fusion	Spain
DRI/Mammogrid	Life Sciences (e-health)	Spain
eIMRT	Life Sciences (e-health)	Spain
FAFNER2	Fusion	Spain
fMRI	Life Sciences (e-health)	Portugal
G-HMMER	Bioinformatics/Genomics	Colombia
G-InterProScan	Bioinformatics/Genomics	Colombia
GAMOS	Life Sciences	Spain
gCSMT	Earth Sciences	France
GenecodisGrid	Bioinformatics/Genomics	Spain
GrEMBOSS	Bioinformatics/Genomics	Mexico
Grid Bio Portal	Bioinformatics/Genomics	Spain
GRIP – Grid Image Processing for Biomedical Diagnosis	Life Sciences	Chile
GROMACS	Life Sciences (Chemistry)	Brazil
gRREEMM	Engineering	Cuba
gSATyrus	Computer Science and Mathematics	Brazil
Heart Simulator	Life Sciences	Brazil
HeMoLab	Life Sciences	Brazil
Industry@Grid	Engineering	Brazil
Integra-EPI	Life Sciences	Brazil
InvCell	Life Sciences	Brazil
InvTissue	Life Sciences	Brazil
LEMDistFE	Engineering	Mexico
MAVs-Study	Engineering	Argentina
META-Dock	Bioinformatics/Genomics	Mexico
Phylogenetics	Life Sciences	Spain
PhyloGrid	Life Sciences	Spain

(continued)

Table 2.1 (continued)

Application	Scientific domain	Country
PILP	Computer Science and Mathematics	Portugal
Portal de Porticos	Engineering	Venezuela
ProtozoaDB	Life Sciences	Brazil
PSAUPMP	Engineering	Mexico
SATCA	Earth Sciences	Mexico
Seismic Sensor	Earth Sciences	Mexico
SEMUM3D	Earth Sciences	France
WAM	Earth Sciences	Ireland
WRF	Earth Sciences	Spain

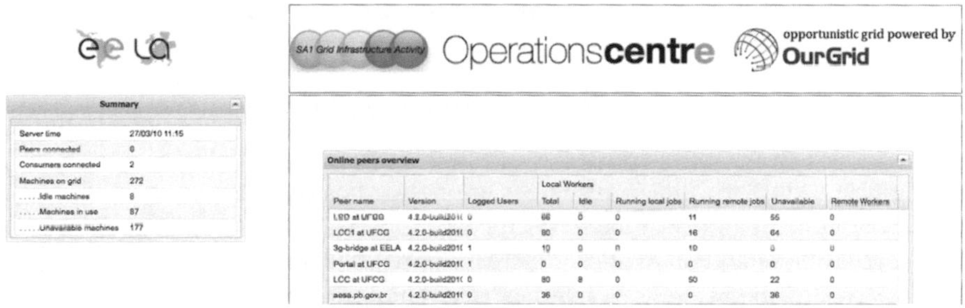

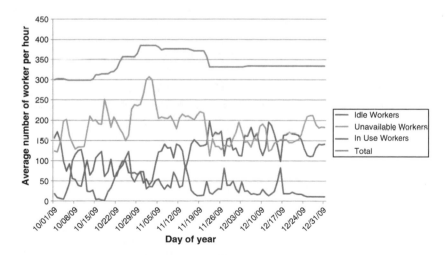

Fig. 2.12 Opportunistic infrastructure monitoring data

Fig. 2.13 Worker Nnodes availability for the opportunistic infrastructure (last quarter of 2009)

Figure 2.14 shows the job submission status for the opportunistic part of the infrastructure during the last quarter of 2009. As it can be seen, the number of failed jobs is fairly small. Moreover, most of the failures are due to the resources becoming

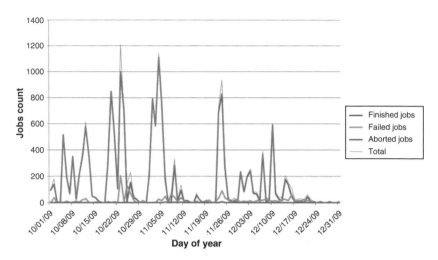

Fig. 2.14 Job submission for the opportunistic infrastructure (last quarter of 2009)

unavailable to the grid (these resources are not dedicated to the grid). This gives evidence of the reliability of the infrastructure.

The other important contribution to increase the reach of the EELA-2 e-Infrastructure was the port of the gLite User Interface, Computing Element, and Worker Nodes components to the Microsoft Windows platform. This allowed resource centers that had staff well trained in managing MS Windows-based system to offer to their users the full power of the gLite middleware – before this port was done, the only option for these system administrators was either to leverage on virtualization technology to run gLite on Scientific Linux systems executed as guest operating systems in virtual machines run on top of the host MS Windows-based system or to provide their resources to the grid using the OurGrid middleware. Currently, there is one resource center (in INFN/Catania) running the MS Windows port of gLite and other resource center should be deployed in the months to come. More importantly, there is already one application (MAVs-Study) benefiting from this development.

2.5.3 Increasing the Usability of e-Infrastructure

The application-oriented services developed in the context of the EELA-2 project helped to solve many common problems related to application deployment and allowed the gridification of some applications with requirements not easy to satisfy using the standard gLite environment. These services have been widely advertised in the EELA-2 Web site, as well as in the various dissemination events organized during the grid schools and the gridification weeks.

The grid schools are closed retreats of 1–2 weeks where application experts work in close collaboration with tutors to interface their applications with the grid

Table 2.2 List of applications that use JRA1 application-oriented services

Service	Application using it	Use description
Digital Archives (GSAF)	gRREEMM	Provide gRREEMM with a Java interface toward the gLite Data Management System
Secure Storage	CardioGrid Portal, HeMoLab, Seismic Sensor, AeroVANT	Applications use this service to manage their confidential data in a secure way inside the Grid infrastructure
Tagging	BRAMS and other SegHidro applications	Help in searching shared data among researchers working on water resources management
Workflow	BRAMS and other SegHidro applications	Several SegHidro applications use it to implement their workflow, starting from the water precipitation prediction provided by BRAMS
Watchdog	CROSS-Fire, InterproScan/HMMER, HeMoLab, AeroVANT, BioMD, Cinefilia	Several applications use it to monitor their long running jobs
Lcg-rec	CROSS-Fire, META-Dock	CROSS-Fire and META-Dock use it to interact in an easier way with the LCG File Catalog
DIRAC	BioMD, PSAUPMP	Ease their execution in sites with different MPI "flavors."

middleware. At the end of the school, the applications involved are able to run on the grid infrastructure.

These events provided us with a good chance to identify applications that could benefit of the additional services. Starting with the applications requirements analysis, we identified the problems that could hinder the applications gridification and the services that could help us to remove these impediments.

For example, applications managing confidential data cannot be easily ported in a grid infrastructure because the standard gLite middleware does not provide users with tools to manage confidential data in a secure way. Instead, profiting of the Secure Storage Service, this obstacle can be removed and these applications are able to run on the grid infrastructure satisfying their requirements. As a result, a number of applications are currently using the services developed and all services are currently been used by at least one application. Table 2.2 gives a summary of this utilization.

2.5.4 Gridify a Windows Application – The MAVs-Study Use Case

In order to allow Windows application to profit from the grid infrastructure, in this section we will provide a detailed description of how we ported the Windows application MAVs-Study on the grid infrastructure. MAVs-Study – Biologically

Table 2.3 MAVs- Study on the grid (JDL and Start Script)

MAVs-Study on the GRID	
JDL	Start Script
Type = "Job"; JobType = "Normal"; Executable = "uvlmRF"; StdOutput = "uvlmRF.out"; StdError = "uvlmRF.err"; InputSandbox = {"uvlm.exe","uvlmRF","CONFIG.DAT", "LS.DAT","RotationAngle.DAT","StrokeDe viation.DAT","StrokePosition.DAT"}; OutputSandbox = {"uvlmRF.err","uvlmRF.out"}; RetryCount = 0; ShallowRetryCount=0;	# Environment variables export PROD=prod.vo.eu-eela.eu export LFC_HOST=lfc.eela.ufrj.br export LCG_GFAL_INFOSYS=bdii.eela.ufrj.br:2 170 export PATH=$PATH:. # Execution date chmod u+x uvlm uvlm # Storage date FILE=results03-00.tar.gz /bin/tar -czf $FILE *.DAT *.Dat *.TEC std.out std.err lcg-cr --vo $PROD -l lfn:/grid/prod.vo.eu-eela.eu/MAVs- Study/test03/$FILE -d lnx097.eela.if.ufrj.br file:$PWD/$FILE # End Date

Inspired, Super Maneuverable, Flapping Wing Micro-Air-Vehicles is an application developed by University of Río Cuarto and University of Córdoba (Argentina) to design micro air vehicles able to be used in different contexts as atmospheric studies, fire detection, inspections of collapsed buildings, hazardous spill monitoring, inspections in places too dangerous for humans, and planetary exploration.

This application is subdivided in three stages: (1) preprocess, (2) process, and (3) post-process. The preprocess stage allows to define the start parameters for the simulation using an interactive application developed in MATLAB. The process stage computes the aerodynamic model using No-linear and no-steady vortex-lattice method (NUVLM). The final stage, developed in FORTRAN 95 and MATLAB, writes the results from the numerical simulations in an appropriate format to be interpreted by other softwares (Table 2.3).

The process stage is a batch and requires a long time to be executed in a normal workstation, about 3/4 days. Then, application developers decided to port the application on the grid infrastructure to benefit of the huge computation resources available. But the process stage has been developed in FORTRAN 95 for Windows Environment and the standard release of the gLite environment supports only Linux. Then, this application couldn't be ported on the grid environment without grid2win, the infrastructure service developed to allow Windows applications to run on gLite.

Using the gLite Windows site installed in the EELA-2 infrastructure, we were able to successfully port MAVs-Study on the grid environment. Above, we have demonstrated the JDL file and Start script used to gridify MAVs-Study while the obtained results about wings position after the first processing cycle are illustrated in Figs. 2.15 and 2.16.

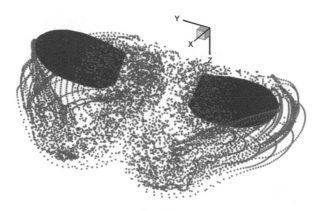

Fig. 2.15 MAVs-study wings position: Isometric view

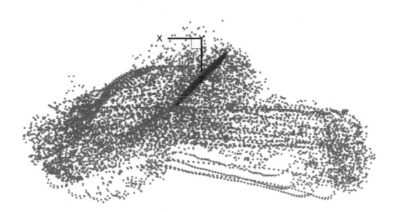

Fig. 2.16 MAVs-study wings position: Right view

2.6   Future Perspectives

The methodology to support e-Science applications introduced in this chapter allowed EELA-2 e-Infrastructure to attract and support several e-Science applications. This infrastructure will continue to be supported in the next years, thanks to new initiatives like new projects funded by the European Commission and local dedicated funds.

Indeed, one of the main objectives of the EELA project was to ensure the long-term sustainability of the e-Infrastructure beyond the term of the project. Several initiatives have been led during the EELA-2 lifetime to reach this target. In particular, we defined a long-term sustainability model, LGI (Latin Grid Initiative) that fits the Latin America reality and could be easily implemented [10, 14].

The described methodology in this chapter will continue to be used in the next years. The EELA-2 e-Infrastructure could be enriched with new additional services and, this way, the number of applications supported could be still increased. Moreover, thanks to the past experiences, the identification and the developing of new services able to satisfy specific applications requirements will be faster. In this way, the EELA-2 e-Infrastructure capabilities will grow in the years, allowing us to approach toward an infrastructure able to support almost all e-Science applications and, moreover, able to quickly adapt to new requirements and needs.

2.7 Conclusion

In this chapter, we described a successful methodology to support e-Science applications on an e-Infrastructure. Enriching the grid middleware adopted with additional services, developed to meet applications requirements, and to increase the appeal of the e-Infrastructure, we set up an e-Infrastructure able to satisfy the heterogeneous requirements of e-Science applications coming from different scientific domains.

We used the EELA-2 use case to show how this methodology can be applied in the real world. First, we introduced the EELA-2 project and the set of applications supported. After then, we described the services developed during the project to enrich the infrastructure. Then, we showed how these services increase the number of applications supported and make faster their deployment on the infrastructure. Finally, we explained how this methodology could evolve in the future, allowing to create an e-Infrastructure able to satisfy almost all the requirements of the e-Science applications.

References

1. Apache Tomcat: http://tomcat.apache.org (2010)
2. Brasileiro, F., Duarte, A., Carvalho, D., Barbera, R., Scardaci. D.: An approach for the co-existence of service and opportunistic grids: the EELA-2 Case. In: Proceedings of the 2nd Latin America Grid International Workshop, Campo Grande, pp. 1–8 (2008)
3. Bruno, R., Barbera, R., Ingrà, E.: Watchdog: a job monitoring solution inside the EELA-2 Infrastructure. In: Proceedings of the 2nd EELA-2 Conference, Choronì (2010)
4. Cardenas-Montes, M., Emmen, A., Marosi, A., Araujo, F., Gombs, G., Terstynszky, G., Fedak, G., Kelly, I., Taylor, I., Lodygensky, O., Kacsuk, P., Lovas, R., Kiss, T., Balaton, Z., Farkas, Z.: Edges: bridging desktop and service grids. In: Proceedings of 2nd Iberian Grid Infrastructure Conference, Porto. http://edges-grid.eu:8080/c/document_library/get_file?p_l_id=29093&fol derId=11075&name=DLFE-201.pdf (2008)
5. CERN Large Hadron Collider (LHC): www.cern.ch/lhc (2010)
6. Cirne, W., Brasileiro, F., Andrade, N., Costa, L., An, A.: Labs of the world unite!!! J. Grid Comput. **4**(3), 225–246 (2006)
7. CREAM (Computing Resource Execution and Management): http://grid.pd.infn.it/cream (2010)
8. EELA: http://www.eu-eela.org/first-phase.php (2006)
9. EELA-2: http://www.eu-eela.eu (2008)

10. EELA-2 DSA1.3: http://documents.eu-eela.eu/record/1119/files/EELA-2-DSA1.pdf?version=1 (2009)
11. EELA-2 general services: http://eoc.eu-eela.eu/docu.php?id=central_services (2008)
12. gLite: http://www.glite.org (2010)
13. Java: http://www.java.com (2010)
14. Marechal, B., Gavillet, P., Barbera, R.: Long-term sustainability of e-Infrastructures in LA: The EELA-2 model. Presented at CCICT Conference, Kingston (2009)
15. MySQL: http://www.mysql.com (2010)
16. OurGrid: http://www.ourgrid.org (2010)
17. Russo, D., Scibilia, F.: Grid2Win: Porting gLite to Windows Based Platforms. In: Proceedings of the 16th IEEE International Workshops on Enabling Technologies: Infrastructure for Collaborative Enterprises, Paris, pp. 300–301. IEEE Computer Society, Evry (2007)
18. Scardaci, D., Scuderi, G.: A secure storage service for the gLite middleware. In: Proceedings of 3rd International Symposium on Information Assurance and Security, Manchester, pp. 261–266. IEEE Computer Society, Washington, DC (2007)
19. Scibilia, F., Barbera, R.: SAGE: storage accounting for grid environments. In: Proceedings of 1st EELA-2 Conference, Bogotá, Colombia (2009)
20. Scifo, S: GSAF: grid storage access framework. In: Proceedings of 16th IEEE International Workshops on Enabling Technologies: Infrastructure for Collaborative Enterprises, Paris, pp. 296–297. IEEE Computer Society, Evry (2007)

Chapter 3
GEMS: User Control for Cooperative Scientific Repositories

Justin M. Wozniak, Paul Brenner, Santanu Chatterjee, Douglas Thain, Aaron Striegel, and Jesús Izaguirre

3.1 Introduction

Data repositories are an integral part of modern scientific computing systems. While a variety of grid-enabled storage systems have been developed to improve scalability, administrative control, and interoperability, users have several outstanding needs: to seamlessly and efficiently work with replicated data sets, to customize system behavior within a grid, and to quickly tie together remotely administered grids or independently operated resources. This is particularly true in the small virtual organization, in which a subset of possible users seek to coordinate subcomponents of existing grids into a workable collaborative system. Our approach to this problem starts with the storage system and seeks to enable this functionality by creating ad hoc storage grids. Modern commodity hardware in use at research labs and university networks ships with an abundance of storage space that is often underutilized, and even consumer gadgets provide extensive storage resources that will not immediately be filled. The installation of simple software enables these systems to be pooled and cataloged into a spacious, parallel ad hoc storage network. While traditional storage networks or tertiary storage systems are isolated behind file servers and firewalls, constricting data movement, we layer the storage service network atop the client consumer network, improving the available network parallelism and boosting I/O performance for data-intensive scientific tasks.

J.M. Wozniak (✉)
Argonne National Laboratory, 9700 S. Cass Avenue, Argonne, IL 60439, USA
e-mail: woznlak@mcs.anl.gov

P. Brenner • S. Chatterjee • D. Thain • A. Striegel • J. Izaguirre
University of Notre Dame, Notre Dame, IN, USA

N.P. Preve (ed.), *Grid Computing: Towards a Global Interconnected Infrastructure*,
Computer Communications and Networks, DOI 10.1007/978-0-85729-676-4_3,
© Springer-Verlag London Limited 2011

Extending scientific repositories out to volunteer data sources and across administrative boundaries using centralized file services, static replica management systems, or peer-to-peer systems is not viable due to the nature of target systems. Heavy scientific workloads, research-oriented usage patterns, and variably collaborative resource networks require new storage architectures.

Our focus application area, computational chemistry simulations, often produce heavy output data sets, transcripts, etc., compared to amount of metadata that is used to specify the data set, such as the simulation configuration, random seed, file names, and access control policy. Metadata may be used to refer to existing data sets but is typically much smaller than the files themselves. Programmatic access to metadata catalogs creates a scientific filesystem that greatly eases access to complex repositories. Our architecture is inspired by typical scientific usage: optimizing system performance for the demands of typical software and interfaces for the mental framework of typical simulation researchers.

The dynamic nature of ad hoc storage networks allows scientific users to easily volunteer storage resources to the system, insert data sets, and manage access control to resources and data. This allows researchers – not just computer administrators – to patch together their own communities of software, data, resources, and users while integrating with a larger repository system and benefiting from semi-autonomic storage management.

Current systems limit user customizability, which enables locally optimal performance, and ease of utility, which enables maintainable software. The solution to these problems is the development of flexible systems, providing a variety of access methods and administrative controls. The policies carried out by flexible ad hoc systems will be reconfigurable at the user level, allowing for integration of grid resources into larger systems and derivation of smaller grids; likewise, enhanced or limited privileges will be administered by users on their own data environments. Applications developed on such a system can make use of this hybridization, enabling system-aware workflow structures.

Our solution to this problem is represented by the Grid-Enabled Molecular Simulation (GEMS) system. Programmatically, GEMS presents a reliable database abstraction atop an uncontrolled network of independent Chirp [9] file servers. GEMS was originally designed for molecular dynamics but has been fully generalized to support any application. In this chapter, we will discuss the advanced usage capabilities of this system for scientific computation and collaboration.

3.2 GEMS Architecture

The GEMS architecture, shown in Fig. 3.1, is intended to provide a quickly deployable organizational framework for a network of independently owned and operated storage services. In an institutional setting, these machines may already be combined into an opportunistic computing system such as Condor, but the available disk space may go unused. The storage services are available on these machines but not usable because of their individual instability. By structuring and controlling these servers,

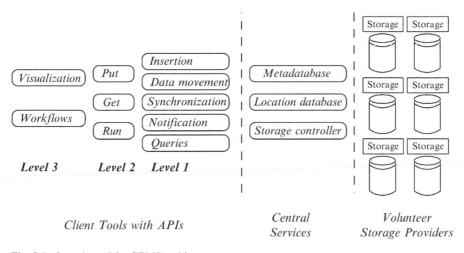

Fig. 3.1 Overview of the GEMS architecture

GEMS gains the utility of the extra disk space as well as the performance offered by a data delivery system that is potentially as scalable as the computing infrastructure.

GEMS delivers the utility of these services as a unified resource, and relies on four major concepts: automated replication, awareness of administrative concerns, distributed access control, and centralized browsability. Replication increases the reliability and parallelism of data sources; in GEMS, a semi-autonomous controller [12] detects and responds to subsystem failure in a priority-driven manner. Additionally, administrative matters are managed within the same control system: disk allocation is balanced with respect to the available space volunteered to the system, and data is removed from disks as their owners fill them. GEMS also manages access control lists in the volunteered space, and provides an authentication mechanism [11] compatible with existing techniques. Observed deviations from system policy are prioritized and repaired [4, 13] without user intervention, by locating, allocating, and using additional available disk space in accordance with user policy. A diagram of example operation is shown in Fig.3.2.

The browsable repository created by GEMS essentially implements a parameter sweep database. This metadata may be used to derive a novel parallel programming model that enables synchronized tuple space communication and parallel data movement, called a data sweep. This framework may be used to build up parameter sweeps, workflows, interactive parameter space exploration, and related hybrid structures.

3.2.1   Runtime Operation

GEMS maintains a replica list for each data file inserted into the system, which asynchronously grows as the file is replicated in accordance with user policy. Management aspects include monitoring the underlying storage for failure, file

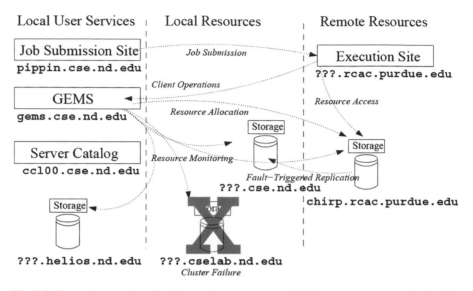

Fig. 3.2 Example operation of replica maintenance system. Replica shortages are repaired while data services to running jobs continue

existence, and file corruption via an MD5 comparison. A diagram of example operation is shown in Fig. 3.2.

Limiting the control software system to user level limits its ability to abuse resource providers and enables the opportunistic use of available storage. While a top-down stovepipe solution might intimidate storage providers, resulting in low volunteer participation, the controller relies on a previously existing intermediary resource discovery service and interacts with registered services as an ordinary user. This promotes the healthy use of ordinary policy negotiation among volunteer resource providers and the consumers of the ad hoc grid [10].

3.2.2   Client Toolkit

While existing tools may be used to access files stored on the underlying system, GEMS enables the orchestration of higher level operations by providing additional tiered client operations as diagrammed in Fig. 3.1. First level utilities enable resource reservation and insertion. This allows a client to reserve a given amount of space on a resource selected by the user or by GEMS for later use. Data movement utilities may be used to transport the data to that location, in addition to the use of existing clients compatible with the storage services. Upon transfer completion, the state of the files is synchronized with the centralized service, which is then entrusted to manage them. Other clients waiting for notification with respect to this data set may then be notified, or the data set may be found and located later by executing metadata-driven queries.

Second level utilities provide simplified access to the system, including FTP-like get and put operations as well as a computation utility to bind existing programs to data sources in the repository without code modification. Third level utilities enable higher level user interaction with the system. Graphical tools include a general-purpose data browser, which is capable of downloading or uploading repository data. Additionally, workflow structures may be built and executed using complex query and notification combinations as discussed below.

3.3   Replica Access

Data replication has multiple benefits. While enhancing data survivability and enabling wide area storage systems as discussed above, it may be combined with computation systems to provide performance benefits. Large-scale computing infrastructures built upon load sharing architectures or Internet peer groups require scalable access to the scientific repositories that enable the application. High-throughput computing requires the elimination of bottlenecks, such as the overuse of a particular file server. A balance in disk usage may intuitively be obtained by balancing data placement: a user-driven process discussed above.

Replica-aware computation has several important aspects. Record naming and identification is an essential user task, which may be greatly eased by appropriate software tools. Data access may be enabled by explicit data transfer or over virtual filesystem technologies, either of which is relevant to this discussion. Ultimately, efficiency and performance must be delivered by proper reference to the replica system.

3.3.1   Data Identification and Access

The underlying complexity of a replica system creates the need for abstract data catalogs that enable scientific data tagging and location. In the case of a simulation repository, for example, each record in the replica system contains the set of data files involved; each record is uniquely identified by a config number. The record may also be tagged by a unique set of key-value pairs, which are typically based on the parameters used to generate the data, such as software settings, scientific coefficients, and random number seeds. The scientific namespace is the set of possible tag combinations that may be mapped to a record.

While abstract naming systems are required in the presence of dynamic data placement, the use of a virtual filesystem creates an additional translation layer that must be overcome. The combination of a config number and a filename represent an abstract name for a file that is location independent with respect to data sources, that is, replica location. The combination of a file server name and a filename represent a virtual name for a file. The resolution of abstract name to virtual name is the essential task of a replica location system, but the existence of both names is useful in replica-aware computation.

The GEMS-based encapsulation of a set of scientific data files inside a logically unified, tagged record provides benefits both scientific and technical. Simulation result files are typically used in concert when performing analysis, and the abstract tagging and naming system simplifies the implementation of postprocessing routines. The naming and access scheme additionally helps mask the complex internals of a distributed database, providing conceptual understanding that may be lacking in a plain filesystem. Common tasks such as retrieving yesterday's results, searching for a critical remote file, or deleting a whole record may be performed with confidence.

Technically, the data structures created by the record system provide guidance when performing maintenance activities. For example, resource consumption may be allocated with respect to discernible data set characteristics, or prioritized with respect to user-defined importance.

3.3.2 Computation in a Replica Management System

Utilization of network topology information with replica access and data insertion is an important technique. When reading from extended data repositories, simple strategies may be employed that benefit from the user-defined storage strategy to obtain access to nearby replicas. In a scientific setting, client software is designed to enable researchers to benefit from fast access to large data sets using a variety of computation tools.

Data access methods may be classed as explicit or implicit techniques: Explicit techniques specifically specify that data is to be moved; Implicit techniques reduce the method to one similar to a local data access method and leave the data movement to an underlying system. Explicit methods are exemplified by FTP and SCP, while implicit methods are exemplified by remote filesystems such as NFS or AFS. Additionally, virtual remote filesystems may be presented to user software using adapters such as Parrot or UFO, allowing implicit access to otherwise explicit services.

Both access methods are expected in extended repositories, and may gain performance improvements due to the available locality and parallelism of data sources. Added complexity and flexibility results when combining traditional local workstation computation with distributed cluster or grid compute engines. Consider the differences in complexity between two potential access patterns: a file retrieval and graphical display on a researcher's local workstation, or a batch of hundreds of parallel computation jobs that analyze hundreds of existing simulations to parameterize and instantiate additional simulations. In both cases, the system must be able to provide access to a nearby copy of a data file for read access. Replica locations must be obtained from the system and sorted with respect to the data consumption site, availability is determined, and data transfer is initiated.

However, in the distributed case, additional optimizations are possible if the data tools are integrated with the computation tools. First, when submitting the job, the abstract name may be used to direct the job submission system to prefer certain computation sites that are more likely to obtain good data access performance. This may be done by inspecting the replica locations that correspond to the abstract record definition upon translation to virtual data names. Next, upon job arrival and start, abstract names are resolved a second time and data access is optimized with respect to the actual job location.

The implementation of multiple name resolution provides benefits in performance and reliability. Performance is achieved by a two-stage process that plants jobs close to their data sources and binds file access to nearby services. Reliability is improved by allowing running jobs to determine replica existence and rebinding the file access with respect to replica availability.

3.3.3   *Formulating Job Submission for Replica Access*

An adapter called Parrot has been previously developed [9] to present a view of multiple remote filesystems as a single local filesystem. By trapping file operations from a running process, the adapter may allow the process to access files from remote servers in a transparent way. This adapter allows for the user to choose the compute site, the input source site, and the output destination site independently. The replica management system is combined with these tools to locate data; however, this increases the complexity faced by the programmer. A client job description framework is needed to locate input sites, find sites to safely store outputs, and obtain a compute site that is not already occupied. To obtain good performance, the three sites should be collocated.

Automated resolution allows clients of the replica management system to map file locations in the searchable, database-like namespace to the physical namespace of the virtual filesystem. In this work, we call the entries in replica namespace the abstract filenames, as opposed to the virtual filenames compatible with the adapter. Name resolution maps abstract names in a /label/path/file format to virtual filenames in a /protocol/host/path/file format. The replica management system provides the additional ability to obtain data set labels by searching over the metadata, providing the ability to perform computation in a completely application-oriented way, as shown in Fig. 3.3.

```
> KEY=$( Match reagents=acidbase )
> GEMSrun --input HCl /$KEY/hcl
          --input NaOH /$KEY/naoh
          --output NaCl salt
          --output HOH water
          reagents=saltwater
          --exec transmute HCl NaOH
                  to NaCl HOH
```

Fig. 3.3 Example simulation script using abstract data locations

The first line of the script uses the client toolkit to locate the data set label required to obtain the necessary input files for the transmute task. The second line invokes the toolkit to resolve the abstract file names to virtual file names compatible with the adapter, and then to submit the user task, `transmute`, to an available compute system, using the adapter to actually perform the file operations. The result of this script is a new entry in the replica system, containing two files, `salt` and `water`, which may be located by using the tag-value pair `reagents=saltwater`.

Clearly, more complex tasks would involve very lengthy command lines. Since existing job schedulers already require users to explicitly define input and output files, simple extensions to the syntax of these job scheduler scripts may be preprocessed by the GEMSrun client to provide a more familiar syntax for job submitters.

3.3.4 Job Submission Methods for Replica

In a replica location system, a service maintains a database of replica locations. This service may be queried in three essential ways: to map metadata tags to data set labels, to map data set labels to a set of file names, or to map a data set label and file name to a storage site. Once the site has been obtained, the data source may be accessed as described above.

While a replica management system does not spawn computation itself, we demonstrate a tool to interface with existing computation systems to access, analyze, and create data in a compatible way.

In this section, we outline four computation modes: ways to effectively perform computation utilizing replica access. These include:

1. Local Computation on Remote Data (LCRD), which allows the local workstation to access remote data sources and create new data in the replica system over a virtual filesystem.
2. Scheduled Computation on Remote Data (SCRD), which interfaces with an existing scheduler to create jobs that access data over a virtual filesystem.
3. Remote Computation on Remote Data (RCRD), which utilizes the ability to directly send jobs to remote systems for processing.
4. Multiple Name Resolution (MNR), which is a more complex scheduled method, guiding the matchmaking process with respect to data locations.

Local Computation on Remote Data (LCRD). In many common cases, the user simply desires to run a single job on the local workstation. The LCRD model enables users to start new jobs that require data access to the replica management system. This mode is based upon a typical command consisting of an operation on abstract data set identities, comprising the input and output locations. These abstract arguments, which do not specify the actual data location, are translated by the replica system into the physical file locations required by the virtual filesystem adapter, in a manner analogous to shell parameter parsing and expansion. Thus, a task that requires access to remote, abstracted data sets may be translated into a local task

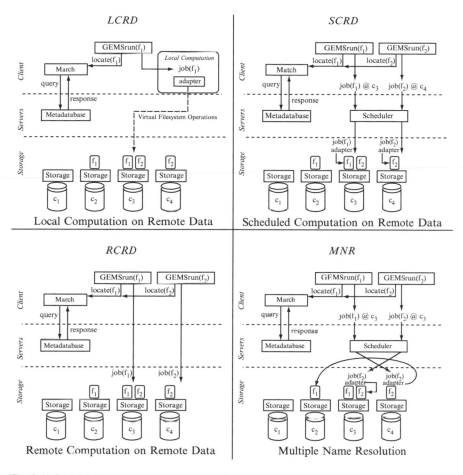

Fig. 3.4 Computation in a replica management system

operating on data that is virtually local. An example execution of this method is shown in Fig. 3.4, in the LCRD frame. Optimizing this operation is quite simple. First, the output data location is determined. The preferred output location is a server on the local host, but if this is not available or not allowed by the relevant access control policy, a server that is not currently busy will be selected. In the worst case, a remote, busy machine will be selected. If any required input files from the system have replicas on a local server, these hosts are selected as data sources. Otherwise, a remote, idle service will be selected to provide the file, and if this is not possible, the worst case behavior of a busy remote server will be selected.

Scheduled Computation on Remote Data (SCRD). We augment the specification for scheduled remote jobs by allowing users to specify input and output locations that reside in the replica management system, and use these locations in the commands and arguments. The GEMSrun client translates this augmented submission script into a submission script compatible with the replica system by making necessary substitutions: resolving the abstract data locations into virtual filesystem locations, and ensuring that the resulting job does in fact run atop the adapter. The data sets required by the resulting job are then location-independent because of the adapter, i.e., no data staging is necessary. As shown in the SCRD frame of Fig. 3.4, jobs are sent to the scheduler with requested destination hosts, illustrated by the "@" markup. The scheduler honors the request and submits the job to the appropriate compute site.

Remote Computation on Remote Data (RCRD). The file server used in this work allows the user to execute jobs inside a server-side execution environment (a Chirp feature). The GEMSrun client makes use of this technique by sending jobs directly to a file server for computation. The method is similar to the scheduled SCRD method. However, we are missing two important concepts: external centralized matchmaking and scheduling. An example of replica access is shown in Fig. 3.4, in the RCRD frame. Two jobs are submitted to the system by the user. Each specifies a target file, f_1 or f_2. The requests are translated into replica location operations. The request for f_1 is received first, and the response indicates that the file can be accessed on host c_3. This host is then marked "busy." The client then submits the job to host c_3. The second response arrives at the server, which locates the file on c_3 and c_4. Since c_3 is busy, the job is sent to c_4.

Multiple Name Resolution (MNR). As seen above, the local computation method selects replicas relative to the given computation site, which is immutable. The scheduled and remote computation methods select replicas relative to a variety of potential compute sites, presenting challenges of interest to designers of grid computing systems.

- In an environment in which replica locations are free to change or fail, replica locations may need to be re-selected after job deployment.
- Specifically for scheduled jobs, if the job is not deployed to the specific host that optimizes the file transfer, it may be beneficial to re-select replica locations to minimize transfer relative to the actual computation site.

Clearly property (1) is a harder constraint than property (2) but both represent essential design issues. A potential solution involves resolving the replica locations twice. A first resolution is performed by the job submission routine, which now selects only the computation site. The computation site is chosen in such a way that the resulting file transfers will be minimized. Then, after deployment, we have a second resolution: the compute job again resolves replica locations, essentially performing an LCRD operation described above. At this point, all replica locations may change due to storage server failure or computation site surprises, but the selection of compute site is fixed, greatly simplifying the choice. This may produce very good throughput at the small but significant cost of a second query to the centralized replica location service.[1]

---

[1] A second query is not absolutely necessary: results from the first query could be packaged, deployed, and reused. There is a fault tolerance tradeoff here that is outside the focus of this chapter.

In summary, we have a scheduled method similar to the SCRD but more robust and efficient because of the complex handling of replica locations. Below, the algorithm for the multiple name resolution method is outlined.

3.3.4.1 Job Submission

The following algorithm is performed by GEMSrun. For each potential compute host c_i, compute the network transfer n_i required to perform computation on that host. Compute appropriate ranks and submit the Late Resolution algorithm as a job to the scheduler.

3.3.4.2 Late Resolution

The following algorithm is performed by the job upon arrival on a compute host:

1. Determine the host this task is occupying
2. Locate all required files, and prefer locations that are on this host
3. Resolve abstract file locations to virtual file locations in the user job argument string
4. Execute the user job atop the adapter

This algorithm is illustrated in Fig. 3.4, in the MNR frame. In a manner similar to the SCRD illustration, the user submits jobs, the replica management system suggests appropriate hosts, and the jobs are sent to the external scheduler. However, the external scheduler places job(f_2) on c_3 first, then places job(f_1) on c_4. Simply applying the SCRD method here would cause two network file accesses: each job would begin accessing files found on a different host. However, using the MNR, job(f_2) utilizes the Late Resolution method and obtains access to the local copy of f_2. job(f_1) utilizes the Late Resolution method, and cannot locate a local copy of f_1 or the originally preferred copy on c_3, but is able to locate the copy on c_2. The net result is that one job obtains access to a local file, and one job must access a file over the network.

3.3.5 Summary

LCRD jobs can be executed in any environment in which a replica location service is available, creating a useful and practical prototyping tool for running simulation in the presence of any replica location system. They even can be submitted to job schedulers, implicitly creating an "unguided" MNR method.

SCRD jobs provide a useful and often requested additional functionality to existing job schedulers: they allow matchmaking based on replica location. However, once the job arrives, it functions as a LCRD job, meaning that if a different compute site is allocated by the scheduler, all file access must occur over the network, because name resolution has permanently occurred.[2]

RCRD jobs require the user to have computer access to the remote machine, over a system such as SSH or Chirp. A special case that could benefit from such a system are Internet computing applications as discussed below, because such applications often require an application-specific job scheduling policy. The RCRD method would allow such applications to use the data locations as an additional guide in the process.

The MNR is a robust and complex method for job scheduling. By both guiding the job to an appropriate compute site and making corrections upon arrival, it gains the benefits of the replicated data sources and the global view of the scheduler. Practically, it relies upon the ability to package additional code as a wrapper around the user job, which may be a constraint in some environments.

3.4   The Repository Model

Scientific repositories create a browsable front-end for user-labeled data sets stored in a scalable back end. With the primary intent of creating a searchable repository, GEMS presents a database-like abstraction over the file sets stored among the storage providers. User applications could access these services directly, but since they are independently managed, their presence in the system is unreliable. Technically, the GEMS system creates a centralized parameter sweep database of application-specific metadata backed up by a churn-aware file replica management backend. By combining the metadatabase with the management system, a quickly deployable tuple space and a survivable and parallelizable data system is therefore implemented. The resulting system is thus a merger of repository tags and parameter sweep entries, which programmatically represents a shared tuple space in which running jobs may communicate, with linkage to a replica location service.

The browsable repository created by GEMS allows users to structure workflows around data sets stored in GEMS. This metadata may be used to derive a novel concurrent programming model that enables synchronized tuple space communication and parallel data movement, called a data sweep. This framework may be used to build up parameter sweeps, workflows, and complex interactive parameter space explorations.

Each entry e in the GEMS contains a tuple of parameter tags and values, formatted as m equations: $e.\text{tuple} = \{p_i = u_i, i = 1....m\}$ (cf. Fig. 3.3). A query set may be formed by creating a similar tuple $\{q_i \mathbf{R}_i w_i, i = 1....n\}$, where $\mathbf{R}_i$ is some relation. The metadatabase respondes to a query set by returning the set $\{e: \forall q_i \exists p_j : p_j = q_i \wedge u_j \mathbf{R}_i w_i\}$. Thus, range queries over the metadatabase may be simply constructed, for example,

---

[2]A variation would be to instruct the scheduler that a given job is only eligible to be run on the specified host, and must otherwise wait, which would provide good collocation but would fill job queues in many applications.

a user may request "all entries of type simulation with temperature above 300." *e* also contains a file management data structure *e*.files, which may be used to obtain file information and replica locations.

3.4.1   Workflows in a Tuple Space

Experimental scientific workloads are more often driven by adaptive parameter investigations than well-known static sequences. Existing popular grid programming models include the parameter sweep and the workflow. In a parameter sweep, the same computation element is independently performed using each eligible point of some parameter domain as input. In a workflow, a partially ordered set of data movement and computation elements is run to completion. An existing example of a hybrid model is the parameter optimization, in which the output of the computation is optimized within a given parameter domain.

While these models are extremely powerful, they fail to capture other important computations such as postprocessing analysis, query-based computing, and interactive computing. Given a computation $y \leftarrow P(x)$, examples for these cases include the following:

- For each completed simulation in category C, compute the average of state variable y_i and store it.
- For each completed simulation $PC(x)$, if the output matches Q, rerun the simulation with parameter modification ∂x.
- Plot the current state of each simulation. Restart a user-selected set of simulations from their last checkpoint after altering state variable x_i.

Workflows built within the GEMS framework are supported by the ability to parameterize workflows, thus seeding the resulting execution. While existing programming tools such as shells support all of the operations performed by workflow tools, workflows are useful for three software engineering-related reasons:

- Encapsulation: Operations performed within a workflow task form a logical group.
- Clarity: The task dependency structure may be described by a simple graph and the state of a running instance may be similarly diagrammed.
- Restartability: Partially completed workflows may be restarted based on previously completed, safely stored work. The ability to quickly determine the minimum amount of new work that must be performed to renew an attempt to achieve a target or explore a new target limits the damage done by faults and enables exploratory interaction.

Any new workflow system functionality should not impede these abilities: without them the user might as well use a fully functional programming language. Thus, the GEMS method alters this model in only a few well-defined ways. First, workflow targets are parameter tuples, not files or operations. The existence of these may be easily queried as shown above. Second, workflow targets may be parameterized, resulting in function call-like tasks. This results in several problems that must be solved by the new framework. Task parameters must be arithmetically manipulated and propagated into the actual task execution. Additionally, operations within workflow targets must be properly parameterized. Inputs and output file locations are also parameterized values that must be linked into the user computation.

Consider a batch of scientific simulations S, over which several random seeds may be used, and the simulation time is broken into manageable, checkpointable segments. Each evaluation $S(u, r, t)$ of the simulation is defined by a user name u, a random seed r, and a time segment t, for m random seeds and n segments. Each evaluation depends on the previous evaluation with respect to time but within the same random seed group.

3.4.2   Dynamic Creation of Workflow Targets

In a static workflow system, the user would have to generate a Makefile-like script containing $m \times n$ workflow tasks with hand-parameterized filenames and other objects. In a parameterized workflow system, this may be framed by simply stating that $S(u, r, t):S(u, r, t-1)$; that is, each segment of execution time is dependent on the previous. A base case $S(u, r, t=0)$ is inserted into the system as an initial simulation state or base case. A target $S(sorin, 312, 100)$ may then be specified, the system would generate the 100 resulting tasks and execute them. Parameters are passed into user code by filtering a user-specified configuration file with `sed`-like operations, then the user task is executed as specified by the workflow node. Thus, each workflow task must contain a header, a dependency list, a mapping from header parameters to metadata values, a mapping from configuration file tokens to header parameters, and an execution string. The resulting example workload fills a rectangular parameter space but includes dependency information as shown in Fig. 3.5a.

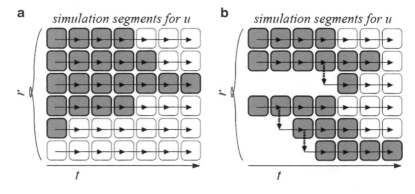

Fig. 3.5 (**a**) In a parameter sweep [1, 3], user jobs typically fill a square parameter space. (**b**) To allow for interactive parameter execution, the system has to allow the dynamic user creation of execution branches

More complex, interactive workflow-like structures may also be simply instantiated within this model. Consider the same molecular simulation example with the addition of user steering: the user may modify the force fields applied within the experiment, thus forking a new trajectory through the parameter space as shown in Fig. 3.5b). In this case, user requests simply create new targets and tasks are launched with respect to the dependency state of the whole workflow. The tree-like search structure is a simple consequence of a minor change to the parameterized dependency rule, such as:

$$S(u,r,t,branch = p):$$
$$S(u,r,t-1,branch = p)$$
$$\text{or } S(identity = p, time = t-1) \qquad (3.1)$$

Thus a branch parameter is added and the segment identity code is referenced. Segments depend on either the previous segment in time or the branch point when appropriate.

3.5   Computing in a Repository of Replicas

The data-driven grid models a compute grid as a set of data sources and sinks of interest, laid out as a potential workspace. Mobile jobs, submitted by data-aware schedulers, interact with the data landscape, consuming existing data objects and storing output data records through unitary operations called transforms [5]. Users of an opportunistic grid of arbitrary size may have temporary access to a large variety of existing storage resources, accessible over standard APIs [2, 6]. However, individual users would typically have difficulty organizing these sites into usable categories, ensuring data survivability in the presence of churn, and efficiently using the resources as data sources and sinks.

3.5.1   Data Placement

While approximately optimal solutions have been attempted for the job/data co-scheduling problem, we focus on the simple case of users attempting to enable grid computing in small collaborative projects. Our model relies upon an external, flat list of available, independently administered storage sites. Users are then capable of organizing the sites into logical clusters, making up a storage map. This reusable per-record process is technically less difficult than typical job placement matchmaking. The maps result in a mentally tangible data environment in which the storage, access control, and data movement policies may be carried out.

Policy negotiation lends itself to existing work on resource matchmaking [7]. However, we extend this model in the storage case by enabling users to specify cluster topology along with the eligibility criterion, called a storage map. This additional information deepens the semantics offered by the given policy information, by labeling the eligible sites as well as defining how to use them. Given a list of available storage sites, the user can select eligible locations and group them into clusters. In typical use cases, whole swaths of available machines at collaborating universities can be pooled together, with simple categorization.

For example, using traditional matchmaking, a controller could be instructed to store two replicas on a given list of eligible sites; with the storage map, one replica would be stored at each of two clusters, and data access operations from a client at either cluster would be directed to the nearest replica. Thus, the simple augmentation can be used to reduce the occurrence of wide area data access performance penalties and increase the availability of replicas in the event of cluster outages. Other consequences of the storage map concept are discussed below.

3.5.2 Data Access

To satisfy these problems, we offer the data sweep as programming model. This model allows users to operate within a data landscape by performing database-like operations. Application checkpoints, job dependencies, user or automatic branches, and ordinary stored data records may be encapsulated and utilized by the researcher. While the high-level approach works with abstract data records stored within the storage map, the underlying system still operates upon the distributed file servers, allowing for the use of existing application codes.

Each data record in the system is correlated to a storage map indicating the cluster topology used by the record. Combining the data sweep computation model with this information allows running jobs to access replicas that are nearest to the computation site with respect to the map. Thus, while not globally optimal, the user level replica placement flexibility offered allows users to create locally optimal systems for their work.

Compiled user codes are unable to accommodate the variety of new and experimental APIs, so new systems must provide tools to connect them to new services. Our approach to this problem builds on previous work that creates abstractions within UNIX-like structures. Since GEMS is primarily a grid controller, it does not deal with these structures directly but provides tools to orchestrate the connections. Additionally, our solutions reinforce the generally held conception that coarse grained, suboptimal performance is achievable by easily portable software while better tools meet portability challenges. In these examples, we consider data access methods for scientific users launching large batches of jobs, which run on a computer network in which an opportunistic storage network is embedded. Experimental cases were performed on a simple archive creation workload and in an actual molecular hyperdynamics application.

3.5.3   Archive Creation

The first experiment measures the time taken to create a simple tar file from a local filespace used by a real-world scientific application, the hyperdynamics experiments. The resulting archive is 3.7 GB and contains 13,934 files. The data storage sites ran Linux 2.6.9 on dual 2.4 GHz 64-bit AMD machines, all on the same institutional network. The GEMS server was located on a dual 2.8 GHz AMD system running Linux 2.4.27.

The three methods were run and profiled; the results are shown in Fig. 3.6.

- G/P Method. GEMS provides a data repository for running scripts through traditional get and put operations. Interleaving these within script operations results in a data staging model similar to that used by Condor and other systems. However, since data records and replicas are stored among the compute sites, there is great potential for data parallelism and locality. This solution is highly portable as it relies only on the GEMS client toolkit, a Java implementation, but relies on significant local disk usage and data copying.
- PIPE Method. Second, GEMS creates data sources and sinks that may be targeted by input and output streams. For example, users may reserve larger amounts of space within the GEMS system than is available on a local client machine, and then use a reference to the reserved location as a streamed output target, enabling the creation of large archives without large local space or data copying.

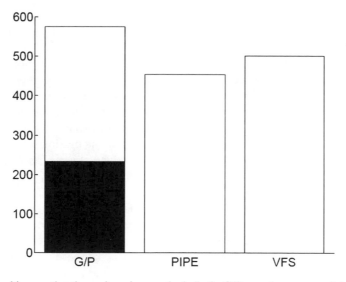

Fig. 3.6 Archive creation times via various methods. In the G/P case, the turnaround time consists of two components, local archive creation (*black*), and archive transfer to the repository (*white*). The other methods perform both operations concurrently

This method offers relatively high performance and an intermediate level of portability and complexity – it again uses only the GEMS client tools but requires interprocess communication connected by the user through UNIX pipes or a similar technique.

- VFS Method. Third, GEMS offers client tools to manage file naming conventions used by the Parrot virtual filesystem. This user space adapter provides system call translation to reformulate ordinary data access methods into distributed filesystem RPCs. GEMS clients simplify user access to this tool when operating within the replica system. While this solution offers the most functionality, it is only available on Linux.

The G/P method created the archive and stored it with the GEMSput repository insertion tool in separate steps. The method PIPE consisted of three steps: creating a repository reservation with GEMSreserve, piping the output of tar into a Chirp I/O forwarding tool, and on completion, committing the repository record with GEMScommit. Each GEMS method took less than 2 s, so the time consumed is not visible. The VFS method created the record using GEMSrun to drive tar execution inside a parrot environment, and managed record construction internally.

Results showed that streaming output methods are slightly better than the two-step method, and that moving data through the pipe was slightly faster than moving data through the virtual filesystem.

3.5.4 Hyperdynamics

The next experiment measures the impact of the GEMS model as overhead on a complex computation. Molecular Dynamics (MD) simulation [8] is a powerful and widely used tool to study molecular motion. Insight into chemical properties of a molecule may be obtained by observing rare conformational transitions from one metastable region of the simulated potential energy surface into another. Typical systems stay in one metastable state for a long time before making a transition into another metastable state, thus considerable computational resources must be allocated to achieve the simulated timescale necessary to reach the transitions. Recently, many approximate methods have been developed to extend the timescale of molecular simulations such as transition path sampling the kinetic Monte Carlo method, the finite-temperature string method, and the hyperdynamics method [14].

In this section, we apply GEMS to a recently developed method in molecular dynamics called hyperdynamics [14]. In hyperdynamics simulation, enhanced storage organization and rapid data access for spacious parameter sweeps are insufficient features for the effective investigation of system behavior. This steered method allows the user to bias the simulation into areas of conformational space yet to be explored.

The hyperdynamics method treated here essentially consists of a search through a parameter space of simulation parameters, including the level of hyperdynamics bias force applied. The method attempts to observe a rare long timescale event quickly by

Table 3.1 Approaches to exploration of the potential energy surface in molecular dynamics and resulting challenges

Name	Approach	Challenge
HYD-DEPTH	Single long run	Numerical performance of scalar system
HYD-BREADTH	Branch search	Scalability of distributed system
HYD-EXPLORE	Interactive	Human interaction with distributed system

applying additional bias forces to the system. The application produces timescale and entropy histograms that indicate whether the simulation has progressed to the point at which applying another bias potential level would be beneficial and free from serious error. Since there is no analytical method to make this determination, tools to enable ad hoc exploration of the parameter space were required.

As described above, our target application involved the generation of simulated molecular trajectories over a range of input parameters, including temperature (T) and density (ρ). These trajectories are independent and thus are an ideal application for parameter sweep toolkits. Figure 3.5a diagrams this method by indicating simulation segments – restartable chunks of simulation progress – as functions of the (T, ρ) input and time t. Each trajectory, shown in the figure as a row, is a sequence of segments over time, each containing the simulated molecular state over a given segment length and encapsulated in the storage system. Applications described above such as transition path sampling (TPS) have already been implemented in such a way [3].

The application described in this chapter differs in that only a subset of the whole parameter space will be explored – it is too large to fully explore and only a part is of interest. However, the area of interest is not known in advance and must be determined by statistical analysis of previously computed segments. The interesting areas of the parameter space are entered by branching from the existing segments, creating a new trajectory that differs from the unmodified sequence in that a new bias potential, described above, is applied. Thus, additional metadata must be stamped on each segment to record the location of the segment in the search tree, as diagrammed in Fig. 3.5b.

Table 3.1 provides an overview of potential approaches to this method. This first, HYD-DEPTH represents the control case of using only traditional molecular dynamics. The second, HYD-BREADTH, automatically explores all possible applications of the method. While this method may employ massive parallelism to obtain a given result quickly, we demonstrate here that it wastes a great deal of resources. A solution is offered in the HYD-EXPLORE method, which allows for the controlled use of parallelism to explore promising paths as well as selective pruning of useless searches. This relies on the technical solution of distributed computing problems such as data management and organization, user feedback and programmability, and job control. Our results demonstrate that user-steered hyperdynamics (HYD-EXPLORE) can improve upon traditional dynamics (HYD-DEPTH) as long as the resource consumption of brute-force techniques (HYD-BREADTH) is restrained.

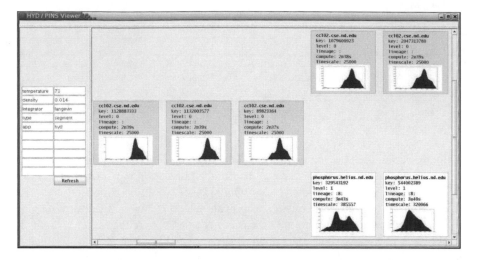

Fig. 3.7 Graphical user interface representation hyperdynamics segments. The tool automates simulation branches and restarts by setting up a hyperdynamics bias. Thumbnails show that entropy distributions in segment 3 and 4, level 0 are similar. Therefore, one can branch from segment 3 to level 1. At level 1, the bias will push the system away from the conformational space already traversed in level 0

As an example, Fig. 3.7 shows a combination of parameter tags from the central database as well as a view of plotted data files. These distributed hyperdynamics executions were followed remotely by Matlab postprocessing, generating and storing simulation output and plots on the remote cooperative system. Parameters include the execution host and output timescale, a hyperdynamics-specific indicator of work performed, and the benefit of the new algorithm. This client also uses parameter tags to arrange the tiles in the frame, and pulls image files from the storage network to provide a high-level view of workflow progress.

In our present application, viewing output on the fly is not enough. The timescale and entropy histogram indicate if the simulation has progressed to the point at which applying another bias potential level would be beneficial and free from serious error. As the algorithm under study is new and there is no analytical method to make this determination, tools to enable ad hoc exploration of the parameter space are required.

As a demonstration of the nontriviality of this process, Fig. 3.8 diagrams the timescale performance as a function of branch location on the time axis. Thus, the researcher controlling the simulation must monitor the output histograms for error and smoothness while selecting branch points that maximize simulation efficiency in terms of timescale. Critically, applying additional bias levels poses hazards. If the bias is too high within a metastable region, the system will not reach a local equilibrium in the biased trajectory and the timescale of the trajectory will be incorrect.

On the other hand, if we apply fewer bias levels, a longer simulation will be required for the system to move from one metastable region to another. It is not known a priori how long one will need to simulate to achieve correct distribution of

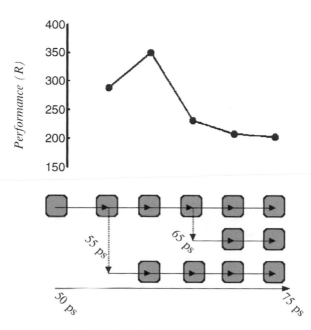

Fig. 3.8 Performance ratio R for various branch points. The ratio is plotted above a diagram indicating two illustrated example branches. R is plotted as a function of branch time. A higher ratio indicates more efficient exploration of the simulated conformation space. The performance ratio is obtainable only as the result of a simulation segment, necessitating interactive workflow control

S for the next bias level. Typically, one would like to run a set of independent hyperdynamics simulations, each with different set of parameters, such as temperature, density, and bias settings.

Since the application of additional bias levels increases computation time per segment, we employ a performance ratio (R) that indicates efficiency: work done measured by timescale per unit of CPU time, or

$$R = \frac{\text{Timescale (simulated femtoseconds)}}{\text{CPU time (real seconds)}} \qquad (3.2)$$

In this perspective, a set of normal single processor hyperdynamics simulations individually run at a baseline performance level. GEMS offers the ability to easily exploit the available parallelism in the method on an opportunistic computing/storage system. Any method to parallelize the set of sequential runs will accumulate some lost communication time; in this section, we consider the communication time consumed as a whole, that is, the time that would not be consumed if running all tasks on a sequential system.

The GEMS framework was used to create a notification-based dependency loop, enabling ordinary workflow programming on parameterized GEMS records, implemented as a data sweep over the required search targets, as diagrammed in Fig. 3.9.

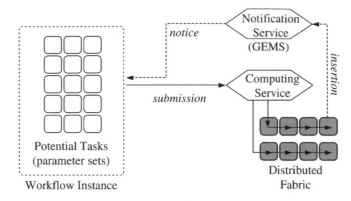

Fig. 3.9 Notification/submission loop parameterized workflow instances in the GEMS framework

3.5.5 Interpretation of Hyperdynamics Results

Running tasks alternate between I/O operations and computation. Here, I/O operations consist of centralized metadata operations as well as data movement operations (Fig. 3.10). A checkpoint, for example, consists of a metadata insertion, a reservation, parallel data movement, and record committal. Computation is fully independent per node. An important measure of system congestion is thus the I/O Ratio (*I*), computed as:

$$ I = \frac{\text{Time spent in GEMS clients}}{\text{Time spent in computation}} \tag{3.3} $$

Where, computation includes PROTOMOL and Matlab operations. This ratio is plotted per segment in Fig. 3.11. Thus, the scalability in terms of number of leaves on the search tree is considered. Plotting the ratio in the segment domain indicates the scalability of the search algorithm. Additionally, individual operations were profiled for performance for a similar, shorter run up to segment 4. The relative server response time, as measured by the server for each operation, is shown in Fig. 3.12. Metadata operations were the most common operation during the run and were also the most expensive.

By extrapolating from the results achieved in this experiment, we can estimate the cost of performing the experiment with another method. Results are tabulated in Table 3.2.

- Employing `HYD-DEPTH` would have required running a single job with traditional dynamics to achieve the target timescale at which the droplet was observed. This would result in 1.8 h of single processor computation.

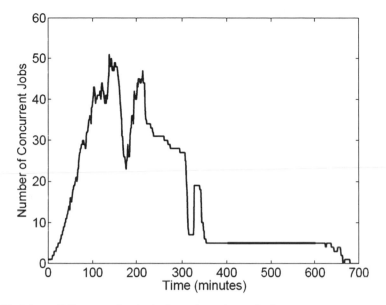

Fig. 3.10 Job parallelism over time in the hyperdynamics methods

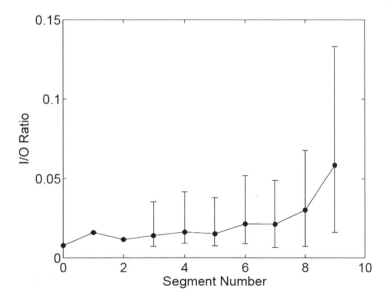

Fig. 3.11 I/O ratio I (Eq. 3.3) per segment. Averages are reported with 95% confidence intervals where appropriate

Fig. 3.12 Centralized time
consumed on the replica
management server per
operation

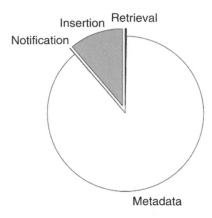

Table 3.2 Experimental results

Name	Total (h)	Turnaround (h)
HYD-DEPTH	1.8[a]	1.8[a]
HYD-BREADTH	5,800[a]	1.4[a]
HYD-EXPLORE	6.2	1.4

[a] Results extrapolated from experiment

- Additionally, a full search of all pathways of length 17 could have been performed, one of which would have resulted in the observed droplet. This would rely on the implementation of perfect parallelism on 216 processors for the final leaves, and ignores the scalability issues mentioned in the previous sections. This idealized computation would result in total resource consumption of 5,800 CPU hours. However, since the path length is still 17, the turnaround time is again only 1.4 h.

This experiment demonstrates that while a centralized metadata system may be employed to efficiently manage workflows that interleave metadata operations with computation, when all tasks request intense synchronization and metadata information simultaneously, performance is greatly affected. Thus, while a full automated search of the parameter space is potentially possible under nominal conditions, selective pruning and interaction with user-identifiable parameter regions should be attempted to gain better resource utility on practical systems.

3.6 Collaboration and Security

Extensible repositories combine user-defined naming schemes, storage strategies, and externally owned and operated storage services into a viable scientific resource. Each operation in the system combines metadata operations on the centralized system with data operations on distributed volunteer systems, and funnels a wide potential usage space through enabling client functionality and tools.

Simple data tagging frameworks are doomed to eventually expire. Different communities of researchers will emphasize different tags due to the varying importance of simulation parameters, local conventions in usage patterns, or obvious application-related reasons. An extensible repository will provide the minimum data tagging tools to make this possible, allowing for new user groups to import existing data sets and naming schemes into the greater system.

The ability to add and remove external storage services during normal system operation from the system is a fundamental feature; thus, users must be capable of determining storage sites that are eligible to store their data. Consequentially, extensible repositories cannot impose data placement strategies on users.

3.6.1   Scientific Collaboration

Extensible repositories are motivated by the conception of collaborating scientists creating a common catalog and management system while maintaining local resource autonomy. Thus, a common ground is instantiated at the intersection of client requests and authorized system services. User and site management is a monumental problem in a large-scale system, and must be localized by data set owners. The global set of users must be able to operate without global data definitions, user lists, host lists, etc., as these are likely to rapidly change. Administrative data structures are thus created on a per-record basis, and represent a usage and management policy followed by the greater system but enforced by the underlying systems trusted by the users. A repository extended over existing resources such as volunteered desktops must be able to respect the ownership of the resource as well as the security of the data objects.

The system allows for the interaction of users in various roles, including data consumer, data provider, storage provider, and replica manager. Note that a person may take on multiple roles. Each has limited knowledge of other users and limited ability to affect the whole system. Individual users may find it quite complex to manage dynamic replica locations, monitoring of user-defined network topology maps, authentication schemes, and large-scale user groups. Thus, simplified concepts are applied and a generalized authentication scheme is employed to enable scientific data sharing when desirable, and tight access restriction otherwise.

3.6.2   User Management and Access Control

Scientific systems operators that wish to share data sets and storage resources with remote users will find that allowing authorized access and prohibiting unauthorized access is of primary importance. These problems are commonly treated as security issues. All users that attempt to access system components must be authenticated. In practice, superficial tests are performed to determine if the user can satisfy a given test based on the subject name claimed by the connecting party. Upon satisfaction,

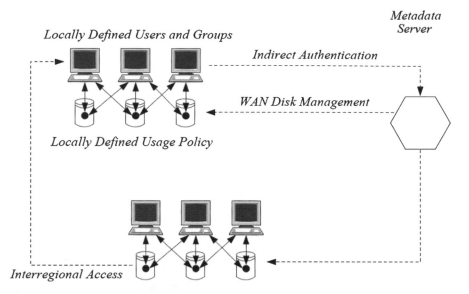

Fig. 3.13 User-specified cluster topology information creates semiautonomous regions on a per-record basis. User and storage providers interact over authenticated connections. Although users have locally defined identities, changes are propagated up to the metadata level as authorized by the record owner.

the system determines if the subject is eligible to perform the requisite operation by consulting an access control list (ACL) (Fig. 3.13).

Wide area extended repositories are designed to support a large number of volatile user groups, data record, and storage devices. The construction and maintenance of a global static list of users and their authentication abilities is not practical. Thus, the authentication process is pushed away from the centralized system and onto the intermediate storage systems with which the users interact. An authentication test may be performed on a storage site relevant and trustworthy with respect to the user and record at hand. The successful completion of the test indicates that the operation is acceptable, and resulting changes are propagated up to the centralized replica management system. More information about this procedure is available in [11].

3.6.3 Semiautonomous Regions

This functionality may be enabled by a careful consideration of all system stakeholders and through the use of appropriate procedures and data structures. Data providers may specify access control rules employing a commonly used tool, the ACL, without referring to a global user list or authentication protocol. Additionally, they may specify which storage providers are eligible to host their data sets. Since data placement is dynamically controlled by the replica manager, pattern matching-based specification structures are employed to include or exclude servers and clusters for individual data records, creating a manageable per-record storage network topology.

The intersection of data and storage providers creates a conceptual semiautonomous region in which data lives. These constructs are autonomous in that the allowable authentication techniques and user lists may be maintained without reference to a global center such as the replica manager or another region.

Data consumers must be able to navigate the distributed data structure created by the data and storage providers. Access to a given record requires satisfaction of the record ACL with respect to a given storage site. Thus, read access is enabled in a pairwise manner, without requiring regulation by the replica manager. Users from multiple regions may interact via these direct connections by regulating access control and consulting the centralized metadata catalog, creating the possibility for efficient, direct data connections and blackboard-style data publication. This creates this potential for simplified collaboration.

3.6.4 Repository Access on the Grid

A founding design feature of grid computing is the ability to allow access resources to users across administrative domain. An administrative domain may be commonly conceived as a local UNIX installation managed by a system administrator. Grid construction allows users outside the local system to run jobs or allocate storage on the resource. A system administrator may enable this by first creating a local user that has access to these services, then installing a grid software system that runs as this user. The new system maintains an independent authentication and authorization scheme intended to scale to many users. For example, the Globus system includes a public key authentication system combined with a virtual organization model to authorize grid operations. This solves the basic grid problem but has certain limitations. Positively, it allows a new abstraction layer – the grid security system – above the operating system layer in a scalable way. However, it shoehorns users into a single authentication scheme orchestrated by administrators, not users. This adds to administrative workloads while restricting the ability of users to share their access to resources with others. Typical systems do not allow users to grant privileges to another user without compromising their own account, by revealing a password or private key. Access control lists allow the addition of user names and permissions but are an authorization scheme. GEMS provides a method to turn arbitrary access control lists into a globally visible authentication scheme as well.

3.6.5 Use Cases

Consider a case in which research group leaders from distant universities desire to construct a relatively secure cooperative database, building upon existing (grid-enabled) resources. This problem is concerned with constructing new grids from existing grids or their fragments, ultimately creating a grid of grids. In the pre-grid era, they would have to agree on a global user list and propagate it out. Using grid tools, they could establish a global security authority and ensure that all components agree to use it. Both solutions are problematic, as global user lists are extremely difficult to manage, and a globalized security system may be overwhelming, limiting the ability of users to create subgroups or employ previous methods (such as UNIX or DNS authentication).

In the distant university case, the construction of the cooperative distributed database should not be taken to mean that within the database all records are equal from a security perspective. In fact, many cases could arise in which users could agree to share resources, say, in a pairwise way within the greater structure. This would involve selecting certain resources for use in the derived system and ensuring the security system works for the users and systems involved: a local procedure, which should have no global side effects. This process again creates a data landscape in which a subgroup of users has access to a subset of possible resources and data records. This use case creates a record-specific grid-within-grid abstraction.

3.6.6 Implementation

The creation of a semiautonomous region starts with the well-known process of matchmaking, a process analogous to selecting rows from a database table. The process is augmented because it results in a new environment: one in which other users can participate. Our simplified implementation begins with a small-scale user process: the selection of the requested resources. Resources may be organized into clusters reflecting network topology or geographical distance to enable certain functionality described below. This information is organized into a storage map and may be stored for later use.

The creation of a data landscape begins when a user combines a data record containing data files and metadata tags with a storage map and Access Control List (ACL), resulting in a config. A typical use of a config is the input and output files of a simulator program, combined with metadata such as the options passed to the program. This config is instantiated, registered with the greater system, and entrusted to its control.

The storage map defines the derived grid resources upon which the data files will reside, defining the data landscape in terms of system-level security and data movement performance. The ACL is propagated to these storage sites and applied to the appropriate files. While this may be performed with existing tools, an important challenge remains: how does information from the config propagate up to the greater system? Users must be able to administer their data at the global level. For example, they must be able to delete a config and its underlying widely replicated files. To do this, they must authenticate to the greater system. The ability to provide metagrid control of diverse resources will constitute our solution to the grid integration problem.

3.6.7   Rendition: An Enabling Technology

The process by which a user performs authenticated operations within the config data landscape is called the rendition protocol. This protocol applies in systems that implement the grid controller model, in which a controller manages the global policy but is agnostic with respect to system specifics such as a password list. In this case, the system may only interact in an authenticated manner with underlying physical storage sites that implement direct authentication protocols. Upon this fabric, we intend to build an indirect protocol that enables the controller to authenticate a channel for a certain user with respect to a config.

Thus, we reiterate our data-driven focus: operations in the system change the data landscape. Critical operations at the controller level must be authenticated through a storage site for a config, because only here is the ACL enforceable and the data stored and protected. The controller model explicitly allows users to use old protocols to interact with the underlying system, relying on direct authentication methods.

The rendition protocol [11] solution allows users to obtain an initially anonymous channel to the controller. The user may then request access to modify a config, at which point the controller creates a challenge, which must be satisfied for the execution of the operation. This challenge typically takes the form of a file operation with respect to the storage site and ACL in question, such as the creation of a numbered marker file in a directory from which all users are restricted except those known to be authorized for the operation by the ACL. Upon the hand over of the file, the controller is notified to inspect the satisfaction of challenge, carry out the operation, and return the appropriate notice.

This protocol may be thought of as similar to other existing indirect protocols that delegate authentication to an external authority, but in fact, rendition offers greater efficacy. The simplicity of the scheme allows ordinary users to delegate authentication to the whole storage fabric, a diverse array of heterogeneous sites, each of which may implement a subset of the available physical authentication protocols. This derivation of responsibility for security enables users to make use of local system knowledge to create ad hoc collaborative systems without global consequences.

As an example, consider the simple collaboration shown in Fig. 3.14. In this case, user B inserts a data record with a config policy that allows storage and access at domain C. Collaboration and shared data administration are possible even though each user is unable to authenticate at a remote site. Moreover, a job submitted by user B running in domain C may access data, perhaps using a simple DNS-based authentication. This reinforces the notion that data replication may be viewed as an asynchronous job pre-staging process.

The rendition-based trust chain infrastructure solves a common problem in trust delegation: trust delegates must not receive too much information from the delegator. Passwords and other credentials simply cannot be passed to a third party. Likewise, the authentication system cannot be globally affected by ordinary users.

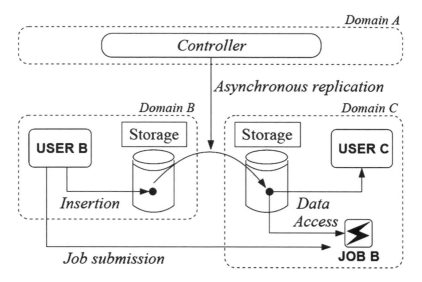

Fig. 3.14 Simple three-domain collaboration

Yet users are able to delegate access to records via an ACL, and the config data structure provides a physical authentication test.

3.7 Conclusion

Observation and design features in this paper are based on experiences with the GEMS system, a replica management system originally designed as a cooperative chemistry simulation repository. The GEMS model provides new practical solutions for active research problems such as autonomous grid control of disparate components, a flexible security model driven by user needs, and services for data access from a variety of possible clients.

GEMS enables the rapid construction of ad hoc storage grids that augment the usability of opportunistic computing systems. The workflow techniques presented here, integrated in the GEMS toolkit, improve the ability to browse intermediate simulation results and guide workflow progress.

The new contribution here is the application of GEMS concepts to general problems in distributed scientific computing, framed as grid integration and derivation problems. While a variety of tools exist to approach these problems, the ad hoc storage grid as presented here proposes a comprehensive solution packaged in a tangible, dynamic data landscape. Additionally, the integration and derivation conception provides a unified methodology for previously fragmented archetypes of matchmaking, access control – providing a platform upon which solutions may be built.

References

1. Abramson, D., Giddy, J., Kotler, L.: High performance parametric modeling with Nimrod/G: Killer application for the global grid. In: Proceedings of the 14th International Parallel and Distributed Processing Symposium, Cancun, pp. 520–528 (2000)
2. Allcock, W., Bresnahan, J., Kettimuthu, R., Link, M., Dumitrescu, C., Raicu, I., Foster, I.: The globus striped GridFTP framework and server. In: Proceedings of the ACM/IEEE Conference on Supercomputing, Seattle (2005). doi: 10.1109/SC.2005.72
3. Brenner, P., Wozniak, J.M., Thain, D., Striegel, A., Peng, J.W., Izaguirre, J.A.: Biomolecular path sampling enabled by processing in network storage. In: Proceedings of IEEE International Symposium in Parallel and Distributed Processing, Long Beach, pp. 1–6 (2007)
4. Brenner, P., Wozniak, J.M., Thain, D., Striegel, A., Peng, J.W., Izaguirre, J.A.: Biomolecular committor probability calculation enabled by processing in network storage. J. Parallel Comput. **34**(11), 652–660 (2008)
5. Foster, I., Voeckler, J., Wilde, M., Zhao, Y.: Chimera: A virtual data system for representing, querying, and automating data derivation. In: Proceedings of the 14th International Conference on Scientific and Statistical Database Management, Edinburgh, Scotland, pp. 37–46 (2002)
6. Rajasekar, A., Wan, M., Moore, R., Kremenek, G., Guptil, T.: Data grids, collections and grid bricks. In: Proceedings of the 20th IEEE/11th NASA Goddard Conference on Mass Storage Systems and Technologies, San Diego (2003). doi:10.1109/MASS.2003.1194830
7. Raman, R., Livny, M., Solomon, M.H.: Matchmaking: Distributed resource management for high throughput computing. In: Proceedings of the 7th International Symposium on High Performance Distributed Computing, Chicago, pp. 140–146 (1998)
8. Schlick, T.: Molecular Modeling and Simulation – An Interdisciplinary Guide. Springer, New York (2002)
9. Thain, D., Klous, S., Wozniak, J.M., Brenner, P., Striegel, A., Izaguirre, J.: Separating abstractions from resources in a tactical storage system. In: Proceedings of the 2005 ACM/IEEE Conference on Supercomputing, Seattle (2005). doi:10.1109/SC.2005.64
10. Wozniak, J.M., Brenner, P., Thain, D., Striegel, A., Izaguirre, J.: Generosity and gluttony in GEMS: Grid-Enabled Molecular Simulation. In: Proceedings of 14th IEEE International Symposium on High Performance Distributed Computing, Research Triangle Park, pp. 191–200 (2005)
11. Wozniak, J.M., Brenner, P., Thain, D.: Access control for a replica management database. In: Proceedings of the 2nd ACM Workshop on Storage Security and Survivability, pp. 41–46 (2006)
12. Wozniak, J.M., Brenner, P., Thain, D., Striegel, A., Izaguirre, J.: Applying feedback control to a replica management system. In: Proceedings of the 38th Southeastern Symposium on System Theory, Cookeville, pp. 472–476 (2006)
13. Wozniak, J.M., Brenner, P., Thain, D., Striegel, A., Izaguirre, J.: Making the best of a bad situation: Prioritized storage management in GEMS. Future Gen. Comput. Syst. **24**(1), 10–16 (2008)
14. Zhou, X., Jiang, Y., Kramer, K., Ziock, H., Rasenmassen, S.: Hyperdynamics methods for entropic systems: Timespace compression and pair correlation function approximation. J. Phys. Rev. (2006). doi:10.1103/PhysRevE.74.035701

Chapter 4
Performance Analysis and Optimization of Linear Workflows in Heterogeneous Network Environments

Qishi Wu and Yi Gu

Abstract The advent of next-generation computation-intensive applications in various science fields is pushing computing demands to go far beyond the capability of traditional computing solutions based on standalone PCs. The availability of today's largest clusters, grids, and supercomputers expedites the development of robust problem-solving environments that marshal those high-performance computing and networking resources and presents a great opportunity to manage and execute large-scale computing workflows for collaborative scientific research. Supporting such scientific workflows and optimizing their end-to-end performance in wide-area networks is crucial to ensuring the success of large-scale distributed scientific applications. We consider a special type of pipeline workflows comprised of a set of linearly arranged modules, and formulate and categorize pipeline mapping problems into six classes with two optimization objectives, i.e., minimum end-to-end delay and maximum frame rate, and three network constraints, i.e., no, contiguous, and arbitrary node reuse. We design a dynamic programming-based optimal solution to the problem of minimum end-to-end delay with arbitrary node reuse and prove the NP-completeness of the rest five problems, for each of which, a heuristic algorithm based on a similar optimization procedure is proposed. These heuristics are implemented and tested on a large set of simulated networks of various scales and their performance superiority is illustrated by extensive simulation results in comparison with existing methods.

Q. Wu (✉) • Y. Gu
Department of Computer Science, University of Memphis, Memphis, TN 38152, USA
e-mail: qishiwu@memphis.edu

N.P. Preve (ed.), *Grid Computing: Towards a Global Interconnected Infrastructure*,
Computer Communications and Networks, DOI 10.1007/978-0-85729-676-4_4,
© Springer-Verlag London Limited 2011

4.1 Introduction

The advance in supercomputing technology is expediting the transition in various basic and applied sciences from traditional laboratory-controlled experimental methodologies to modern computational paradigms involving complex numerical model analyses and extreme-scale simulations of physical phenomena, chemical reactions, climatic changes, and biological processes as shown in Fig. 4.1. These computation-based simulations and analyses have become an essential research and discovery tool in next-generation scientific applications and are producing colossal amounts of data, on the order of terabyte at present and petabyte or even exabyte in the predictable future. Other scientific data of similar scales generated in broad science communities include real-world environmental data such as satellite climate data [19], multimodal sensor data, etc., and high-throughput experimental data such as Spallation Neutron Source (SNS) [50], Large Hadron Collider (LHC) [46], etc. No matter which type of data is considered, one crucial task would be to develop an effective and efficient end-to-end solution for geographically distributed users to transfer, process, visualize, analyze, and synthesize the data (raw datasets, intermediate results, or final outputs) in heterogeneous network environments for collaborative research (Report SLAC-R-782, 2004) [41, 42].

Many scientific computing workflows can be modeled as linear computing pipelines consisting of a number of sequential modules, where each module represents a subtask and each directed edge represents the execution dependency between two adjacent modules. In some context, a computing module is also referred to as an activity, a job, a transformation, a stage, or a program. Each module, except for the first module and the last module, is considered as an autonomous computing

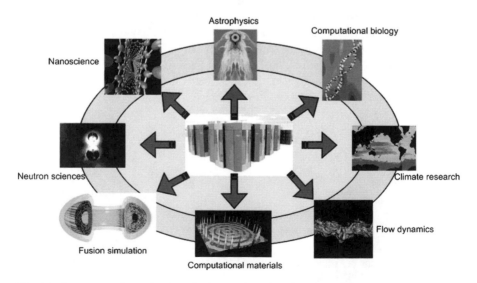

Fig. 4.1 Supercomputing technology for large-scale scientific applications

Fig. 4.2 An example of pipeline applications in remote visualization

agent: it receives data as input from the preceding module, executes a predefined processing routine on the input data, and sends the results as output to the succeeding module. We assume that the first module serves as a data source that does not perform any computing task and the last module serves as a terminal job that does not require any data transfer, and further assume that neither can a module start execution until its required input data arrive, nor send out the results until the execution is completed. For a small-scale standalone application where an end user accesses a local data source, the entire computing pipeline may be executed on a single computer. However, in large-scale distributed applications where data sources are not located at the same site as end users, we are faced with a significant challenge to support increasingly complex computing pipelines over wide-area networks with heterogeneous computer nodes and network links. The remote visualization pipeline, as shown in Fig. 4.2, in scientific applications such as Terascale Supernova Initiative (TSI) [52] is a typical example, where the simulation datasets on the order of terabytes for now and petabytes in the predictable future generated on a remote supercomputer must be retrieved, filtered, transferred, processed, visualized, and analyzed by a collaborative team of geographically distributed scientists. Note that a computing pipeline with only two end modules reduces to a traditional client/server-based computing paradigm.

We consider the network environment as an overlay computer network consisting of heterogeneous computer nodes interconnected by disparate network links. The overlay network can be represented by a directed weighted graph, whose topology may be complete as in the case of the Internet based on layer-3 IP routing, or not as in the case of most dedicated research testbed networks using layer-1 or 2 circuit/lambda switching techniques. Note that even in Internet environments, the network topology may not be always complete because the network connectivity or facility accessibility could be largely affected by firewall settings on either routers or end systems. We would also like to point out that computer nodes are of different processing capabilities and network links are of different transport properties in terms of bandwidth and minimum link delay in most wide-area computer networks.

We consider two types of large-scale distributed applications with linear computing pipelines: (1) Single-input applications where a single dataset is sequentially processed along a pipeline. Typical examples include an interactive parameter update on a remote visualization system that triggers a sequence of subtasks for data filtering, isosurface extraction, geometry rendering, image compositing, and final display. (2) Streaming applications where a series of datasets are continuously fed through a pipeline. Typical examples include a video-based real-time monitoring system for detecting criminal suspects at an entrance that performs feature extraction and detection, facial reconstruction, pattern recognition, and identity matching on images that are continuously captured. The performance of a computing task highly depends on how efficiently these modules are mapped to network nodes. Our goal is to find an efficient mapping scheme that allocates the modules of a computing pipeline to computer nodes in an underlying network to achieve minimum end-to-end delay (MED) for fast system response in single-input applications with a single instance of input dataset or maximum frame rate (MFR) for smooth data flow in streaming applications with multiple (e.g., time-serial) instances of input datasets. The frame rate (FR), also referred to as throughput, is the data production rate at the last module. The application performance in terms of MED or MFR is determined by the module execution time on computer nodes and the data transfer time over network links. Note that in the streaming applications, if multiple modules are mapped onto the same node (i.e., node reuse), the node's computing resource could be shared in a fair manner by concurrently running modules on that node with multiple input datasets. The fair share of CPU cycles is supported by many modern operating systems that employ a round-robin type of CPU scheduling algorithm. Similarly, the bandwidth of a network link is equally shared by multiple data transfers that take place concurrently over the same link with multiple input datasets. The fair share of link bandwidths is supported by the wide use of TCP-friendly transport protocols in wide-area networks. The difficulty of this mapping problem essentially arises from the topological matching nature in the spatial domain, which is further compounded by the resource sharing complicacy in the temporal dimension if multiple modules are deployed on the same node. Supporting such scientific workflows in those computational or data grids and optimizing their end-to-end network performance are crucial to the success of large-scale collaborative scientific applications and the utilization of massively distributed heterogeneous resources.

We formulate the pipeline mapping problems in heterogeneous network environments as optimization problems and categorize them into six classes with two mapping objectives (MED and MFR) and three network constraints on node reuse or resource share: (1) MED with No Node Reuse (MED-NNR), (2) MED with Contiguous Node Reuse (MED-CNR), (3) MED with Arbitrary Node Reuse (MED-ANR), (4) MFR with No Node Reuse or Share (MFR-NNR), (5) MFR with Contiguous Node Reuse and Share (MFR-CNR), and (6) MFR with Arbitrary Node Reuse and Share (MFR-ANR). Here, contiguous node reuse means that multiple contiguous modules along the pipeline may run on the same node and arbitrary node reuse imposes no restriction on node reuse. We prove that MED-ANR is polynomially solvable and the rest are NP-complete. We further prove that there does not exist any θ approximation solution to MED/MFR-NNR/CNR unless $P = $ NP. We propose a set of solutions, named Efficient Linear Pipeline Configuration (ELPC), in which an optimal solution based on Dynamic Programming (DP) is developed to solve MED-ANR, and a heuristic algorithm is designed for each of the rest five NP-complete problems. The simulation results illustrate the performance superiority of the proposed algorithms over the existing ones.

4.2 Background Survey

Many parallel and distributed applications in science fields face a major workflow optimization problem to map or schedule the subtasks of a workflow in distributed computing environments. This workflow mapping or scheduling problem has attracted a great deal of attention from researchers in various disciplines [1, 3, 5, 6], Susarla and Vairavan, 1975 [7, 8, 14–16, 23, 30–32, 37, 48, 53, 54, 58, 60] and continues to be the focus of distributed computing due to its theoretical significance and practical importance. There exist two types of problems for optimizing distributed tasks: one is to assign the component subtasks in a workflow to an appropriate set of computing nodes, which is referred to as workflow mapping and is the focus of this chapter, and the other is to decide the order of task executions on a specific node or processor, which is referred to as task scheduling and is out of the scope of this chapter.

In the early years, when shared network resources were still scarce, many research efforts were focused on static workflow mapping on multiprocessors considered as identical/homogeneous resources [3]. Over the years, workflow mapping problems in heterogeneous environments have been increasingly identified and investigated by many researchers to facilitate more convenient and comprehensive collaborations among different institutes and domains across wide-area networks [8, 9, 33]. However, some of these works only consider independent subtasks in the workflow [11] or assume independent/fully connected nodes in the network [8, 53], which may not be sufficient to model the complexity of real applications.

The grid environments provide compositional programming and execution models to enable the resource interactions that support large-scale scientific applications by supplying the mechanisms to access, aggregate, and manage the network-based infrastructure of science. Such grid-based scientific applications include Large Hadron Collider (LHC) [46] supported by the Worldwide LHC Computing Grid (WLCG) [57], climate modeling supported by the Earth System Grid [24], and NASA's National Airspace Simulation supported by the Virtual National Airspace Simulation (VNAS) grid [34, 39]. Many other grid systems such as Open Science Grid (OSG) [43] ASKALON [51, 56], TeraGrid, GridCOMP, and Legion are under rapid development and deployment. Due to the pervasive deployment of networked resources based on grid infrastructures, a significant amount of efforts have been devoted to workflow mapping or job scheduling in grid environments under different mapping and resource constraints [1, 12, 13, 44, 56]. Grid initiative and projects such as the Globus Toolkit [26, 27], Pegasus [22], and Condor/DAGMan [21, 36] provide toolkits and infrastructures to deploy grid computing systems, and several visualization applications were built using these services. Note that for steaming applications, in the pipeline workflow mapping problem considered in this chapter, each module only has a single copy processing datasets sequentially on its mapping node, while in Condor/DAGman, each module could be dispatched multiple times to process different datasets concurrently on different nodes. Similar mapping problems are also studied in the context of sensor networks. In [47] Sekhar, Manoj, and Murthy have proposed an optimal algorithm for mapping subtasks onto a large number of sensor nodes based on an A^* algorithm.

The heuristic workflow mapping algorithms can be roughly classified into the following five categories [38, 53]: (1) Graph-based methods [20, 40]. Among the traditional graph mapping problems in theoretical aspects of computing, subgraph isomorphism is known to be NP-complete while the complexity of graph isomorphism still remains open. (2) List scheduling techniques, in which the most commonly used is critical path method [35, 37, 44]. (3) Clustering algorithms [9, 29], which assume an unlimited number of processors and thus are not very feasible for practical use. (4) Duplication-based algorithms [2, 10, 45], most of which are of a high computational complexity. For example, in [10], the complexity of the algorithm DBUS is of $O(m^2n^2)$, where m and n are the number of tasks in the workflow and the number of nodes in the network, respectively. (5) Guided random search methods such as genetic algorithm [3, 55] and simulated annealing [49] where additional efforts are often required to determine an appropriate termination condition and usually there is no performance guarantee.

Several pipeline mapping studies are closely related to the mapping problems considered in this chapter. Particularly, Benoit and Robert [8] have presented the mapping of computing pipelines onto different types of fully connected networks with identical processors and links (fully homogeneous platform), with identical links but different processors (communication homogeneous platform), or with different processors and links (fully heterogeneous platform). They also discussed three versions of pipeline mapping problems, i.e., one-to-one, interval, and general mappings, all of which are NP-complete in fully heterogeneous platforms. The problem they studied maps each module or stage (including input, processing, and output) onto one node in a serial manner, which is defined as a one-port model. A hierarchical end-to-end analysis technique has been proposed in [14] that decomposes a very complex heterogeneous multi-resource scheduling problem into a set of single-resource scheduling problems with well-defined interactions. An approach to optimally configure sessions has been proposed in [18], in programmable networks by converting the session configuration problem to the problem of finding a shortest path in a special layer-constructed graph [18]. The NP-completeness of this problem was further studied considering capacity constraints of each link and processing node and a heuristic solution using extended Dijkstra's algorithm [17].

The main differences between our work and the aforementioned efforts stem from the facts that we consider: (1) an exhaustive problem formulation with different performance optimization objectives and mapping constraints on node reuse; (2) networks with arbitrary topology and heterogeneous computing nodes and network links; (3) a multi-port model where one node can receive, process, and send data simultaneously; (4) resource sharing among multiple concurrent module executions on the node or data transfers over the link in streaming applications; and (5) unknown time cost on each node and link until a mapping scheme is determined.

4.3   Objective Functions and Problem Formulations

A number of large-scale distributed applications in various scientific, engineering, and medical fields require efficient execution of computing tasks that consist of a sequence of linearly arranged modules, which form a so-called computing pipeline between a data source and an end user. The pipeline mapping problems in our work are to find an efficient mapping scheme that maps the computing modules onto a set of strategically selected nodes to: (1) minimize end-to-end delay for single-input applications where a single dataset is processed sequentially along a computing pipeline, and (2) maximize frame rate for streaming applications where multiple datasets are fed into a computing pipeline in a batch processing mode to sustain continuous data flow. We construct cost models for pipeline and network components to facilitate a mathematical formulation of optimization problems and mapping objective functions.

4.3.1   Cost Models for Computing Pipelines and Computer Networks

We consider a computing pipeline consisting of m sequential modules, $w_0, w_1, \ldots , w_{m-1}$. The computing dependency between a pair of adjacent modules w_{i-1} and w_i is represented by a directed edge $e_{i-1,i}$ between them. Module w_i receives a data input $z_{i-1,i}$ from its preceding module w_{i-1} and performs a predefined computing routine whose complexity is modeled as a function $\lambda_{wi}(\bullet)$ on the input data size $z_{i-1,i}$ as shown in Fig. 4.3a. The complexity of a module is an abstract quantity that not only depends on the computational complexity of the algorithm defined in the module but also the implementation details such as the specific data structures used in the program. Once the routine is executed successfully in its entirety, module w_i sends a different data output $z_{i,i+1}$ to its succeeding module w_{i+1}. We assume that a module cannot start its execution until its required input data arrive. For an application with multiple source or destination modules, we could convert it to this model by inserting a virtual starting or ending module of complexity zero connected to all source or destination modules with zero-sized output or input data transfers.

We model the overlay computer network as an arbitrary weighted graph $G_c = (V_c, E_c)$, consisting of $|V_c| = n$ computer nodes interconnected by directed network links. We use a normalized variable p_i to represent the overall processing power of a computer node v_i without specifying its detailed system resources such as processor frequency, bus speed, memory size, storage performance, and presence of coprocessors. The network link $l_{i,j}$ between nodes v_i and v_j has Bandwidth (BW) $b_{i,j}$ and minimum link delay (MLD) $d_{i,j}$ as shown in Fig. 4.3b. The transfer time of a large dataset is mainly constrained by BW, while MLD could be a significant overhead for the transfer of a dataset whose size is comparable to the maximum transmission unit (MTU) of the underlying network. In practical applications, we may employ a linear regression-based method to estimate the BW and MLD of a network link [59].

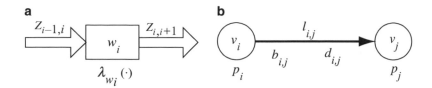

Fig. 4.3 Analytical cost model: (**a**) module and edge and (**b**) node and link

Table 4.1 Parameters used in the cost models

Parameters	Definitions
$w_0, w_1, \dots, w_{m-1}$	Computing pipeline
m	The number of modules in the computing pipeline
w_i	The i-th computing module
$e_{i,j}$	Dependency edge from module w_i to w_j
$z_{i,j}$	Transferred data size over dependency edge $e_{i,j}$
$\lambda_{wi}(\bullet)$	Computational complexity of module w_i
$G_c = (V_c, E_c)$	Computer network
n	The number of nodes in the computer network
v_i	The i-th network or computer node
v_s	Source node
v_δ	Destination node
p_i	Processing power of node v_i
$l_{i,j}$	Network link between nodes v_i and v_j
$b_{i,j}$	Bandwidth of link $l_{i,j}$
$d_{i,j}$	Minimum link delay of link $l_{i,j}$

We specify a pair of source and destination nodes (v_s, v_d) to run the starting module w_0 and the ending module w_{m-1}, respectively, and further assume that module w_0 serves as a data source without any computation and module w_{m-1} performs a terminal task without any data transfer. We estimate the execution time of module w_i running on computer node v_j as $T_{comp}(w_i, v_j) = \dfrac{\lambda_{w_i}(z_{i-1,j})}{p_j}$ and the data transfer time of dependency edge $e_{i,j}$ over network link $l_{h,k}$ as $T_{tran}(e_{i,j}, l_{h,k}) = \dfrac{z_{i,j}}{b_{h,k}} + d_{h,k}$.

For convenience, we tabulate the problem input parameters in Table 4.1.

4.3.2 End-to-End Performance Metrics

The application performance in terms of MED or MFR is determined by the module execution time on computer nodes and the data transfer time incurred over communication links. An efficient mapping scheme must account for the temporal constraints

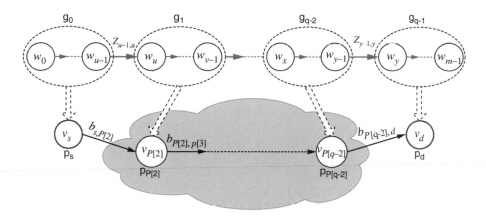

Fig. 4.4 A mathematical model of a general pipeline mapping

in the form of execution order of computing modules and spatial constraints in the form of geographical distribution of network nodes and their connectivity. Based on the analytical cost models presented in the previous section, we consider the following performance metrics.

End-to-end delay (ED) is the total completion time of the entire pipeline from the time when the original dataset is fed into the first module to the time when the final result is generated at the last module, which is an important performance requirement in time-critical applications especially for single-input operations. A general mapping scheme divides the pipeline into q groups of modules denoted by $g_0, g_1, \dots, g_{q-1}$ ($1 \leqslant q \leqslant m$), and maps them onto a selected network path P of not necessarily distinct q nodes (depending on mapping constraints), $v_{P[0]}, v_{P[1]}, \dots, v_{P[q-1]}$ from source $v_s = v_{P[0]}$ to destination $v_s = v_{P[q-1]}$, as shown in Fig. 4.4. Once a mapping scheme is determined, the ED is calculated as the total time cost incurred on the pipeline mapped to a network path, defined as:

$$T_{ED}\left(\text{path } P \text{ of } q \text{ nodes}\right) = T_{comp} + T_{tran} = \sum_{i=0}^{q-1} T_{g_i} + \sum_{i=0}^{q-2} T_{e(g_i, g_{i+1})}$$

$$= \sum_{i=0}^{q-1} \left(\sum_{j \in g_i, j \geq 1} \frac{w_j(z_{j-1,j})}{p_{P[i]}} \right) + \sum_{i=0}^{q-2} \left(\frac{z(g_i, g_{i+1})}{b_{P[i],P[i+1]}} + d_{P[i],P[i+1]} \right), \qquad (4.1)$$

where we assume that the inter-module transfer time within one group on the same node is negligible. We use $z(g_i, g_{i+1})$ to denote the transferred data size from group g_i to group g_{i+1}, which is the same as the data size generated by the last module in group g_i.

Frame Rate (FR) or throughput, i.e., the inverse of the global Bottleneck (BN) of the workflow, is the most critical performance metric for streaming applications that process multiple instances (e.g., time serial) of datasets. The bottleneck time

T_{BN} could be on either a computing module running on a computer node or a data transfer over a network link, defined as:

$$T_{\mathrm{BN}}(\text{Path } P \text{ of } q \text{ nodes}) = \max_{\substack{\text{Path } P \text{ of } q \text{ nodes} \\ i=0,1,\ldots,q-2}} \begin{pmatrix} T_{\mathrm{comp}}(g_i) \\ T_{\mathrm{tran}}(e(g_i, g_{i+1})) \\ T_{\mathrm{comp}}(g_{q-1}) \end{pmatrix}$$

$$= \max_{\substack{\text{Path } P \text{ of } q \text{ nodes} \\ i=0,1,\ldots,q-2}} \begin{pmatrix} \dfrac{\alpha_{P[I]}}{p_{P[I]}} \max_{j \in g_i, j \geq 1}(\lambda_{w_j}(z_{j-1,j})) \\ \dfrac{\beta_{P[I],P[i+1]} \cdot z(g_i, g_{i+1})}{b_{P[I],P[i+1]}} + d_{P[I],P[i+1]} \\ \dfrac{\alpha_{P[q-I]}}{p_{P[q-I]}} \max_{j \in g_{q-i}, j \geq 1}(\lambda_{w_j}(z_{j-1,j})) \end{pmatrix} \qquad (4.2)$$

where $\alpha_{P[i]}$ denotes the number of modules running simultaneously on node $v_{P[1]}$, and $\beta_{P[1],P[i+1]}$ is the number of datasets transferred concurrently over link $l_{P[1],P[i+1]}$ between nodes $v_{P[i]}$ and $v_{P[i+1]}$.

Objective Functions
The objective function of MED is defined as:

$$\min_{\text{all possible mappings}}(T_{\mathrm{ED}}) \qquad (4.3)$$

which is the minimum sum of time costs along the pipeline among all possible mappings. Similarly, the objective function of MFR is defined as:

$$\max_{\text{all possible mappings}}\left(\frac{1}{T_{\mathrm{BN}}}\right) \qquad (4.4)$$

which is achieved by identifying and minimizing the time T_{BN}, on a computing module or a dependency edge among all possible mappings. We maximize FR to produce the smoothest data flow in streaming applications when multiple instances of input datasets are continuously generated and fed into the pipeline.

4.4 Linear Pipeline Optimization

We first formulate and categorize the pipeline mapping problems into six classes with two mapping objectives (MED/MFR) and three network constraints (NNR/CNR/ANR), and then present a set of mapping solutions, Efficient Linear Pipeline Configuration (ELPC), in which an optimal solution is designed for MED-ANR and heuristic algorithms are proposed for the rest five NP-complete problems.

4.4.1   Problem Categorization and Complexity Analysis

For both MED and MFR, we consider three different types of mapping constraints as shown in Fig. 4.5: (1) NNR, where a node on the selected path P executes exactly one module, (2) CNR, where multiple contiguous modules along the pipeline are

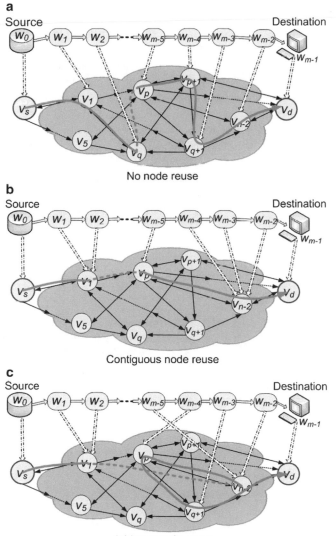

Fig. 4.5 Three network constraints on pipeline mappings

Objective Function / Constraints	Minimum End-to-end Delay	Maximum Frame Rate
No Node Reuse	NP-complete	NP-complete
Contiguous Node Reuse	NP-complete	NP-complete
Arbitrary Node Reuse	Polynomial (Dyn. Prog.)	NP-complete

Fig. 4.6 Complexities of six pipeline mapping problems

allowed to run on the same node, and (3) ANR, where multiple modules, either contiguous or noncontiguous, are allowed to run on the same node.

These mapping problems and their complexities are tabulated in Fig. 4.6.

We show that MED/MFR-NNR/CNR are NP-complete by reducing to them from the problem of finding two vertex-disjoint paths in a directed graph. This allows us to prove that these problems cannot be approximated by any constant factor, unless $P = NP$ [32]. For ANR, the difficulty of finding disjoint paths does not occur anymore since the mapping scheme can reuse some nodes that are used for previous modules. Indeed, MED-ANR is close to a shortest path problem and we are able to develop a polynomial time optimal solution to this problem using a DP-based procedure. However, we prove MFR-ANR to be NP-complete by reducing to it from the Widest-path with Linear Capacity Constraints (WLCC) problem [61].

4.4.2 An Optimal Solution to MED-ANR

In MED applications, since a single dataset is processed and there is only one module being executed at any particular time, nodes can be reused but are not shared concurrently among different modules on the same dataset. We present a Dynamic Programming (DP)-based polynomial time optimal algorithm to solve MED-ANR and provide its correctness proof.

Let $T^{-1}(v_j)$ denotes the MED with the first j modules mapped to a path from the source node v_s to node v_i in the network. We have the following recursion leading to the final solution $T^{m-1}(v_d)$:

$$
T^{j-1}(v_i) \underset{j=2 \text{ to } m, v_i \in V_c}{=} \min \left(\begin{array}{l} T^{j-2}(v_i) + \dfrac{\lambda_{w_{j-1}}(z_{j-2,j-1})}{p_i} \\[4mm] \min\limits_{v_u \in adj(v_j)} \left(T^{j-2}(v_u) + \dfrac{\lambda_{w_{j-1}}(z_{j-2,j-1})}{p_i} + \dfrac{z_{j-2,j-1}}{b_{u,i}} + d_{u,i} \right) \end{array} \right) \quad (4.5)
$$

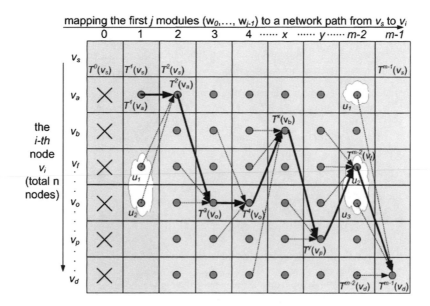

Fig. 4.7 Construction of 2D table based on DP

Where adj(v_i) denotes the set of preceding (adjacent) neighbors of node v_i, with the base condition computed as:

$$T^1(v_i)_{v_i \in V_c, \text{ and } v_i \neq v_s} = \begin{cases} \dfrac{\lambda_{w_i}(z_{0,1})}{p_i} + \dfrac{z_{0,1}}{b_{s,i}} + d_{s,i}, & \text{if } l_{s,i} \in E_c \\ +\infty, & \text{otherwise} \end{cases} \quad (4.6)$$

on the second column of a 2-dimensional (2D) table as shown in Fig. 4.7, where modules are listed in order along the horizontal axis and nodes are arranged along the vertical axis, as constructed by a typical DP-based method.

In Fig. 4.7, every cell $T^{j-1}(v_i)$ in the 2D DP table represents an optimal mapping solution that maps the first j modules in the pipeline to a path between the source node v_s and node v_i in the network. In MED-ANR, each cell is calculated from the intermediate mapping results up to its adjacent nodes or itself, which are stored in its left column $T^{j-2}(\bullet)$. The pseudocode of this algorithm is presented in Algorithm 1 and its complexity is $O(m \times E_c|)$, where m denotes the number of modules in the computing pipeline and $|E_c|$ is the number of communication links in the computer network.

Algorithm 1 ELPC for MED-ANR

Input: A linear pipeline with m computing modules, a heterogenous computer network $G = (V_c, E_c)$, where $|V_c| = n$, and a pair of source and destination nodes (v_s, v_d).

Output: The MED of the pipeline mapped onto a selected network path P from v_s to v_d.

1: Initialize the first column of 2D table: $T_{[0][0]} = 0.0$, $T_{[i][0]} = NULL$, $i = 1, 2, \ldots, n - 1$;
2: **for all** nodes v_i from $i = 0$ to $n - 1$ with only two modules w_0 and w_1 **do**
3:      **if** $e_{s,i} \in E$ **then**
4:          Calculate MED for cell $T_{[i][1]}$ in the 2nd column as the base condition;
5:      **else**
6:          $T_{[i][1]} = \infty$;
7: **for all** modules w_j from $j = 2$ to $m - 1$ **do**
8:      **for all** nodes v_i from $i = 0$ to $n - 1$ **do**
9:          **if** module w_{j-1} is mapped to node v_i **then**
10:             Map module w_j to node v_i, calculate ED D_1;
11:         **else**
12:             **for all** nodes $adj(v_i)$ directly connected to v_i **do**
13:                 Map module w_j to node v_i, calculate ED $D(adj(v_i))$;
14:             Choose the minimum total delay among all neighbor nodes of
                v_i: $D_2 = \min(D(adj(v_i)))$;
15:             $T_{[i][j]} = \min(D_1, D_2)$;
16: **return** $T_{[n-1][m-1]}$ as the final MED.

Theorem 4.1 *The DP-based solution defined in Eq. 4.5 to MED-ANR is optimal.*

Proof. At each recursive step, there are only two sub-cases, the minimum of which is chosen as the MED to fill in a new cell $T^{j-1}(v_i)$: (1) In sub-case 1, we run the new module on the same node running the last module in the previous mapping sub-problem $T^{j-2}(v_i)$. In other words, the last two or more modules are mapped to the same node v_i. Therefore, we only need to add the computing time of the last module on node v_i to the previous total delay, which is represented by a horizontal incident link from its left neighbor cell in the 2D table. (2) In sub-case 2, the new module is mapped to node v_i and the last node v_u in a previous mapping subproblem $T^{j-2}(v_u)$ is one of the neighbor nodes of node v_i, which is represented by a slanted incident link from a neighbor cell on the left column to node v_i. In Fig. 4.7, a set of neighbor nodes of node v_i are enclosed in a cloudy region in the previous column. We calculate the ED for all mappings using slanted incident links of node v_i and choose the minimal one, which is further compared with the one calculated in sub-case 1 using the horizontal incident link from the left neighbor cell. The minimum of these two sub-cases is selected as the MED for the partial pipeline mapping to a path between nodes v_s and v_i. Since each cell provides an optimal partial solution to a subproblem and mapping a new module does not affect the optimality of any previously computed partial solutions, this DP-based procedure provides an optimal solution to MED-ANR.

4.4.3 Complexity Analysis of MED/MFR-NNR/CNR and MFR-ANR

4.4.3.1 MED/MFR-NNR/CNR

We first define MED/MFR-NNR/CNR as decision problems:

Definition 4.1. Given a linear computing pipeline of m modules, a directed weighted computer network G and a bound T, does there exist a mapping scheme of the pipeline to the network with NNR or CNR such that the T_{ED} or T_{BN} does not exceed T?

Note that here we consider bottleneck cost T_{BN}, the inverse of frame rate, to make the problem definitions uniform among these four problems.

Theorem 4.2. *MED/MFR-NNR/CNR are NP-complete.*

Proof. We use a reduction from DISJOINT-CONNECTING-PATH (DCP) [28] which is NP-complete even when restricting to two paths in the case of directed graphs (2DCP) [25]. The mapping problems clearly belong to NP: given a division of the pipeline into q groups and a path P of q nodes, we can compute T_{ED} or T_{BN} in polynomial time using Eqs. 4.1 and 4.2, and check if the bound T is satisfied. We prove their NP-hardness by showing that $2DCP \leq_p MED/MFR-NNR/CNR$.

Consider an arbitrary instance I_1 of 2DCP, i.e., a network graph $G = (V,E)$, $n = |V| \geq 4$ and two disjoint vertex pairs (x^1, y^1), $(x^2, y^2) \in V^2$. We ask if G contains two mutually vertex-disjoint paths, one going from x_1 to y_1, and the other going from x_2 to y_2. We can create the following instance I_2 of our mapping problems (MED/MFR-NNR/CNR). The pipeline consists of $m = 2n + 1$ modules and the computational complexity of each module w_i is $\lambda_{wi}(z) = 1$ for $0 \leq i \leq 2n$, $i \neq n$ and $\lambda_{wi}(z) = n^2$. In other words, only module w_n has a much higher complexity than all other modules. The network consists of $|V| + 1 + (n-1)(n-2)$ nodes and $|E| + n(n-1)$ links, and is constructed as follows: starting from graph G, we add a new node t, which is connected to G with an incoming link from y_1 to t, and an outgoing link from t to x_2. We also add $0 + 1 + 2 + \ldots + (n-2)$ additional nodes between y_1 and t and their corresponding links to connect y_1 to t through a set of $n-1$ paths of length l (in terms of the number of nodes, excluding two end nodes y_1 and t), $0 \leq l \leq n-2$, as shown in Fig. 4.8.

Similarly, additional nodes and links are added between t and x_2 such that there exist a set of $n-1$ paths of length l, $0 \leq l \leq n-2$, between nodes t and x_2. The processing capability of each node v_j V' in the new graph $G' = (V', E')$ is set to $p_j = 1$ except for node t, whose processing power is set to be n^2, which is much higher than all other nodes. All link bandwidths are set to be sufficiently high so that transfer time between nodes is ignored compared to computing time. The source and destination nodes v_s and v_d are set to be x_1 and y_2, respectively. We ask if we can achieve an T_{ED} that does not exceed $T_{MED} = 2n + 1$ or T_{BN} that does not exceed $T_{MFR} = n$. Obviously, this instance transformation can be done in polynomial time.

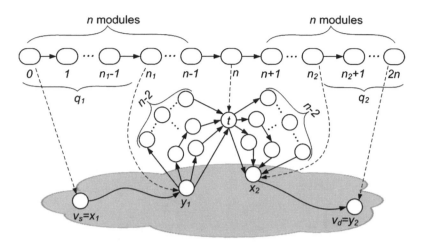

Fig. 4.8 Reduction from 2DCP problem

We show that given a solution to I_1, we can find a solution to I_2 of four mapping problems. Let q_i be the length of the path from x_i to y_i (including two end nodes), $i = 1, 2$. We have $2 \le q_i \le n$ for both paths, and paths are vertex-disjoint. The mapping solutions are derived in two cases under different mapping constraints, i.e., NNR and CNR, as follows:

1. Steps for deriving mapping solutions to NNR

   (a) We map the first q_1 modules starting from module w_0 one-to-one onto q_1 nodes of the path from x_1 to y_1 with NNR. Thus, w_0 is mapped on the source node $x_1 = v_s$ and w_{q_1-1} is mapped on node y_1.

   (b) We map the next $n - q_1$ modules from w_{q_1} to w_{n-1} along the pipeline one-to-one onto a path between y_1 and t (excluding two end nodes y_1 and t) of length $n - q_1$ with NNR. There must exist such a mapping path since $0 \le n - q_1 \le n - 2$. Obviously, each of the first n modules from w_0 to w_{n-1} incurs a delay of 1.

   (c) We map module w_n with a complexity of n^2 to the fast node t, which also incurs a delay of $n^2 / n^2 = 1$.

   (d) Similar to the first n modules, we map the last n modules from w_{n+1} to w_{2n} one-to-one onto the path of length $n - q_2$ from t to x_2 (excluding two end nodes) and then on the path of length q_2 from x_2 to y_2 (including two end nodes) with NNR. Each of the last n modules also incurs a delay of 1.

2. Steps for deriving mapping solutions to CNR

   (a) Same as Step 1 in the case of NNR, we map the first q_1 modules starting from module w_0 one-to-one onto q_1 nodes of the path from x_1 to y_1 with NNR, where each module incurs a delay of 1 (excluding module w_{q_1-1}).

   (b) We map all of the next $n - q_1$ modules from w_{q_1} to w_{n-1} along the pipeline to node y_1, together with module w_{q_1-1}, where each module incurs a delay of $\frac{1}{(1/(n-q_1+1))} = n - q_1 + 1$ due to resource sharing.

(c) Same as Step 3 in the case of NNR, we also map module w_n with a complexity of n^2 to the fastest node t, which incurs a delay of $n^2 / n^2 = 1$.

(d) Similar to the first n modules, we map all of $n - q_2$ modules in the last n modules starting from w_{n+1} to node x_2, and then map the last q_2 modules one-to-one onto the path of length q_2 from x_2 to y_2 (including two end nodes) with NNR. Each module on node x_2 incurs a delay of $\frac{1}{(1/(n - q_2 + 1))} = n - q_2 + 1$ due to resource sharing and each of the modules mapped on the path from x_2 to y_2 (excluding those mapped on x_2) incurs a delay of 1.

Obviously, the above-derived mapping solutions meet the requirements of NNR/CNR since we use the solution to I_1: two paths from x_1 to y_1 and from x_2 to y_2 are disjoint, so either no node is reused or only contiguous modules are mapped to the same node (either y_1 or x_2). For MED problems, since each module incurs a delay of 1 with no resource sharing and there are $2n + 1$ modules in total, the T_{ED} of this mapping solution is $2n + 1 \le T_{MED}$ in both NNR and CNR; while for MFR problems: (1) in the case of NNR, since all modules have an identical delay of 1, the T_{BN} of the entire pipeline is $1 \le n = T_{MFR}$; (2) in the case of CNR, all modules incur an identical delay of 1 except those mapped on nodes y_1 and x_2, where each module on node y_1 has a delay of $n - q_1 + 1$ and each module on node x_2 has a delay of $n - q_2 + 1$ because of resource sharing. The T_{BN} of the entire pipeline is either $n - q_1 + 1 \le n - 2 + 1 < n = T_{MFR}$ if $q_1 \le sq_2$, or $n - q_2 + 1 \le n - 2 + 1 < n = T_{MFR}$ if $q_1 > q_2$. Therefore, we find a valid solution to I_2 of all four mapping problems.

Reciprocally, if I_2 has a solution, we show that I_1 also has a solution. We prove that the mapping of I_2 has to be of a similar form as the mapping described above (or similar but with CNR in some instances of the problem), and thus that there exists disjoint paths $x_1 \rightarrow y_1$ and $x_2 \rightarrow y_2$. This property comes from the fact that node t must be used in the mapping. Indeed, if node t is not used to process module w_n, this module will incur a delay of n^2, thus the T_{ED} will be at least $n^2 + 4$ (each of 4 nodes, i.e. x_1, y_1, x_2, and y_2, incurs a delay of 1), which is larger than the total delay bound $T_{MED} = 2n + 1$, and also becomes the T_{BN} with cost larger than the bound $T_{MFR} = n$. Since the T_{ED} of I_2 is less than $2n + 1$, or the T_{BN} is less than or equal to n, module w_n must be mapped on node t in the solution to I_2. Note that the only way to reach node t involves using one of the $n - 1$ paths going from y_1 to t. Thus, there is at least one module mapped on y_1. Let w_{n_1} be the last of these modules: $n_1 < n$, and $w_{n_1 + 1}$ is not mapped on y_1. Similarly, all paths departing from t go through x_2, thus there is at least one module mapped on x_2. Let w_{n_2} be the first of these modules: $n_2 > n$, and $w_{n_2 - 1}$ is not mapped on x_2. Moreover, source and destination nodes x_1 and y_2 are also used, since w_0 is mapped on x_1 and w_{2n} is mapped on y_2. Therefore, the entire mapping scheme is made up of the following three segments: (1) modules w_0 to w_{n_1} are mapped on a path between x_1 and y_1 (including two end nodes); (2) modules $w_{n_1 + 1}$ to $w_{n_2 - 1}$ are mapped on a path between y_1 and x_2 (excluding two end nodes) going through t; and (3) modules w_{n_2} to w_{2n} are mapped on a path between x_2 and y_2 (including two end nodes). Since only contiguous modules along the pipeline can be deployed on the same node, or NNR is performed at all in this mapping, nodes in both paths $x_1 \rightarrow y_1$ and $x_2 \rightarrow y_2$ should be distinct, and they are connected only by the edges in G according to the construction of I_2. Thus, we find two disjoint paths, which constitute a solution to I_1.

Theorem 4.3. *Given any constant $\theta > 0$, there exists no θ-approximation to the MED/MFR-NNR/CNR problems, unless $P = NP$.*

Proof. Given θ, assume that there exists a θ-approximation to one of the four problems. Let I_1 be an instance of 2DCP (see proof of Theorem 2). We build the same instance I_2 as in the previous proof, except for the speed of the fast node t and the computational complexity of module w_n, both of which are set to be θn^2 instead of n^2.

We use the θ-approximation algorithm to solve this instance I_2 of our problem, which returns a mapping scheme of ED or bottleneck cost T_{alg} such that $T_{alg} \leq \theta T_{opt}$, where T_{opt} is the optimal T_{ED} or T_{BN}. Then we prove that we can solve 2DCP in polynomial time. We need to differentiate the cases of T_{ED} and FR (inverse of T_{BN}) as follows:

1. MED problems

   (a) If $T_{alg} > \theta(2n+1)$, then $T_{opt} > 2n+1$ and there does not exist two disjoint paths; otherwise, we could achieve a mapping of T_{ED} equal to $2n+1$. In this case, 2DCP has no solution.
   (b) If $T_{alg} \leq \theta(2n+1)$, we must map w_n on t; otherwise, it would incur a delay of $\theta n^2 > \theta(2n+1) \leq T_{alg}$, which conflicts with the condition. Hence, the mapping is similar to the one described in the proof of Theorem 2, and we conclude that 2DCP has a solution.

2. MFR problems

   (a) If $T_{alg} > \theta n$, then $T_{opt} > n$ and there does not exist two disjoint paths; otherwise, we could achieve a mapping of FR equal to n. In this case, 2DCP has no solution.
   (b) If $T_{alg} \leq \theta n$, we must map w_n on t; otherwise, it would incur a delay of $\theta n^2 > \theta n \leq T_{alg}$, which conflicts with the condition. Hence, the mapping is similar to the one described in the proof of Theorem 2. We conclude that 2DCP has a solution.

Therefore, in both cases, if 2DCP has a solution in polynomial time, then $P = NP$, which establishes the contradiction and proves the non-approximability result.

Because of the arbitrary node reuse, the non-approximability result is not directly applicable to MFR-ANR. We conjecture that MFR-ANR can be approximated, for instance, by modifying classical bin packing approximation schemes [4].

4.4.3.2 MFR-ANR

The NP-completeness proof for MFR-ANR is based on the Widest-path with Linear Capacity Constraints (WLCC) problem, which is shown to be NP-complete in [61].

An LCC-graph is a three-tuple $(G = (V,E),C,b)$, where the capacity of each link $e \in E$ is a variable x_e, and (C,b) represent a set of m linear capacity constraints $Cx \le b$, C is a $0 - 1$ coefficient matrix of size $m \times |E|$, x is a $|E| \times 1$ vector of link capacity variables, and $b \in R^m$ is a capacity vector. Each link $e \in E$ has a capacity $c(e) > 0$. Given an LCC-graph (G,C,b), the width $\omega(P)$ of a path $P = (e_1,e_2,...,e_k) \subset G$ is defined as the bottleneck capacity x_{BN} subject to $x_{e_j} = 0$, $\forall e_j \notin P$, $Cx \le b$, and $x_{e_1} = x_{e_2} = \cdots = x_{e_k} = x_{BN}$. We define WLCC as a decision problem: Given an arbitrary instance $(G = (V,E),C,b)$ of WLCC, two nodes $v_s, v_d \in V$ and a positive integer $K \le \max\{b_i\}$, does there exist a path p from v_s to v_d whose width, i.e., bottleneck capacity x_{BN}, is no less than K?

We first define MFR-ANR as a decision problem:

Definition 4.2. Given a linear computing pipeline of m modules, a computer network G and a bound B, does there exist a mapping scheme of the pipeline to the network with ANR such that the FR, i.e., the inverse of the T_{BN}, is no less than B?

Theorem 4.4. MFR-ANR is NP-complete.

Proof. For a given solution to an instance of MFR-ANR, we can go through the entire path to calculate the FR and check if it satisfies the bound in polynomial time, which means that MFR-ANR $\in$ NP. We prove its NP-hardness by showing that WLCC $\le_p$ MFR-ANR.

Given an arbitrary instance I_1 in WLCC, in which there are several LCCs among the links, as shown in Fig. 4.9a, we can transform it into an instance I_2 of MFR-ANR, i.e., $I_1 \in$ WLCC $\Rightarrow I_2 = F(I_1) \in$ MFR-ANR, where $F(\cdot)$ is a polynomial-time transformation function. We first construct a pipeline that consists of $|V|$ identical modules w, whose computational complexity is denoted as a function $\lambda_w(\cdot)$ of the same input data size z. We then make a copy of the entire topology of G and denote it as graph $G' = (V',E')$, where $V' = V$ and $E' = E$. Any vertex $v \in V$ in G not on a constrained link and any link $e \in E$ in G not in constraints (C,b) remain unchanged in V' and E', respectively, including the capacity of each link. We consider three types of LCCs:

Case 1 of adjacent LCC
If there are η constrained links within one LCC that are all adjacent, their corresponding vertices in V' are bundled together and replaced with a virtual node v_{vir}, which contains the same number of self-loops as that of contiguously adjacent constrained links defined in the LCC. The power p of the virtual node is set to $\lambda_w(z) \cdot \gamma$, where γ is the LCC capacity. For example, in Fig. 4.9, the links $e_{1,2}$, $e_{2,3}$ and $e_{3,4}$ have an LCC $x_{e_{1,2}} + x_{e_{2,3}} + x_{e_{3,4}} \le \gamma_1$ among them, so we have $\eta = 3$ and $\gamma = \gamma_1$.

Case 2 of nonadjacent LCC
If there are ζ constrained links within one LCC that are all nonadjacent, their corresponding vertices in V' are bundled together and replaced with a virtual node v_{vir}. The power p of the virtual node is again set to $\lambda_w(z) \cdot \gamma$, where γ is the LCC capacity. For example, in Fig. 4.9a, the links $e_{i+1,i+2}$ and $e_{j+2,j+3}$ have an LCC $x_{e_{i+1,i+2}} + x_{e_{j+2,j+3}} \le \gamma_2$ between them, so we have $\zeta = 2$ and $\gamma = \gamma_2$.

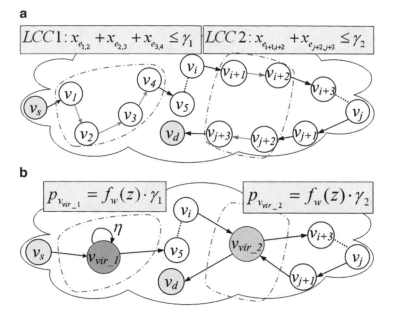

Fig. 4.9 Reduction from WLCC: (**a**) Example of LCC-graph, (**b**) LCC-graph replaced with virtual nodes

Case 3 of mixed LCC
This is a combination of the first two cases. The corresponding vertices in V' of all adjacent and nonadjacent constrained links within one LCC are bundled together and replaced with a virtual node v_{vir}, whose properties (self-loops and processing power) are treated the same way as in the first two cases.

Furthermore, the processing power of all other nodes is set to infinity. The newly constructed graph G' with one adjacent LCC and one nonadjacent LCC is shown in Fig. 4.9b. Finally, we select a bound $B = K$. Obviously, this process can be done in polynomial time. The question for MFR-ANR is: does there exist a mapping path p' from v'_s to v'_d in G' that provides FR no less than B?

We show that given a solution to WLCC problem, we can find a solution to the MFR-ANR problem. Suppose that there exists a path p from v_s to v_d in G of width no less than K. We first identify a path p' in G' corresponding to path p in G, and then sequentially map the modules in the pipeline onto the nodes along the path p' from v'_s to v'_d, with the first module mapped onto source node v_s and the last module mapped onto destination node v_d. Between v'_s and v'_d, we sequentially map each module onto a regular node along the path, and when a virtual node is encountered, we have three different mapping schemes:

Case 1 of adjacent LCC
If this virtual node is converted from η adjacent constrained links, among which η' ($\eta' \le \eta$) links are on path p, we map η' contiguous modules to it.

Case 2 of nonadjacent LCC

If this virtual node is converted from ζ nonadjacent constrained links, among which ζ' ($\zeta' \le \zeta$) links are on path p, we map one module to it every time when the path passes through it for total ζ' times.

Case 3 of mixed LCC

If this virtual node is converted from both adjacent and nonadjacent constrained links, we map modules to it according to a combination of the mapping strategies for virtual nodes converted from either a single adjacent LCC or a single nonadjacent LCC as specified in the first two cases.

Any remaining contiguous modules are mapped onto the non-virtual destination node v_d. If the destination node v_d itself is a virtual node in G', we can create a special node with infinite processing power and connect the destination node v_d to it with infinite bandwidth on the link. This special node is then considered as the new destination node to run the last module and all remaining unmapped modules. We consider the following four cases:

Case 1: Where the maximum capacity of path p is not on any LCC link: the FR in G' is equal to the corresponding maximum capacity in G. Therefore, path p' from v_s' to v_d' in G' provides FR that is no less than $K = B$.

Case 2: Where the maximum capacity of path p is on one of the adjacent LCC links: we calculate the FR on the virtual node in G' as $1/(\lambda_w(z)/\frac{p}{\eta'})$. After plugging in $p = \lambda_w(z)\cdot\gamma$, the FR becomes: $1/(\lambda_w(z)/\frac{\lambda_w(z)\cdot\gamma}{\eta'}) = \frac{\gamma}{\eta'}$. In WLCC problem, the bottleneck bandwidth x_{BN} of the widest path p has the following inequality: $K \le x_{BN} \le \frac{\gamma}{\eta}$ since all constrained links share the capacity γ. Hence, the corresponding mapping path p' from v_s' to v_d' in G' provides FR at $\frac{\gamma}{\eta'} \le K = B$.

Case 3: Where the maximum capacity of path p is on one of the nonadjacent LCC links: we calculate the FR on the virtual node in G' as $1/(\lambda_w(z)/\frac{p}{\zeta'})$. After plugging in $p = \lambda_w(z)\cdot\gamma$, the FR becomes: $1/(\lambda_w(z)/\frac{\lambda_w(z)\cdot\gamma}{\zeta'}) = \frac{\gamma}{\zeta'}$. In WLCC problem, the bottleneck bandwidth x_{BN} of the widest path p has the following inequality: $K \le x_{BN} \le \frac{\gamma}{\zeta}$ since all constrained links share the capacity γ. Hence, the corresponding mapping path p' from v_s' to v_d' in G' provides FR at $\frac{\gamma}{\zeta'} \le K = B$.

Case 4: Where the maximum capacity of path p is on one of the mixed LCC links: we calculate the FR on the virtual node in G' as $1/(\lambda_w(z)/\frac{p}{\eta'+\zeta'})$. After plugging in $p = \lambda_w(z)\cdot\gamma$, the FR becomes: $1/(\lambda_w(z)/\frac{\lambda_w(z)\cdot\gamma}{\eta'+\zeta'}) = \frac{\gamma}{\eta'+\zeta'}$. In WLCC problem, the bottleneck bandwidth x_{BN} of the widest path p has the following inequality: $K \le x_{BN} \le \frac{\gamma}{\eta'+\zeta}$ since all constrained links share the capacity γ. Hence, the corresponding mapping path p' from v_s' to v_d' in G' provides FR at $\frac{\gamma}{\eta'+\zeta'} \le K = B$.

Therefore, we conclude that the mapping path p' is the solution to the instance I_2 of MFR-ANR problem. Now we show that if there is a solution to MFR-ANR problem, we can also find a solution to WLCC problem in polynomial time.

Given a path p' from v'_s to v'_d in G' with FR $\leq B$, we first identify a corresponding path p in G. We also consider the following four cases:

Case 1: Where the FR is incurred on a network link in G', the corresponding link in G has the bottleneck bandwidth of the widest path in WLCC;

Case 2: Where a virtual node converted from an adjacent LCC incurs the FR as: $1/(\lambda_w(z)/\frac{p}{\eta'}) = 1/(\lambda_w(z)/\frac{\lambda_w(z)\cdot\gamma}{\eta'}) = \frac{\gamma}{\eta'} \leq 1$, the corresponding path p in G has the bottleneck bandwidth $x_{BN} = \frac{\gamma}{\eta'} > B = K$ of the widest path in WLCC;

Cases 3 and 4: Where the solution derivation steps are very similar to those in case 2, except for replacing η' with ζ' and $\eta'+\zeta'$, respectively.

Therefore, we conclude that path p in G from v_s to v_d is the solution to the instance I_1 of WLCC problem.

4.5 Heuristics for NP-Complete Problems

We develop heuristic solutions by adapting the optimal DP-based method for MED-ANR to the NP-complete MED mapping problems with some necessary modifications. The heuristics for MED-NNR/CNR are similar to that defined in Eq. 4.5 except that (1) in MED-CNR, we skip the cell of a neighbor node (slanted incident link) in the left column whose solution (path) involves the current node to ensure a loop-free path, and (2) in MED-NNR, we further skip the immediate left neighbor cell (horizontal incident link) to ensure that the current node is never reused. Such path backtracking and cell exclusion reflect the heuristic nature of these algorithms since the skipped cells might lead to the actual optimal solution.

For streaming applications, we use $1/T_{BN}^{j-1}(v_i)$ to denote the MFR with the first j modules mapped to a path from source node v_s to node v_i in the computer network, and the following recursion leads to the final solution $T_{BN}^{m-1}(v_d)$:

$$T_{BN}^{j-1}(v_i) = \min_{j=2\,to\,m, v_i \in Vc} \left(\begin{array}{c} \max\left(\dfrac{\lambda_{w_{j-1}}(z_{j-2,j-1})\cdot\alpha_i}{p_i} \right) \\[3em] \min_{v_u \in adj(v_i)} \left(\max\left(\begin{array}{c} \dfrac{\lambda_{w_{j-1}}(z_{j-2,j-1})\cdot\alpha_i}{p_i} \\[2em] \dfrac{z_{j-2,j-1}\cdot\beta_{u,i}}{b_{u,i}} + d_{u,i} \end{array} \right) \right) \end{array} \right) \quad (4.7)$$

with the base condition computed as:

$$
T_{\mathrm{BN}}^1(v_i) \atop {\scriptstyle v_i \in V_c,\ and\ v_i \neq v_s} = \begin{cases} \max\left(\dfrac{\lambda_{w_1}(z_{0,1})}{p_i} + \dfrac{z_{0,1}}{b_{s,i}} + d_{s,i} \right), & \forall l_{s,i} \in E_c \\[2ex] +\infty, & \text{otherwise} \end{cases}
\tag{4.8}
$$

on the second column of the 2D table and we have $T_{\mathrm{BN}}^0(v_s) = 0$. Note that α_i denotes the total number of input datasets for different instances concurrently running on computer node v_i and $\beta_{u,i}$ denotes the total number of input datasets for different instances concurrently transferred over the communication link $l_{u,i}$ between nodes v_u and v_i. In MFR-NNR, we have $\alpha = 1$ and $\beta = 1$. The steps for filling out the 2D table for MFR problems are similar to those for their corresponding MED problems but differ in the following aspects: at each step, we ensure that the processing power of reused nodes be equally shared and calculate T_{BN} of the path instead of T_{ED}. These solutions are heuristic in nature because: (1) in MFR-CNR/ANR, the share of resources affects the optimality of previously computed partial solutions, and (2) in MFR-NNR, when a node has been selected by all its neighbor nodes at previous steps, we may miss an optimal solution if this node is the only one leading to the destination node or obtain a suboptimal solution if there are multiple nodes leading to the destination. Based on our extensive experiments, we would like to point out that the occurrences of unsuccessful mapping solutions due to backtracking are quite rare and all these heuristics achieve satisfactory mapping performance on a large number of simulated pipelines and networks of different scales.

4.6   Performance Evaluation and Comparison

In this section, we illustrate the superiority of the proposed optimal and heuristic algorithms through extensive performance comparison using simulated computing pipelines and computer networks by varying their topology and data size from small to large scales.

4.6.1   Algorithms in Comparison

Besides the proposed algorithms, ELPC, we also implement other two algorithms for comparison, namely, Streamline [1] and Greedy algorithms on the same Windows XP desktop PC equipped with a 3.0 GHz CPU and 3 Gbytes memory.

- *Streamline Algorithm (SL)*. A grid scheduling algorithm, Streamline, for graph-structured dataflow scheduling in a network with n resources and $n \times n$ communication links [1]. The Streamline algorithm considers application requirements in terms of per-stage computation and communication needs, application constraints on co-location of stages (node reuse), and availability of computation and communication resources. Two parameters, rank and blevel, are used to quantitate these features. Rank calculates the average computation and communication cost of a stage, and blevel estimates the overall remaining execution time of a data item after being processed by a stage. Based on these two parameters, the stages are sorted in a decreasing order of resource needs and the nodes are sorted in a decreasing order of resource availability. This scheduling heuristic works as a global greedy algorithm that expects to maximize the throughput of an application by assigning the best resources to the most needy stages in terms of computation and communication requirements at each step. The complexity of this algorithm is $O(m \times n^2)$, where m is the number of modules in the graph and n is the number of nodes in the network.

- *Greedy Algorithm.* A greedy algorithm iteratively obtains the greatest immediate gain based on certain local optimality criteria at each step, which may or may not lead to the global optimum. We design a heuristic mapping scheme based on a naive greedy algorithm that calculates the end-to-end delay for mapping a new module onto the current node or one of its succeeding neighbor nodes and chooses the minimal one based on computation and communication cost. This greedy algorithm makes a module mapping decision at each step only based on the current information without considering the effect of this local decision on the mapping performance in later steps. Since other links are not considered at each step except for the current one, this algorithm might fail to find a feasible mapping solution due to the topology restrictions. The complexity of this algorithm is $O(m \times |E_c|)$, where m is the number of modules in the computing pipeline and $|E_c|$ is the number of communication links in the computer network.

We conduct an extensive set of performance comparison between our proposed algorithms and the above heuristics in terms of MED or MFR based on a large number of simulated computing pipelines and computer networks. These simulation datasets are generated by randomly varying the following parameters of the computing pipelines and computer networks within a suitably selected range of values: (1) the number of modules and the complexity of each module, (2) the data size between two modules, (3) the number of nodes and the processing power of each node, and (4) the number of links and the BW and MLD of each link.

4.6.2 Comparative Performance Evaluation

We perform mapping experiments using ELPC, Streamline, and Greedy algorithms with various mapping constraints under 20 different problem sizes (from 4 modules, 6 nodes and 29 links to 100 modules, 200 nodes and 39790 links), indexed from 1 to 20. The topology and data size of 20 simulated computing pipelines and computer networks and their corresponding performance measurements, MED in milliseconds (ms) and MFR in frames/s (f/s), are tabulated in Tables 4.2 and 4.3, respectively,

Table 4.2 MED performance measurements of 20 problem cases

Problem index	Problem size m, n, $|E_c|$	MED-NNR (ms)			MED-CNR (ms)		MED-ANR (ms)		
		ELPC	Greedy	Streamline	ELPC	Greedy	ELPC (optimal)	Greedy	Streamline
1	4, 6, 29	90.12	90.13	103.15	89.59	105.86	33.31	33.31	36.44
2	6, 10, 86	122.83	246.57	340.11	85.80	111.19	52.65	58.97	92.08
3	10, 15, 207	204.82	220.37	439.11	97.28	139.83	95.69	95.70	226.96
4	13, 20, 376	227.39	252.50	557.03	96.84	96.85	106.02	147.43	144.48
5	15, 25, 597	349.35	378.49	548.19	153.66	219.68	144.12	144.13	174.37
6	19, 28, 753	341.78	362.34	931.62	128.20	128.21	166.76	254.11	267.88
7	22, 31, 927	439.21	485.46	925.35	175.71	181.26	196.26	274.52	255.04
8	26, 35, 1180	495.95	528.09	727.95	205.62	214.21	194.02	194.02	340.13
9	30, 40, 1558	551.77	586.55	1346.74	228.67	263.58	247.92	276.19	505.91
10	35, 45, 1963	664.16	712.59	1424.02	255.64	271.54	309.66	414.94	495.82
11	38, 47, 2153	699.79	776.09	1148.48	281.68	401.21	284.01	302.71	451.73
12	40, 50, 2428	716.60	811.62	1161.81	335.86	609.92	320.03	386.29	377.18
13	45, 60, 3520	864.32	924.21	1592.16	394.91	452.03	361.32	378.02	630.51
14	50, 65, 4155	881.78	920.12	2094.98	436.48	486.37	386.21	488.36	537.89
15	55, 70, 4820	960.48	1050.60	1584.84	557.42	682.77	417.29	424.43	949.11
16	60, 75, 5540	1087.21	1232.20	2127.81	548.25	571.79	421.76	751.70	834.16
17	75, 90, 7990	1392.05	1503.61	3206.72	658.31	706.55	599.00	599.00	729.48
18	80, 100, 9896	1564.58	1673.24	3248.07	744.00	753.38	648.79	674.36	979.86
19	90, 150, 22346	1484.32	1594.28	2811.84	746.07	805.52	700.54	744.47	1340.25
20	100, 200, 39790	1552.42	1604.69	3325.08	789.81	850.87	752.46	760.73	2057.51

Table 4.3 MFR performance measurements of 20 problem cases

Problem index	Problem size $m, n, |E_s|$	MED-NNR (f/s)			MED-CNR (f/s)		MED-ANR (f/s)		
		ELPC	Greedy	Streamline	ELPC	Greedy	ELPC	Greedy	Streamline
1	4, 6, 29	33.47	10.97	28.15	11.36	11.36	22.10	10.97	4.75
2	6, 10, 86	47.93	36.50	16.19	48.54	39.19	36.50	36.50	26.31
3	10, 15, 207	54.33	24.81	6.10	60.15	54.06	63.33	59.31	4.18
4	13, 20, 376	56.67	30.44	5.68	54.21	12.58	76.01	56.67	26.50
5	15, 25, 597	37.64	5.07	8.48	51.25	46.18	36.98	35.33	26.23
6	19, 28, 753	48.92	19.77	3.21	54.21	50.07	48.92	48.92	48.90
7	22, 31, 927	47.62	25.85	6.51	49.52	32.62	67.95	53.74	57.82
8	26, 35, 1180	38.70	30.95	10.33	21.42	14.61	61.52	57.90	47.41
9	30, 40, 1558	52.51	32.13	2.42	40.61	6.13	96.49	57.90	13.63
10	35, 45, 1963	36.46	24.09	3.65	32.19	7.70	36.46	36.46	27.17
11	38, 47, 2153	45.09	24.97	7.69	61.45	57.86	45.09	15.18	45.09
12	40, 50, 2428	27.43	25.65	8.07	60.57	55.57	27.43	27.43	27.42
13	45, 60, 3520	52.59	18.61	4.62	34.34	32.25	61.01	49.53	55.24
14	50, 65, 4155	43.92	10.61	2.10	52.50	16.99	89.65	59.70	56.56
15	55, 70, 4820	50.80	22.20	5.85	40.97	34.13	50.80	50.80	35.45
16	60, 75, 5540	43.41	25.19	3.95	50.23	49.92	94.00	53.82	45.19
17	75, 90, 7990	35.35	29.04	4.17	50.52	50.02	15.35	15.35	15.35
18	80, 100, 9896	32.60	18.32	6.96	54.25	32.38	32.60	28.90	32.59
19	90, 150, 22346	55.63	35.58	6.52	56.07	41.54	88.95	55.49	24.47
20	100, 200, 39790	56.70	18.35	4.86	56.86	34.31	84.94	55.98	20.68

where each problem size is represented by a three-tuple $(m, n, |E_c|)$: m computing modules in the pipeline, and n computer nodes and $|E_c|$ communication links in the computer network. The measured MED of these algorithms vary from milliseconds for small-scale problems to seconds for large-scale ones in terms of MED. The relative performance differences of these three algorithms observed in other cases are qualitatively similar. For MED, since only one single dataset sequentially flows through each module along the path, the resource of a reused node is not shared by multiple modules at any time; while for MFR, node reuse causes resource share and may affect the optimality of the partial mapping scheme carried out in the previous steps in the 2D DP table. We would like to point out that these heuristics may miss a feasible mapping solution in certain cases.

For a visual comparison, we also plot the performance measurements of MED and MFR produced by these three algorithms under three network constraints (NNR/CNR/ANR) in Figs. 4.10a–c and 4.11a–c, respectively. We observe that ELPC exhibits comparable or superior performances in terms of MED and MFR over the other two algorithms in all the cases we studied. We do not compare with Streamline in the case of CNR because Streamline does not allocate the resources by the sequence numbers of stages (modules), so we may not know the previous

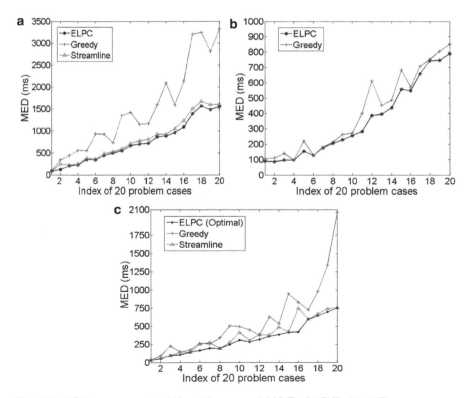

Fig. 4.10 MED measurements of 20 problem cases: (**a**) NNR, (**b**) CNR, (**c**) ANR

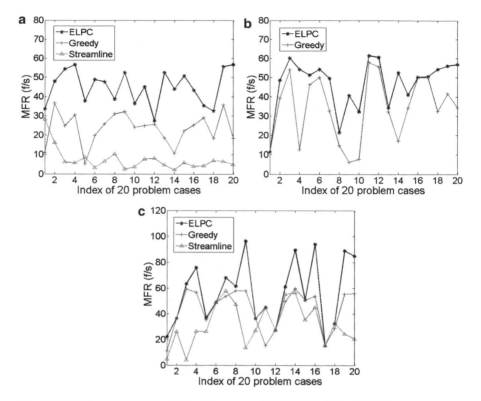

Fig. 4.11 MFR measurements of 20 problem cases: (**a**) NNR, (**b**) CNR, (**c**) ANR

node when the current one is being allocated. Since the MED represents the total delay from source to destination, a larger problem size with more network nodes and computing modules generally (not absolutely, though) incurs a longer mapping path resulting in a longer ED, which explains the increasing trend in Fig. 4.10a–c. On the other hand, the MFR, i.e., the reciprocal of the bottleneck cost on a selected mapping path, is not particularly related to the path length, and hence the performance curves in Fig. 4.11a–c lack an obvious increasing or decreasing trend in response to varying problem sizes.

4.7 Future Research Directions

In the cost models for computer nodes and network links, we used a normalized quantity to represent the processing power and bandwidth for simplicity. However, a single constant is not always sufficient to describe node computing and link transfer capability, which highly depend on the type and availability of system and network resources, and could be time-varying in a dynamic environment. The time-varying nature of system and network resources' availability makes it even more challenging to perform an accurate prediction or estimation of the execution time of a computing module or the transfer time of a network link in real networks. It is of our future interest to investigate sophisticated cost models to characterize real-time node and link behaviors in dynamic network environments. Also, the fairness in resource sharing may not necessarily lead to the best end-to-end performance. More sophisticated methods are needed to schedule the execution of multiple concurrent modules on the same node or multiple concurrent data transfers over the same links for further performance improvement. It would also be of our future interest to extend the mapping problems from linear pipelines to more general graph-structured workflows.

4.8 Conclusion

In this chapter, we did an extensive background survey of the classical and state-of-the-art mapping schemes for pipeline workflow optimization. We constructed analytical cost models to quantitate the characteristics of computing modules and dependency edges in computing pipelines as well as computer nodes and network links in overlay computer networks, and conducted an exhaustive investigation on the data-intensive computing pipeline mapping problems in distributed heterogeneous networks with different objectives and mapping constraints. We proved that MED-ANR can be solved in polynomial time, while the rest five problems are NP-complete.

Moreover, we proved that all MED and MFR problems with NNR and CNR cannot be approximated by any constant factor (unless $P = $ NP). We designed a set of ELPC algorithms for these mapping problems and tested them on a large set of simulated computing pipelines and computer networks. The extensive simulation results show that the ELPC scheme exhibits superior mapping performance over other existing algorithms, Streamline and Greedy, in terms of both MED and MFR.

References

1. Agarwalla, B., Ahmed, N., Hilley, D., Ramachandran, U.: Streamline: A scheduling heuristic for streaming application on the grid. In: Proceedings of the 13th Multimedia Computing and Networking Conference, San Jose (2006)
2. Ahmed, I., Kwok, Y.: On exploiting task duplication in parallel program scheduling. IEEE Trans. Parallel Distrib. Syst. **9**, 872–892 (1998)
3. Annie, S.W., Yu, H., Jin, S., Lin, K.C.: An incremental genetic algorithm approach to multiprocessor scheduling. IEEE Trans. Parallel Distrib. Syst. **15**, 824–834 (2004)
4. Ausiello, G., Crescenzi, P., Gambosi, G., Kann, V., Marchetti-Spaccamela, A., Protasi, M.: Complexity and Approximation: Combinatorial Optimization Problems and Their Approximability Properties. Springer, Berlin (1999)
5. Bajaj, R., Agrawal, D.P.: Improving scheduling of tasks in a heterogeneous environment. IEEE Trans. Parallel Distrib. Syst. **15**, 107–118 (2004)

6. Bashir, A.F., Susarla, V., Vairavan, K.: A statistical study of the performance of a task scheduling algorithm. IEEE Trans. Comput. **32**(12), 774–777 (1975)
7. Benoit, A., Hakem, M., Robert, Y.: Optimizing the latency of streaming applications under throughput and reliability constraints. In: Proceedings of the 2009 International Conference on Parallel Processing, Vienna, pp. 325–332, (2009)
8. Benoit, A., Robert, Y.: Mapping pipeline skeletons onto heterogeneous platforms. J. Parallel Distrib. Comput. **68**(6), 790–808 (2008)
9. Boeres, C., Filho, J.V., Rebello, V.E.F.: A cluster-based strategy for scheduling task on heterogeneous processors. In: Proceedings of the 16th Symposium on Computer Architecture and High Performance Computing, Foz Do Iguacu, pp. 214–221 (2004)
10. Bozdag, D., Catalyurek, U., Ozguner, F.: A task duplication based bottom-up scheduling algorithm for heterogeneous environments. In: Proceedings of the 20th International Parallel and Distributed Processing Symposium, Rhodes Island, pp. 12 (2006). doi:10.1109/IPDPS.2006.1639389
11. Braun, T.D., Siegel, H.J., Beck, N., Boloni, L.L., Maheswaran, M., Reuther, A.I., Robertson, J.P., Theys, M.D., Yao, B., Hensgen, D., Freund, R.F.: A comparison of eleven static heuristics for mapping a class of independent tasks onto heterogeneous distributed computing systems. J. Parallel Distrib. Comput. **61**(6), 810–837 (2001)
12. Buyya, R., Abramson, D., Giddy, J.: Nimrod/G: An architecture for a resource management and scheduling system in a global computational grid. In: Proceedings of the 4th International Conference/Exhibition on the High Performance Computing in the Asia-Pacific Region, vol. 1, Beijing, pp. 283–289 (2000)
13. Cao, J., Jarvis, S.A., Saini, S., Nudd, G.R.: GridFlow: Workflow management for grid computing. In: Proceedings of the 3rd IEEE/ACM International Symposium on Cluster Computing and the Grid, Tokyo, pp. 198–205 (2003)
14. Chatterjee, S., Strosnider, J.: Distributed pipeline scheduling: End-to-end analysis of heterogeneous, multi-resource real-time systems. In: Proceedings of the 15th International Conference on Distributed Computing Systems, Washington, DC, pp. 204–211 (1995)
15. Chaudhary, V., Aggarwal, J.K.: A generalized scheme for mapping parallel algorithms. IEEE Trans. Parallel Distrib. Syst. **4**(3), 328–346 (1993)
16. Chen, L., Agrawal, G.: Resource allocation in a middleware for streaming data. In Proceedings of the 2nd Workshop on Middleware for Grid Computing (2004). doi:10.1145/1028493.1028494
17. Choi, S.Y., Turner, J.: Configuring sessions in programmable networks with capacity constraints. In: Proceedings of IEEE International Conference on Communications, Anchorage, pp. 823–829 (2003)
18. Choi, S.Y., Turner, J., Wolf, T.: Configuring sessions in programmable networks. In: Proceedings of IEEE INFOCOM, Anchorage, pp. 60–66 (2001)
19. Climate and Carbon Research Institute (CCR): Retrieved from http://www.ccs.ornl.gov/CCR (2010)
20. Cordella, L.P., Foggia, P., Sansone, C., Vento, M.: An improved algorithm for matching large graphs. In: Proceedings of the 3rd IAPR-TC-15 International Workshop on Graph-Based Representations, Venice (2001)
21. Deelman, E., Callaghan, S., Field, E., Francoeur, H., Graves, R., Gupta, N., Gupta, V., Jordan, T.H., Kesselman, C., Maechling, P., Mehringer, J., Mehta, G., Okaya, D., Vahi, K., Zhao, L.: Managing large-scale workflow execution from resource provisioning to provenance tracking: The cybershake example. In: Proceedings of the e-Science Conference, Amsterdam (2006). doi:10.1109/E-SCIENCE.2006.99
22. Deelman, E., Singh, G., Su, M., Blythe, J., Gil, Y., Kesselman, C., Mehta, G., Vahi, K., Berriman, G.B., Good, J., Laity, A., Jacob, J.C., Katz, D.S.: Pegasus: A framework for mapping complex scientific workflows onto distributed systems. J. Sci. Program. **13**, 219–237 (2005)
23. Dogan, A., Özgüner, F.: Matching and scheduling algorithms for minimizing execution time and failure probability of applications in heterogeneous computing. IEEE Trans. Parallel Distrib. Syst. **13**(3), 308–323 (2002)

24. Earth System Grid (ESG): Retrieved from http://www.earthsystemgrid.org (2010)
25. Fortune, S., Hopcroft, J., Wyllie, J.: The directed subgraph homeomorphism problem. Theor. Comput. Sci. **10**, 111–121 (1980)
26. Foster, I.T.: Globus toolkit version 4: Software for service-oriented systems. J. Comput. Sci. Technol. **21**(4), 513–520 (2006)
27. Foster, I.T., Kesselman, C., Tuecke, S.: The anatomy of the grid – Enabling scalable virtual organizations. Int. J. Supercomput. Appl. **15**(3), 200–222 (2001)
28. Garey, M.R., Johnson, D.S.: Computers and Intractability: A Guide to the Theory of NP-Completeness. Freeman, New York (1979)
29. Gerasoulis, A., Yang, T.: A comparison of clustering heuristics for scheduling DAGs on multiprocessors. J. Parellel Distrib. Comput. **16**(4), 276–291 (1992)
30. González, D., Almeida, F., Moreno, L., Rodríguez, C.: Towards the automatic optimal mapping of pipeline algorithms. J. Parallel Comput. **29**(2), 241–254 (2003)
31. Gu, Y., Wu, Q.: Optimizing distributed computing workflows in heterogeneous network environments. In: Proceedings of the 11th International Conference on Distributed Computing and Networking, San Jose (2010). doi: 10.1007/978-3-642-11322-2_17
32. Gu, Y., Wu, Q., Benoit, A., Robert, Y.: Optimizing end-to-end performance of distributed applications with linear computing pipelines. In: Proceedings of the 15th International Conference on Parallel and Distributed Systems, Shenzhen (2009)
33. Ilavarasan, E., Thambidurai, P.: Low complexity performance effective task scheduling algorithm for heterogeneous computing environments. J. Comput. Sci. **3**(2), 94–103 (2007)
34. Johnston, W.E.: Computational and data grids in large-scale science and engineering. J. Future Generation Comput. Syst. **18**(8), 1085–1100 (2002)
35. Kwok, Y.K., Ahmad, I.: Dynamic critical-path scheduling: An effective technique for allocating task graph to multiprocessors. IEEE Trans. Parallel Distrib. Syst. **7**(5), 506–521 (1996)
36. Litzkow, M., Livny, M., Mutka, M.: Condor – A hunter of idle workstations. In: Proceedings of the 8th International Conference on Distributed Computing Systems, San Jose, pp. 104–111 (1988)
37. Ma, T., Buyya, R.: Critical-path and priority based algorithms for scheduling workflows with parameter sweep tasks on global grids. In: Proceedings of the 17th International Symposium on Computer Architecture on HPC, Rio de Janeiro, pp. 251–258 (2005)
38. McCreary, C., Khan, A.A., Thompson, J.J., McArdle, M.E.: A comparison of heuristics for scheduling DAGs on multiprocessors. In: Proceedings of the 8th International Symposium on Parallel Processing, Cancun, pp. 446–451 (1994)
39. McDermott, W.J., Maluf, D.A., Gawdiak, Y., Tran, P.B.: Airport simulations using distributed computational resources. DOI: 10.4271/2001-01-2650 (2001)
40. Messmer, B.T.: Efficient graph matching algorithms for preprocessed model graphs. Ph.D. thesis, Institute of Computer Science and Applied Mathematics, University of Bern, Bern, Swtzerland (1996)
41. Mezzacappa, A.: Scidac Scientific discovery through advanced computing. J. Phys. Conf. Ser. **16**, 536–540 (2005)
42. NSF Grand Challenges in eScience Workshop, 2001 (NSF): Retrieved from http://www2.evl.uic.edu/NSF/index.html (2010)
43. Open Science Grid (OSG): Retrieved from http://www.opensciencegrid.org (2010)
44. Rahman, M., Venugopal, S., Buyya, R.: A dynamic critical path algorithm for scheduling scientific workflow applications on global grids. In: Proceedings of the 3rd IEEE International Conference on e-Science and Grid Computing, Bangalore, pp 35–42 (2007)
45. Ranaweera, A., Agrawal, D.P.: A task duplication based algorithm for heterogeneous systems. In: Proceedings of IEEE International Parallel and Distributed Processing Symposium, Los Alamitos, pp. 445–450 (2000)
46. Relativistic Heavy Ion Collider (LHC): Retrieved from http://www.bnl.gov/rhic (2010)
47. Sekhar, A., Manoj, B.S., Murthy, C.S.R.: A state-space search approach for optimizing reliability and cost of execution in distributed sensor networks. In: Proceedings of International Workshop on Distributed Computing, Kharagpur, pp. 63–74 (2005)

48. Shirazi, B., Wang, M., Pathak, G.: Analysis and evaluation of heuristic methods for static scheduling. J. Parallel Distrib. Comput. **10**, 222–232 (1990)
49. Shroff, P., Watson, D.W., Flann, N.S., Freund, R.F.: Genetic simulated annealing for scheduling data-dependent tasks in heterogeneous environments. In: Proceedings of Heterogeneous Computing Workshop, Honolulu, pp. 98–104 (1996)
50. Spallation Neutron Source (SNS): Retrieved from http://www.sns.gov (2010)
51. Taylor, I.J., Deelman, E., Gannon, D.B., Shields, M. (eds.): Workflows for e-Science: Scientific Workflows for Grids. Springer, Berlin (2007)
52. Terascale Supernova Initiative (TSI): The office of science data-management challenge, Mar.-May 2004. Report from the DOE Office of Science Data-Management Workshops. Technical Report SLAC-R-782, Stanford Linear Accelerator Center, Stanford. Retrieved from http://www.phy.ornl.gov/tsi (2010)
53. Topcuoglu, H., Hariri, S., Wu, M.Y.: Performance effective and low complexity task scheduling for heterogeneous computing. IEEE Trans. Parallel Distrib. Syst. **13**(3), 260–274 (2002)
54. Ullman, J.D.: NP-complete scheduling problems. J. Comput. Syst. Sci. **10**(3), 384–393 (1975)
55. Wang, L., Siege, H.J., Roychowdhury, V.P., Maciejewski, A.A.: Task matching and scheduling in heterogeneous computing environments using a genetic-algorithm-based approach. J. Parallel Distrib. Comput. **47**, 8–22 (1997)
56. Wieczorek, M., Prodan, R., Fahringer, T.: Scheduling of scientific workflows in the ASKALON grid environment. ACM SIGMOD Record J. **34**(3), 56–62 (2005)
57. Worldwide LHC Computing Grid (WLCG): Retrieved from http://lcg.web.cern.ch/LCG (2010)
58. Wu, Q., Gu, Y., Zhu, M., Rao, N.S.V.: Optimizing network performance of computing pipelines in distributed environments. In: Proceedings of the 2008 IEEE International Parallel & Distributed Processing Symposium IPDPS 2008
59. Wu, Q., Rao, N.S.V.: On transport daemons for small collaborative applications over wide-area networks. In: Proceedings of the 24th IEEE International Performance Computing and Communications Conference, Phoenix, pp. 159–166 (2005)
60. Wu, Q., Zhu, M., Gu, Y., Rao, N.S.V.: System design and algorithmic development for computational steering in distributed environments. IEEE Trans. Parallel Distrib. Syst. **21**(4), 438–451 (2009)
61. Zhu, Y., Li, B.: Overlay network with linear capacity constraints. IEEE Trans. Parallel Distrib. Syst. **19**, 159–173 (2008)

Part II
Resource Management, Allocation, and Monitoring

Chapter 5
Resource Management and Service Deployment in Grids

Christos Chrysoulas and Nicolas Sklavos

Abstract Semantic grid refers to an approach to grid computing in which information, computing resources, and services are described in standard ways that can be processed by computer. This makes it easier for resources to be discovered and joined up automatically, which helps bring resources together to create virtual organizations. By analogy with the Semantic Web, the Semantic grid can be defined as an extension of the current grid in which information and services are given well-defined meaning, better enabling computers and people to work in cooperation. Because semantic grids represent and reason about knowledge declaratively, additional capabilities typical of agents are then possible including learning, planning, self-repair, memory organization, meta-reasoning, and task-level coordination. These capabilities would turn semantic grids into cognitive grids. Only a convergence of these technologies will provide the ingredients to create the fabric for a new generation of distributed intelligent systems. Inspired from the concept of Autonomous Decentralized Systems, we propose that the above-mentioned goals can be achieved by integrating FIPA multi-agent systems with the grid service architecture and hence to lay the foundation for semantic grid. Semantic grid system architecture is aimed to provide an improved infrastructure by bringing autonomy, semantic interoperability, and decentralization in the grid computing for emerging applications.

C. Chrysoulas (✉)
Technological Educational Institute of Patras, Notara 92 Street, Patras 26442, Greece
e-mail: cchrys@ece.upatras.gr

N. Sklavos
Informatics & MM Department, Technological Educational Institute of Patras,
Notara 92 Street, Patras 26442, Greece
e-mail: nsklavos@ieee.org

N.P. Preve (ed.), *Grid Computing: Towards a Global Interconnected Infrastructure*,
Computer Communications and Networks, DOI 10.1007/978-0-85729-676-4_5,
© Springer-Verlag London Limited 2011

5.1 Introduction

Owing to the increase in both heterogeneity and complexity in today's networking systems, the need arises for new network-based services architectures. They must provide flexibility and efficiency in the definition, deployment, and execution of the services and, at the same time, handle the adaptability and evolution of such services. In this paper, we present an approach that applies a Web Service-based resource management framework. It enables the provision of parallel applications as Quality-of-Service (QoS) aware applications, whose performance characteristics may be dynamically negotiated between a client application and service providers. Our component model allows context dependencies to be explicitly expressed and dynamically managed with respect to the hosting environment, computational resources, and dependencies on other components. In such a model, the resource management, in terms of representation, allocation, and management of the resources, plays a vital role regarding the efficiency of the entire dynamic service deployment architecture.

Network and service management fields nowadays find themselves at crossroads with middleware technologies, new network architectures, and emerging research directions. Middleware technologies like web services have reached maturity and enjoy wide deployment and adoption. Network architectures and infrastructures built for different purposes are well on their way toward Internet Protocol (IP) convergence, giving rise to new integrated and more complex architectures. Finally, recent ambitious research directions like autonomic computing and communications have already made a dynamic appearance in the networking community, increasing the challenges even further.

This activity has coincided with the end of an era in network and service management during which vast experience has been accumulated and numerous lessons have been learned. It is based on what constitutes the past state of the art in telecommunications and in data networks, realized by many as Common Object Request Broker Architecture (CORBA)-based distributed management platforms and Simple Network Management Protocol (SNMP)-based platforms, respectively.

This produces speculation and activity about redefining/reassessing the initial requirements that drove the developments in network and service management in the past and about the "shape" of management when projected into the future.

As network infrastructure is shifting toward service-centric networks, a number of architectural characteristics are likely to influence management operations and functionality and dictate specific choices of technologies for the realization thereof. In our opinion, three such characteristics are going to play a crucial role in the coming years:

- *Federated network architectures.* In an effort to provide seamless end-to-end connectivity that meets customer demands, networks/service providers have started forming federations of networks wherein a number of operations, such as Authentication, Authorization, and Accounting (AAA), monitoring and Service-Level Agreement (SLA) support, are treated in a homogeneous way in a heterogeneous environment.

- *Network architectures with distinct separation of concerns.* The most representative example is the separation of control from the forwarding plane, which allows the two to evolve separately. The binding element between the two is a set of open interfaces that abstract functionality and allow access to vendor-independent functionalities and resources.
- *Distributed network node architectures.* Individual network nodes and other devices are clustered together to form more complex and extensible distributed architectures that operate as one integrated node. Such constellations provide the means of adding resources as needed and foster dynamic service deployment, namely, the injection of new functionality into the network.

In such a context, management faces a number of challenges originating from the increasing complexity and size of networks, the heterogeneity of devices and technologies that must coexist, and the high degree of flexibility required in services. The common denominator is the management functionality that injects services and components on demand and configures the network end-to-end. Unless we address these challenges with sufficient and complete technical solutions first, it is difficult to see how new research initiatives, e.g., autonomic networking, can be brought to a successful outcome.

We have based our designs on web services as the de facto standard technology in networks with high integration capability and one of the most promising approaches to future management technologies.

Grid computing is the aggregation of networked-connected computers to form a large-scale distributed system used to tackle complex problems. By spreading the workload across a large number of computers, grid computing offers enormous computational, storage, and bandwidth resources that would otherwise be far too expensive to attain within traditional supercomputers. High-performance computational grids involve heterogeneous collections of computers that may reside in different administrative domains, run different software, be subject to different access control policies, and be connected by networks with widely varying performance characteristics. The security of these environments requires specialized grid-enabled tools that hide the mundane aspects of the heterogeneous grid environment without compromising performance. These tools may incorporate existing solutions or may implement completely new models. In either case, research is required to understand the utility of different approaches and the techniques that may be used to implement these approaches in different environments.

This chapter gives a fairly comprehensive resource management and service deployment overview in grid computing. The main purpose is for the reader to obtain knowledge of resource management in high-performance computing. In grid technology, resource management tools are concerned with establishing the identity of users or services (authentication), protecting communications, and determining who is allowed to perform what actions (authorization), as well as with supporting functions such as managing user credentials and maintaining group membership information.

Semantic grid refers to an approach to grid computing in which information, computing resources, and services are described in standard ways that can be processed by computer. This makes it easier for resources to be discovered and joined up automatically, which helps bring resources together to create Virtual Organizations (VOs). By analogy with the semantic web, the semantic grid can be defined as an extension of the current grid in which information and services are given well-defined meaning, better enabling computers and people to work in cooperation. Because semantic grids represent and reason about knowledge declaratively, additional capabilities typical of agents are then possible, including learning, planning, self-repair, memory organization, meta-reasoning, and task-level coordination. These capabilities would turn semantic grids into cognitive grids.

Only a convergence of these technologies will provide the ingredients to create the fabric for a new generation of distributed intelligent systems. Inspired from the concept of Autonomous Decentralized Systems, we propose that the above-mentioned goals can be achieved by integrating FIPA multi-agent systems with the grid service architecture and hence to lay the foundation for semantic grid. Semantic grid system architecture is aimed to provide an improved infrastructure by bringing autonomy, semantic interoperability, and decentralization in the grid computing for emerging applications.

The rest of the chapter is organized as follows. The next section presents related work in the field of semantic grid. The followed sections outline an abstract architecture of proposed system while they present a detailed design of agent web gateway for integration of software agents with web services framework. The final section presents the experimental results and the conclusions.

5.2   Related Work

Agent systems such as ACL and RETSINA employ powerful advertisement languages with inferencing capabilities so that behavioral specifications of agents can be described. In contrast to the knowledge-based representations used in these systems, the proposed solution uses an EXtensible Markup Language (XML) representation of the available, needed resources. XML is simple and lightweight allowing efficient and robust implementation.

Much effort has been devoted to developing information systems for publishing, aggregating, and supporting queries against collections of service descriptors (SNMP, LDAP, MDS, UDDI) [9]. Such systems differ in various dimensions, such as their description syntax (e.g., MIBs, LDAP objects), query language (e.g., SQL, XQuery, LDAP query) [5, 13], and the techniques used to publish and aggregate service descriptions (e.g., soft state vs. stateful servers). However, these systems all have in common that the service agent–consumer interaction is asymmetric: the agent-published description of its resources (properties) is queried by the consumer to identify candidates prior to generating requests for service. Such strategies require that service provider policy to be enforced only after candidate services are selected by the incoming customer, which can result in a wasted effort.

Distributed component models, such as CORBA or DCOM, are widely used, mainly in the context of commercial applications. The Common Component

Architecture developed within the CCA Forum defines a component model for high-performance computing based on interface definitions. XCAT3 [10] is a distributed framework that accesses grid services, e.g., OGSI [4], based on CCA mechanisms. It uses XSOAP for communication and can use GRAM for remote component instantiation. The Vienna Grid Environment (VGE) [1] is a web service-oriented environment for supporting high-performance computing applications. The VGE has been realized based on state-of-the-art grid and web service technologies, Java and XML. Globus Toolkit 4 (GT4) is an environment that mostly deals with the discovery of services and resources in a distributed environment rather than the deployment of the services themselves. Our model clearly addresses the above issue regarding the dynamic deployment of new services.

Goble and De Roure in [6], and Goble et al. in [7] have presented a high-level architecture for knowledge-oriented grids, as well as descriptions of some case studies where semantic grid ideas can be applied. Besides, projects like InteliGrid and myGrid have made significant attempts to provide either such architectural principles or to show how explicit metadata can be used in the context of existing grid applications, respectively.

Goble et al. in [7] already discuss the fact that semantics in grid applications cannot be placed in a separated layer, different from other resources like data, computational resources, etc. On the contrary, semantics permeate the full virtual vertical extent of grid applications and infrastructure. This proposal distinguishes several macro components that work together: knowledge networks (our knowledge entities); knowledge generating services (our semantic binding provisioning services); knowledge-aware, knowledge-based or knowledge-assisted grid services (our semantic aware grid services); and grid knowledge services (our ontology and reasoning services). However, the proposal does not go into more detail about the actual mechanisms to be used to deliver and consume semantics.

The myGrid [16] project is a pioneering semantic grid effort, which has developed a suite of tools and services to enable workflow-based composition of diverse biological data and computational resources. Within the project, semantic web technologies have been applied to the problems of resource discovery and workflow results management. A characterizing aspect of these solutions is their focus on user orientation, which has resulted in: (1) Semantic aware decision-support components instead of decision-making components, and (2) User-facing tools that keep the human in the loop during metadata generation and querying. The project has identified the need for specialized components for storage of ontologies and metadata (semantic provisioning services), and for service discovery (an example of a semantically aware grid service).

InteliGrid [14] have proposed an architecture based on three layers: conceptual, software, and basic resource. At the conceptual layer, we find descriptions of knowledge entities such ontologies, notions, graphs, etc., while the software layer consists of software that consumes the knowledge entities found in the conceptual layer; this is equivalent to the semantic aware grid services from our architecture). The basic resource layer includes the low-level infrastructure and resembles the notion of the grid fabric. Ontology services, situated in the software layer, play a central role in this architecture as they are considered as interoperability services that support multiple functionalities such as data consistency, service discovery, Virtual Organization (VO) set-up management, etc.

There are also other ongoing projects where the use of explicit metadata is identified as a key issue in the next generation of grid application development. However, they do not provide specific proposals or mechanisms on how to expose and deliver this metadata in application development, or they focus on very specific advanced knowledge-intensive functions like service discovery. Furthermore, none of those projects addresses the issue of manageability, soft-state aspects related to metadata. Examples of such projects are NextGrid, AkoGrimo, K-WF Grid [11], or KnowledgeGrid [17].We believe that all of these projects could benefit from the application of the architecture described in this paper, and we are aiming at providing support to them as part of EU Grid concertation activities.

From the Semantic Web Service (SWS) perspective, we can also perceive some similarities and differences with respect to the work that has been presented in this paper, some of which were already pointed out in the introduction. In general, we can argue that SWS approaches like WSMO or OWL-S are mainly focused on solving complex problems like discovery, composition, and negotiation.

If we analyze SWS approaches with respect to our design principles, we can conclude that these approaches do not focus on parsimony, extensibility, and uniformity, but mainly on the aspects of diversity (SWS execution environments can exewwcute both web services and SWS) and heterogeneity (the problems of language, content, and process heterogeneity are overcome by mediation techniques). That is, they provide heavyweight complete solutions (e.g., the WSMX environment, IRS-III [3], or the OWL-S virtual machine [12] that may make the uptake of their approach more difficult. Finally, even if the platforms follow the enlightenment principle, this is not usually addressed in the sample applications that are being developed with these approaches.

In this respect, the main conclusion is that the approaches presented in the proposed approach and in SWS are complementary: proposed system can be used for the grid-compliant exposure and delivery of semantics provisioned and used by SWS approaches.

5.3   Web Services

5.3.1   Web Service Technology

Interoperability across heterogeneous platforms, in particular the need to expose all or part of a particular application to other applications on different platforms or on different technologies, is the driving force for developing a web service architecture.

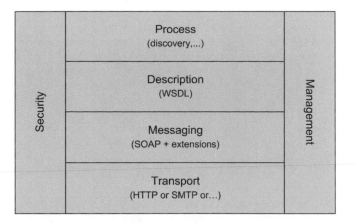

Fig. 5.1 An abstract view of the various specifications that define the web service architecture

Web services standardize the messages that entities in a distributed system must exchange to perform various operations. At the lowest level, this standardization concerns the protocol used to transport messages (typically HTTP), message encoding (SOAP), and interface description (WSDL). A client interacts with a web service by sending a SOAP message; the client may subsequently receive response message(s) in reply. At higher levels, other specifications define conventions for securing message exchanges (e.g., WS-Security), for management (e.g., WSDM), and for higher-level functions such as discovery and choreography. Figure 5.1 presents an overview of these different component technologies.

5.3.2   Web Service Implementation

From the client's perspective, a web service is simply a network-accessible entity that processes (Simple Object Access Protocol) SOAP messages. To simplify service implementation, it is common for a web service implementation to distinguish the following:

- The hosting environment, i.e., the logic used to receive a SOAP message and to identify and invoke the appropriate code to handle the message, and potentially also to provide related administration functions.
- The web service implementation, i.e., the code that handles the message.

The SOAP message is typically transported via Hypertext Transfer Protocol (HTTP), thus an HTTP engine or web server is required, and a SOAP engine is needed in order to process the SOAP messages. Figure 5.2 illustrates these various components.

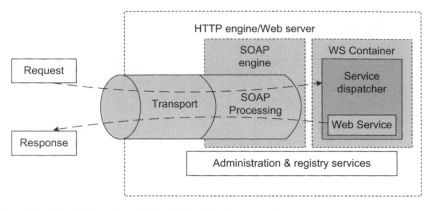

Fig. 5.2 Web service high-level view of functional components

5.3.3   XML-Based Architecture

Several EXtensible Markup Language (XML)-based network management techniques have recently emerged toward overcoming the limitations of SNMP management in configuration operations. Since XML documents can have much higher-level semantics than SNMP, they are more appropriate for bulk configuration operations.

Exporting XML interfaces for network management has also other advantages since:

• XML is easy to generate, parse and process, supports sophisticated data structuring, and can therefore handle complex organizations of management information.
• XML DTD (Document Type Definitions) and XML Schemas specify and validate the structure of XML documents, thus alleviating developers of network management applications from tedious tasks.
• XML comes with numerous W3C technologies supporting rapid development of network management applications (e.g., Extensible Stylesheet Transformations (XSLT), which transform XML documents to other XML formats and XPath/XQuery discovering XML elements subject to criteria).

XML management systems with SOAP interfaces constitute an emerging architecture for WS-based network management. This architecture leverages the advantages of XML systems with respect to the programmability and cost-effectiveness of the management operations. The drawbacks on XML-based architectures lie in the processing overhead incurred by the parsing and construction of XML messages and files, which can lead to performance penalties. XML gateways tend to increase response time for management operations.

While this is a disadvantage of XML management per se, it becomes less important when SOAP interfaces are used. This is because the fact that XML gateways deal with XML documents is eliminating the additional overhead imposed by SOAP.

SOAP constitutes a more natural interface for XML management systems that already handle XML messages. This is a significant incentive for using SOAP in XML systems. Note that SOAP interfaces are anyway very likely to proliferate, since SOAP is an open standard with a growing community of developers and vendors supporting it.

5.4 Dynamic Service Deployment in FlexiNET

5.4.1 Distributed Router Architecture

The idea behind the distributed router architecture as proposed by Hitachi Ltd [8] is the separation of basic forwarding and packet delivery functionality from the service/control logic that may reside in access nodes in order to foster service creation by means of service deployment capabilities.

As depicted in Fig. 5.3, it is comprised of two blocks: the basic block, and the extended block. Each one of the functional blocks may also be composed of several modules. This is the architecture adopted to build the FWAN FlexiNET node instance.

The basic function block has packet-processing modules, which classify received packets, retrieve routing tables, and reroutes or terminates packet flows to extensible function block modules for further processing. The extended function block has service modules, which handle the processing for service-specific functions and control and management modules, which process the routing protocols, management agent functions. These modules are inserted and removed as required for performance or for service provision by the node.

The two blocks are loosely connected by a generic physical interface such as a Gigabit Ethernet network interface, and communicate each other by exchanging packets that include control messages across this interface.

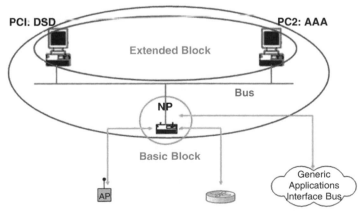

Fig. 5.3 A distributed network node architecture

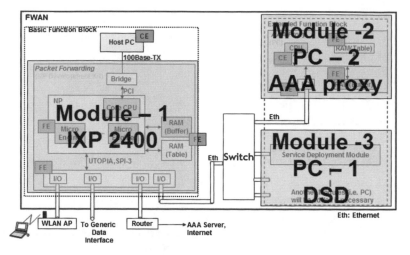

Fig. 5.4 Internal configuration of the node

The advantage of this architecture is that new modules may be dynamically added to the extensible block as needed. As a result, flexibility and scalability is greatly improved since the modules to be added form a pool of resources that are capable of hosting new functionality in the form of new services and components thereof. This feature is exploited when we describe the DSD architecture. Figure 5.4 illustrates the internal configuration of the current node.

5.4.2   DSD Architecture

The DSD architecture performs two major tasks: (1) the decision where to deploy the services upon reception of a service request, and (2) the execution of a service deployment decision.

The former task is based on a matchmaking algorithm that implements different strategies. In order for the matchmaking algorithm to run, it first needs to be fully aware of the node environment within which deployment is going to take place. This includes, the amount of resources, the capabilities as open interfaces, and the composition (operating systems, programming environments supported), of each of the modules in the distributed environment. Second, it must be able to understand the service requirements in terms of resources, code modules, and location thereof that require deployment. The two sets of information are compared to each other in order to find out which module meets the service deployment criteria in the most efficient manner.

The latter task comprises all the mechanisms and interfaces necessary to carry our deployment by contacting the code server, downloading, loading and running the code, and finally, configuring the local networking environment not only according to service requirements but also user profile that stores the signed SLA of the customer.

5.4.3   Proposed DSD Architecture

Figure 5.5 depicts the proposed DSD architecture comprised of the following components.

Web Services Server
The web services server component supports communication for exchanging messages between DSD and all those services deployed in the various modules found in the extensible block of the distributed router. Such services must also be implemented using web services technologies. The web service server component has all the necessary functionality to register a web service in a Universal Description, Discovery and Integration (UDDI) directory. This component also is capable of finding other web service interfaces.

DSD Manager
The DSD manager has been assigned the tasks of coordinating a series of operations supported by the DSD controller that relate with service deployment as well as the downloading of user profiles from the DGWN in order to find out the services this particular user is registered to, in order to initiate their deployment and configuration according to its SLA. To this end, the DSD manager is also responsible for user-related management operations like checking whether a user has terminated the connection, stopping a service, deleting a user's personal configuration.

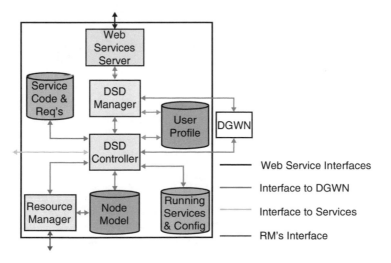

Fig. 5.5 DSD architecture

DSD Controller

The DSD controller component has the following duties: it receives specific service requests from the DSD manager, communicates with the DGWN in order to download the service code and the service requirements, retrieves the available resources by making use of the data held by the node model, performs the matchmaking algorithm in order to find the most suitable resources, and finally deploys the service. The DSD controller is responsible for the services in three steps: download, deploy, and configure.

Resource Manager

The resource manager component discovers and monitors the resources. With the help of the resource manager interface, it collects information from all the modules of the distributed router according to the data definitions captured in the node model. It also communicates with the DSD controller in order to feed the matchmaking algorithm with the current state of the node model.

Node Model

The node model is responsible for keeping all information for every module that comprises the distributed router in order to maintain a complete view thereof. Such information includes availability and usage of physical resources, as well as data on running services. The node model is an essential part of the proposed DSD architecture and its functionality as it is equivalent of information models like MIBs or CIM only customized for the purposes of service deployment. More details on the structure and the information captured by the node model are provided later in the text.

User Profile

The user profile is a data storage facility where the downloaded user profile is stored in order to keep track of the active users.

Service Code and Requirements

The service code and requirements is another data storage facility responsible for storing the downloaded code and its requirements (in terms of physical resources) that describe a service.

Running Services and Configuration

Finally, the running services and configuration data storage facility is responsible for storing data about running services and their current configuration.

5.5   Proposed System

Open systems like grid are capable of dynamically changing and hence the resources are not known in advance, rather they can change over time and are highly heterogeneous [15]. It gives rise to the need of technologies that support negotiation, cooperation in which multi-agent systems have proven to be effective.

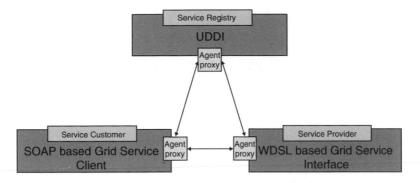

Fig. 5.6 Layered structure of the semantic grid

The entities in grid environment should not just act as a dumb receptor of task descriptions, but should cooperate with the user and with other entities to achieve their goal. Hence, there is need of agents acting as expert assistants or delegate with respect to some services, knowledgeable about both the grid environment and the requirements of user in the form of an agenda of tasks and capable of negotiating with other agents (owner of different services), establishing contracts, performing service composition to achieve user's goals (Fig. 5.6).

The semantic web presents a conceptual perspective in the way distributed knowledge can be viewed, in terms of creation, consumption, dissemination, and management. Concepts can be defined within extensible, open ontologies published using standard protocols with instances and properties being asserted at arbitrary locations across the Internet. Semantic grid is the ultimate extension of semantic web, for sharing resources and services based on the machine-understandable information and knowledge.

Multi-agent systems, in contrast, provide methodologies for consuming, processing, creating, and disseminating both information and knowledge within a distributed framework. Moreover, the construction and coordination of heterogeneous agent communities itself requires complex management of data; the interpretation of which may be ambiguous without semantic structure or reasoning.

It is therefore, necessary to integrate agents with web services to realize the vision of semantic web, and semantic grid. Devising solution to such integration problem has been quite challenging. The proposed system testbed is composted by four PCs. The characteristics of each PC are the following:

- Operating System: Linux Fedora Core 8
- RAM: 1,024 MB
- Globus Toolkit 4.0.5 with semantic MDS support
- Ganglia

We used Protégé for writing the needed ontologies.

5.5.1 Proposed Architecture

This section describes the detailed design of proposed system in which the most important technical challenges are solved, i.e., without changing any specification and implementation of grid and agents, enabling two-way service discovery, service publishing (service description transformation), and communication protocol conversion among software agents and grid.

This level of integration will undoubtedly create new challenges for both agents and grids. However, the result could be frameworks for constructing robust, large-scale, agile distributed systems that are qualitatively and quantitatively superior to the best current practice today.

5.5.2 Software Agent Interaction with Grid Service

In this section, detailed design as shown in Fig. 5.7 that enables FIPA-compliant software agents interact with W3C-compliant SOAP-based grid computing environment entities, including grid services and grid clients by performing service discovery in UDDI, understanding grid service, and invoking a grid service.

5.5.2.1 Agent Performing Service Discovery in UDDI

A middleware is designed that makes services visible to software agents (see Fig. 5.2). Whenever a software agent searches some service, it performs lookup for the agent in Directory Facilitator (DF) of multi-agent system. If DF does not have the required

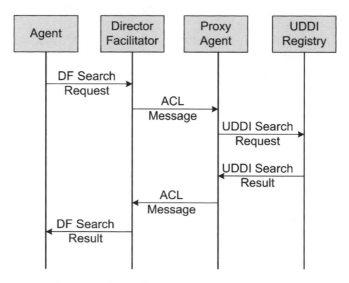

Fig. 5.7 Agent searching for needed service

agent registered, it redirects its search to the middleware by sending an Agent Communication Language (ACL) message.

As soon as the middleware input interface receives message, it passes it to protocol converter that extracts out the service name and passes it a component named as ACL2SOAP converter in the middleware. It performs transformation of the ACL-based search query into SOAP-based UDDI search query and forwards to UDDI where the required service is expected.

A search is performed in UDDI and if required service is found, a message is returned by the UDDI as SOAP-based search query response to the middleware where the component SOAP2ACL converts that result into valid ACL-based search response message and sends back to DF. The DF further forwards the message to software agent that requested for search. In this way, the middleware has helped a software agent to search for the services in UDDI with an illusion that it is searching agent services in DF of agent platform.

5.5.2.2   Agent Understanding a Grid Service

In previous section, the software agent has come to know about the existence and address of the required service and now the agent is required to consume the service. In order to consume the service, software agent is needed to know about the ontology, agent action schema, predicate schema, and concept schema, etc. On the other hand, middleware as the address for Web Services Description Language (WSDL) file. WSDL analyzer gets the WSDL file of required web service and analyzes portTypes, SOAP bindings for service, and extracts out useful information from it.

This extracted information is then passed to three components, which participate in generating the code for proxy agent. First of all, agent class code is generated in contains necessary behaviors. Second component generates ontology file for proxy agent on the basis of portTypes of WSDL file of actual web service. The third component generates necessary Agent action and predicate schema based on information from web service. In this way, complete proxy agent along with its ontology is generated.

Translation of WSDL services is performed into a form (proxy agent) that software agents can understand. Agent shares the newly generated ontology of proxy agent with itself with an illusion that the proxy agent is providing the required service. In this way, we have made the web service description published in agent platform in order to make it understandable for software agents.

5.5.2.3   Agent Invoking Grid Service

In previous sections, middleware has helped the software agent to search and understand services. Now the software agent is ready to consume the service. Software agents share ontology with proxy agent (generated in previous step) with an illusion that proxy agent is providing the required services. After sharing ontology, software agent sends an ACL request message (according to the shared ontology with proxy agent) having input parameters to middleware.

Input interface receives the message and passes it to ACL2SOAP protocol converter. This converter extracts out the input parameters from ACL request message and creates an equivalent SOAP message. The SOAP client at middleware is directed to send the generated SOAP request message to the web service at remote web server providing required services.

The service after receiving SOAP request message processes the input parameters and then returns the output in the form of SOAP response message to the SOAP client at middleware, which, upon receiving the SOAP response message, passes it to SOAP2ACL protocol converter, which extracts outputs from SOAP message and generates a ACL response message. The generated ACL message is then sent to the software agent. In this way, the middleware helps the software agent search, understand, and consume web services.

5.5.3   Grid Entities Interaction with Software Agents

In this section, the shown detailed design enablesW3C-compliant SOAP-based grid computing environment entities including grid services, and grid clients interact with FIPA-compliant software agents by performing service discovery in DF, understanding services provided by a software agent, and consuming services from software agents.

5.5.3.1   Agent Understanding a Grid Service

Whenever SOAP-based grid client needs some service, it performs lookup for the service in UDDI, if the UDDI does not have the required service, it redirects its search to the middleware by sending a simple SOAP-based UDDI search request message. As soon as the middleware input interface receives message, it passes it to protocol converter that extracts out the service name and passes it to proxy agent present at middleware. This proxy agent creates and sends a valid ACL-based DF search request message to remote agent platform from where the required service is expected.

DF of the remote agent platform performs a search. If required service is found, a message is returned by the DF of that remote agent platform to the agent at our middleware, which is further passed to the ACL2SOAP protocol converter.

This converter transforms ACL-based DF search response back to SOAP-based UDDI search response and sends to the UDDI lookup service, which further forwards message to the web service client requested for the search as shown in Fig. 5.8. In this way, the middleware helps the web service client to search for the services at agent platform. The SOAP response message contains the address of the middleware, which means that web service client is given an illusion that the required service is available as grid service at middleware.

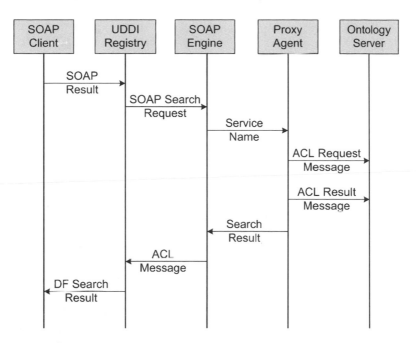

Fig. 5.8 Grid client searching for needed service

5.5.3.2 Grid Client Understanding Services Provided by Software Agent

Up till now, grid client has come to know about the existence and address of the required agent and now the client is required to consume the service. In order to consume the service, the client is needed to know about the functions, input parameters, and outputs of the service. Since the client has already got the address of the service from the previously received SOAP response message, that is why, this time, client sends request message to middleware to get the agent service published in UDDI. Middleware translates the agent service into WSDL. How this translation will occur at middleware is given below.

The SOAP request message of the web service client is received by the SOAP Engine. The service name for which the WSDL file is required is taken out and is passed to an agent. This agent then contacts the ontology server of the remote agent platform in order to share the ontology used by the agent at remote platform providing the required services.

Agent at middleware gets the ontology of the agent of remote platform shared by the ontology server and informs the ontology code generator, which is present at the middleware. The ontology code generator gets instance of the shared ontology and using reflection, generates the equivalent java code of the ontology instance. This generated java code of ontology class contains information about methods, input parameters, and outputs provided by the agent, providing the required services in order to consume the service.

The java code is passed to Java to WSDL converter in order to translate the interface code into a WSDL to make it understandable for web service clients. WSDL file is generated and sent to web service client and may be used for the preparation of SOAP requests. The same WSDL file can be published in UDDI. This will make the agent publish its services in the web services world in order to make these services understandable for web service clients.

5.5.3.3 Grid Client Accessing

Up till now, the middleware has helped the web service client to search and understand the services provided by agents. Now the web service client is ready to consume the services provided by the agent. This time, web service client communicates with the middleware with an illusion that it is the required web service.

The client generates a SOAP request message (according to the service description which it got in WSDL) having input parameters. This SOAP request message is sent to the middleware. Input interface receives the message and passes it to SOAP2ACL protocol converter. This converter extracts out the input parameters from SOAP input message and creates an equivalent ACL message. The agent at middleware is directed to send the generated ACL request message to the agent at remote platform providing required services.

The agent after receiving ACL request message processes the input parameters and then returns the output in the form of an ACL response message to the agent at middleware. The agent at middleware upon receiving the ACL response message passes it to ACL2SOAP protocol converter that extracts outputs from ACL message and generates a SOAP response message. The SOAP response message is finally sent to the web service client. In this way, the middleware helps the web service client search, understand, and consume services provided by software agents.

5.6 Experimental Results

The primary scope of our work was to present a model that will be in position to adequately monitor and give a real view of a semantically grid-based environment.

According to the trials we have made, we manage to succeed much better times regarding resource gathering. We also succeed better time regarding the time needed for new PCs getting into our environment and to be fully operative.

The experimental results were properly compared with the experimental results we had got from another implementation we did during our elaboration with the FlexiNET IST [2].

According to our trials, it takes an average time of 13 ms (standard deviation is 1.9 ms) for gathering the resources in the agent-based (FlexiNET) approach and only 9 ms (standard deviation is 1.2 ms) in the proposed semantic grid-based approach (Fig. 5.9).

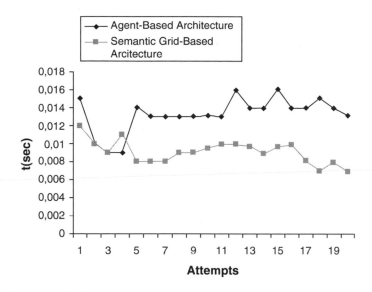

Fig. 5.9 Resource gathering

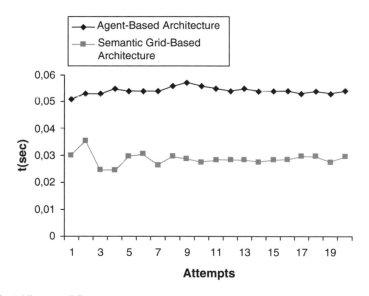

Fig. 5.10 Adding new PCs

The average time for three new PCs to be added and be fully operational is 28 ms (standard deviation is 2.2 ms), while in the old architecture the average time was 54 ms (standard deviation is 1.3 ms), Fig. 5.10. By fully operative, we mean that the system is in a position to accept the deployment of a new service.

5.7   Conclusions and Future Work

Dynamic, heterogeneous, and distributively owned resource environments present unique challenges for resource representation, allocation, and management. In this chapter, we have introduced a resource management and a service deployment system supported by a simple matchmaking algorithm to address the problem of heterogeneous resource co-allocation, motivated by the intent of solving a real problem encountered during designing and testing.

Our contribution is in designing an adequate resource management system and accompanying implementation of the resource manager itself and a matchmaking algorithm that proves the feasibility of the proposed solution. The implementation of the model regarding resource management has now been realized, even though it requires further refinement and analysis. As future work, we plan to provide a more sophisticated model for service deployment and selection based on QoS properties.

A significant goal of our future work is to incorporate preferences into the matchmaking algorithm. In this way, more sophisticated algorithms will be able to cope with the possibility of more demanding services. Agent systems embody current AI research on distributed intelligent systems. Yet, agent systems have drawn in very limited ways from distributed computing, which hinders their scalability and long-lived operations. Grids, in turn, aim to develop similarly intelligent capabilities but from the bottom up, and have concentrated more on managing low-level resources than higher-level tasks. Cross-cutting research across both areas would enable significant progress in grids as well as agents research.

References

1. Benkner, S., Brandic, I., Engelbrecht, G., Schmidt, R.: VGE-A service-oriented environment for on-demand supercomputing. In: Proceedings of the 5th IEEE/ACM International Workshop on Grid Computing, Pittsburgh, pp. 11–18 (2004)
2. Chrysoulas, C., Haleplidis, E., Kostopoulos, G., Haas, R., Denazis, S., Koufopavlou, O.: Towards a service-enabled distributed router architecture. IET Circuits Devices Syst. **2**(1), 60–68 (2008)
3. Domingue, J., Cabral, L., Hakimpour, F., Sell, D., Motta, E.: IRS-III: A platform and infrastructure for creating WSMO-based Semantic Web Services. In: Proceedings of Workshop of the 1st WSMO Implementation Workshop (WIW), Frankfurt (2004)
4. Foster, I., Kesselman, C., Nick, J.M., Tuecke, S.: The physiology of the grid: An open grid services architecture for distributed systems integration. Technical report, Global Grid Forum. Retrieved from http://globus.org/alliance/publications/papers/ogsa.pdf (2002)
5. Garsia-Molina, H., Ullman, J.D., Widom, J.: 2002 Database Systems: The Complete Book (GOAL Series). Prentice Hall, Englewood Cliffs (2002)
6. Goble, C., De Roure, D.: The semantic grid: Myth busting and bridge building. In: Proceedings of the 16th European Conference on Artificial Intelligence, Valencia, pp. 1129–1135 (2004)
7. Goble, C., De Roure, D., Shadbolt, N., Fernandes, A.: Enhancing services and applications with knowledge and semantics. In: Foster, I., Kesselman, C. (eds.) The GRID 2: Blueprint for a New Computing Infrastructure, pp. 431–458. Morgan Kaufmann, San Francisco (2004)

8. Hirata, T., Mimura, I.: Flexible service creation node architecture and its implementation. In: Proceedings of the 18th Annual Workshop on IEEE Computer Communications, Newport Beach, pp. 166–177 (2003)

9. Howes, T.A., Smith, M.C., Good, G.S.: Understanding and Deploying LDAP Directory Services. Addison-Wesley Professional, Boston (2003)

10. Krishnan, S., Gannon, D.: A Framework for CCA Components as OGSA Services. In: Proceedings of the 9th International Workshop on High-Level Parallel Programming Models and Supportive Environments, pp. 90–97, Santa Fe (2004)

11. K-WF Grid Project: Knowledge-based workflow system for grid applications. Retrieved from http://www.kwfgrid.eu (2010)

12. Paolucci, M., Ankolekar, A., Srinivasan, N., Sycara, K.: The DAML-S virtual machine. In Proceedings of the 2nd International Semantic Web Conference, Sandial Island, pp 290–350 (2003)

13. Scott, B., Chamberlin, D.D., Fernandez, M.F., Florescu, D., Robie, J., Simeon, J.: XQuery 1.0: an XML query language. The World Wide Web Consortium (W3C). Retrieved from http://www.w3.org/TR/2007/REC-xquery-20070123 (2007)

14. Turk, Z., Stankovski, V., Gehre, A., Katranuschkov, P., Kurowski, K., Balaton, E., Hyvarinen, J., Dolenc, M., Klinc, R., Kostanjsek, J., Velkavrh, J.: Semantic grid architecture. InteliGrid Project. Retrieved from http://inteligrid.eu-project.info/data/works/att/d13_1.content.00913. pdf (2004)

15. Wolski, R., Brevik, J., Plank, J., Bryan, T.: Grid resource allocation and control using computational economies. In: Berman, F., Fox, G., Hey, A.J.G. (eds.) Grid Computing: Making the Global Infrastructure a Reality, pp. 747–772. Wiley, Chichester (2003)

16. Wroe, C., Goble, C.A., Greenwood, M., Lord, P., Miles, S., Papay, J., Payne, T., Moreau, L.: Automating experiments using semantic data on a bioinformatics grid. IEEE Intell. Syst. 19(1), 48–55 (2004)

17. Zhuge, H.: China's e-science knowledge grid environment. IEEE Intell. Syst. 19(1), 13–17 (2004)

Chapter 6
Social Grid Agents

Gabriele Pierantoni, Brian Coghlan, and Eamonn Kenny

Abstract Social grid agents are a socially inspired solution designed to address the problem of resource allocation in grid computing, they offer a viable solution to alleviating some of the problems associated with interoperability and utilization of diverse computational resources and to modeling the large variety of relationships among the different actors. The social grid agents provide an abstraction layer between resource providers and consumers. The social grid agent prototype is built in a metagrid environment, and its architecture is based on agnosticism both regarding technological solutions and economic precepts proves now useful in extending the environment of the agents from multiple grid middlewares, the metagrid, to multiple computational environments encompassing grids, clouds and volunteer-based computational systems. The presented architecture is based on two layers: (1) Production grid agents compose various grid services as in a supply chain, (2) Social grid agents that own and control the agents in the lower layer engage in social and economic exchange. The design of social grid agents focuses on how to handle the three flows (production, ownership, policies) of information in a consistent, flexible, and scalable manner. Also, a native functional language is used to describe the information that controls the behavior of the agents and the messages exchanged by them.

6.1 Introduction

The complexity of resource allocation in grid computing, and more broadly, in every distributed computational system, consists in meeting the expectations of different actors that have different concepts of optimality within an environment divided into

G. Pierantoni (✉) • B. Coghlan • E. Kenny
Department of Computer Science, Trinity College Dublin, Ireland
e-mail: gabriele.pierantoni@cs.tcd.ie; pierang@cs.tcd.ie

N.P. Preve (ed.), *Grid Computing: Towards a Global Interconnected Infrastructure*,
Computer Communications and Networks, DOI 10.1007/978-0-85729-676-4_6,
© Springer-Verlag London Limited 2011

geographically dispersed and different administrative domains and thus unsuited to supporting centralized management systems. The complexity of the problem is further increased by the fact that the scientific community has created different grids with different standards, focuses, and technologies.

This problem closely resembles that of an economy and has consequently been investigated with economic paradigms, leading to models that are often tailored to one or more specific situation. We speculate that an approach reflecting the social structures that support economic models could allow different models to coexist as they do in the real world. We also speculate that a successful solution should be able to encompass different grids both present and future.

In order to achieve this, the modeling of the different actors is inspired by some behaviors that are common in societies; to encompass different grids; the environment of the actors is modeled as a metagrid: a conceptual space encompassing different existing middlewares and border regions where interoperability issues are tackled by a combination of abstraction and translation.

The resource allocation system we propose is based on topologies, agents, and policies. The topologies employ agents to model different philosophies that arise both in the real world and in grid computing; the agents constitute the nodes of the topologies and their behavior is defined by sets of policies. The proposed architecture currently uses four different kinds of topologies: (1) Production Topologies, (2) Social Topologies, (3) Control Topologies, and (4) Value and Price Topologies.

The aim of such approach is to allow a resource allocation system to be capable of being agnostic to the technology of the different middlewares it uses and to the economic philosophies of the different allocation mechanisms employed.

6.2   Resource Allocation in Grid Computing

Although the various solutions [3, 10] envisaged by the scientific community to tackle the complexities of resource brokerage and allocation in grids encompass genetic algorithms, simulated annealing, and hybrid solutions [1], we focus this survey on resource allocation approaches that are economy-based, ranging from competitive liberalism to cooperation, from uncontrolled markets [3, 19] to centralized controlled economies [7].

Wolsky et al. in [22, 23] have presented an attempt to analyze the problem of economic-based resources (only CPU and disk space are taken in account) allocation in grid computing (at times referred to as Computational Economies), both at a theoretical and practical level through simulations. A set of assumptions for Computational Economics are defined and two main pricing mechanisms, commodity market and auctions, are analyzed in different market conditions. The conclusion of the authors is that, although auction-based systems are widely used, the commodity market models perform better in most market conditions. The authors suggest that this is due to the relative simplicity of the implementation of auction-based systems.

Although most of the economic-based solutions and analysis [3, 4, 6, 8] of the problem of resource allocation in grid computing rely, implicitly or explicitly, on the belief that the General Equilibrium Theory is useful to describe real life economics and that, by extension, it is useful to tackle similar problems in grid computing, the study conducted in [17] contradicts this belief on different counts. The main problems raised by the authors are of different kinds: first General Equilibrium Theory does not offer any explanation for cases in which the markets fail; second the differences between real and computational markets may result in an even higher probability of failure; last, General Equilibrium.

Theory does not take into account aspects such as the role of government policies, or the necessity for trust between the agents that are relevant in grid computing. Buyya et al. in [3, 4] have presented a survey of the market models that could be possibly applied to grid computing. These are deemed to be:

- Commodity Market Models where the price of a resource is set directly and solely by the owner of the resource.
- Posted Price Models similar to the Commodity Market with the extension of special offers that a resource provider can post to attract new costumers.
- Bargaining Models where the price is defined by a negotiation of two parties.
- Tendering/Contract-Net Models where the party requesting a resource publishes its requirements and collects offers from the resource owners.
- Auction Models that define a one-to-many negotiation where a party offers resources to many possible buyers.
- Community and Coalition Models where the resources are shared among the members of a community from a common pool.
- Bid-based proportional sharing models where the percentage of a resource that each requester can get is a proportion of the price it offered during the bidding process.
- Monopoly, Oligopoly where the price is set by one or few resource owners that can define prices without competition.

There are many different resource allocation implementations being proposed, investigated, and actively used in the grid community, some of which are inspired by economic and even social ideas. Although the following list does not pretend in any way to be conclusive or omni-comprehensive, it includes the resource allocation mechanisms that are closer, in their philosophy, to social grid agents (SGA).

6.2.1   SweGrid and SGAS

The SGAS [7] system focuses on interoperability and fair-share allocation. Interoperability is achieved by offering plugin points for adapters specific to different environments. SGAS is somehow inspired by a socialist perspective where great importance is attributed to the fairness of the allocation.

To achieve this, SGAS implements a centralized economic model where a central authority grants different amounts of credits to the various users of the system. This solution allows a fair allocation of resources (provided that the central authority is fair), in the sense that all users may be given a fair amount of credits; unfortunately, in the absence of a correcting mechanism, there is no guarantee that the credits can be really converted into services. SGAS successfully tackles this problem by time-stamping the allocation credits and by reducing their validity to a certain time frame. This discourages clients from hoarding credits and the possibility that they are used all at once.

6.2.2   SORMA

The SORMA project [21] attempts to adopt self-organization. The project proposes an economic model called Decentralized Local Greedy Mechanism inspired by the neo-liberist belief that a population of agents acting in the pursuit of their exclusive self-interest will eventually reach an equilibrium of economic efficiency that no single agent planned for at the beginning.

The model is further enriched in [18] to take Service Level Agreements (SLA) agreements into account. An Economic Enhanced Resource Manager (EERM) uses a predictive model to foresee the impacts on the resources it manages of accepting a certain task. The model uses the concepts of Revenue (the amount of credits that are to be paid if SLA terms are met), Penalty (the amount of credits that are to be paid if SLA terms are not met), and Gain (the difference between Revenue and Penalty). The EERM will decide whether to violate or not SLA terms, basing its decisions on the foreseen effects on resources and the financial outcome.

6.2.3   CATNETS

CATNETS [5, 9] offers a theoretical analysis and simulation experiments of a market model based on the concept of a self-organizing population of agents. CATNETS implements a two-step economic model whereby a call for proposals is followed by a negotiation. The simulation also encompasses two different types of markets for resources and services. This approach allows the evaluation of a free market allocation topology where no central broker exists.

6.2.4   GESA

Minoli in [16] has described an OGSA-based architecture that supports grid economic services, the Grid Economic Services Architecture (GESA). The proposal was not tailored to any specific economic model but offers an OGSA compliant architecture to support different economic models and to build effective, standardized economic-based applications in grids. The architecture is harmonized with the architectural proposals of several Global Grid Forum (OGF) [14] working groups on Resource Usage Services, Grid Resource Allocation Agreement Protocols, and Usage Records. GESA architecture is flexible and comprehensive; it describes resources as well as complex payment issues such as compensation, refunding, and support for multiple currencies.

6.2.5   The Gridbus Project

The Gridbus Project [15] project is the continuation of the Grid Economy Project [13] that produced an economic-aware infrastructure sitting on top of existing middlewares. The overall architecture is composed of different layers where economy-aware components are present except in the bottom (grid fabric hardware) and top (grid application) layers.

The architecture of Gridbus allows for the implementation of economic models that are mainly Quality-of-Service (QoS), budget, and time driven at every level from low-level scheduling with Libra to high-level interactions with markets, banks, and workflow engines. It is worth noticing that, although the current implementation highlights time and budget constrained allocation modalities, its paradigm and the philosophy underlying its architecture is inspired by a broader analysis of many different economic models [3, 4].

6.2.6   ArguGRID

Although it relies on Peer to Peer computing-oriented resources rather that grid middleware, the ArguGRID [2] (funded by the European Commission under Framework Programme 6) proposes an interesting agent-based approach. Its design is inspired by Service-Oriented Architecture and is based on a set of agents capable of argumentation to cope with incomplete knowledge and conflicting information for decision-making.

The most innovative aspect of ArguGRID is that intelligent agents use argumentation to negotiate with each other to produce contracts that describe task allocations and workflow descriptions.

6.3   The Social Grid Agents

The architecture of Social Grid Agents (SGA) is based on two layers as described in Fig. 6.1, one where production grid agents compose various grid services and another layer where the social grid agents that control the agents in the lower layer engage in social and economic exchange.

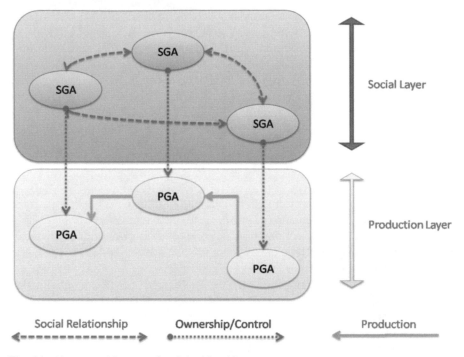

Fig. 6.1 Abstract architecture of social grid architecture

Social grid agents describe the usage of existing grid services with the concept of a production chain that goes from the basic goods, or factors, to intermediate commodities and, in the end, to the final service, or produced commodity. At each step of the production chain, services are combined into higher-level ones by one or more actors. We call these actors production grid agents or, as an abbreviation, production agents, reflecting society's conception of an agent. These agents are defined without implying any sense of agent technology as commonly understood in computer science.

To describe the concepts of ownership and control, let us add a new layer: the social layer. Now the paradigm is composed of two interacting layers, one where production takes place and another that hosts agents owning and/or controlling the production entities. Each layer can be complex or even hierarchical, but the production layer does not have social properties, whereas the social layer does. Agents in the social layer can own, control or use none, one or more production agents. A social agent should also be able to exchange and trade the use of, or the services produced by, the production agents it controls.

This allows our socioeconomic paradigm to exhibit behavior such as the purchase of services, the rent of production agents, and the exchange of ownership

of one or more related production agents. SGAs model the relations between social
and production agents as:

- Ownership. When social agents own production agents, they have complete control
  over them; they can sell, rent, or donate them; they can set access rights for controllers and users and they can set policies to regulate the production process.
- Control. When social agents control production agents, they have partial control
  over them. They can set access rights for users and set, possibly a subset, of
  production policies.
- Usage. When social agents use production agents, they can access only the
  services that they were granted by a controller or an owner.

6.3.1   Topologies of Social Grid Agents

As shown in Fig. 6.2, this design allows for some variety of connection topologies
among the social and production agents.

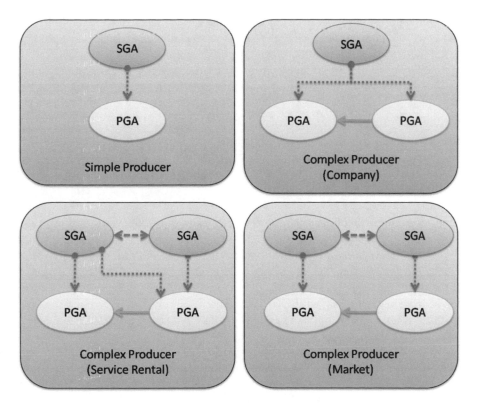

Fig. 6.2 Simple examples of production topologies

6.3.2   Simple Producer

The simplest of these topologies is the simple producer shown in Fig. 6.2, where a client contacts a social agent and negotiates the acquisition of a grid service. When the social or economic transaction is accepted by the two parties, the social agent gives instructions to the production agent it controls to execute the required service. Even such a simple example can be implemented in many different ways. From a social and economic perspective, there may be or not a payment required for the service, depending on the relationship between the agents. There can be different payment policies such as pay beforehand, pay after the service is executed, pay only if the service is successfully executed, etc. All these different ways are defined by the policies that control the agent's behavior and by the modalities that define how services are to be executed.

6.3.3   Service Rental

A slightly more complex control topology is the service rental as shown in Fig. 6.2. Here two social agents exchange the services of one or more production agents. After the social or economic agreement, the grantor social agent instructs the production agent to accept requests from the grantee agent with a certain modality, e.g., current SGA implementations allow for modalities based on tokens, time slots, deadlines, or combinations thereof. The grantee is now capable of directly using the production agent.

6.3.4   Companies and Markets

These two simple topologies can be combined to describe companies and markets. A company is a control topology where a social agent controls one or more production agents. The control exerted by the social agent lets it define the topology of the production flow. Current SGA implementations allow the ownership and the control of the production agents to be absolute or relative based on tokens or time. A company can avail itself of the services of production agents it does not control directly, provided that it can either obtain partial control of them or be able to purchase their services from their social agents.

When the production agents are controlled by different social agents, their services and/or partial control can be exchanged in a market. In this case, a social agent engages in exchange with other social agents to create the production topology it needs for the services it wishes to produce.

6.3.5 Complex Topologies

Finally, these two topologies can be combined in topologies of a higher complexity. In Fig. 6.3, a client *C* asks for a complex service, the execution of which requires different grid resources (*P1*, *P2*, *P31*, and *P32*). These resources can represent different job submission systems and a workflow engine or, in other cases, storage devices and computational power. The social agent *S1* interacting with the client *C* directly controls only the grid resource *P1* through one of its production agents. When the social agent receives the request from the client, it checks if the other social agents, with which it has a relation, are able to fulfill the needed services. If so, a social arrangement is made to allow the social agent to gain control of other production agents (*P2*, *P31*, or *P32*) for the necessary time. The social agent then instructs its production agent about the other production agents it can use for the completion of the complex service. The service is then executed and the result is sent back to the client.

In production topologies, social agents control production agents; a similar process is possible among social agents, thereby forming social topologies. Although more complex, the possible control topologies amongst the social agents are similar in nature to those between social and production agents. Owners can set policies and access rights for controllers; controllers can set policies for clients. Such policies can encompass, among other information, the nature of the social behavior of the agents such as the type of purchase to which an agent is entitled, e.g., purchase for free, special prices, full price, or the maximum credit/debit it is entitled to.

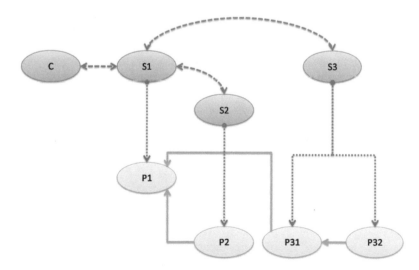

Fig. 6.3 A complex production topology encompassing markets and companies

In this social topology, also termed as simple purchase, an owner or controller sets the pricing policies of a social agent. The social agent then responds to the requests of its clients accordingly.

6.3.6 Tribe

In a tribe, the social agents accept the pricing and access policies of the tribe, usually free or discounted prices for all the members of the tribe. Then, all social agents can use part of the resources of the tribe to fulfill their needs. This topology is called a tribe as its allocation mechanism is similar to that of a tribe, where all active members of the society share part of their resources with the other members in compliance of the rules dictated by a tribal authority.

6.3.7 Pub

In a pub social topology, two or more social agents agree to share part of their resources. This topology is similar to the tribe but it is not centralized as the agents can define private sharing modalities that do not need to be approved or defined by the other members. This topology is called a pub topology as its allocation mechanism is similar to that of the behavior of friends that go regularly to a pub. If one of the friends lacks the money, the others will gladly pay for his consumption under the assumption that the same would be done for them. If one of the parties consistently fails to help the others for a certain period, it is usually not granted help any more.

6.3.8 Keynesian Scenario

In this scenario, the social agents accept pricing and access policies from an authority; these pricing and access policies usually refer to a subset of all the clients of the social agents. This topology is called a Keynesian scenario in a loose fashion without implying any direct link with the work or theory of John Maynard Keynes to describe a scenario where one of the actors (Keynesian authority) can provide resources directly or indirectly to a community and/or is delegate to define some of the economic parameters for the society.

6.3.9 Value and Price

Two basic concepts used in social grid agents are value and price. These concepts can be very loosely borrowed from economics and used in a similar fashion but without the strictness and formality of economics.

Price is a mathematical entity expressed in a unit (a currency that has to be recognized by all parties involved) on which two parties agree on an economic transaction. It is easy to define the concept of price for digital goods.

Unfortunately, it is difficult to define strategies solely based on price when not entirely economic behaviors arise. In grid computing, there are social behaviors that cannot be easily described within an economics-based paradigm. Cooperation may require decisions entailing financial losses to maintain social relations. As informal cooperation and "charity" mechanisms are present in grid computing, it is necessary to find another, more private, metric to describe how an individual agent perceives the "worthiness" of a resource, a service, or an action. Let us call this value, an entity to be used both to define prices and to help the decision-making process.

Value is used in control topologies where one or more social agents are in complete control of a production chain and, therefore need not use a widely accepted currency. Price, on the other hand, is used in exchanges among social agents that do not share control topologies that can define value.

One useful simplification is to say that the production layer is only aware of value. The value of services and resources could be either inferred or directly set by the social layer. In the paradigm, a production agent could be constrained to make decisions only on value. It would be possible, as an example, for a production agent to perform a service up to a certain value or to report to its owners or controllers the value of a performed service. The value of a service could be defined or it could be inferred from metrics through a defined function.

On the other hand, the social layer might not only define the value of the services it controls but might also infer a price from it. A social agent may map values into prices without considering the buyer's identity as done in supermarkets or instead it might define a price depending on the value and also the buyer's identity like a seller who decides to offer a discount to a good costumer or, finally, it might decide to donate services up to a given value because the social relation is deemed worthy of such financial sacrifice.

The topology for the definition of value and price can be further divided into top-down and bottom-up depending on the main direction of the flow of information. Figure 6.4 describes these two different approaches. In the top-down approach described in the left part of the figure, the social grid agent determines arbitrarily the value of the production resources it controls and their price.

The bottom-up approach is more complex and flexible. In it, the social grid agent determines the function to compute the price from the value and the metrics and the function to compute the value from the metrics in a top-down fashion but there then occurs an opposite bottom-up flow of information that provides the parameters of the functions.

A more flexible way to compute the value of a service is to define it as a function of two different sets of metrics: Service Metrics that provide information on the abstract service, and Resource Metrics that provide information on the resources that have been used by a specific execution of a service.

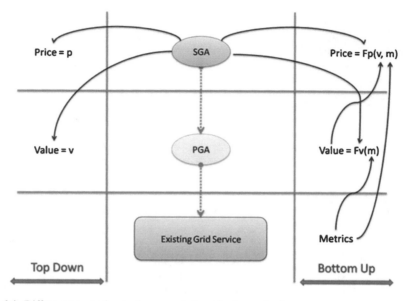

Fig. 6.4 Different approaches to the computation of value and price

6.4 Policies and Social Grid Agents

Social grid agents exchange information in the form of messages that, at least, contain:

- A Subject, that often is the sender of the message.
- An Action, describing what must be done. An action might be an execution, a request for information, the definition of behavioral patterns of the agent or the cancellation of some action.
- An Object, describing the object of the action. An object could be an action itself in the case of complex actions.
- A Set of Modalities, describing how the action has to be carried out.
- Optionally the Identity of the Beneficiary, i.e., the ultimate requester: Describing the identity of the agent that initially requested the action.

The agents that process these messages then take decisions based on their relationship with the subject of the message. A request of the type "Execute job j with modalities m" should be accepted or rejected on the basis of the compatibility of the actions and their modalities with the status and relationship of the agents, and especially, how it wishes to handle such requests, i.e., its policies.

As described in Fig. 6.5, every agent supports a set of policies, the set SP which encompasses all the possible policies that can be enforced during the execution of a certain action. The nature of the relation between the agents defines a subset GP of policies that can be granted. Finally, the modalities with which the action is to be

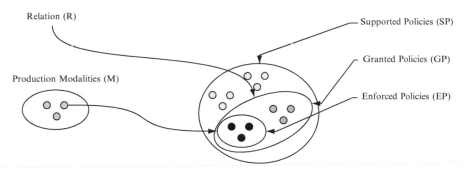

Fig. 6.5 Policies and modalities

executed define a final subset *EP* of policies that will be enforced. If the subset of enforced policies is empty, the action cannot and will not be executed by the agent.
   The policies consist of:

- Authentication policies: that define how authentication is to be executed.
- Authorization policies: that define if and how the actions specified in a message are to be executed. It would not be unusual for authorization policies to be defined in terms of other policies.
- Allocation policies: that describe allocation parameters that define the execution of a certain task.
- Execution policies: that describe specific execution parameters such as timeouts.
- Value policies: that describe the value of the services offered by the production agents.
- Accounting policies: that describe if and how an action is to be accounted for.
- Pricing policies: that describe how resources and services are priced with regard to the relationships with the other social agents.
- Selection policies: that describe how resources and services must be selected.
- Billing policies: that describe how credit transactions are to be performed and if they must be performed through a bank or whether a simple transfer of credit is sufficient.

6.5   Architecture of the Agents

Agents act as nodes that connect different information flows (production, control/ownership, social, and price/value) and react to their changes; they also manipulate and react to social information flows that describe their relationships. An abstract view of the architecture, described in Fig. 6.6, is as a set of message transformers that communicate and compose services.

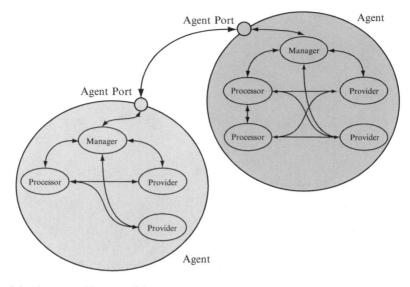

Fig. 6.6 Abstract architecture of the agents

Transformers can be further subdivided into sub-entities:

- Providers: that simply process a message; they constitute the simplest tile of the architecture. A provider interface is used to wrap the message-based SGA architecture around a service. An example of a provider can be a wrapper around a job submission system or a piece of code capable of performing some clearly defined operation.
- Processors: that map messages into sequences of messages that unfold in time; a simple example of a processor is a workflow engine. A very informal description is that processors map messages to messages in time.
- Managers: that map messages to providers in space; managers are basically indexing services.

These three sub-entities are composed to create structures of the required complexity and sophistication. A fourth concept, the agent, describes a set of message transformers that share an identity. Agents themselves are transformers and expose the same behaviors: Processing agents behave as workflow engines orchestrating complex services, managing agents offer indexing services such as markets or yellow pages whilst agents wrapping existing services such as job submission are pure provider agents. All agents and service providers expose a minimal interface composed of a single method process(message) that returns another message. The agents are simple message transformers, where the transformation is defined in a native language.

6.5.1   Agent Implementation

The conceptual architecture of the agents is independent of its realization. Several implementations have been realized each with its own native technology and language. The native technology of the current implementation is Java, while its native language is ClassAd.

6.5.2   Messaging

Agents communicate through messages that reflect the division into layers. Social agents communicate with each other through social messages, production agents accept and send production messages and, finally, service providers communicate through service provider messages or, for the sake of conciseness, execution messages. Messages contain a description expressed in the native language and possibly attached data in a service-specific format.

Execution messages can contain the information needed to execute the various services; either by native agent code or by existing grid services, or they can convey information regarding the service provider to the production layer. This information can be condensed, filtered, and enriched by additional production information when it is exchanged by production agents. Finally, production messages can join social information in social messages. In every layer, there can also be messages that contain only information pertaining to that level like pure social messages, pure production messages, and social messages containing pure production messages.

6.5.3   Service Providers

Service providers can be interfaces to existing grid services or to native services for the grid agents. In the first category, there are interfaces to existing grid services, such as job submission. Messages received by the service providers are usually simple wrappers containing necessary information for the execution of a service.

6.5.4   Behavior Engines

All service providers are managed by a component called the Agent Behavior Engine described in detail in Fig. 6.7. When a message is received by an Agent Behavior Engine, its Manager checks whether there is any Processor able to manage it. A processor is a class that contains the "knowledge" of what to do with one or more messages. The processor will execute a series of actions that can use other processors or service providers.

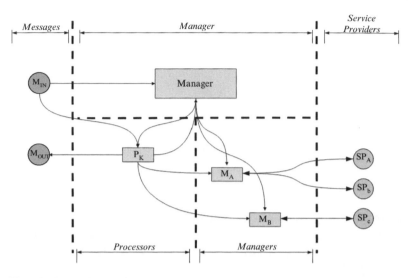

Fig. 6.7 Behavior engine architecture

The manager is capable of matchmaking a processor to a message through a mapping function. The processor then analyzes the message and engages in a series of steps; when it needs external providers, it requests them from the manager (SP_A and SP_B in Fig. 6.7) that instantiates them using the same mechanism as that which was used to obtain the processor. The processor executes all the necessary steps and returns a message (M_{OUT}).

These maps are used to describe relations that link message types and message values, including the identity of the requester (and sometimes, the beneficiary), to policies and processors capable of handling them.

This mapping technique is described in Fig. 6.8. First, a message m is received by the agent from a sender s. The first step in the mapping process is to link the sender and the beneficiary to a relationship. Then the action requested in the message and the relationship is mapped to the set of granted policies. Then the modalities requested for the action and the set of granted policies are mapped to an enforced policy. Finally, the requested action and the enforced policy are mapped to a processor.

6.5.5 Processors

Processors are a key component of the Agent Behavior Engines; they must be able to perform sequences of actions in response to received messages and they must also be able to react to messages whilst performing actions. In order to do so, processors contain a map based on the native language, which itself must be capable of

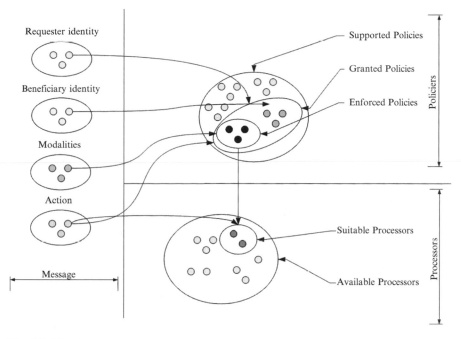

Fig. 6.8 Mapping a message to a processor

mapping the current action, parts of the status of the processor, and messages eventually received into the next step action. Processors are of two kinds:

1. Synchronous processors that react to messages with a predefined sequence of actions and return results at the end of this sequence. Obviously, this behavior is acceptable only if the sequence of actions can be executed in a short and predictable amount of time.
2. Asynchronous processors that inherit their behavior from a threading model but extend it with a synchronous sequence of actions at start-up. This design feature is to allow rapid, predictable sequences of actions to be performed in a synchronous fashion before starting the thread.

6.5.6   Managers

Processors, both synchronous and asynchronous, are managed by Managers. The purpose of these components is to provide the right processors upon the reception of a message. They do this by mapping processors and messages in maps. While synchronous processors are easily managed, asynchronous processors need to be managed more carefully in order to allow them to be retrieved when necessary. To allow this, a Processor Manager stores both types and instances of an asynchronous processor.

6.6   Language of the Agents

Agents have to make decisions driven by external elements and their own behavioral characteristics. They must decide whether to accept or reject requests from other agents depending on their social relations, they must assess the price of a service, and they must execute actions in order to perform services. The architecture of social grid agents offers a software infrastructure capable of mapping a message into policies and a sequence of actions.

Policies, maps, and action sequences are expressed in a native language, which in the current implementation of social grid agents is based on the ClassAd language [20]. The ClassAd Language is a strongly typed, side-effect-free functional language whose main characteristic is its ability to support matchmaking of different entities. The two ClassAd expressions ClassAd A and ClassAd B can be matchmaked against each other using the combined namespaces of both expressions. This means that we can define if and how much ClassAd A and ClassAd B are compatible. This is achieved by two particular functions of the ClassAd Language: (1) The Requirements function and (2) The Rank Function.

The current implementation of social grid agents uses the ClassAd Language extensively. Agents often map entities to other entities: actions are mapped to other actions in processors, messages are mapped to processors in managers and, finally, messages, relationships, and modalities are mapped to policies and actions in agents. Agents map messages to providers, either simple service providers or more complex processors. This operation is performed inside managers.

As previously mentioned, processors are engines capable of executing sequences of actions. They can perform this either in synchronous or asynchronous mode. The ClassAd language is used both to define the single actions and their sequences. Every processor has a description in ClassAd, which contains the current action and some data related to its status. The engine of the processor will use this information to determine the next action.

Let us illustrate an example of the steps that usually arise in the handling of a message in an agent:

- The Acceptance Action is always the first action performed when a message is received by an agent. It accepts as Input the message itself and returns one that has been modified in the fields relating to the Authentication of the sender (the sender must have a valid X509 certificate in order to have its message accepted) and the status of the message.
- The Action contained in the message is then extracted from the accepted message and a suitable processor (if any) is found in the manager.
- The Action is then mapped to a set of Policies by a Policies Mapping Provider.
- The Action with the constraints represented by the Policies is then usually processed by a Policies Enforcement Provider that defines the subset of constraints defined by the Policies and Modalities.
- The Action with the constraints represented by the Enforced Policies is then usually passed again to the manager to find a suitable provider; this operation can yield yet another action or an object.

6.6.1   Policies and Modalities

Agents receive, assess, and possibly accept messages requesting execution of services. These requests are detailed with modalities. On the other hand, agents providing the services define a set of policies. If these two sets overlap, then the service can be executed. The architecture of the social grid agents is multilayered and it cannot be assumed that every layer has a perfectly overlapping namespace. In fact, the various layers of the architecture share only subsets of their namespaces.

Let us describe an arbitrary level i. The requester will define its request and modalities with the ClassAd expression $\mathrm{expr}_{\mathrm{req}}^{i}$ that defines a set of values P_{r}^{i}, a requirement and a rank function:

$$\mathrm{Requirements} = f_{\mathrm{r}}^{i}(V \times V) \to Q$$

$$\mathrm{Rank} = g_{\mathrm{r}}^{i}(V \times V) \to K$$

Conversely, the *provider* will define its services and policies with the ClassAd expression $\mathrm{expr}_{\mathrm{p}}^{i}$ that defines a set of values P_{p}^{i}, a Requirement and a Rank function:

$$\mathrm{Requirements} = f_{\mathrm{p}}^{i}(V \times V) \to Q$$

$$\mathrm{Rank} = g_{\mathrm{r}}^{i}(V \times V) \to K$$

At level i, the matchmaking process will have two possible outcomes: it can evaluate or not. Unless the Requirements and Rank functions use directly the function *is_defined* to handle cases in which values are undefined, they will evaluate to *UNDEFINED* if any of the used expressions are not defined in the Cartesian product of the namespaces of $\mathrm{expr}_{\mathrm{p}}^{i}$ and $\mathrm{expr}_{\mathrm{r}}^{i}$: $P_{\mathrm{p}}^{i} \times P_{\mathrm{r}}^{i}$. In the latter case, at least one of the functions will evaluate to *UNDEFINED*, so the agent will not be able to make a decision and will have to delegate it to a lower level.

The provider at level i will then act as a requester of level $i - 1$, issuing a request that defines a set of values P_{r}^{i-1} (that contains all the needed values of the level i and $i - 1$), a requirements and a rank function:

$$\mathrm{Requirements} = f_{\mathrm{r}}^{i-1}(V \times V) \to Q$$

$$\mathrm{Rank} = g_{\mathrm{r}}^{i-1}(V \times V) \to K.$$

where:

$$f_{\mathrm{r}}^{i-1} = f_{\mathrm{p}}^{i} \, \& \& f_{\mathrm{r}}^{i}$$

$$g_{\mathrm{r}}^{i-1} = F(g_{\mathrm{r}}^{i}, g_{\mathrm{p}}^{i})$$

Where F is any function that combines the ranking functions and where $\&\&$ is the implementation offered by ClassAd of the Boolean AND function. This implementation also supports the *ERROR* and *UNDEFINED* values as described by Table 6.1.

Table 6.1 ClassAd extension of the Boolean AND Function

	TRUE	FALSE	ERROR	UNDEFINED
TRUE	TRUE	FALSE	ERROR	UNDEFINED
FALSE	FALSE	FALSE	ERROR	UNDEFINED
ERROR	ERROR	ERROR	ERROR	ERROR
UNDEFINED	UNDEFINED	UNDEFINED	ERROR	UNDEFINED

At each step, the requirements and rank functions are to be partially evaluated. A ClassAd function evaluates to *UNDEFINED* if any of its parts is *UNDEFINED*, and this possibility is not taken into account with the *is_undefined* special function. This makes it impossible to perform a detailed partial evaluation in which only the values defined at each step are evaluated and all the others are propagated to the other steps. This problem has been solved by writing a Partial Evaluation Parser that parses a ClassAd expression and substitutes only the values that are defined.

6.7 Environment of the Agents

If we imagine that the different grids occupy segments of a space, then another space can be conceived as a generic interoperability space. We call the latter a metagrid space. Since workflow engines are users of grids, not an intrinsic element of any one grid, it is useful to conceive of these as distinctly different entities, yielding three distinct spaces: Grids, workflow engines, and the metagrid space. Communication between the metagrid and a grid or workflow middleware flows through the border regions, where two or more technologies coexist.

Social grid agents and metagrid are mutually beneficial paradigms. In a metagrid SGAs can, among other things, perform two major roles: border agents or native metagrid agents.

In borders, the SGA capability of expressing and enforcing different policies helps to allow the coexistence of different middleware. SGAs prove their usefulness in two main respects: they can act as standards bridges and they can act as policy enforcement points for those responsible for the existing middleware. Border agents can translate different standards. While these translation capabilities of the agents are mostly useful at a production level, the social level of the agents is useful in describing the ownership and control topologies of the different middlewares, allowing those responsible to define suitable policies to reflect the agreed cooperation levels. As an example, a middleware requiring complete traceability of the issuer of the job will instruct its border agents with appropriate authorization and delegation policies whilst middleware with a different security policy might allow border agents to submit jobs without bothering to fully trace back the delegation chain. In this case, a control topology of a production border agent can be used to scope areas in the metagrid space where different security policies coexist.

On the other hand, inside the metagrid space, social grid agents can be used to enforce the policies required by the border agents and to control ancillary services such as indexes, markets, and exchanges. The metagrid space presents obvious opportunities for further exploration.

The generic nature of SGAs finds a natural complement in a metagrid environment where its native language can be translated into different dialects of grid middleware by border agents. This capability allows for the definition of policies (and resulting behaviors) that are not tied to any particular middleware but that can be translated (sometimes accepting the loss of some information) into the specific languages. The adoption of a native language implies that the number of translating agents grows with N, where N is the number of supported middleware, and not with N^2.

An interesting feature of this view is that the production layer is a border region with the existing middleware, and production grid agents are wrappers of the different services; this allows for scalable expansion of the encompassed middleware as well as a single point of translation.

6.8   Behavior of the Agents

Figure 6.9 represents a simple experiment to demonstrate the behavior of the agents. A workload is submitted to an agent that belongs to four different topologies. The agent's behavior is determined by a policy that states which resource is to be chosen first and, consequently, which topology is to be preferred under different conditions.

The testbed comprises eight agents of whom four are Production Agents (*PGA1*, *PGA2*, *PGA3*, *PGA4*) and four are Social Agents (*SGA1*, *SGA2*, *SGA3*, *SGA4*).

The agents are arranged in different topologies:

- Simple Producer relationship encompassing *SGA1* with *PGA1*, *SGA2* with *PGA2*, *SGA3* with *PGA3*, and *SGA4* with *PGA4*.
- Pub relationship encompassing the four agents *SGA1*, *SGA2*, *PGA1*, and *PGA2*.
- Simple Purchase encompassing three couples of agents: Client with *SGA1*, *SGA1* with *SGA3*, and *SGA1* with *SGA4*.

Agent *SGA1* chooses between its resources, *PGA1* which it directly controls, *PGA2* which can be reached through a Pub agreement and *PGA3* and *PGA4*, which can be purchased, as dictated by the following policies.

- Price Policy. The resource can be used by anybody provided that the offered price is sufficient, 10 credits per submission.
- Execution Policy enforced on Production Agent *PGA1*. The resource can be used on the condition that at least one job slot is left available.
- Selection Policy enforced on Social Agent *SGA1*. The first resource to be used is the one that is directly controlled (*PGA1*), then the one that is accessible through pub relations, then it can be purchased at the same price for which it was bought and finally, as a last resort, it can be purchased from the more expensive resource but on the condition that the endowment be above a certain threshold.

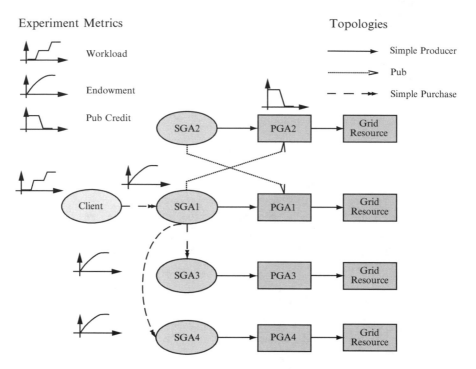

Fig. 6.9 Experiment testbed

Agent *PGA2* accepts or not jobs from *SGA1* based on the following policies:

- Execution Policy. The resource can be used on the condition that at least one job slot is left available.
- Authorization Policy. The resource can be used by *SGA1* only if the "Pub Credits" are greater than zero. Each time it performs a job on behalf of *SGA1*, the balance of its tokens is decreased by a unit.

Agent *SGA3* accepts or not jobs from *SGA1* based on the following policies:

- Price Policy. The resource can be used by anybody provided that the offered price is sufficient, 10 credits per submission.

Agent *SGA4* accepts or not jobs from *SGA1* based on the following policies:

- Price Policy. The resource can be used by anybody provided that the offered price is sufficient, 12 credits per submission.

The initial conditions of the testbed were:

- *SGA1*'s Endowment was set to 100 credits.
- *SGA3*'s Endowment was set to 0 credits.
- *SGA4*'s Endowment was set to 0 credits.
- *PGA2*'s Token was set to 5 units.

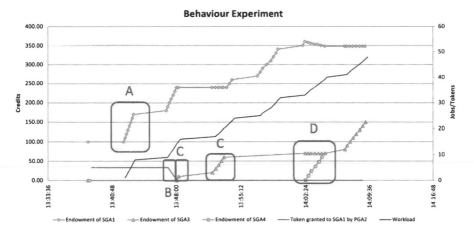

Fig. 6.10 Metrics of the experiment

This set of initial conditions was chosen in order to explore all the possible behaviors of the agents. A Direct Control execution policy was set to always leave a free slot, Pub tokens were set to a low number (and not zero) so that they could be used but not suffice for heavy workload, leaving the two Simple Purchase relations as the last viable solutions.

The results of the experiment are shown in Fig. 6.10. There are three main phases of the experiment:

In a phase A, the workload of agent *SGA1* can be met entirely by the resource, Production Agent *PGA1*, it is in control of. As specified by its Selection Policy, all jobs are then executed by this resource until one job slot remains free.

During phase B, the directly controlled resource *PGA1* does not match any more the execution policy of having one free job slot. The Selection Policy dictates that, in this case, the Production Agent *PGA2* that can be reached through a Pub topology has to be used. This behavior is sustainable until the number of available tokens is greater than zero.

During Phase C, the pub resource is not available anymore and the Selection Policy dictates that a Simple Purchase topology is to be used. As the price paid to agent *SGA3* to perform the execution is the same that the Client paid to *SGA1*, the endowment of *SGA1* remains constant while the endowment of *SGA3* increases.

During Phase D, the cheap simple purchase resource is not available and the Selection Policy dictates that a last resort Simple Purchase topology is to be used provided that the endowment is above a certain threshold. In this case, is the initial endowment of 100 credits.

The results of this simple experiment show how *SGA1* is able to sort its economic-driven relations with regard to their cost and to make decisions accordingly. In this case, the decision criteria were to use cheaper resources first and to use the more expensive only as a last resort and only if the endowment is above a certain threshold. The set of policies of the agents allowed for the definition of an opportunistic behavior where the endowment was to be increased or, at least, kept constant and where the agent preferred to use its own resources, those accessible through pub relationships and only as a last resort, those accessible through a market.

6.9 Conclusions

The core criteria that the agents should be capable of encompassing different coexisting allocation philosophies has been proven by behavioral experiments that show how different policies of the agents result in different coexisting allocation philosophies.

This proves to be valuable when one recognizes that grid is becoming a means to distribute computational power in an increasing number of scenarios and that some of the challenges posed by this expansion (coexistence of actors with different aims) can clearly be tackled with the SGA paradigm.

Although the current implementation of social grid agents yields useful results, its full potential may yet to be fully discovered, as discussed below.

In SGAs, actions are described with the use of modalities and a rather primitive; one-step form of negotiation is offered by the intersection of policies and modalities that defines how the action is really executed. Social grid agents will certainly be much more interesting if they have a more advanced approach leading to formal Service Level Agreements (SLA) and Negotiation Protocols. For the latter, it could be feasible and profitable to encompass some existing technology and to delegate the act of negotiation to it.

As yet, only relatively simple social topologies and their policies have been developed for the agents. In the future, research should embrace more complex topologies. At a microeconomic level, the existing solutions may be enriched by insurance agents that compensate with credits when middleware fails. Currently, agents define prices based only on the data from the supply side without taking into account demand. This doesn't allow the definition of realistic price models and thus some mechanism capable of gathering demand-related information would prove very profitable for the implementation of more sophisticated agents. A much more advanced topic that is still to be tackled is the relation between the credit system used by the agents and the real economy. For the present, there is no direct connection between the credits that are used among the agents and real currencies. This is a serious limitation that prevents agent's societies from being connected to the real economy. Whether a connection between these two economies would yield positive or negative outcomes for one or both is a very open question that could constitute a propitious field for future enquiries.

At present, social grid agents allow a limited implementation of Service Level Agreements. They consist only in the data that specify both the functionalities and policies for the execution of jobs. On the other hand, the functional characteristics of the agents native language should allow more sophisticated implementation of Service Level Agreements.

As an example, a deadline requested for the completion for a job may not only influence the resource allocated but also the modality with which the status of the job is queried. Theoretically, the homogeneous nature of the agent's internal and external language allow for the creation of arbitrarily complex mappings between action, policies, modalities, and behaviors; the difficulty of reading and debugging the ClassAd code may represent, on the other hand, a strong constraint to the level of complexity of these patterns.

The assumptions behind the conception of social grid agents that no economic model is proven to be optimal under any circumstance and that no grid middleware is proven, again, to be optimal for every computational scenario proved to be useful in tackling the diversity of sharing and allocation approaches and, also, in allowing social grid agents to harness different middleware. These assumptions on economic and technological agnosticism are now proving useful in expanding the same architecture to encompass distributed computational systems such as clouds- and volunteer-based systems. The economic agnosticism is a paradigm that helps social grid agents to connect with computational platforms designed around different social concepts such as volunteer-based or revenue-based allocation philosophies while the abstraction layer provided by the border agents provides a natural interoperability infrastructure for different computational platforms as it did for different grid middleware.

References

1. Abraham, A., Buyya, R., Nath, B.: Nature heuristics for scheduling jobs on computational grids. In: Proceedings of the 8th IEEE International Conference on Advanced Computing and Communication, Cochin, pp. 45–52 (2000)
2. ArguGRID Project: Retrieved from http://www.argugrid.eu (2010)
3. Buyya, R.: Economic-Based Distributed Resource Management and Scheduling for Grid Computing. Monash University, Melbourne (2002)
4. Buyya, R., Abramson, D., Giddy, J., Stockinger, H.: Economic models for resource management and scheduling in grid computing. J. Concurr. Comput. Pract. Exp. **14**, 1507–1542 (2002)
5. CATNETS Project: Retrieved from http://www.catnets.uni-bayreuth.de (2010)
6. Davies, A.: Computational intermediation and the evolution of computation as a commodity. Appl. Econ. **36**(11), 1131–1142 (2004)
7. Elmroth, E., Gardfjall, P.: Design and evaluation of a decentralized system for grid-wide fair-share scheduling. In: Proceedings of the 1st International Conference on e-Science and Grid Computing, Melbourne, pp. 221–229 (2005)
8. Ernemann, C., Hamscher, V., Yahyapour, R.: Economic scheduling in grid computing. In: Revised Papers from the 8th International Workshop on Scheduling Strategies for Parallel Processing, Edinburgh, pp. 128–152 (2002)
9. Eymann, S.H., Streitberger, W., Hudert, S.: CATNETS – Open market approaches for self-organizing grid resource allocation. In: Proceedings of the 4th International Conference on Grid Economics and Business Models, Rennes, pp. 176–181 (2007)
10. Foster, I., Kesselman, C., Lee, C., Lindell, B., Nahrstedt, K., Roy, A.: A distributed resource management architecture that supports advanced reservation and co-allocation. In: Proceedings of the 7th International Workshop on Quality of Service, London, pp. 27–36 (1999)
11. Foster, I., Kesselamn, C., Nick, J.M., Tuecke, S.: The Anatomy of the Grid. Int. J. High Perform. Comput. Appl. **15**(3), 200–222 (2001)
12. Foster, I., Kesselamn, C., Nick, J.M., Tuecke, S.: The Physiology of the Grid: an open grid services architecture for distributed systems integration. Retrieved from http://www.globus.org/alliance/publications/papers/ogsa.pdf (2002)

13. Grid Economy Project: Retrieved from http://www.buyya.com/ecogrid (2010)
14. Global Grid Forum: Retrieved from http://www.globalgridforum.org (2010)
15. Gridbus Project: Retrieved from http://www.gridbus.org (2010)
16. Minoli, D.: A Network Approach to Grid Computing. Wiley-Interscience, Hoboken (2004)
17. Nakai, J., Van Der Wijngaart, R.F.: Applicability of markets to global scheduling in grids. Retrieved from http://www.nas.nasa.gov/News/Techreports/2003/PDF/nas-03-004.pdf (2003)
18. Puschel, B.M.: Economically enhanced resource management for Internet service utilities. Lect. Notes Comput. Sci. **4831**, 335–348 (2007)
19. Sherwani, J., Ali, N., Lotia, N., Hayat, Z., Buyya, R.: Libra: A computational economy-based job scheduling system for clusters. Softw. Pract. Exp. **34**(6), 573–590 (2004)
20. Solomon, M: The ClassAd Language Reference Manual. Retrieved from http://www.cs.wisc.edu/condor/classad/refman.pdf (2008)
21. SORMA Project: Retrieved from http://www.im.uni-karlsruhe.de/sorma/index.htm (2010)
22. Wolski, R., Brevik, J., Plank, J.S., Bryan, T.: Grid resource allocation and control using computational economics. In: Berman F., Fox G., Hey A.J.G (eds.) Grid Computing: Making the Global Infrastructure a Reality, Wiley and Sons. pp. 747–772 (2003)
23. Wolski, R., Plank, J.S., Brevik, J., Bryan, T.: Analyzing market-based resource allocation strategies for the computational grid. Int. J. High Perform. Comput. Appl. **15**, 258–281 (2001)

Chapter 7
Monitoring and Controlling Grid Systems

Ciprian Dobre

Abstract An important part of managing global-scale distributed systems is a monitoring system that is able to monitor and track in real time many site facilities, networks, and tasks in progress. The monitoring information gathered is essential for developing the required higher level services, the components that provide decision support and some degree of automated decisions, and for maintaining and optimizing workflow in large-scale distributed systems. In this chapter, we present the role, models, technologies, and structure of monitoring platforms designed for large-scale distributed systems. It also aims to realize a survey study of existing work and trends in distributed systems monitoring by introducing the involved concepts and requirements, techniques, models, and related standardization activities.

7.1 Introduction

Monitoring can be defined as the process of dynamic collection, interpretation, and presentation of information concerning the characteristics and status of resources of interest. In case of large-scale distributed systems, monitoring is an important process that facilitates management activities such as performance management, configuration management, fault management, security management, etc. In this case, the monitoring consists in gathering data about the behavior of the system. This information is further used to make management decisions and perform the appropriate control actions on the system.

C. Dobre (✉)
Computer Science Department, Faculty of Automatic Controls and Computers,
University Politehnica of Bucharest,
Office EG303, Spl. Independentei, 313, Sect. 6, Bucharest 060042, Romania
e-mail: ciprian.dobre@cs.pub.ro

N.P. Preve (ed.), *Grid Computing: Towards a Global Interconnected Infrastructure*, 171
Computer Communications and Networks, DOI 10.1007/978-0-85729-676-4_7,
© Springer-Verlag London Limited 2011

In this chapter, we present models and requirements that describe the monitoring process in large-scale distributed environments. We present core components, such as production, processing, dissemination, and presentation of monitoring information of systems designed to support the monitoring of distributed systems, particularly grid related. These components may describe a layered model, having the monitoring production at the lowest level and the presentation on top of other layers, or other particular architecture.

Monitoring is effectively used in many systems but has specific roles in grids and other large-scale distributed platforms. The monitored data is used by services interested in taking decisions based on the state of the system, but it can be further used even for prediction and learning purposes, e.g., scheduling of jobs according to a measured execution profile, avoiding bad schedules, and so on. For clarity, in this chapter we consider the following terms [31], an entity is any networked resource, e.g., processors, memories. An event is a collection of time-stamped, typed data, associated with an entity, and represented in a specific structure; an event type is an identifier, which uniquely maps to an event structure; an event schema defines the typed structure and semantics of all events so that, given an event type, one can find the structure and interpret the semantics of the corresponding event; and a sensor is a process monitoring an entity and generating events.

In a distributed environment, a large number of monitoring events are generated by the system components during the execution or interaction with external objects, such as users or processes. Monitoring such events is necessary for observing the run-time behavior of the large-scale distributed system and for providing status information required for debugging, tuning, and managing processes. However, correlated events are generated concurrently and can be distributed in various locations, which complicates the management decisions process. In this chapter, such problems are detailed based on case studies learned while implementing one of the most complex monitoring frameworks, capable of running and already being used in production in several of the largest grid systems worldwide, MonALISA [25]. This monitoring framework is one of the most complex platforms, which offers a large set of monitoring services and supports resource usage accounting, optimization, and automated actions. MonALISA service provides a distributed framework for monitoring and optimizing large-scale distributed systems. It is based on a Dynamic Distributed Service Architecture and is largely applicable to many fields of data-intensive applications. Specialized distributed agents are used for global optimization and guidance in large systems. A key point is its scalability coming for the distributed multi-threaded engines that host a variety of loosely coupled, self-describing dynamic services, capable of dynamic registration and discovery. It is implemented mainly in Java and is using JINI and WSDL technologies.

The rest of this chapter is organized as follows. In Sect. 7.2, we present a background on the domain of monitoring solutions designed for large-scale distributed systems. Sect. 7.3 presents architectural models for such monitoring systems, together with a comparison study of the most important models currently being used. Section 7.4 presents a selection of techniques for collecting and publishing data, followed by standards and solutions for representing the monitoring information in Sect. 7.5. Section 7.6 presents solutions to the problem of visualization of monitoring information, and we conclude in Sect. 7.7 with a presentation of case studies on the role of monitoring instruments for control and optimization in large-scale distributed systems. In the final Sect. 7.8, we conclude.

7.2 Background

Distributed systems have become very useful especially for complex scientific applications, involving the processing of very large data volumes, in a very short amount of time, as well as the storage of these data. Taking into account the tremendous popularity of complex distributed systems, favored by the rapid development of computing systems, high-speed networks, and the Internet, it is clear that it is imperative, in order to achieve adequate performances in the utilization of these systems, to pick optimal architectures and solutions for designing and deploying distributed systems. In large-scale distributed systems, monitoring in particular is essential to improve the quality of the management and production control processes. The process of developing, maintaining, and operating distributed applications can be complex.

Currently, there are many forms of distributed system architectures. Computing in the late 1990s has reached the state of Web-based distributed computing. A basis of this form of computing is distributed computing, which is carried out on distributed computing systems. Several new innovations in networked computing have brought it into the eyes of the public and business, as well as academics. Various levels of hype have surrounded all these ideas at some point, but each of them is still relevant and they form the foundations of grid computing. Among the first modern distributed architectures were the cluster systems. A cluster, a parallel or distributed system that consists of a collection of interconnected computers, is utilized as a single, unified computing resource. Distributed Computing or Internet Computing has been given much publicity by the SETI@Home project [3]. The project harnesses idle computing resources to analyze radio signals from space in the hope of finding messages from intelligent extraterrestrial life.

The peer-to-peer (P2P) networking model [3] forms a completely decentralized system, where every host, or peer, has equal status to any other peer. P2P systems enable direct communication between any two symmetric peers. The most common types of P2P applications are file sharing, distributed computing, and storage applications. Projects such as JXTA are developing P2P protocols to enable P2P applications to operate between anything from PCs to mobile devices. Many of the new-generation file sharing applications use decentralized indexing servers, making them true P2P applications.

Grid computing is considered to be the next phase of distributed computing. It represents an evolving area of computing, where standards and technology are still being developed to enable this new paradigm. All over the world computational grids are being constructed so that distributed resources can be aggregated and shared among different users and organizations. This development has been driven by the scale of many current and future scientific projects in which the amount of data produced and the computational resources required to analyze it are far greater than previously seen. With such requirements, it is not possible to use traditional cluster computing or supercomputing at a single location, and scientists are looking to link geographically distributed resources together to form grids. The hype around grid computing is not about replacing current technologies but harnessing them all together (cluster computing, web services, P2P, etc.) to work as one unified utility. Grid computing incorporates many of these technologies, together with their characteristics.

The next-generation distributed environment, Cloud Computing, describes a new supplement, consumption, and delivery model for Information Technology (IT) services based on the Internet, and it typically involves the provision of dynamically scalable and often virtualized resources as a service over the Internet. It is a computing capability that provides an abstraction between the computing resource and its underlying technical architecture (e.g., servers, storage, networks), enabling convenient, on-demand network access to a shared pool of configurable computing resources that can be rapidly provisioned and released with minimal management effort or service provider interaction.

An efficient monitoring of such systems is an essential mechanism to produce good-quality applications, that are reliable, robust, secure, and of high performance. The necessity of monitoring significantly increases when using large-scale distributed systems since they are more susceptible to many issues such as reliability and performance degradation and also more difficult to debug and steer. There are several motivations for monitoring complex distributed systems [11]; debugging and testing, performance tuning, fault recovery, security, correctness checking, performance evaluation, and resource utilization.

Large-scale distributed systems often experience unexpectedly low performance, the reasons for which are usually not obvious. The bottlenecks can be found in the applications, the operating systems, the disks or network adapters, the network switches and routers, or any other part of the system. The solution to find and correct the problem consists in the use of highly instrumented monitoring systems that provide precision timing information and analysis tools. Such systems also help other crucial components of the system. The scheduling could not schedule jobs for execution without having monitoring information about existing resources; the security component also relies on the monitoring subsystem to find possible intrusion attempts; monitoring is an important component in ensuring resilience in case of various failures; and the list can continue. Therefore, the monitoring subsystem is an important building block for any large-scale distributed system.

The monitoring of complex distributed systems is not a trivial task to accomplish because of several aspects. The resources are geographically dispersed; however, to make a decision about the state of the distributed system, one needs to consider a consistent snapshot of all the resources. Then, there is the diversity of hardware and software systems composing the environment. These resources are under different policies and decision-making mechanisms, as a distributed monitoring infrastructure can spread outside the border to a single organization and span multiple administrative domains over the Internet. The monitoring system itself must not compete for system resources with the monitored objects.

In order to overcome such challenges, a distributed monitoring system must meet several important requirements.

The system should be able to analyze and process vast amounts of data. This potentially huge amount of data might be collected from a vast number of nodes, scattered around the entire system. Thus, scalability of the monitoring system is an important characteristic. This generally implies using a high-performance filtering mechanisms to reduce the traffic, and distributing the monitoring operations. A hierarchical organization of the communication can also help with this requirement.

The system of the distributed system being monitored also influences the manageability of the monitoring system. The system should incur management overheads that scale slowly with the number of nodes. For example, managing the system should not require a linear increase in system administrator time as the number of nodes in the system increases. Manual configuration should also be avoided as much as possible.

Accuracy is another important aspect. The system should provide both real-time and history-collected information. This information must be correct and up-to-date, as it must accurately reflect how the large system performs. However, the monitoring system should provide increased accuracy without too much overhead. The system should incur low per-node overheads for all scarce computational resources including CPU, memory, I/O, and network bandwidth. For high-performance systems, this is particularly important since applications often have enormous resource demands. The monitoring system should be highly re-configurable to handle dynamic consumer requests (run-time add, delete, and modify) with minimal performance overhead.

The monitoring system should facilitate interaction with other technologies and middleware components that are part of the distributed system such as the security infrastructure, resource brokers, schedulers, etc. For that, the system should be easily extendable. This means it should be extensible enough to allow the integration of new types of monitoring events. In fact, one cannot know a priori everything that might want to be monitored. The system should allow new data to be collected and monitored in a convenient fashion.

Standardization is another important factor. The data being used by the system should employ standard representations. This can facilitate the adoption of the system in larger systems. This is related to portability, meaning that the system should be designed such that to support a large variety of operating systems and CPU architectures.

Finally, robustness of the monitoring system is another important aspect. The system should be made robust to various failures, hardware, and software, occurring in both nodes and network links. As systems scale in the number of nodes, failures become both inevitable and commonplace. The system should be able to localize such failures; it should continue to operate and deliver useful services even in the presence of failures.

7.3 Architectural Models for Monitoring Systems

Monitoring large-scale distributed systems typically includes four stages [22]:

1. Generation of monitoring events, that is, sensors capture events and encode the measurements according to a given schema.
2. Processing of generated events may take place during any stage of the monitoring process.
3. Distribution refers to the transmission of the events from the source to interested parties.
4. The presentation typically involves some further processing so that the overwhelming number of received events will be eventually provided in a series of abstractions in order to enable an end user to draw conclusions from the operation of the monitored system.

Typical examples of the processing taking place in the second stage include filtering according to some predefined criteria, or summarizing a group of events (i.e., computing the average). In the fourth state, the presentation can be in either human form or event consumption. For humans, the presentation is typically provided in the form of a Graphical User Interface (GUI) application making use of visualization techniques. It may either use a real-time stream of monitoring data or a recorded trace usually retrieved from an archive. However, for components using the monitoring data, the last stage takes the form of consumption, since the users of the monitoring information are not necessarily humans and therefore visualization may not be involved.

Several architectural models for monitoring systems were developed over the last years. The de-facto standard proposed by the Open Grid Forum was among the first. It was soon followed by the relational model, developed starting from it. The most widely used architecture today is, however, the functional model.

7.3.1 GGF Grid Monitoring Architecture

Among the first standardized architectures for monitoring systems was the Grid Monitoring Architecture (GMA) [4]. Being proposed by the Global Grid Forum, the architecture promotes interoperability between grid monitoring systems. Not necessarily a standard, the architecture consists of several components:

- A producer is a process that makes performance data available (a performance event source).
- A consumer is a process that receives events by using an implementation of at least one consumer API.
- A discovery service is a lookup service that allows producers to publish the event types they generate, and consumers to find out the events they are interested in. Additionally, a registry holds the details required for establishing communication with registered parties (e.g., address, supported protocol bindings, security requirements).

The GMA handles monitoring event transmitted as time-stamped (performance) events. Each event is defined by an event schema. The events are sent directly from the producer to a consumer. The architecture supports both a streaming publish/subscribe model and a query/response model. For both models, producers or consumers that accept connections publish their existence in the directory service.

Consumers can use the directory service to discover producers of interest, and producers can use the directory service to discover consumers of interest. Either a producer or a consumer may initiate the connection to a discovered component. Communication of control messages and transfer of performance data occurs directly between each consumer/producer pair without further involvement of the directory service.

7.3.2   Relational Architecture

A relational implementation of GMA components and their interfaces is Relational Grid Monitoring Architecture (R-GMA) [9]. According to this architecture, the information and monitoring system is similar to a large relational database which can be directly queried as such. Anyone supplying or obtaining information from R-GMA does not need to know about the Registry, the Consumers, and the Producers, and the way they are managed behind the scenes. This approach allows both static and dynamic data handling because Producers have two important views: database producers for static data stored on disk in relational databases and stream producers for dynamic data stored in memory buffers.

Using this model, producers use SQL statements to announce their data availability "create tables" and publish monitoring data "insert into." Consumers collect the data using queries "select." In order for a component to act as either a consumer or a producer, it has to instantiate a remote object (agent) and invoke methods from the appropriate (consumer or producer) API. This schema allows for dynamic creation and dropping of new relations in addition to the core set. The relations and views are then further stored by the registry, which also holds the global schema.

In the original proposal, the registry is a centralized component. However, efforts for a distributed implementation are under way. In the architecture, also, a mediator uses the information available in the registry and cooperates with consumers to dynamically construct query plans for queries that cannot be satisfied by a single relation; that involve "joins" from several producers, for example.

7.3.3   Hierarchical Architecture

Lately, another architectural model converged. This model is centered on a hierarchy of components and services. This hierarchical approach is best suited for efficient data collection, federation, and aggregation. The model is based on creating a tree of monitoring connections and keeping the monitored system's load at a minimum by transmitting changes in monitoring levels only to local monitors.

The Ganglia system [23] implements this hierarchical architecture, targeting at federation of clusters and using a tree of point-to-point connections. The approach considers that each leaf represents a node in a specific cluster being federated, with nodes higher up in the tree specifying aggregation points and logically representing sets of clusters. Multiple cluster nodes are specified for each leaf to ensure reliability. Aggregation at each point in the tree is done by using the reception of a heartbeat as a sign that a node is available and the non-reception of a heartbeat over a small multiple of a periodic announcement interval as a sign that a node is unavailable. Each node monitors its local resources and sends multicast packets containing monitoring data on a well-known multicast address whenever significant updates occur.

The Globus Toolkit's Monitoring and Discovery System (MDS) [12] also forms a hierarchical structure and uses a pull model for data propagation. Starting with Globus MDS-4, subscription is also supported. MDS2 has a hierarchical structure that consists of three main components. A Grid Index Information Service (GIIS) provides an aggregate directory of lower-level data. A Grid Resource Information Service (GRIS) runs on a resource and acts as a modular content gateway for a resource. The Information Providers (IPs) interface from any data collection service and then talk to a GRIS. Each service registers with higher level services using a soft-state protocol that allows dynamic cleaning of dead resources. MDS4 implements a standard web services interface to different local monitoring tools and various information providers. Besides the implemented query/subscription/notification protocols and interfaces defined by the WS Resource Framework (WSRF), MDS4 also provides higher level services: An Index service, which collects and publishes aggregated information about information sources, and a Trigger service, which collects resource information and performs actions when certain conditions are triggered. These services are built on a common Aggregation Framework infrastructure that provides common interfaces and mechanisms for working with data sources, following the hierarchical model.

7.3.4   Case Study: The MonALISA Architecture

The MonALISA system is designed as an ensemble of autonomous self-describing agent-based subsystems, which are registered as dynamic services [20]. These services are able to collaborate and cooperate in performing a wide range of distributed information gathering and processing tasks. An agent-based architecture of this kind is well-adapted to the operation and management of large-scale distributed systems, by providing global optimization services capable of orchestrating computing, storage, and network resources to support complex workflows. By monitoring the state of the grid-sites and their network connections end-to-end in real time, the MonALISA services are able to rapidly detect, help diagnose, and in many cases, mitigate problem conditions, thereby increasing the overall reliability and manageability of the

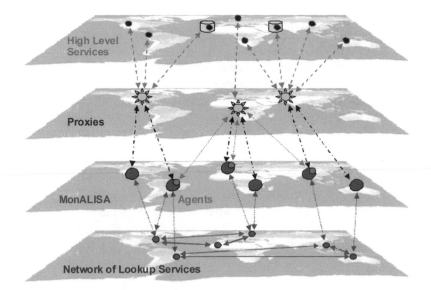

Fig. 7.1 The four layers, main services, and components of the MonALISA framework

distributed computing systems. The MonALISA architecture [19] is based on four layers of global services (Fig. 7.1).

The network of Lookup Discovery Services (LUSs) at the bottom provides dynamic registration and discovery for all other services and agents. MonALISA services are able to discover each other in the distributed environment and to be discovered by the interested clients. The registration uses a lease mechanism. If a service fails to renew its lease, it is removed from the LUSs and a notification is sent to all the services or other application that subscribed for such events. Remote event notification is used in this way to get a real overview of this dynamic system.

The second layer represents the network of MonALISA services that host many monitoring tasks and loosely coupled agents that analyze the collected information in real time. The collected information can be stored locally in databases. Agents are able to process information locally and to communicate with other services or agents to perform global optimization tasks. A service in the MonALISA framework is a component that interacts autonomously with other services, either through dynamic proxies or via agents that use self-describing protocols. By using the network of lookup services, a distributed services registry, and the discovery and notification mechanisms, the services are able to access each other seamlessly. The use of dynamic remote event subscription allows a service to register an interest in a selected set of event types, even in the absence of a notification provider at registration time.

The third layer consists of a collection of proxy services. This layer provides an intelligent multiplexing of the information requested by the clients or other services and is used for reliable communication between agents. The communication between clients and the selected services is performed through this set of proxy services.

The proxy services register their existence in the lookup services and are dynamically discovered. The usage of proxies for the communication has multiple advantages. First, the data from a service can be sent only once and is multiplexed to all the interested clients connected to the same proxy. This reduces the load on the service and on the network, in case of many clients. It also provides a natural way of scaling the system, to support a large number of clients. Second, this has an extremely valuable practical advantage: the services do not require incoming network connectivity when clients running outside service's domain connect to the service. This distributed architecture is fault tolerant because it does not have a single point of failure. All the core services (lookup and proxy services) are replicated in different locations worldwide.

Higher level services and client access the collected information using the proxy layer of services. A load balancing mechanism is used to allocate these services dynamically to the best proxy service. The clients, other services or agents can get real-time or historical data by using a predicate mechanism for requesting or subscribing to selected measured values. These predicates are based on regular expressions to match the attribute description of the measured values a client is interested in. They may also be used to impose additional conditions or constraints for selecting the values. The subscription requests create a dedicated priority queue for messages. The communication with the clients is served by a pool of threads. The allocated thread performs the matching tests for all the predicates submitted by a client with the monitoring values in the data flow. The same thread is responsible to send the selected results back to the client as compressed serialized objects. Having an independent thread for clients allows sending the information they need, in a fast and reliable way, and it is not affected by communication errors, which may occur with other clients. In case of communication problems, these threads will try to reestablish the connection or to clean up the subscriptions for a client or a service, which is no longer active.

The main aim for developing the MonALISA system was to provide a flexible framework capable to use in near real-time the complete monitoring information from large number of jobs, computing facilities, and wide area networks to control and optimize complex workflows in distributed systems. Most of the monitoring tools currently used are dedicated to specific activities. In the MonALISA system, we provide the functionality to easily collect any type of information. This leads to a more synergetic approach, necessary to control and optimize the execution of data-intensive applications on large-scale distributed systems.

7.4   Techniques for Collecting and Publishing Data

Independent of the architectural model used, the main process of a distributed monitoring system consists of the tasks of retrieving, organizing, and providing the monitoring information. In the following, we distinguish between three important steps related to monitoring data retrieving: collection, handling, and discovery.

7.4.1 Data Collection

At this level, a specific component gathers data obtained either directly or by a monitoring tool. Usually, direct retrieving of monitoring data involves parsing applications' and services' log files, inspecting system files, pushing results from third-party external applications or protocols (e.g., Simple Network Management Protocol (SNMP) for network links, routers, and switches monitoring) in order to acquire the interesting monitoring events. One common approach to implement this consists in a component-based engineering approach, where different modules are constructed for different needs. In this approach, the data collection is performed by a set of monitoring modules that are able to be dynamically loaded and can execute a procedure (or runs a script/program, performs a request) to collect parameters (monitored values) by properly parsing the output of the procedure. In general, a monitoring module is a simple application, which is using a certain procedure to obtain a set of parameters and report them in a simple, standard format. Monitoring modules can be used for pulling data or to install pushing scripts (programs). The former solution assumes that the monitoring modules are executed with a predefined frequency (i.e., a pull module, which queries a web service). In the latter, the monitoring modules send the monitoring results periodically back to the main monitoring service (usually to a collection engine).

Allowing to dynamically load these modules from a (few) centralized sites simplifies the management process of the monitoring system because new functionalities are dynamically added only when needed. Users can also easily implement new dedicated modules and use them to adapt the framework according to their needs. This approach is successfully used by the MonALISA monitoring system and, as a consequence, the number of tracked parameters has continuously evolved over time. Moreover, the types of monitored parameters are quite diverse, closely related to the domains where it is used: system parameters, network, jobs, user accounting, Virtual Organization (VO) accounting, P2P key parameters, physical sensors, etc.

The second approach is to use the information provided by an existing monitoring tool and push its results back into the monitoring framework. The core of such an implementation consists of a module capable of interfacing monitoring applications and tools. We present some of the most frequently used low-level monitoring tools (Hawkeye and Ganglia) and batching systems (Condor, PBS, SGE, LSF). These resource managers have in common the capability to provide monitoring information to third-party applications.

Hawkeye [17] is a tool designed for grid and distributed applications. It is flexible and easy to deploy, and provides automated detection and timely alerts of problems. Hawkeye is based on Condor technology and uses ClassAds and matchmaking mechanisms for collecting, storing, and using information about computers and further management of systems. The system monitors various attributes: system load, I/O, usage, watching run-away processes, monitoring the health of the job pool, the status of the grid sites, the grid modules check on jobs, etc. In short, Hawkeye is essentially a Condor that has been modified to achieve monitoring and publish information in ClassAds. However, in the evaluation performed [32], the Hawkeye Manager performed poorly in the response transmission and connection phases, but has the best performance when searching for ClassAds in the processing phase. Hawkeye is currently being used to monitor systems on the US/CMS testbed and is also integrated in other monitoring tools. For example, MonALISA uses specially designed Hawkeye modules to collect information. However, the project lost its support since 2006, and its modules were last updated back in 2004.

Ganglia [23] is a scalable distributed monitoring system for high-performance computing systems, such as clusters and grids. It is based on a hierarchical design targeted at federations of clusters. The system relies on a multicast-based listen/ announce protocol to monitor state within clusters. It also uses a tree of point-to-point connections amongst representative cluster nodes to federate clusters and aggregate their state. Its main advantages are: availability on many platforms, wide use with many users and set-ups, global and local views available, highly customizable via modules, fine granular statistics, monitored data stored in Round Robin Databases, easily extendible, support to add new data types. However, there is no official support available, it provides no automation support while some setups require extensive work and the monitoring daemon is basically a distributed redundant database, which can imply more overhead than necessary.

Condor [8] is a workload management system specialized for computing intensive jobs. One of its advantages is the ability to perform opportunistic computing (harnessing CPU power from idle desktop workstations). Also, Condor provides a flexible mechanism for matching resource requests with resource offers (called ClassAds). It includes mechanisms for dynamic checkpointing and migration, for interfacing with the Globus middleware, and with gLite MD. However, Condor is not adequate for parallel applications, and its checkpointing mechanism only works for batch jobs.

The Portable Batch System (PBS) [15] is based on the classical client–server model. A client makes job execution requests to a batch server, and the server handles the execution of the jobs in a cluster by placing them in queues. Among the features that PBS provides are the possibility to set priorities for jobs and to specify interdependencies between them, automatic file staging, and multiple scheduling algorithms. Recently, the focus of development has shifted to clusters and basic parallel support has been added. In addition, the Maui scheduler has been ported to act as a plug-in scheduler to the PBS system. This combination is proving successful at scheduling jobs on parallel systems. For example, while the resource manager and scheduler are able to reserve multiple processors for a parallel job, the job startup, including the administrative scripts, is performed entirely on one node.

Sun Grid Engine (SGE) [27] is an open source resource management system able to schedule the allocation of distributed resources such as processors, memory, disk space, and software licenses. Its features include resource reservation, job checkpointing, the implementation of the DRMAA job API and multiple scheduling algorithms, and flexible scheduling policies. It allows monitoring and controlling of jobs and queues and also provides accounting information through special plug-ins (e.g., APEL, producing CPU job accounting records). SGE is currently

Table 7.1 Resource managers and the metrics they provide

	Condor	LSF	PBS	SGE
CPU time	Yes	Yes	Yes	Yes
Run time	Yes	Yes	Yes	No
Job size	Yes	Yes	No	Yes
Disk space	Yes	No	No	No

used in the EGEE grid. However, its SGE Information Provider needs to improve its flexibility and take into account overlapping queues/virtual queues definitions.

Load Sharing Facility (LSF) [21] is a commercial resource management system based on the Platform Enterprise Grid Orchestrator (EGO). The system provides a way to orchestrate all the enterprise applications into a single cohesive system using virtualization and automation. The LSF system has flexible job scheduling policies, an advanced resource management component (i.e., capable to support checkpointing, job migration, and load balancing), a good graphical interfaces to monitor cluster functionalities and also allows easily integration with a vast majority of grid platforms. However, it is an expensive commercial product, and it is not suitable for small computing clusters.

We summarize in Table 7.1, the metrics we can obtain from these resource managers.

At this level, MonALISA provides a set of monitoring services. These services are capable of monitoring a large number of entities (hosts, services, applications, network). In fact, the system support using simultaneously several modules, which interact actively with the entities or passively listen for information, or interface with other existing monitoring tools.

The system monitors and tracks site computing clusters, applications and network links, routers, and switches. It dynamically loads modules, a capability that allows it to interface with other existing monitoring applications and tools. The core of the monitoring service is based on a multi-threaded system used to perform the many data collection tasks in parallel, independently. The modules used for collecting different sets of information, or interfacing with other monitoring tools, are dynamically loaded and executed in independent threads.

In MonALISA, a Monitoring Module is a dynamic loadable unit, which executes a procedure or runs a script/program or performs a SNMP or TL1 request, or collects a set of parameters (monitored values) by properly parsing the output of the procedure. In general, a monitoring module is a simple class, which is using a certain procedure to obtain a set of parameters and report them in a simple, standard format. Monitoring Modules can be used for pulling data and in this case, it is necessary to execute them with a predefined frequency or pushing programs (scripts), which are sending the monitoring results (via SNMP, UDP, or TCP/IP) periodically back to the Monitoring Service.

MonALISA includes modules that integrate monitor information collected from Ganglia, Lemon, MRTG, Nagios, and Spectrum [20]. To monitor the execution of jobs, it includes dedicated modules that collect data from batch systems such as LSF, Condor, PBS, and Sun Grid Engine. Any monitoring module can be dynamically loaded from the local system or from a (few) central repositories in a secure way. The functionality to dynamically load these modules from centralized sites when they are needed makes much easier to keep large monitoring systems updated and to provide new functionalities dynamically.

The collection of services available in MonALISA also include filtering and aggregation of the monitoring data, providing additional information based on several data series. They provide storage for short period of time of the monitoring information, in memory or in a local database. This way, the clients can also get a history of the monitoring information they are interested in, besides the real-time monitored events. MonALISA also allows the integration of various triggers, alerts, and actions based on the monitored information. This way, the system is capable to react immediately when abnormal behavior is detected.

The system provides web services for direct access to the monitored data, from the monitoring service. This way, local clients can get the information directly, without following the whole chain. MonALISA also provides advanced controlling using dedicated modules that allow to perform complicated actions, that cannot be taken only by the local flow of information. This way, the service can act based on monitoring information from several services at the command of a controlling client, or direct or indirect users request.

7.4.2 Handling Monitoring Data

The transmission of monitoring data events from the source to the interested parties is generally made possible using several basic models: push/pull mechanisms, data filters, periodic/aperiodic, unicast/one-to-many.

The push/pull models are the most common mechanisms, being used by a broad variety of monitoring systems. In the "Pull" approach, the data consumer is responsible with pulling the data of interest (usually from a browser or an application). In the "Push" approach, a publish/subscribe notification service mediates the interaction between the publisher and the interested consumer. In both these approaches, after an initial discovery step, the client connects directly with the data producer for receiving monitoring information. The client can further get real-time of historical events using a matching scheme for requesting or subscribing to selected measured values. The matching scheme depends on the data representation models being used.

Monitoring data requests based on a push/pull mechanism makes possible the using of the WSDL/SOAP bindings from clients or services written in other languages. The attributes of the interested monitoring values are described in WSDL and any client can create dynamically and instantiate the objects it needs for communication. However, currently, the web services technology does not provide the functionality to register as a listener and to receive the future measurements a client may want to receive. This motivates the approach of periodic vs. aperiodic monitoring data requests. These models are intensively used by monitoring engines like GridIce [1] or MonALISA as the main solution for data distribution. Although the query matching is implemented differently (GridIce uses GLUE schema for data representation, whilst MonALISA uses a proprietary regular expression predicate), the core of the dissemination engine is similar at an architectural level.

Data Filters are an alternative to the traditional push/pull model. In this case, filters insert a selection mechanism into the monitoring service, collecting for consumers only the relevant information. In order to reduce the transmission of unneeded monitoring data, these models usually include a subscription mechanism. This allows clients to select the collectors from which they are interested in receiving data instead of receiving it from every collector in the system. The consumers express their monitoring interests through a filter program, which contains information about their monitoring requests. This is similar to a subscription process aiming at an event-driven model. The monitoring services receive the monitoring demands and configure their components accordingly. This has the advantage of relieving the consumers from receiving and processing a large volume of monitoring data as it is the case in push/pull approach, which may overwhelm the consumers as well as the network links. Compared to the previous model, filters introduce a higher control on the granularity of the monitoring process by limiting the monitoring operations on observing specific system components or events. They also enhance applications' performance and reliability providing faster responses since the reaction can be instant.

The preferred solution used by various monitoring systems consists in composing the push/pull approach for data collection with data filtering. In RGMA, for example, users can easily model their requests with custom "select" queries: in order to act as a data consumer, they instantiate a remote object (agent) and invoke methods from the appropriate consumer API. The global schema includes a core set of these relations, while new relations with filtering arguments can be dynamically created and dropped by consumer and producers.

In MonALISA, clients can send several types of requests to the services: history requests, served from the service local database and subscription for new data events. Filtering is expressed using predicates written using regular expressions with a simple syntax. The general filtering and data collection model used by the vast majority of monitoring systems [25] is presented in Fig. 7.2.

New custom filters can be implemented and deployed dynamically, producing derived values that can be stored along or instead of the original values. The custom filters can be implemented to intercept received data (or particular subsets of it) and act on the values. For example, in case of monitoring the ALICE experiment [2], special filters were developed to store the names of raw data files produced by the experiment in separate database tables, while the size and count values go to the default storage structures and the standard views are used to display them. This is an example of how the data can be customary stored and accessed using the constructs available.

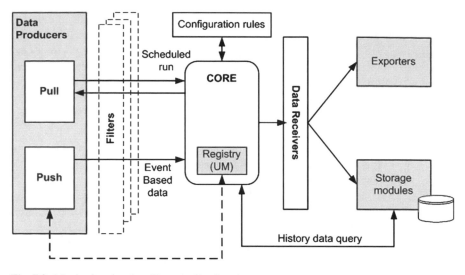

Fig. 7.2 Monitoring data handling at collection site

7.4.3   Registration and Discovery Services

Once the important monitored events are collected by sensors, their dissemination to the appropriate users or processing agents generally relies on the use of a discovery service. Its role is to discover the monitoring services and to consequently mediate the interaction between data consumers and data producers. While the former uses the service to find appropriate monitoring information sources, the latter registers with the data being provided. This can be hard to achieve in a distributed environment, where there is hard-to-find lasting statuses in case of nodes and sites. In this case, an automated resource and service discovery process must be launched at a frequency compatible with the frequency of updates on the status of the distributed system's elements.

There are several problems that make it difficult to construct a reliable registration and discovery service for such an environment. First, the system consists of users and resources highly dynamic and geographically distributed; these are connected by unreliable networking links. The resources can enter or exit the system without any notification or coordination. There are variable grouping of users and resources. In fact, there are many Virtual Organizations (VOs) involved and sometimes there is unclear the partition of the grid. They are under various security policies: the many production sites involved in a grid have their own security policies and system administration principles and procedures; a global discovery system must be efficient and not intrusive with respect to security policies and should not interfere with site local rules like logging and auditing.

One of the key concepts in case of a registration and discovery service is the concept of VO. The service should work well in environments spanning various VOs, which group together resources and users in related communities. As VOs enable sharing of resources and stress the non-locality of participants, they have an inherent dynamic nature, which has to be handled by the R&D system: VOs come and go, resources can join and leave VOs, resources can change status and fail, they have community-wide goals, and must not interfere with each other. Scalability in this context implies not only large numbers of users and independent resources, but also service dependability, ensuring as much function possible, a "graceful degradation of service" [7], tolerating partitions, and pruning failures. Although resources have discovery information (published by themselves, e.g., in the form of WSRF-based services, or collected by a separate probe, such as GridFTP), there is a need for a separate service to collect and publish this information in order not to increase the local load. This translates to some additional requirements needed by a reliable R&D system: support for community-specific discovery, specialized views and policies, scalability and replication for fault tolerance purposes. We detail how these requirements are met by some of the most common used registration and discovery services.

The Monitoring and Discovery System 4 [24] consists of a framework of web services aiming at monitoring and discovering services and resources in grids. Integrated in Globus Toolkit 4, it basically implements a standard web services-based interface to local monitoring tools and various information sources. MDS services provide query and subscription interfaces to highly heterogeneous resources data and a trigger interface configurable to take action when specific conditions are satisfied. The services included acquire their information through this extensible interface, which can be used to query WSRF services for resource property information, execute a program to acquire data, or interface with third-party monitoring systems.

MDS4 is built around a layered architecture known as a "protocol hourglass." It uses standard schemas, such as GLUE, and standard interfaces for subscription, registration, and notification. At the higher level, reside the applications that use the information from the sources the MDS4 interacts with: schedulers, portals, warning systems, etc. At the lower level, MDS4 interfaces with various information providers using a uniform interface, which translates diverse schemas into standard (whenever possible) XML schemas. Currently, it supports as information providers cluster monitors such as Ganglia, Hawkeye, Clumon, Nagios, services such as GRAM, RFT, RLS, and queuing systems, such as PBS, LSF, and Torque. The Hawkeye Information Provider gathers data about the Condor pool resources using the XML mapping of the GLUE schema and reports it to a WS GRAM service, which further publishes it as resource properties. The Ganglia information providers do the same for cluster data from resources running Ganglia. The WS GRAM is the job submission service component of GT4; its WSRF service publishes information about the local scheduler. WSRF is also used for publishing by the RFT – Reliable File Transfer service component of the GT4 and CAS – Community Authorization Services with information identifying the VO that is serves.

JINI technology [18] comes as a natural choice for use in discovery services in large-scale distributed environments. It enables service-based architectures, provides spontaneous networking (assembled into working group of objects – Federations), abstracts the distinction between hardware and software (through objects), and also provides a distributed computing infrastructure to make writing distributed programs easier. Moreover, JINI offers a Lookup Service for service finding and resolution, which makes it suitable for monitoring services registration and discovery purposes. The lookup service in JINI acts as a repository of available services, which maps interfaces indicating the functionality provided by a service to sets of objects that implement the service. In addition, descriptive entries associated with a monitoring service allow more fine-grained selection of data producer services based on some user-defined properties. The lookup service is built around a hierarchical model, as objects in a lookup service may be federated with other lookup services. The basic lookup service interface provides registration, access, update, search, and removal. The JINI discovery protocols are used to find and join group of services, which advertise their capabilities. It is based on UDP multicast and establishes a reference with lookup services; this multicast mechanism allows Jini clients and services on relatively close network segments to find each other without prior knowledge. The unicast discovery is also supported and the locator mechanism allows prior knowledge to be used to directly access a Jini lookup service, which can be used to find services of interests.

The main design issue with both JINI and MDS is their scalability. JINI was initially designed to be used in LAN settings, dependant on multicast. The infrastructure for supporting JINI communities distributed over wide area networks is poor. Solutions used in this case include P2P technology with JXTA technology, JINI gateways, or designing new protocols. For example, MonALISA adopted JINI for a fully distributed and replicated implementation of the LookUp services used by the monitor clients and sensors. In MonALISA, services are able to discover each other in the distributed environment and to be discovered by the interested clients. Each MonALISA service registers itself with a set of Lookup Services as part of one or more groups and it publishes some attributes that describe it. Consequently, any interested application can request MonALISA services based on a set of matching attributes. The registration uses a lease mechanism provided by JINI. If a service fails to renew its lease, it is removed from the LUSs and a notification is sent to all the services or other application that subscribed for such events. Remote event notification is used in this way to get a real overview of this dynamic system. Lookup services maintain replicated information, so a monitoring service has to be registered in two or more distributed lookup services, because if one fails responding, interested clients can find the services registered in the other online lookup services. Thus, the single point of failure problem can be avoided and a more reliable network for registration of services can be achieved in the distributed environment. The JINI technology used allows dynamically adding and removing Lookup Services from the system. Security is addressed by restricting services' registration based on authorized X.509 certificates.

7.5 Standards and Solutions for Representing the Monitoring Information

Each information source publishes its monitoring information using a specific format according to some schema. Due to the diversity of data producers and grid resources, which may define different schemas, important collaborative efforts are underway to define common schemas and abstract models for distributed resources. Such a schema should meet some key requirements [6]: adequate size – in order to capture all the relevant information but abstracting from all unnecessary details; flexibility – to be able to represent the heterogeneous software and resources in use; precision – as the semantics should be clearly defined; simplicity – the attributes are to be easy to understand and use; calculability – the attributes must be capable of being calculated in real systems in a relatively short time; extensibility – to allow evolution over time with as little overhead as possible. As the authors note, these properties are, to some extent, in conflict with each other, so it generally is necessary to find a reasonable compromise. This is the case with the schemas presented in the following.

The GLUE Schema [16] is an abstract data model for grid resources and their mapping to concrete schemas that can be used in grid information services; it creates a standardization framework for the publication of information about grid sites. The schema is defined using a subset of UML, in terms of objects with attributes and relations to other objects. Although there are several mappings into LDAP, relational (R-GMA), XML, and Condor ClassAds, these implementations are significantly different and impose constraints on the possible structure of the schema. The schema specification presents a description of core grid resources at the conceptual level by defining an information model that is an abstraction of the real world into constructs that can be represented in computer systems (objects, properties, behavior, and relationships). Thus, the proposed information model is not tied to any particular implementation and can be profitably used to exchange information among different knowledge domains. From a high level, we distinguish four categories of the schema, in which parameters are grouped. The GlueSite is an administrative concept used to aggregate a set of services and resources usually installed and managed by the same set of administrators. The GlueSite can further aggregate GlueServices (a general representation of a service, network, etc.), Storage Elements (attributes and objects related to storage systems in the original schema, now enhanced with a complex protocol [28] to manage large-scale grid-enabled storage), and Computing Elements (defined to map a queue in a batching system enhanced with grouping capabilities as the VOView).

GLUE schema is used by the MDS information model, which organizes information into well-defined collections – each entry representing an instance of some type of object. There are several projects that are participating in the GLUE schema activity: EGEE, LCG, OSG, Globus, NorduGrid, GridICE. While its main advantages are the collection of all GLUE information, plotted in a useful way and giving both a detailed and a general overview of the grid, the notification service and the support for custom graphs, a significant drawback is its close relation to the schema as statistics are not present in the GLUE schema and, therefore, are not analyzed by GridIce. However, the experience of the schema with other grids has proven that evolution of the grid technology itself also implies changes in the schema. Current efforts are now underway toward a major upgrade of the GLUE schema (2.0 specification is in planning), which should unify all relevant modeling efforts in the grid context and provide a firm foundation for grid interoperability.

As the GLUE schema, the Common Information Model (CIM) [14] is also an object-oriented information model. However, CIM is more complex, aiming at standardization for publishing IT environment information and specification for all available components. It was proposed by the Distributed Management Task Force (DMTF) [14] as a management standard and has the advantage of being user-extensible. CIM models both physical attributes and logical abstractions as users, dependencies, administration policies, and hardware capabilities. Like GLUE schema, CIM has different format implementations, including xmlCIM, the representation in XML format used by the DMTF. The widespread use of CIM is mainly caused by its possibility to express relations such as inheritance or other dependencies as opposed to flat information models expressed, for instance, in Management Information Base (MIB). Indeed, relevant CIM information is hold by classes organized in a hierarchy-based on inheritance. Instances can relate through an association model, containing regular and referential properties. Hence, the key innovations of CIM compared to other information models [30] are: reduced complexity of the models based on the performed abstraction and classification of the problem domain defining high level and fundamental concepts, common characteristics and their relationships as baseline for the specific objects; utilization of object-oriented concepts such as object inheritance or the use of associations to depict relationships between the objects; use of semantic annotations of the associations allowing to express common characteristics and features; definition of abstract behavior independent of the underlying hardware; common model across the whole management environment and potentially custom defined other problem spaces.

These features motivate the current research [13] on making CIM even more accessible and providing it a query service for resource management information in grid systems. The efforts are toward integrating CIM with MDS4. This involves publishing the CIM information on the MDS4 and the development of a query engine that supports queries with arbitrary navigation depth on a CIM instance tree. This approach benefits applications needing structured and interrelated information models as the one ensured by CIM. It also makes possible the specification of complex expressions through the query implementation, which could not be formulated on other information models, like GLUE, without ad hoc code, as authors observe.

Despite the effort to integrate these schemas into monitoring implementations, practice shows that some developers of such systems prefer using particular schemas. This has the advantages of easy extensibility and flexibility in mapping to specific application constrains. Nagios [29] is a system and network monitoring application built around a central core providing scheduling and using plug-ins to access resources. It is designed to be extensible and easy customizable hence plug-ins can be used to create user-defined metrics (using virtually any language available). The Simple Network Management Protocol (SNMP) monitors and manages the network components. It maintains a set of management information following the specific format described in a Management Information Base (MIB). The information is held in a hierarchical manner with unique identifiers. However, for very large MIBs, performance quickly degrades. In MonALISA, the system has the ability to transport and store different types of monitoring data; this data is user-definable, so any service user can easily implement its own data type, extending a base object: MLData. The new defined data only has to be self-describing so that the database engine can store it in transparent manner.

7.6 Visualization of Monitoring Information

The highest level of a monitoring system consists in the presentation layer, at which the monitoring information is visualized by users in formats that meet their application requirements. Such a visual interface should be able to cope with the high rate of data updates involved by a real-time monitoring system, the large amounts of data produced, and with the various levels of abstraction needed for both global and particular detailed views. The main techniques for displaying monitoring information identified in [22] are: textual data presentation (which involves simple text with special format rendering the monitored information), time series diagrams (the most commonly used in web interfaces), and animations. Recently, new chart types have emerged with higher expressivity: pies, multiple axes charts, spider graphs, bars for real-time information, geo map monitoring information (monitoring data rendered on maps to highlight the locations of the captured data), flash views. However, no single view is always sufficient for monitoring purposes, so more often, in various monitoring systems, one can find combinations of these presentation techniques.

In Ganglia, for example, the web interface is built around Apache HTTPD server in PHP and uses presentation templates that make the interface easily customizable. It presents an overview of all nodes within the grid or cluster, and also detailed individual charts both in textual and graphical views. The interface uses the RRDTool – Round Robin Database Tool [26], a storage and trend graphing tool. It defines fixed-size databases that hold data of various configurable granularities. Thus, it enables high-performance data logging and graphing systems for time series data due to the constant and predictable data storage size and the automatic data consolidation over time. This is achieved through the use of various Round Robin Archives (RRA), which hold data points at decreasing levels of granularity. Multiple data points from a more granular RRA are automatically consolidated and added to a courser RRA.

In GridIce, the highest layer of the architecture is the Presentation Service, a web-based interface designed according to a role-based strategy, which renders different views depending on the type of consumer: Grid Operations Center (GOC) view, targeting at the whole set of grid resources managed by a GOC; the Site view, whose target is the set of resources belonging to a certain site; and the Virtual Organization view, whose target is the whole set of grid resources that can be accessed by users of a certain VO.

In MonALISA the overall status of the dispersed systems being monitored is provided by either a GUI client or through specialized web portals, called Repository. A similar technique as the one used in Ganglia is also being used by the MonALISA Repository. In this case, data is written in the database only at the end of an aggregation interval, using asynchronous operations to minimize the impact of I/O operations over the main monitoring tasks. Upon request, the system automatically selects the most appropriate storage structure, depending on the time interval and the number of data points requested.

For example, a yearly report generated by the repository takes data from the structure having the lowest resolution, while looking in detail over a few hours around the time of an event that happened a week ago will use the highest resolution structure.

If a single structure cannot cover the entire request length, then data from multiple structures can be aggregated to form the response. A data reduction scheme like this one has the advantage of conserving disk space while providing enough detail for recent events.

The interactive clients in MonALISA have the role of representing, in a human readable and viewable form, the information gathered from several monitoring services. Using the interactive clients, the user has an intuitive graphical and global interface of the states of the distributed monitored systems. For this purpose, MonALISA provides several ways to visualize the data (Fig. 7.3).

7.7 Using the Monitoring Tools for Control and Optimization: Case Studies

The main purpose of a distributed monitoring infrastructure is the ability to invest the system with control capabilities and some degree of automated management, as the large amounts of data and vast resources harnessed by these applications make the task of administration only through user interaction not a trivial one. The goal is to develop new building blocks based on the existing infrastructure and using the collected monitoring information to control remote resources and applications in a standardized way. The Resource Management Systems are the most likely to use monitoring information to perform their functionalities, but the application field is not limited to them: anomaly detection, diagnosis, pattern detection, predictions, automated actions, and alarms use the information from monitoring services to perform a distributed control. In the following, we present several case studies of using the monitoring data to make control decisions in MonALISA.

7.7.1 Network Monitoring and Management

Network monitoring is vital to ensure proper network operations over time, and MonALISA was successfully used to provide its monitoring services to control a vast majority of the data-intensive processing tasks used by the LHC experiments. In order to build a coherent set of network management services, it is very important to collect, in near real-time, information about the network traffic volume and its quality, and analyze the major flows and the topology of connectivity.

Access to both real-time and historical data, as provided by MonALISA, also is important for developing services able to predict the usage pattern, to aid in efficiently allocating resources globally across a set of network links. A large set of MonALISA monitoring modules has been developed to collect specific network information (SNMP, TL1, ICMP) or to interface it with existing monitoring tools (NetFlow, sFlow, MRTG, and Nagios). These modules have been field-proven to function with a very high level of reliability over the last few years.

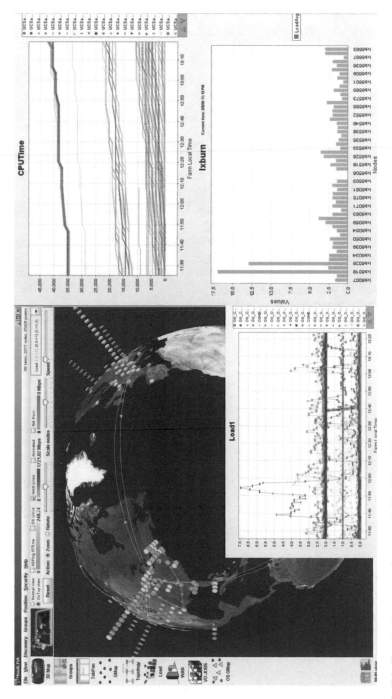

Fig. 7.3 The visual representations provided by MonALISA

MonALISA is used, for example, to provide reliable, real-time monitoring in case of the USLHCNet infrastructure [10]. In each center part of this infrastructure (GVA, AMS, CHI, NYC), a MonALISA service monitors all the links, the network equipment, and the peering with other networks. These services keep locally the history of all the measurements. A global aggregation, for long-term history, is also kept in a MonALISA repository. Dedicated TL1 modules for various optical switches were also developed to collect specific information on topology, dynamic circuits, and operational status.

MonALISA is used to monitor the status of all WAN links and peering connections. The repository analyzes the status information from all the distributed measurements, for each segment, to generate reliable status information. Measurements are done every approximately 45 s, and the full history is kept in the repository database. The system allows to transparently change the way a WAN is operated and is able to keep consistent history. Figure 7.4 shows the panel that allows analyzing the links availability for any time interval.

The MonALISA framework is used to construct, in near real-time, the network topology for different types of technologies currently used in the High Energy Physics infrastructure. For the routed networks, MonALISA is able to construct the overall topology of a complex wide area network, based on the delay on each network segment determined by tracepath-like measurements from each site to all other sites. The combined information from all the sites allows one to detect asymmetric routing or links with performance problems. For global applications, such as distributing large data files to many grid sites, this information is used to define the set of optimized replication paths.

7.7.2   Monitoring ALICE Distributed Computing Environment

The ALICE collaboration, consisting of 86 institutes, grouped together specialists interested in the LHC experiments at CERN to study physics using a large-scale distributed environments for processing the tremendous amounts of data. The project is strongly dependent on a distributed computing environment to perform its physics program. The computing centers around the world provide many different computing platforms, operating systems flavors, and storage solutions. The software and operating conditions are rapidly changing and evolving. In these conditions, MonALISA is used to monitor the global state of the grid down to the individual building blocks, both hardware and software. It traces the resource usage, software performance, and, in fact, any event of interest for the developers, operators, and users.

According to the ALICE Computing Model, each site member of the collaboration provides a machine dedicated to running VO-specific services [5]. The distributed computing infrastructure is controlled by AliEn (ALIce Environment), a software package that has two main sets of services: central services that deal with job submission, file catalogue, scheduled transfers, users, authentication, and so on, and site services that manage local site resources (jobs, storage, and software packages).

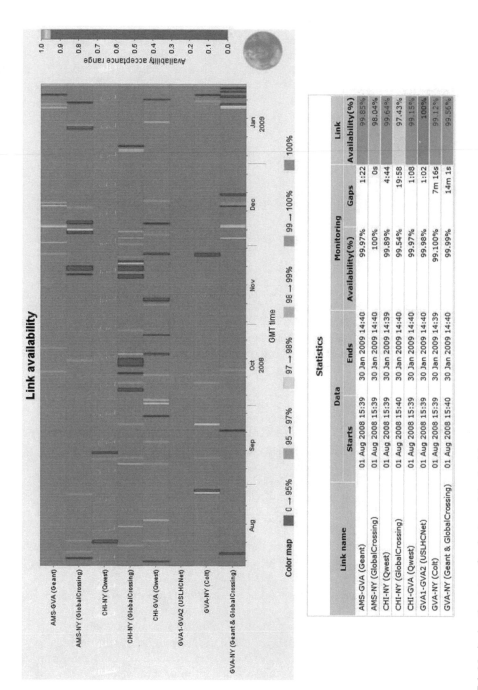

Fig. 7.4 Monitoring the status of major trans-Atlantic links

196 C. Dobre

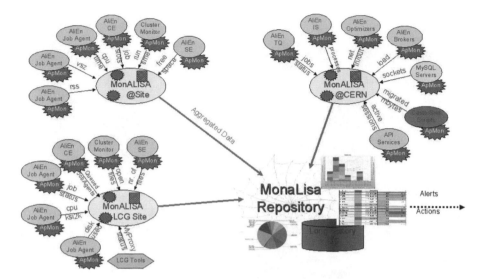

Fig. 7.5 MonALISA service on each VoBox

A MonALISA service instance is installed on each VoBox (Fig. 7.5) and on each of the machines running central services. These services are used to collect monitoring information from each active job, transfer, or service, and make available to any client the information in raw or aggregated form. For example, the full information about each job is available on demand, but values like number of jobs in each state or total CPU power consumed by all the jobs running on that site are also available. AliEn components (central services, such as the Task Queue, Information Service, Optimizers, and APIService; site services, such as Cluster Monitor, Computing and Storage Elements, and Job Agents) send monitoring information to the MonALISA service at the site. The AliEn Job Agents send information about their status (such as requesting job, running job, finishing). Other, non-AliEn services are also monitored using a small external ApMon-based script.

The overall status page from the MonALISA repository, shown in Fig. 7.6, presents the status of all services running on a site. It is also the starting point for expert debugging of a problem. The experts can immediately see which component is not working properly and what the cause of the failure is. In addition, automatic e-mail notification is sent to a pre-configured list of people (individual for every site) when a service failure is detected.

Another monitoring module is used to perform simple tests that check the status and availability of the grid middleware services and authorization credentials (grid proxies), needed to interact with these services. In the ALICE system, jobs are executed within Job Agents, which are also enabled to send monitoring information to the configured MonALISA service. They send data about the current job status (such as started, running, saving, etc.) and about the resource usage of the job itself (e.g., how much memory, disk space, CPU time, CPU SpecInt units the job consumes). Nodes where critical AliEn services are running are also monitored to assure an immediate detection of a service failure or other critical events.

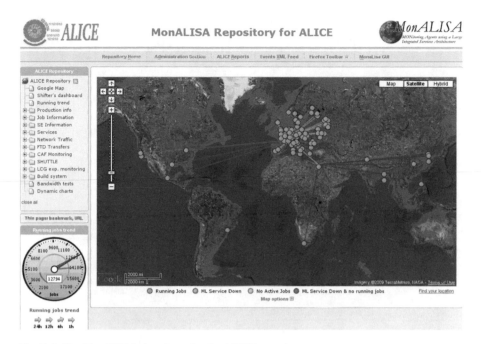

Fig. 7.6 The MonALISA repository for the ALICE experiment

AliEn Job Agents, like all the other AliEn services, read their configuration from a central LDAP directory. In the site service configuration, there is an entry for the MonALISA service that should receive the monitoring information from all the services and the jobs running in that site. The MonALISA services running on each site comprise several monitoring modules that receive the local monitoring data and an Agent Filter that aggregates it. The Agent Filter receives and aggregates the information collected by the monitoring modules, for example, in the form of how many jobs are running in each of the possible states, what is the total CPU usage on this site, what is the average memory usage of the jobs, how many agents are currently waiting to receive a job, how many queued agents were submitted in the batch queuing system.

Following the model for the possible status for AliEn jobs, the monitoring system provides various views of these job categories: site views, user views, and task queue. In site views, one can plot summary retrospective and near real-time job or job agent information for each site. Visualizations at various aggregation levels of the usage for the set of resources available to members are also available: consumed CPU time for ALICE jobs, total CPU SPECint2000 units, Wall time, jobs efficiency in time (CPU time/Wall time), and SPECint2000 units (CPU SI2K/Wall SI2K). The used CPU power in SI2K is normalized taking into account the node's parameters (processor type, cache size, core frequency). Network traffic is also monitored (incoming/outgoing), as well as key system parameters: memory usage by the jobs at each site, virtual memory usage, system memory usage, opened files, sizes of the working directories, disk and CPU usage. An example of site view is shown in Fig. 7.7.

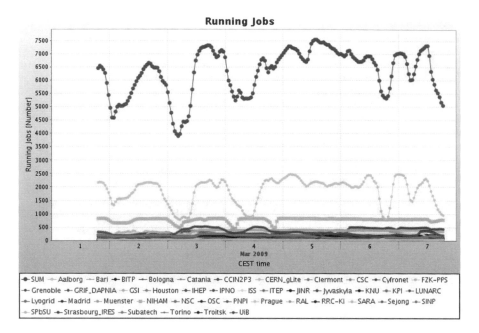

Fig. 7.7 Running jobs statistics from the ALICE MonALISA Repository

The chart presents the average number of running jobs at each site for a week. The user can select from the interface the sites of interest for detailed view, as well as the time interval of the plot, the representation model (series, stacked areas, pie charts). The system also allows adding operational annotations for specific events relevant to the currently plot data sets.

Using the monitoring information received from sites, the repository can be instructed to automatically take actions based on simple politics. The simplest action is to send an alert (MonALISA currently includes protocols for e-mail and instant messenger) when something has stopped working (an AliEn site or central service, storage element, critical machines, and so on). From the web interface, the user can subscribe to receive notifications in each category and (in some cases) for each particular site or for all sites.

Another kind of automated action is maintenance of central services load balancing. The load balancing is DNS-based, with the repository updating the CERN DNS servers with the list of IP addresses where various central services are available to service remote site services/jobs/users, etc. The lists are dynamically generated, so newly added services that pass the functional tests are automatically added to the load balancing, while non-responding or overloaded services are immediately removed. So this function not only maintains the load-balancing, but also protects the central services from a flood of requests.

The repository is also responsible for the MonteCarlo data production [2]. By continuously monitoring the number of queued jobs in the system and reacting when the number goes below a threshold, new production jobs are automatically submitted in AliEn and jobs finishing in various error states are resubmitted for execution. The jobs to be executed are taken from a list of production requests made according to the relative priority between the requests and keeping track of the number of events that were produced for a given job type.

From this central point, the site services are also controlled. By an SSL channel established between the repository and each remote service, failing AliEn services are automatically restarted, but with additional constraints like verifying that all the central services are functional. This feature, combined with e-mail alerts sent to site administrators and grid operators when problems cannot be automatically solved, has improved a lot, the overall availability of the system.

7.8 Conclusion

In this chapter, we presented a set of models and requirements that describe the monitoring process in large-scale distributed environments. We identified a set of core components (production, processing, dissemination, presentation of monitoring information) and discussed their implementations and the issues raised. These components may describe a layered model with data production as the lowest level and the presentation on top of other layers. However, as presented, current monitoring systems may perform these activities with some restrictions or additional features, in different places and various interactions in order to meet specific monitoring requirements.

The presented issues were detailed in analogy with case studies learned while implementing one of the most complex monitoring frameworks, capable of running and already being used in production in several of the largest grid systems world-wide, MonALISA. This monitoring framework is one of the most complex platforms, which offers a large set of monitoring services and supports resource usage accounting, optimization, and automated actions.

The MonALISA services currently deployed are used by the HEP community to monitor computing resources, running jobs and applications, different grid services, and network traffic. The system is used to monitor detailed information on how the jobs are submitted to different systems, the resources consumed, and how the execution is progressing in real-time. It also records errors or component failures during this entire process. MonALISA and its APIs are also used for the CMS dashboard, and by all the job submission tools for analysis and production jobs.

As of this writing, more than 350 MonALISA services are running throughout the world. These services monitor more than 20,000 servers, and thousands of concurrent jobs. More than 1.5 million parameters are currently monitored in near real-time with an aggregate update rate of approximately 15,000 parameters per second.

This information also is used in a variety of higher-level services that provide optimized grid job-scheduling services, dynamically optimized connectivity among the EVO reflectors, and the best available end-to-end network path for large file transfers. Global MonALISA repositories are used by many communities to aggregate information from many sites, to properly organize them for the users and to keep long-term histories. During the last year, the entire repository system served more than 15 million user's requests.

References

1. Aiftimiei, C., Andreozzi, S., Cuscela, G., Donvito, G., Dudhalkar, V., Fantinel, S., Fattibene, E., Maggi, G., Misurelli, G., Pierro, A.: Recent evolutions of GridICE: a monitoring tool for grid systems. In: Proceedings of the 2007 Workshop on Grid Monitoring, Boston (2007)
2. ALICE Website: Retrieved from http://aliceinfo.cern.ch (2010)
3. Anderson, D.: SETI@Home Peer-To-Peer: Harnessing the Benefits of a Disruptive Technology. O'Reilly, Sebastopol (2001)
4. Aydt, R., Smith, W., Swany, M., Taylor, V., Tierney, B., Wolski, R.: A grid monitoring architecture. Retrieved from http://www-didc.lbl.gov/GGF-PERF/GMA-WG/papers/GWD-GP-16-3.pdf (2001)
5. Bagnasco, S., Cerello, P., Barbera, R., Buncic, P., Carminati, F., Saiz, P.: AliEn – EDG Interoperability in ALICE. In: Computing in High Energy and Nuclear Physics, La Jolla (2003)
6. Burke, S., Andreozzi, S., Field, L.: Experiences with the GLUE information schema in the LCG/EGEE production grid. In: International Conference on Computing in High Energy and Nuclear Physics. J. Phys. Conf. Ser. **119**, 062019 (2008)
7. Clifford, B.: Globus monitoring and discovery. In: Proceedings of GlobusWORLD, Argonne (2005)
8. Condor: Project Official Homepage. Retrieved from http://www.cs.wisc.edu/condor (2008)
9. Cooke, A.J., Gray, G., Ma, L., Nutt, W., Magowan, J., Oevers, M., Taylor, P., Byrom, R., Field, L., Hicks, S., Leake, J., Soni, M., Wilson, A., Cordenonsi, R., Cornwall, R., Djaoui, A., Fisher, S., Podhorszki, N., Coghlan, B., Kenny, S., O'Callaghan, D.: R-GMA: An information integration system for grid monitoring. In: Proceedings of the 11th International Conference on Cooperative Information Systems, Catania, pp. 462–481 (2003)
10. Costan, A., Dobre, C., Cristea, V., Voicu, R.: A monitoring architecture for high-speed networks in large scale distributed collaborations. In: Proceedings of the 7th International Symposium on Parallel and Distributed Computing, Krakow, pp. 409–416 (2008)
11. Cristea, V., Dobre, C., Pop, F. (eds.): Large-Scale Distributed Computing and Applications – Models and Trends. IGI Global, Hershey (2010)
12. Czajkowski, K., Kesselman, C., Fitzgerald, S., Foster, I.: Grid information services for distributed resource sharing. In: Proceedings of the 10th IEEE International Symposium on High Performance Distributed Computing, (HPDC'01), San Francisco, pp. 181 (2001)
13. Diaz, I., Fernandez, G., Martinm, M.J., Gonzalez, P., Tourino, J.: Integrating the common information model with MDS4. In: Proceedings of the 2008 9th IEEE/ACM international Conference on Grid Computing, Washington, DC, pp. 198–303 (2008)
14. Distributed Management Task Force, Inc. Common Information Model (CIM) standards: Retrieved from http://www.dmtf.org/standards/cim (2008)
15. Feng, H., Misra, V., Rubenstein, D.: PBS: A unified priority-based scheduler. In: Proceedings of the 2007 ACM SIGMETRICS international Conference on Measurement and Modeling of Computer Systems, San Diego, pp. 203–214 (2007)

16. Glue Schema Website: Retrieved from http://www.globus.org/toolkit/mds/glueschemalink. html (2010)
17. Hawkeye Official Website: Retrieved from http://www.cs.wisc.edu/condor/hawkeye (2004)
18. JINI Website: Retrieved from http://www.jini.org (2010)
19. Legrand, I.C., Newman, H.B., Voicu, R., Cirstoiu, C., Grigoras, C., Toarta, M., Dobre, C.: MonALISA: An Agent Based, Dynamic Service System to Monitor, Control and Optimize Grid based Applications. CHEP04, Interlaken (2004)
20. Legrand, I.C., Newman, H.B., Voicu, R., Cirstoiu, C., Grigoras, C., Dobre, C., Muraru, A., Costan, A., Dediu, M., Stratan, C.: MonALISA: An agent based dynamic service system to monitor, control and optimize distributed systems. Comput. Phys. Commun. **180**(12), 2472–2498 (2009)
21. Lumb, I., Smith, C.: Scheduling attributes and platform LSF. In: Nabrzyski, J., Schopf, J.M., Weglarz, J. (eds.) Grid Resource Management: State of the Art and Future Trends, pp. 171–182. Kluwer, Boston (2004)
22. Mansouri-Samani, M., Sloman, M.: Monitoring distributed systems. In: Sloman, M. (ed.) Network and Distributed Systems Management, pp. 303–347. Addison-Wesley Longman, Boston (1994)
23. Massie, M.L., Chun, B.N., Culler, D.E.: The ganglia distributed monitoring system: Design, implementation, and experience. Parallel Comput. **30**, 817–840 (2004)
24. MDS4 Website (2010) The GT4 monitoring and discovery system. Retrieved from http://www. globus.org/toolkit/mds
25. MonALISA Official Website: Retrieved from http://monalisa.caltech.edu (2010)
26. RRDTool Website: Retrieved from http://oss.oetiker.ch/rrdtool (2010)
27. SGE Website: Retrieved from http://www.sun.com/software/sge (2009)
28. SRM Website: SRM: Storage Resource Manager. Retrieved from http://sdm.lbl.gov/srm-wg/ documents.html (2010)
29. Velt, S.: Neues vom schutzheiligen: Nagios in version 3.0 freigegeben. Technical report, IX (2008)
30. Wesner, S.: Integrated Management Framework for Dynamic Virtual Organizations. Höchstleistungsre-chenzentrum, Universität Stuttgart. Retrieved from http://elib.uni-stuttgart. de/opus/volltexte/2009/3868/pdf/disswesner_final_as_printed.pdf (2008)
31. Zanikolas, S., Sakellariou, R.: A taxonomy of grid monitoring systems. Future Gener. Comput. Syst. **21**, 163–188 (2005)
32. Zhang, X., Freschl, J.L., Schopf, J.M.: Scalability analysis of three monitoring and information systems: MDS2, R-GMA, and Hawkeye. J. Parallel Distrib. Comput. **67**(8), 883–902 (2007)

Part III
Grid Services and Middleware

Chapter 8
Service Level Agreements for Job Control in Grid and High-Performance Computing

Roland Kübert

Abstract Service Level Agreements (SLAs) are electronic contracts that are used to describe service levels for a plethora of tasks and situations, regardless of them being consumed offline or online. SLAs are being investigated already for a long time in the area of grid computing and, as well, by classical High-Performance Computing (HPC) providers. Most often, these investigations are either only on a high logical level above or at the middleware or on a low physical level below the middleware. In the first case, components are at best placed in the middleware layer but are not directly communicating with lower level resources; in the second case, SLAs are only used below the middleware and are not visible above. This work presents an approach for a solution to job submission and scheduling, called job control, using SLAs as long-term contracts in an integrated fashion across layers.

8.1 Introduction

On high-performance computing resources, job scheduling is still realized in most cases through simple batch queues, for example, OpenPBS [4] or TORQUE [7]. Submitted jobs are queued, possibly in different queues, and a scheduler selects jobs to run from the given queues; this can happen using different algorithms, for example, the simple First-Come-First-Served (FCFS) where jobs that are taken from the highest priority queue in the order in they were put in and, only once there are no jobs left in a high-priority queue, lower priority queues are emptied.

On job submission, parameters can be specified as well, like the number of desired CPUs, the maximum walltime or the maximum runtime on all processors of

R. Kübert (✉)
High Performance Computing Center Stuttgart (HLRS),
Nobelstraße 19, Hochstleistungsrechenzentrum, Stuttgart 70569, Germany
e-mail: kuebert@hlrs.de

N.P. Preve (ed.), *Grid Computing: Towards a Global Interconnected Infrastructure*,
Computer Communications and Networks, DOI 10.1007/978-0-85729-676-4_8,
© Springer-Verlag London Limited 2011

the job. OpenPBS, for example, sorts jobs per default by walltime, maximum run time on all CPUs, and maximum run time on any single CPU. Except requesting special nodes or queues, there is no further possibility for the user to specify requirements for his job. This can be augmented by the use of advanced reservation, which enables users to precise start and end times, but this leads to a fragmented schedule where special algorithms are needed to fill the resulting holes.

The fact that there are only few functional parameters that can be specified when submitting jobs and that there is basically no way for the user to know how the parameters are honored runs contrary to the fact that more and more interactions in distributed systems are described using specific Quality-of-Service (QoS) guarantees. These guarantees are most often stated in service level agreements (SLAs), mutual treatments between parties which specify service levels, rights, obligations, bonuses, and penalties for all parties. Service level agreements are used for defining miscellaneous interactions and can be used to enhance job scheduling in the Grid and High-Performance Computing (HPC) area.

As SLAs may describe quite many diverse parameters to be taken into account, new algorithms for job scheduling respecting the assured service levels need to be developed and integrated with middlewares and low-level resource managers and schedulers. This allows the user to request specific fine-grained parameters through service level agreements and results in the provider changing the main task of its scheduling system to satisfying the service levels.

8.2   Background and Related Work

This chapter deals with the intersection of three different fields: (1) Service Level Agreements (SLAs), (2) Job submission, and (3) Scheduling and SLA management. This section shortly introduces these areas and gives information about relevant work that has taken place in each of these.

8.2.1   Service Level Agreement Languages

Service level agreements have originated from the telecommunications industry but have found broad uptake in diverse fields where they are used offline or online. Nowadays, SLAs are, for example, used in describing the characteristics of IT Help Desks [28] or call centers [38], defining metrics for IT outsourcing [16], provisioning in optical networks [14], web and e-mail hosting [23], or more recently, Cloud Computing [1, 27]. Even patents have been issued regarding the use of service level agreements [13, 26].

The diverse scenarios in which SLAs are used show that there probably can be no single definition that is valid for service level agreements in all cases. The more specific a definition is, the more it is focused on one area. An accepted base definition seems to be that SLAs are contracts between a service provider and a customer, specifying details of the provided service, where details can be both functional – what the service does – and nonfunctional – how the service does what it does. SLAs are seen both as contracts in their own right as well as subcontracts of greater framework contracts [5, 25].

In IT, SLAs are mostly regarded as subcontracts. This makes the usage of SLAs easier, as contractual aspects need to be only treated briefly as there is already a contract in place that is assumed to take care of legal and financial issues. The SLA itself can thus be made more concise and can concentrate on aspects directly related to the service provisioning and consumption.

There have been various proposals for the syntax of SLAs where the three most prominent ones are IBM's Web Service Level Agreement (WSLA) [20], the Open Grid Forum's Web Services Agreement Specification (WS-Agreement) [2], and the SLA language (SLAng) [21]. WSLA's main usage is for checking the adherence of web services to service guarantees through monitoring; it allows the specification of performance metrics, performance targets, and actions to be performed when performance is not met. WS-Agreement provides a more generic framework for service level agreements, defining only high-level content and leaving most of the input to domain-specific extensions. On the one hand, this leaves users a great degree of freedom in designing their structure but makes the interchange with others users more prone to error, as interoperability is not likely to be found easily. SLAng proposes a syntax for the definition of service level agreements that can be used to describe end-to-end quality of service and complex agreements between various kinds of services, therefore going into much more detail in its specification than WS-Agreement.

The implementation of electronic SLAs depends on the framework in which they exist and on the requirements the syntax needs to fill. If SLAs are just subcontracts of a broader framework, they can have a minimalistic structure, focusing on the expression of all technically relevant aspects, referencing the framework contract. Needless to say, even in this form SLAs need to be nonambiguously matchable to both the framework contract and the participating parties, but this task can be achieved by employing a suitable communications framework, which ensures the integrity and nonrepudiation of messages. Having a framework contract, a legally valid document between all parties, that governs aspects broader than the scope of the SLAs themselves as well as how and when agreements can be formed removes the burden of using SLAs themselves as legally binding contracts, an, up to now, seldom investigated possibility.

8.2.2   Service Level Agreements for Job Submission and Scheduling

In the area of job submission and job scheduling, the concrete syntax of SLAs is often not considered. This seems logical, as most work deals with SLAs as per-job contracts that solely define quality of service requirements or parameters specified per job. All of the previously mentioned syntaxes can be used to specify parameters for job submission, but service level agreements do not need to take one of the forms presented before but can be of any structure that fits the needs of all involved parties. A simple, self-defined schema might therefore be sufficient and easier to handle than more complex schemata whose features are not used at all.

The investigation of SLAs solely under the aspect of job submission is rarely done. One prominent exception to this rule is presented by Sakellariou and Yarmolenko in [33], who analyze the flexibility of the WS-Agreement specification in regard to job submission and come to the conclusion that enhancement to the specification could lead to fewer negotiation overheads and less failed agreements. The fact that job submission on its own is often not considered may come from the fact that publications discussing job scheduling also (at least briefly) deal with the procedure of how the job is submitted. Additionally, it seems that the Job Submission Description Language (JSDL) [3] is a language for describing the requirements of computational jobs for submission to resources, particularly in Grid environments and it is widely accepted as it is usually referred to for job submission.

While the area of SLAs for job submission is only sparsely treated, the investigation of SLAs for the scheduling of jobs is of more research interest, as much more publications regarding this area can be found. There are various approaches to the usage of service level agreements for job scheduling. While they differ in many respects (detail of the presentation, assumed parameters, implementation level, etc.), they all share the fact that they treat SLAs as agreements on a per-job basis. That means that, for each job to be submitted, a unique SLA is established before the job can be submitted.

Yarmolenko and Sakellariou in [40], after having identified the fact that SLA-based scheduling is not researched as intensively as it could be, investigate the influence of different heuristics on the scheduling of parallel jobs. SLAs are identified as a means to provide more flexibility, to increase resource utilization, and to fulfill a larger number of user requests. Parameters either influence timing (earliest job start time, latest job finish time, job execution time, number of CPU nodes) or pricing. They present a theoretical analysis of scheduling heuristics and how they are influenced by SLA parameters; however, they do not investigate how the heuristics might be integrated into an already existing set-up. The same authors identify, in a later work, the need to provide greater flexibility in service levels offered by high performance, parallel, supercomputing resources [34]. In this work, they present an abstract architecture for job scheduling on the Grid and come to the conclusion that new algorithms are necessary for efficient scheduling in order to satisfy SLA terms but that little research has been published in this area. MacLaren et al. in [24] have led to a similar conclusion, stating the necessity for SLAs in an architecture supporting efficient job scheduling on grids.

Yeo and Buyya in [41] have investigated SLAs that contain a job's deadline as a parameter and are used for deadline-constrained job admission control in a cluster. The main findings were that these SLAs depend strongly on accurate run time estimates, but it is difficult to obtain good run time estimates from job traces. Djemame et al. in [9] have presented a way of using SLAs for risk assessment and management, thereby increasing the reliability of Grids. The proposed solution is discussed in the scope of three use cases: a single-job scenario, a workflow scenario with a broker that is only active at negotiation time, and a workflow scenario with a broker that is responsible at run time. It is claimed that risk assessment leads to fewer SLA violations, thus increasing profit, and to increased trust into Grid technology. Dumitrescu et al. in [12] have explored a specific type of SLAs, usage SLAs, for scheduling of Grid-specific workloads using the bioinformatics BLAST tool with the GRUBER scheduling framework. Usage SLAs are characterized by four parameters: a user's Virtual Organization (VO) membership, group membership, required processor time, and required disk space.

Raimondi et al. in [30] have described how it is possible to monitor the timeliness, reliability, and request throughput of web services at run time. Monitors can automatically be derived from SLAs using a software module. SLAs are, in this case, used to describe web services whose main attributes are timeliness, reliability, and throughput conditions.

Sandholm [35] described the general requirements of an accounting-driven computational Grid, the Swedish national Grid, and how the Grid can be made aware of SLAs. It is presented how the architecture can be extended with SLAs and it is stated the greatest benefit would be achieved by insisting on formally signed agreements.

A comprehensive overview of resource management systems and the application of SLAs for resource management and scheduling is given by Seidel et al. in [36]. The main summary is that service level agreements will lead to increased interoperability.

8.2.3   Service Level Agreement Management Frameworks

Scheduling takes places on a low layer, the resource layer. This layer is directly related with the distribution of jobs on Grid and HPC resources. The client does not communicate directly with the resource layer but uses the middleware layer, which provides high-level functionality. For example, the ability to negotiate service level agreements and to submit jobs in reference to SLAs, as it is illustrated in Fig. 8.1.

The approach to the management of SLAs on this layer is very diverse and usually supports the whole lifetime of an SLA (once again, service level agreements are regarded as on a per-job or per-task basis and not as long-time contracts). There is no accepted standard and various research projects have developed their own service level agreement management framework.

The NextGRID project, which aimed at the generation of an architecture for next-generation Grids, developed a framework for SLA management that supported discovery, negotiation, and management of service level agreements [29]. The aim in NextGRID was to not let the client deal with SLAs in their normal, machine-readable way but to let the customer specify business objectives, requirements, and preferences on a higher level, for example, providing choices like "gold," "silver," and "bronze," which are then mapped to service levels. Transactions around the establishment

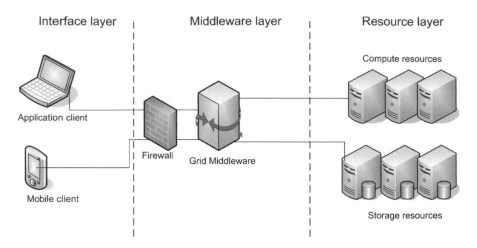

Fig. 8.1 An example of a three-layered grid middleware architecture

of an SLA were automated as far as possible. As NextGRID was mainly concerned with the architecture level (there were, of course, proof-of-concept implementations), its SLA management framework is only realized on a high layer.

The Highly Predictable Cluster for Internet-Grids [17] project aimed at developing an SLA-aware resource management system to allow resource sharing adhering to service levels in Virtual Organizations (VOs). HPC4U uses a planning-based approach, in contrast to queue-based approaches that are normally used; planning-based approaches do not only consider the current time but also preassign waiting jobs. SLAs are established through a multiphase negotiation on a per-job basis.

A Grid Usage Service Level Agreement-based BrokERing Infrastructure (GRUBER), presented by Dimitrescu et al. presents an architecture as well as a toolkit for the specification of SLAs for resource usage and enforcement [10]. Properties for a job are inferred out of the membership the submitter has in groups and virtual organizations. The SLAs do not contain quality of service agreements but only basic job information: processor time, permanent storage or network bandwidth resources, and the user's membership in groups and virtual organizations. DI-GRUBER enhanced GRUBER to work in a distributed fashion and mainly analyzed the performance of distributed decision making [11].

IRMOS (Interactive Real-time Multimedia Applications on Service-Oriented Infrastructures) investigates the usage of service level agreements for the provisioning of real-time capable services over a service-oriented infrastructure [19]. IRMOS uses a combination of Infrastructure as a Service (IaaS) and Platform as a Service (PaaS) to separate high-level and low-level requirements and to enable the client to not having to deal with low-level parameters. To this intent, two interlinked service level agreements are used in order to not disclose unwanted information to parties by including all parties in a contract.

8.3   Using Service Level Agreements for Job Control

This section gives an analysis of the related work presented in Sect. 8.2 and shows the gaps that motivate this work, followed by the presentation of the selected approach that ameliorates said problems.

8.3.1   Problem Statement

As the previous section has shown, SLAs have been researched in various fields that are relevant to the topic discussed in this chapter. Two great gaps can be identified when perusing the research up to date: there is a strong tendency to only take into account service level agreements that are negotiated on a per-job basis and there is little interest in regarding the whole process of SLA management and job control (submission and scheduling) in an integrated fashion. Regarding the first issue, it is certainly a valid approach to regard SLAs as negotiated on a per-job basis, but this is not the only possible solution.

Current practice at HPC provider is to have contracts that formulate the conditions that govern the usage of computing and storage resources in an overall way (see [31]); single jobs are then submitted in reference to these contracts, therefore there is no need to perform individual negotiation for each single job. It is certainly possible to have a mixture of both systems; this would give the flexibility to dynamically negotiate contracts but ensure to the user that there is already a contract that can be used to submit jobs, therefore eliminating the possibility that the client cannot come to an agreement with a provider and would be unable to submit jobs.

With regard to the second issue, it can be said that due to the complexity of the topics involved, it makes sense to investigate issues on their own; however, making use of preexisting results and combining them into an integrated solution combines the achieved results and can lead to a whole that is worth more than the sum of its parts.

This section will present an integrated approach that supports the use of SLAs as long-term contracts on provider side for all relevant tasks:

- Formulation of contracts as SLAs, either prenegotiated or negotiated from scratch.
- Job submission in reference to SLAs.
- Acceptance of jobs depending on SLAs.
- Scheduling of jobs in accordance with pre-negotiated parameters.

8.3.2   High-Level Architecture Overview

Figure 8.2 shows the high-level components that are realizing the task mentioned beforehand.

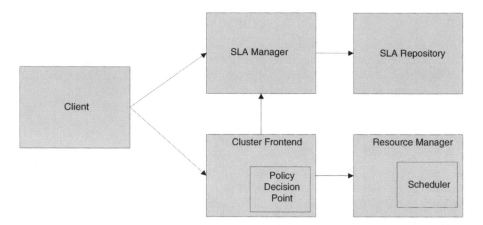

Fig. 8.2 High-level component overview

It is obvious that there are only very few additional components necessary on the provider side compared to a normal set-up. Thus, the architecture adheres to the KISS (Keep It Simple, Stupid) Principle or in other words, "Il semble que la perfection soit atteinte non quand il n'y a plus rien à ajouter, mais quand il n'y a plus rien à retrancher" [8]. Although this solution may seem too simple, a prototypical realization has been developed and is functioning well. The advantage of this simplicity is the simple integration on the provider side with only two components, as it can be done quickly and there are only few dependencies that need to be configured.

The cluster front end can usually be customized through plug-in mechanisms and does not necessarily need to be changed programmatically in itself [37]. As for the resource manager, depending on the realization, a scheduling algorithm may not be necessary as a correct queue configuration can suffice, but in general, a new scheduling algorithm will need to be implemented, which will probably require recompilation and reinstallation of the resource manager. The client may be kept backward compatible and thus need not be modified, but then it cannot make use of SLA capabilities. Modifications, which will be detailed later, can easily be performed and may be integrated into custom clients as well, without difficulties.

8.3.3 Component Descriptions

The SLA manager is the core component of the SLA management framework. Through the SLA manager, the service provider can offer service level agreement templates, which are boilerplate contracts than can be either directly filled in by the customer or customized and then submitted back to the provider as an offer. Furthermore, the SLA manager offers basic negotiation functionality and is the central point of contact for all SLA-related information. The SLA manager's negotiation capabilities can be changed at run time through a plug-in mechanism, which allows the provider to react dynamically on changing conditions and contracts.

Table 8.1 Interface of the cluster front end

Operation	Description
create Managed Job	Submits a job to the provider; if submission is successful, a web service referring to the job resource is created and the endpoint reference pointing to it is returned, along with the current time on the provider side and the termination time of the resource
Get Multiple Resource Properties	Allows the retrieval of multiple resource properties of the submission service
Get Resource Property	Allows the retrieval of a single resource property of the submission service
Query Resource Properties	Allows the retrieval of multiple resource properties of the submission service by specifying a query

The SLA repository is primarily storage for agreed-upon contracts. Furthermore, it can be used to store any kind of (eXtensible Markup Language – XML) data that needs to be available on the provider side, for example, templates, endpoint references, etc.

The cluster front end is the point of access to the client once an SLA is in place and jobs will be submitted. The front end can be queried for information and allows the client to submit jobs; successful submission will lead to the creation of a web service resource for the given job. Table 8.1 shows the operations offered by the job submission front end of the Globus Toolkit to clients.

The resource manager is a preexisting software component on the provider side that provides control over batch jobs and distributed computing nodes. It has basic scheduling capabilities built in, but different scheduling software can be normally plugged in as well. It is invoked by the cluster front end and gets passed the job submitted by the client to the service provider. A Policy Decision Point (PDP) can ensure that only jobs referencing an SLA can be submitted; for the sake of backward compatibility, the PDP may map jobs that are submitted without a reference to an SLA to an SLA only existing internally or these jobs may be allowed but treated differently.

The client encapsulates functionality that might be used for SLA negotiation. If this is not the case, SLAs need to be preexisting and can then be used when submitting jobs, which is another functionality of the client. Additionally, it might want to be able to receive notifications when the job state changes and thus will need to implement corresponding functionality (for the Globus Toolkit, this can be done by implementing the corresponding interfaces of the WS-Notification specification) [15].

8.3.4   Job Submission Sequence

Now that we have explained the functionality of the high-level components, we can have a more detailed look on the steps that are performed (see Fig. 8.3), starting with an optional negotiation of a service level agreement in steps 1–8; the negotiation is optional in the case that an SLA already exists, regardless of it having been negotiated

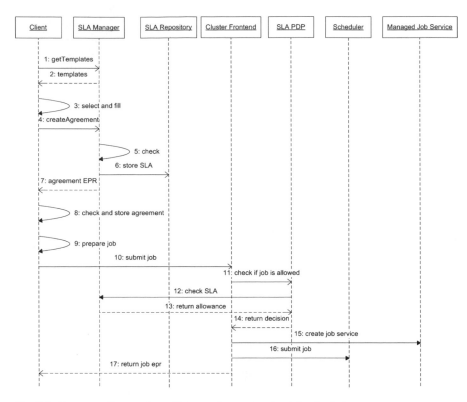

Fig. 8.3 Sequence diagram from SLA template retrieval to job submission

before or being an representation of a previous paper contract. Steps 9–16 then
show the steps necessary for job submission in relation to an SLA.

Negotiation of SLAs is not the focus of this work, so it has been decided to keep
the SLA negotiation simple, and, thus, a simple one-shot negotiation protocol has
been used. If this may seem overly simplified, it can be noted that even with these
protocols, optimizations can be performed in order to better fit templates or offers
to the opposite side [32]. Additionally, in many cases, contracts will already exist,
as Grid and HPC providers are mostly (at least currently) not participating in highly
dynamic markets and users have to fulfill specific requirements in order to be able
to submit jobs, for example, being part of an institute having established a contract.
That is, SLA with the provider.

However, negotiation starts with the client obtaining SLA templates from the
provider's SLA manager. For simplicity reasons, the SLA manager implements negotiation capabilities as well. The templates are service level agreements that are filled
in from the provider and that provide different combinations of services offered by the
provider. The client then selects a template and fills it with recommended values, for
example, contact information, bank account data, etc. This converts the template into
an offer, which is sent to the provider's SLA manager (step 4).

The provider then checks the received offer against the published templates. Additionally, as there could have been free-ranging values or values that allowed a selection by the client, these values need to be checked as well. If the values are not complying with the template or possible values, the offer is rejected. The provider will as well check already existing service level agreements which may relate to the current offer – offering urgent computing capabilities, for example, to multiple customers, may be very difficult to fulfill. Otherwise, the document is turned into an agreement, a web service instance representing this agreement is created and the agreement service's endpoint reference is returned to the client. This concludes the negotiation process.

Job submission starts with the client preparing a job to submit. This includes not only the general preparation of the job that is always necessary before submission but also the inclusion of an id referencing an SLA in the endpoint reference. A client might have different contracts in place, for example, one guaranteeing immediate access (urgent computing) and one for regular queue access. The client would then only use the urgent computing SLA if it is really necessary, but in general has the option to choose any already established SLA. The SLA contract id can be specified in the endpoint reference pointing to the job submission service like this (the code shown in bold is the actual code specifying the SLA id):

```
ns1:EndpointReferenceType xsi:type="ns1:EndpointReferenceType"
    xmlns:ns1="http://schemas.xmlsoap.org/ws/2004/03/addressing"
xmlns:xsi="http://www.w3.org/2001/XMLSchema-instance">
 <ns1:Address xsi:type="xsd:anyURI"
xmlns:xsd="http://www.w3.org/2001/XMLSchema">
https://gt4.dgrid.hlrs.de:8443/wsrf/services/
    ManagedJobFactoryService
</ns1:Address>
 <ns1:ReferenceProperties xsi:type="ns1:ReferencePropertiesType">
  <ns2:slaId xsi:type="xsd:string"
xmlns:ns2="http://www.hlrs.de/namespaces/services/job_submission"
xmlns:xsd="http://www.w3.org/2001/XMLSchema">
5deeef17-2816-4c23-874f-a1630c8d1fd2
  </ns2:slaId>
 </ns1:ReferenceProperties>
 <ns1:ReferenceParameters
xsi:type="ns1:ReferenceParametersType"/>
</ns1:EndpointReferenceType>
```

The prepared job is then submitted to the specified endpoint reference which, besides the SLA id, specifies the address of the job accepting service; in the case of the Globus Toolkit, this is the *ManagedJobFactoryService*. A PDP is invoked before the service itself is invoked and extracts the SLA id and, first of all, checks if the submitting entity is allowed to submit jobs referring to this SLA contract. This can, for example, be guaranteed by the submitter presenting an appropriate certificate, for example one delegated by the signer of the SLA. If the client is allowed to submit jobs in reference to the presented SLA id, the SLA manager is called in order to check the SLA to see if a job can be submitted for this SLA. An SLA may state, for example, that only one job can be queued at a time or that only a certain number of jobs can be submitted in a certain time frame and obligations like these on the client need to be checked. This can be either done internally in the SLA manager, which, for example, can keep count of submitted jobs or by querying other entities, for example the resource manager. If the SLA manager acknowledges that the job can be submitted, this decision is returned to the PDP, which in turn returns a positive decision. The elegant solution that can be performed is to integrate this PDP check with other PDPs already in place. Usually, a gridmap file or something similar, stating allowed certificates and mapping them to a local user name, is already in place. An algorithm where the final decision mechanism is that a deny decision takes precedence ensures that the system respects the previously necessary authentication mechanism.

The service passing the job to the local resource manager may not need to be modified in order to correctly pass the job to the resource manager. If the resource manager's scheduling algorithm is modified accordingly and the SLA PDP stores relevant information in a way that it can be accessed by the scheduler, the service can stay unmodified. To ensure backward compatibility, jobs which are submitted without an SLA id can be allowed to be submitted and can be internally sorted into a specially prepared generic queue. The client finally receives an endpoint reference of a service representing the submitted job and can query this service. Additionally, it can subscribe for notifications which are sent out by the service provider when the job state changes.

8.3.5 Job Scheduling

Exactly how scheduling will be performed on the service provider's side is a complex task and cannot be answered generally. As it has been shown, different heuristics lead to different rates in satisfied service level agreements and in revenue for the provider, so the provider has to find a trade-off [40] between these options. Currently, scheduling is often performed in a fair-share manner that ensures that clients that have consumed fewer resources get a greater share of resources. With the usage of Service Level Agreements for scheduling, the equal treatment of users will no longer be the only option. Instead, users can be prioritized or not based on the service level agreement against which they have submitted. Instead, users can be prioritized or not based on the service level agreement against which they have submitted jobs. Whereas currently there is only a single type of charges [31], various billings can be introduced that reflect priorities; cheap computing power, for example, may be associated with a best-effort queue that only can schedule jobs if the system is otherwise idle, whereas a higher prices SLA may result in jobs being scheduled with priority. This enables the support for urgent computing as well, as an even higher service level might result in immediate execution of a submitted job. Naturally, this will be expensive as potentially other service level agreements have to be broken in order to fill the urgent job.

Apart from the above-mentioned prioritized access, many more possibilities for quality of service options can be specified [39]:

- Pricing models – submitting jobs in relation to specific SLAs enables the customer to make use of price benefits or to trade price versus priority.
  - Timed access – resource access or job running at a certain point in time.
  - Exclusive access – exclusive access for jobs to one resource (e.g., a whole supercomputer).
- The implementation realized in this work has performed a proof-of-concept implementation of a simple model using prioritized access where there are three service levels:
  - Platinum – having immediate access (urgent computing)
  - Gold – high-priority jobs
  - Silver – best-effort jobs

This scheduling model is obviously very simple but already shows some issues: how to deal with competing platinum jobs? How to prevent job starvation of low-priority jobs [6]? How to prioritize competing gold jobs? All of these issues can be tackled in various ways; the introduction of business policies on the service provider side is a first possibility that immediately comes to mind. Unfortunately, these issues are too complex to be discussed in this chapter. Suffice to say that the usage of service level agreements for scheduling not only offer up new possibilities but also presents new problems.

The benefit of regarding service level agreements as long-term contracts, which are referenced by submitted jobs, is that longer term planning is possible for both sides. The service provider knows already existing contracts and can already predict resource usage as he knows about SLAs that are in place. The greatest advantage for the client is that a contract is already in place, which prevents the possibility that occurs when negotiating dynamically, that no resources might be obtained. Of course, the client has to take care that the resources guaranteed by the service provider are not already used up; even then, there is still the possibility to negotiate new SLAs.

8.4   Future Research Directions

Service Level Agreements (SLAs) also having being researched for quite some time, still generally offer a wide area of research that can be performed. Even so, the topic discussed in this chapter is rather specific, there being many opportunities of research. This is because of the fact that this subject has not been treated as extensively as some other areas using SLAs – agreement schemata or negotiation strategies, just to name two areas that have been widely covered. Research on a fully integrated approach of SLAs covering all aspects from job submission to billing and accounting with real integration in the scheduling layers is new, even though all of these topics have been discussed on their own, as has been shown in the analysis of related work.

An obvious area of research is the closer inspection of business policies for influencing scheduling. SLAs can be closely linked to business policies, but this topic has only been touched lightly here. It may be of interest how different policies influence the scheduling and satisfaction of SLAs, how flexible policies can be easily integrated into the presented concept and, even more interesting, the effect of different policies for different customers. With regard to scheduling, a very interesting research and implementation opportunity is the development of a more mature scheduler. Currently, a basic scheduler is used and the scheduling decision is solely based on a simple model of prioritized access. Other schedulers might implement more fine-grained mechanisms, which will lead to more complex components, but this may well be worth the effort; the different service levels previously described can be implemented in a scheduler as well.

The concept presented here has been realized using the popular combination of the Globus Toolkit and the TORQUE resource manager. This combination of grid middleware and resource management software is in use at many HPC providers[1] and was therefore an obvious choice for investigating the feasibility of the concept. Nonetheless, integration of the concept or even whole components into different middlewares and resource managers is an apparent possibility for future work. As the Globus Toolkit is currently undergoing major changes – in the current release, version 5.0, the web services container is no longer part of the release and will be released later using a different framework – investigation of a feasible platform, which probably may even be nonWSRF, is obviously needed. As changes in the area of HPC computing are seldom ill conceived but rather well thought through, the adoption of new concepts, of which it cannot be foreseen easily which benefits they bring, tends to be slow, so this is possibly not as pressing an issue as it seems.[2]

While quick changes in existing and well-working software set-ups are unlikely, hardware still changes very rapidly. The advent of processors with multiple cores, starting from dual cores, has gained much momentum, where the current height seems to be the "Single-chip Cloud Computer," uniting 48 cores on one chip [18]. Developments like this might lead to very diverse hardware at HPC providers, more so than it exists at the moment. One can envision a manifold variety of chips with different sizes of cores and other specialized capabilities, even more so than today where already various CPU architectures and GPUs are offered as resources. Apart from that, the presented approach only assumes simple resources and does not take special resources into account. For example, nodes with different RAM, varying processor sizes and speed, or the usage of Graphical Processing Units (GPUs), which are an interesting research topic [22].

---

[1] For example, at the German high-performance computing centers in Jülich, Munich, and Stuttgart.

[2] The High-Performance Computing Center Stuttgart, as well as the infrastructure provided by the German grid initiative D-Grid is, for example, still using the Globus Toolkit version 4.0, although this has been superseded by version 4.2 in February 2008 and version 5.0 in January 2010.

Support for real-time capable software, at least for soft real-time, is now coming to service-oriented provisioning of services as well (IaaS and PaaS). This is a highly demanding field for service providers but can offer great revenues. It is an interesting approach to see to what extent it is possible to offer real-time capable hardware through service level agreements and if this is even possible with the approaches used until today.

8.5   Conclusion

In this chapter, the usage of Service Level Agreements (SLAs) for job control (i.e., the submission, overall management, and scheduling of computing jobs) has been discussed for Grid and HPC. It has been shown how an approach integrating SLAs on a high-level – preexisting or dynamically negotiated SLAs referenced in submitted jobs – as well as on a low level – influencing scheduling decision – can be realized, assuming just a standard set-up with a common middleware and a common resource manager. Even existing contracts can be modeled as service level agreements; therefore, it is ensured that the solution can be easily integrated into a Grid or HPC provider's set-up. The proof-of-concept implementation presented above focuses on simplicity, therefore requiring only minimal set-up and configuration, which differentiates it from other SLA management approaches. Nonetheless, it is easy to extend, so that additional components can be integrated without too much effort. It has been shown that presented concept is feasible, can be used productively, and that service level agreements can offer new possibilities for the control of jobs for Grid and HPC providers and that they offer very flexible approaches which can be influenced through business policies.

References

1. Amazon Web Services LLC: Amazon EC2 SLA. Retrieved from http://aws.amazon.com/ec2-sla (2008)
2. Andrieux, A., Czajkowski, K., Dan, A., Keahey, K., Ludwig, H., Nakata, T., Pruyne, J., Rofrano, J., Tuecke, S., Xu, M.: Web services agreement specification (WS-Agreement). OpenGridForum, pp. 1–81. Retrieved from https://forge.gridforum.org/sf/go/doc14574?nav=1 (2007)
3. Anjomshoaa, A., Brisard, F., Drescher, M., Fellows, D., Ly, A., McGough, S., Pulsipher, D., Sawa, A.: Job Submission Description Language (JSDL) specification, version 1.0. OpenGridForum, pp. 1–72. Retrieved from http://www.gridforum.org/documents/GFD.56.pdf (2005)
4. Argonne National Laboratories: OpenPBS Public Home. Retrieved from http://www.mcs.anl.gov/research/projects/openpbs (2010)
5. Boniface, M., Phillips, S.C., Surridge, M.: Grid-based business partnerships using service level agreements. In: Proceedings of Cracow Grid Workshop, Cracow, pp. 16–18 (2006)
6. Chakrabarti, A.: Grid Computing Security. Springer, New York (2007)
7. Cluster Resources Inc.: TORQUE resource manager. Retrieved from http://www.clusterresources.com/products/torque-resourcemanager.php (2010)

8. De Saint-Exupery, A.: Terre des hommes. Gallimard Education, Paris (1999)
9. Djemame, K., Gourlay, I., Padgett, J., Birkenheuer, G., Hovestadt, M., Kao, O., Voss, K.: Introducing risk management into the grid. In: Proceedings of the 2nd IEEE International Conference on E-Science and Grid Computing, Amsterdam (2006). doi:10.1109/E-SCIENCE.2006.92
10. Dumitrescu, C., Raicu, I., Foster, I.: The design, usage, and performance of GRUBER: A GRid Usage Service Level Agreement based BrokERing Infrastructure. J. Grid Comput. 5(1), 99–126 (2005a)
11. Dumitrescu, C., Raicu, I., Foster, I.: DI-GRUBER: a distributed approach to grid resource brokering. In: Proceedings of the ACM/IEEE 2005 Conference on Supercomputing, Seattle, p. 38 (2005b). doi:10.1109/SC.2005.23
12. Dumitrescu, C.L., Raicu, I., Foster, I.: Usage SLA-based scheduling in grids: Research articles. Concurr. Comput. Pract. Exp. 19(7), 945–963 (2007)
13. Ernest, L.M., Hamilton, R.A., Moraca, W.L., Seaman, J.W.: Managing compliance with service level agreements in a grid environment (No. 7668741). Retrieved from http://www.freepatentsonline.com/7668741.html (2010)
14. Fawaz, W., Daheb, B., Audouin, O., Du-Pond, M., Pujolle, G.: Service Level Agreement and provisioning in optical networks. IEEE Commun. Mag. 42(1), 36–43 (2004)
15. Graham, S., Hull, D., Murray, B.: Web services base notification 1.3. Retrieved from http://docs.oasis-open.org/wsn/wsn-ws_base_notification-1.3-spec-os.pdf (2006)
16. Hayes, I.S.: Metrics for IT outsourcing Service Level Agreements. Clarity Consulting Publications. Retrieved from http://www.clarity-consulting.com/MetricsforIToutsourcing.pdf (2004)
17. HPC4U (Highly Predictable Cluster for Internet-Grids) Consortium: HPC4U project home page. Retrieved from http://www.hpc4u.org (2006)
18. Intel Inc.: Single-chip cloud computer. Retrieved from http://techresearch.intel.com/UserFiles/en-us/File/terascale/SCC-Overview.pdf (2009)
19. IRMOS (Interactive Realtime Multimedia Applications on Service-Oriented Infrastructures) Consortium: IRMOS project home page. Retrieved from http://irmos-project.eu (2010)
20. Keller, A., Ludwig, H.: The WSLA framework: Specifying and monitoring service level agreements for web services. J. Netw. Syst. Manage. 11(1), 57–81 (2003)
21. Lamanna, D.D, Skene, J., Emmerich, W.: Slang: a language for defining service level agreements. In: Proceedings of the 9th IEEE Workshop on Future Trends of Distributed Computing Systems, San Juan, pp 100–106 (2003)
22. Lupton, G., Thulin, D.: Accelerating HPC using GPU's. Retrieved from http://www.hp.com/techservers/hpccn/hpccollaboration/ADCatalyst/downloads/accelerating_HPC_Using_GPU%27s.pdf (2008)
23. Lux Scientiae Inc.: Service level agreement for shared email & web hosting. Retrieved from http://luxsci.com/extranet/shared-sla.html (2010)
24. MacLaren, J., Sakellariou, R., Krishnakumar, K.T., Garibaldi, J., Ouelhadj, D.: Towards service level agreement based scheduling on the grid. In: Proceedings of the 2nd European across Grids Conference, Nicosia, pp. 100–102 (2004)
25. Mahler, T., Arenas, A., Schubert, L.: Contractual frameworks for enterprise networks and virtual organizations in e-learning. In: Cunnigham, P., Cunningham, M. (eds.) Exploiting the Knowledge Economy: Issues, Applications, Case Studies, vol. 2. IOS Press, Amsterdam (2006)
26. Mangipudi, K., Basani, V.: Method and apparatus for implementing a service level agreement (No. 7058704). Retrieved from http://www.freepatentsonline.com/7058704.html (2006)
27. Microsoft Corporation: Download details: Windows Azure Compute SLA document. Retrieved from http://go.microsoft.com/fwlink/?LinkId=159704 (2010)
28. New Jersey City University, Department of Information Technology: Policy & procedures: Help desk Service Level Agreement (SLA). Retrieved from http://www.njcu.edu/dept/it/documents/helpdesk_sla-employees_sp08.pdf (2008)
29. NextGRID Consortium: NextGRID project home page. Retrieved from http://nextgrid.org (2008)
30. Raimondi, F., Skene, J., Emmerich, W.: Efficient online monitoring of web-service SLAs. In: Proceedings of the 16th ACM SIGSOFT International Symposium on Foundations of Software Engineering, Atlanta, pp. 170–180 (2008)

31. Resch, M: Entgeltordnung für die nutzung der rechenanlagen und peripheren geräte des höchstleistungsrechenzentrums Stuttgart (HLRS) an der Universität Stuttgart. Retrieved from http://www.hlrs.de/fileadmin/_assets/organization/sos/puma/services/Entgeltordnungen/ Entgeltordnung_16-09-2008.pdf (2008)
32. Saha, S., Biswas, A., Sen, S.: Modeling opponent decision in repeated one-shot negotiations. In: Proceedings of the 4th International Joint Conference on Autonomous Agents and Multiagent Systems, Utrecht, pp. 397–403 (2005)
33. Sakellariou, R., Yarmolenko, V.: On the flexibility of WS-agreement for job submission. In: Proceedings of the 3rd International Workshop on Middleware for Grid Computing, vol. 117, Grenoble, pp. 1–6 (2005)
34. Sakellariou, R., Yarmolenko, V.: Job scheduling on the grid: towards SLA-based scheduling. In: Grandinetti, L. (ed.) High Performance Computing and Grids in Action. IOS Press, Amsterdam (2008). Retrieved 03 Mar 2010 from http://www.cs.man.ac.uk/~rizos/papers/hpc08.pdf
35. Sandholm, T.: Service level agreement requirements of an accounting-driven computational grid. Tech. Rep. No. TRITA-NA-0533. Royal Institute of Technology, Stockholm (2005)
36. Seidel, J., Wäldrich, O., Wieder, P., Yahyapour, R., Ziegler, W.: Using SLA for resource management and scheduling – a survey. In: Talia, D., Yahyapour, R., Ziegler, W. (eds.) Grid Middleware and Services – Challenges and Solutions. Springer, New York (2008)
37. Siebenlist, F., Welch, V.: The Globus toolkit authorization framework. Retrieved from http://www.globus.org/alliance/events/sc06/AuthZ.pdf (2006)
38. University of California, Los Angeles: Cts call center service level agreement. Retrieved from http://www.cts.ucla.edu/pdfs/CallCenterSLA.pdf (2010)
39. Wesner, S.: Integrated management framework for dynamic virtual organizations. Dissertation, Universität Stuttgart, Stuttgart (2008)
40. Yarmolenko, V., Sakellariou, R.: An evaluation of heuristics for SLA based parallel job scheduling. In: Proceedings of the 20th International Parallel and Distributed Processing Symposium, Rhodes Island, p. 8 (2006)
41. Yeo, C.S., Buyya, R.: Managing risk of inaccurate runtime estimates for deadline constrained job admission control in clusters. In: Proceedings of the 2006 International Conference on Parallel Processing, Columbus, pp. 451–458 (2006)

Chapter 9
Composable Services Architecture for Grids

**Vassiliki Pouli, Yuri Demchenko, Constantinos Marinos,
Diego R. Lopez, and Mary Grammatikou**

Abstract Grids provide collaborative environments for integration of the distributed heterogeneous resources and services running on different operating systems (OSs), e.g., Unix, Linux, Windows, embedded systems; Platforms, e.g., J2EE, .NET; and Devices, e.g., computers, instruments, sensors, databases, networks. Such environments need platform-independent technologies for services to communicate across various domains. These kinds of technologies are offered by Service-Oriented Architectures (SOA) that provide an architectural framework for loosely coupled set of services and principles to be used within multiple heterogeneous domains. Based on SOA, another architecture, the Open Grid Services Architecture (OGSA), was built to offer semantics and capabilities to services that reside in grid environments. Examples of such capabilities are statefulness and notifications. As evolution of the existing architectures, in this chapter, we will introduce a service-oriented architecture, the Composable Services Architecture (CSA), aimed to support dynamic service provisioning and integration in grid environments.

V. Pouli (✉) • C. Marinos • M. Grammatikou
Network Management and Optimal Design Laboratory (NETMODE), School of Electrical
and Computer Engineering (ECE), National Technical University of Athens (NTUA),
9 Iroon Polytechneiou Str., GR 157 80, Zografou, Athens, Greece
e-mail: vpouli@gmail.com; vpouli@netmode.ntua.gr

Y. Demchenko
University of Amsterdam (UvA), Leuvenstraat 92, Amsterdam 1066HC, The Netherlands

D.R. Lopez
RedIRIS, Spain

N.P. Preve (ed.), *Grid Computing: Towards a Global Interconnected Infrastructure*,
Computer Communications and Networks, DOI 10.1007/978-0-85729-676-4_9,
© Springer-Verlag London Limited 2011

9.1   Introduction

Grid environments constitute one of the most promising computing infrastructures in computational science. One of their main goals is to tackle current and upcoming complex, large-scale problems, by enabling seamless sharing of computational resources.

Grid computing has emerged as a key infrastructure for flexible, secure, coordinated resource sharing among dynamic collections of individuals, institutions, and resources [20]. It is finalized to the aggregation of resources into Virtual Organizations (VOs) [24, 27]. Scientific communities embraced grid technologies to run projects involving distributed resources and using massive data sets, in the context of the so-called e-Science. Main goals are the improvement of the collaboration across distributed research groups, sharing experimental results that must be submitted to compute-intensive analysis, and optimizing the use of computational and storage resources.

Key to the realization of the grid goals is standardization. Standardization enables the creation of interoperable, reusable, and portable components used in a common way across heterogeneous systems. Service-Oriented Architectures (SOA) address this need for standardization and offer integration of heterogeneous systems and reduce the complexity of managing diverse environments. Based on SOA, the Open Grid Services Architecture (OGSA) adds extra features and capabilities to a service-oriented architecture, which are needed to model and manage grid services and resources.

This chapter intends to explore how current advances in Service-Oriented Architectures (SOA) can be applied to realize the grid promise of seamless inter-working of distributed, heterogeneous systems, and to even bring it further through an architecture fully covering dynamic service life cycle.

At the beginning of this chapter, we will present grid environments and their characteristics, following we will deal with Service-Oriented Architectures (SOA and OGSA) that offer solutions to the federated and dynamic nature of grids and at the end, based on these characteristics, we are going to introduce our architecture, the Composable Services Architecture (CSA), that aims to integrate services in two ways: either OGSA services among them or OGSA infrastructures with different services coming from various environments. In this way, it provides an interoperation for federated environments in a dynamic and seamless way.

9.2   Grid and Service Architectures – Overview

9.2.1   Grid

Grid [6] can be defined as a large-scale generalized network system distributed across multiple organizations and administrative domains. It is a system that coordinates distributed resources using standard, open, general-purpose protocols and interfaces to deliver high qualities of service. It also integrates and coordinates resources and users that live within different control domains (e.g., the user's desktop vs central computing, different administrative units of the same company, and/or different companies), and addresses the issues of security, policy, payment, membership, etc. that arise in these settings. Otherwise, we are dealing with a local management system.

In less than a decade, grids have developed from initial research idea to production ready technology and infrastructure. The initial grid definition in one of the grid foundational papers, the Anatomy of the Grid [7], actually described the goal of this new technology at that time: Grid systems and applications aim to integrate, virtualize, and manage resources and services within distributed, heterogeneous, dynamic Virtual Organizations (VOs) [7]. The more detailed grid definition developed in later works included such main components as distributed infrastructure, dynamics, virtualization, and user-defined security – the components that provide a framework for coordinated collaborative resource sharing in dynamic, multi-institutional VOs [7, 8].

The software enabling seamless distribution of resources and services, referred to as middleware, is the key to grid's functionality. Open source middleware toolkits were created by the Globus Alliance [7]. Grid middleware is intended to provide this layer of grid service harmonization and orchestration. However, many times grid workflows may require the use of services from existing, third-party systems which are not fully compatible with the grid middleware, due to specific implementation technology.

Recently, the grid definition is extended to scalable, distributed computing across multiple heterogeneous platforms, locations, and organizations [26]. The document also defines the following characteristics and goals of grids in general:

- Dynamic resource provisioning: dynamically determine where, for how long, and how many resources will be acquired
- Management of Virtualized Infrastructure
- Resource pooling and sharing: grouping together of resources to maximize their advantage
- Self-monitoring and improvement
- Highest quality of service

The following grid types are identified depending on usage and required common functionality:

- Cluster Grids: have predominantly homogeneous structure and focus on shared use of high-performance computing resources.
- Collaboration Grids: are targeted at supporting collaborative distributed group of people over multiple domains and involving heterogeneous resource.
- Data Center Grids: are actually adding provider-specific aspects in managing resources, users, their associations, and supporting whole provisioning life cycle.

Most of today's grids are used for executing sequential applications that follow a batch processing approach. However, some users require interactive access when running jobs on grid sites. Execution of these applications on a grid environment is a challenging problem that requires the cooperation of several middleware tools and services. Additional problems arise when this interactive support is intended for parallel applications, which may run remotely across several sites. The Interactive European Grid project aims to provide transparent and reliable support for such applications.

Currently, grids found their place as a technology to build problem or project-oriented collaborative environment that combine high-end compute, storage, and visualization resources. However, wider grids usage is limited by the complexity of the grid resources set-up and management. Cloud computing is emerging as targeting simpler use cases and potentially wider user community that require large volume but simpler computation. A recent informational document by OGF positions clouds as providing higher level abstraction to access grid and compute cluster resources [25].

Grids have to deal with fundamental problems of authentication, authorization, resource discovery, and access across different services in heterogeneous environments. To offer interoperability across these diverse domains and create portable applications, standard protocols and interfaces need to become available. Standardization can realize the grid goals and offer seamless access to services, create reusable components and systems, and provide general management of resources as in a single domain.

The Open Grid Services Architecture (OGSA) [9] is a service-oriented architecture that addresses this need for standardization by defining a set of core capabilities and behaviors that address key concerns in grid systems. The Open Grid Services Architecture v1.5 (OGSA) published by the Open Grid Forum (OGF) in [9] defining the grid as: A system that is concerned with the integration, virtualization, and management of services and resources in a distributed, heterogeneous environment that supports collections of users and resources (Virtual Organizations) across traditional administrative and organizational domains (Real Organizations).

9.2.2 Service-Oriented Architecture

Service-Oriented Architecture (SOA) can be considered as an evolution of distributed computing based on the request/response design paradigm for synchronous and asynchronous applications. An application's business logic or individual functions are modularized and presented as services for consumer/client applications. SOA is essentially a collection of services most suitable for loosely coupled distributed applications. These services communicate with each other to offer interoperability between distributed systems. It is an architecture that enables interoperability between heterogeneous and diverse systems and reduces the complexity of administering heterogeneous systems.

SOA enables developments of the software components for on-demand consumption with Web services establishing itself as the popular connection technology.

SOA principles also influence the business logic of services by encouraging good design, i.e., promoting modular and dispersed components that can be separately developed and maintained. Services exposed as Web services can be integrated into complex services that may span multiple domains and organizations.

SOA, viewed as a tool for the integration of distributed resources, plays a significant role, not only as manager of computational resources, but increasingly as aggregator of measurement instrumentation and pervasive large-scale data acquisition platforms, e.g., sensor networks. In this context, the functionality of a service-oriented architecture allows managing, maintaining, and exploiting heterogeneous and geographically sparse instrumentation and acquisition devices in a unified way, by providing standardized interfaces and common working environments to their users. This is achieved through the properties of isolation from the physical network and from the peculiarities of the instrumentation, granted by standard middleware, together with secure and flexible mechanisms to seek, access, and aggregate distributed resources.

The Service-Oriented Architectures concepts that build upon Web Service Architecture (WSA) abstractions are typically specified using XML-based standards and recommendations and have the following key characteristics:

- WSA services have self-describing interfaces in platform-independent XML documents. Web Services Description Language (WSDL) [2], is the standard one for service description when services are SOAP based, whilst Web Application Description Language (WADL) is the standard XML-based format for RESTful Web services. There is also Universal Service Description Language (USDL) [2], a language for formally describing the semantics of Web services in order to become more practical so that users and applications can discover, process, deploy, and synthesize services automatically.
- WSA services communicate with messages formally defined via XML Schema (also called XSD). Communication among consumers and providers or services typically happens in heterogeneous environments, with little or no knowledge about the provider. Implementers commonly build SOAs using Web services standards, such as Simple Object Access Protocol (SOAP) [2]. SOAP is the most common network message format and encapsulates the specific communications between a requestor agent and a service (and also, possibly, routing intermediaries). SOAP is an open, standard protocol developed by the W3C and supported by the main IT players (Sun, Microsoft, HP, IBM, Oracle, BEA). SOAP adds a further application level to the TCP/IP stack, so that SOAP messages can be transported by any Internet application protocol (HTTP, SMTP, FTP, etc.). SOAP is also an extensible format: additional directives for security, reliability, addressing, and similar higher level qualities of service are added as supplemental information to the SOAP header. Apart from SOAP, one can, however, implement SOA communication using any service-based technology, such as REST [23]. The acronym REST stands for REpresentational State Transfer, an architectural style for the design of large-scale distributed software, inspired on a subset of World Wide Web functionality. REST services stringently avoid issues of exposed state

and provide a single programming interface, essentially, HTTP GET, PUT, DELETE, and POST, for all services. REST services operate on URIs, which may respond with XML messages as well as other formats. XML payloads may be in any format. News feeds using RSS and Atom formatting are typical examples. These are best known as news feed formats, but they can be used as general purpose envelopes for conveying sequential data; similar to SOAP. JavaScript Object Notation (JSON) is an alternative to XML for message exchange. The combination of clients to multiple services in a single application is called a mash-up. REST services are purposefully simpler and have less sophisticated interaction patterns than WS-* services, relying on human developers rather than tooling to construct applications. The RESTful implementation of a service, compared to the corresponding SOAP protocol solution, has an important difference: the design and implementation of an additional application layer is not required, because the HTTP protocol already provides the primitives for service access. URIs, natively supported by HTTP, provide a unique, uniform, and universal addressing mechanism; at the same time, the system components are tied by loose coupling, granting a high degree of scalability. The architecture of a RESTful Web service is simple because, at most, it involves the extension of the client-side and server-side functionalities for the management of the XML responses.

- WSA services are maintained in the enterprise by a registry that acts as a directory listing in order to store and publish services. The Universal Description, Definition, and Integration (UDDI) [2] specification defines a registry for service publication and service discovery. It is platform-independent and designed to store WSDL Web service descriptions of the bindings and formats required to call the services.

9.2.3 Open Grid Services Architecture

Based on the Service-Oriented Architecture, the grid SOA was developed because the grid architects decided that there were enough requirements in their services-oriented architecture that were not met by the service-oriented standards. Thus, the Open Grid Forum (OGF) was formed to standardize a services-based infrastructure for the grid environments, named OGSA (Open Grid Services Architecture) [9].

OGSA represents an evolution toward a grid system architecture based on Web services concepts and technologies by introducing semantics and capabilities to Web services, statefulness, stateful interactions, transient instances, lifetime management, introspection, and notification on state changes at the resources.

OGSA provides, through a framework of specifications that undergo a community review process, a precise definition of grid computing. Key capabilities include the management of application execution, data, and information. Security and resource state modeling are examples of crosscutting capabilities in OGSA. Many grid middleware stacks (Globus, gLite, Unicore, OMII, Willow, Nareji, GOS, and Crown) are available. Web and grid services are typically atomic and general purpose. Workflow tools, including languages and execution engines [10], are used to compose multiple general services into specialized tasks. Collections of users, services, and resources form virtual organizations that are managed by administrative services.

The numerous Web service specifications that constitute grids and Web service systems are commonly called "WS-*." WS technologies combined with a Service-Oriented Architecture (SOA) approach can serve as the base for building highly reliable and flexible distributed systems. OGSA is mainly based on Web service technologies, like WSDL, SOAP, XML, but it aims to be largely agnostic in relation to the transport-level handling of data.

Generally, OGSA provides state-aware, continuous availability for service applications, data, and processing logic. It is based on architecture that combines horizontally scalable, database-independent, middle-tier data caching with intelligent parallelization and an affinity of business logic with cache data. This enables newer, simpler, and more efficient models for highly scalable service-oriented applications that can take full advantage of service virtualization and event-driven architectures that exist in grid environments. It provides uniform mechanisms to discover and query resources, while it simplifies the administration and management of heterogeneous systems and resources by offering common management and virtualization capabilities.

The OGSA document [9] describes an OGSA grid in terms of the following capabilities/services:

- Execution Management Services: services that are concerned with the problems of instantiating and managing different components of work.
- Data Services: those OGSA services that are concerned with the management of, access to, and update of data resources, along with the transfer of data between resources.
- Resource Management Services: resource management performs several forms of management on resources in a grid.
- Security Services: security services facilitate the enforcement of the security related within an organization (grid).
- Self-Management Services: in a self-management environment, system components – including hardware components, such as network and storage devices – are self-configuring, self-healing, and self-optimizing.
- Information Services: the ability to access and manipulate information about applications, resources, and services.

OGSA is a distributed interaction and computing architecture based around services, assuring interoperability on heterogeneous systems so that different types of resources can communicate and share information. OGSA has been described as a refinement of the emerging Web services architecture, specifically designed to support grid requirements. The Open Grid Services Architecture also defines, in terms of Web Services Description Language (WSDL) interfaces and associated conventions, mechanisms required for creating and composing sophisticated distributed systems, including lifetime management, change management, and notification. Service bindings can support reliable invocation, authentication, authorization, and delegation, if required.

Grid environments tend to be heterogeneous and distributed, encompassing a variety of hosting environments (e.g., J2EE, .NET), operating systems (e.g., Unix,

Linux, Windows, embedded systems), devices (e.g., computers, instruments, sensors, storage systems, databases, networks), and services, provided by various vendors. In addition, they are frequently intended to be long-lived and dynamic, and may therefore evolve in ways not initially anticipated. OGSA must enable interoperability between such diverse, heterogeneous, and distributed resources and services as well as to reduce the complexity of administering heterogeneous systems. Moreover, many functions required in distributed environments, such as security and resource management, may already be implemented by stable and reliable legacy systems. It will rarely be feasible to replace such legacy systems; instead, we must be able to integrate them into the grid. The need to support heterogeneous systems leads to requirements that include the following, as they were described in the OGSA document:

• Resource virtualization: essential to reduce the complexity of managing heterogeneous systems and to handle diverse resources in a unified way.
• Common management capabilities: simplifying administration of a heterogeneous system requires mechanisms for uniform and consistent management of resources. A minimum set of common manageability capabilities is required.
• Resource discovery and query: mechanisms are required for discovering resources with desired attributes and for retrieving their properties. Discovery and query should handle a highly dynamic and heterogeneous system.
• Standard protocols and schemas: important for interoperability. In addition, standard protocols are also particularly important as their use can simplify the transition to using grids.

9.3   Basic Composable Services Architecture Design Principles

In this chapter, we will provide a short overview of the related to the proposed Composable Services Architecture industry standards and will discuss the basic CSA design principles, in particular, those related to SOA, and the Open Service Environment (OSE) concept, as defined by ITU-T Next-Generation Network (NGN) [13, 17, 18].

9.3.1   Compliance with Standard SOA Frameworks

CSA is based, by definition, on and supports the basic SOA architectural principles and services interaction models [1, 4]. As correctly noted in [11], SOA is based on business requirements and aligns IT and business so that IT systems work the way the business does, helping to ensure that IT produce business value. From the service design point of view, this means that SOA-based services and the service design and deployment process should allow and use different levels of abstraction and ensure the whole services delivery life cycle.

In its evolution and gradual development, CSA is going to adopt SOA best practices and comply with the Open Group Services Integration Maturity Model (OSIMM) [22]. The OSIMM defines a grid of seven maturity level and seven dimensions that describe provisioned services and SOA-related properties.

The seven OSIMM maturity levels include:

- (OSIMM1) Silo
- (OSIMM 2) Integrated
- (OSIMM 3) Componentized
- (OSIMM 4) Services
- (OSIMM 5) Composable services
- (OSIMM 6) Virtualized services
- (OSIMM 7) Dynamically reconfigurable services

The seven dimensions define different presentation layers and aspects of the services such as Business view, Governance and Operations, Methods, Applications, Architecture, Information, Infrastructure and Management.

In the Applications dimension, the SOA-based applications deal with the different components and building blocks mapped to the above-defined maturity levels: modules (OSIMM1), objects (OSIMM2), components (OSIMM3), services (OSIMM4), applications comprised of services (OSIMM5), process integration via services (OSIMM6), and dynamic application assembly (OSIMM7).

Starting from the level "OSIMM4 – Services," the information or data are represented as information as a service (OSIMM4), data dictionary and repository (OSIMM5), virtualized data services (OSIMM6), and semantic data vocabularies, (OSIMM7).

Table 9.1 provides a summary of the services presentation models at the different OSIMM levels. In accordance with SOA and OSIMM [22], composable services can be positioned at the highest level.

9.3.2 Next-Generation Network (NGN) Services Convergence Based on Web Services

A number of the recent ITU-T recommendations related to the Next-Generation Network (NGN) provide a basis for transport/network and Information Technology (IT) convergence based on NGN. The Next-Generation Networks (NGN) concept is introduced by ITU-T as a next step in creating a global information infrastructure.

The NGN reference model, according to ITU-T Y.2011 Recommendation [14], suggests the separation of the transport network and application services and defines them as NGN service stratum and NGN transport stratum consisting of a User plane, a Control plane, and a Management plane. Any modern networking environment is characterized by the integration between services and network infrastructure, increasing use of Internet protocols for interservice communication, services "digitizing," and integration with higher level applications.

Table 9.1 SOA components presentation at different OSIMM levels [22]

OSIMM levels and dimensions	OSIMM1 Silo	OSIMM2 Integrated	OSIMM3 Componentized	OSIMM4 Services	OSIMM5 Composable services	OSIMM6 Virtualized services	OSIMM7 Dynamically reconfigurable services
Business view	Isolated business lines	Business process integration	Componentized business	Componentized business offers services	Processes through services composition	Geographical independent service centers	Mixed match business and context-aware capabilities
Organization	Ad hoc IT strategy and Governance	Ad hoc enterprise strategy and Governance	Common Governance process	Enabling SOA Governance	SOA and IT Governance Alignment	SOA and IT Infrastructure Governance Alignment	Governance through policy
Methods	Structured analysis and design	Object-oriented modeling	Component-based development	Service-oriented modeling	Service-oriented modeling	Service-oriented modeling for infrastructure	Business grammar-oriented modeling
Applications	Modules	Objects	Components	Services	Applications comprised of services	Process integration via services	Dynamic assembly, context-aware invocation
Architecture	Monolithic architecture	Layered architecture	Component architecture	Emerging SOA	SOA	Grid-based SOA	Dynamically reconfigurable architecture
Information	Application specific	LOB or enterprise specific	Canonical models	Information as a service	Enterprise business data dictionary and repository	Virtualized data services	Semantic data vocabularies
Infrastructure (and Management)	LOB platform specific	Enterprise standards	Common reusable infrastructure	Project-based SOA environment	Common SOA environment	Virtual SOA environment, S&R	Dynamic sense, Decide and Respond
	OSIMM1	OSIMM2	OSIMM3	OSIMM4	OSIMM5	OSIMM6	OSIMM7

The ITU-T Recommendations Y.2012 [16] and Y.2201 [17] specify high-level requirements and functional architecture of the NGN Release 1 [16, 17]. The described NGN service architecture proposes a service and network separation principle and defines functional components of the Transport stratum and Service stratum. The NGN Y.2012 [16] architecture also defines the Application Network Interface (ANI) that provides an abstraction of the network capabilities and is used as a channel for applications to access network services and resources.

The NGN convergence service model is defined by ITU-T Recommendation Y.2232 [18] and suggests the major scenario by means of Web services. The NGN Open Service Environment (OSE) defined by ITU-T Recommendation Y.2234 [15] is based on Web services and actually implements basic SOA principles in defining a service integration model. The definition of the OSE and Web services convergence model is targeted to provide a common framework for both application and provider service developers.

The Y.2201 [17]/Y.2234 [15] NGN OSE is required to satisfy such requirements as independence from transport network providers, independence from manufactures, location transparency, network transparency, and protocol transparency. The OSE should provide the following capabilities to support effective services integration and operation: service coordination, interworking with service creation environment, service discovery, service registration, policy enforcement, and development support. The latter capability actually suggests that OSE should support the full life cycle of components, ranging from installation, configuration, administration, publishing, versioning, maintenance, and removal.

In a natural step, another set of ITU-T standards prescribe NGN convergence model based on Web services, and require NGN capabilities to support OSE. Web service-enabled NGN transport networks provide a native environment for integrating applications, services, and resources that can be provisioned on demand.

Composable Service Architecture (CSA) has been motivated and can be positioned as a framework for implementing the Open Service Environment (OSE) concept, as defined by ITU-T Next-Generation Network (NGN), which demonstrates the present trend to using service-oriented concepts in the modern telecommunication industry [13, 14].

9.3.3 Composable Services Life Cycle Management

SOA-based technologies provide a good basis for creating composable services which, in case of advancing to dynamically reconfigurable services, should also rely on a well-defined Services Life cycle Management (SLM) model. Most of the existing services development and life cycle management frameworks and definitions are oriented toward rather traditional human-driven services development and composition [12, 21, 30]. Dynamically provisioned and reconfigured services will require rethinking of existing models and proposing new security mechanisms at each stage of the provisioning process.

9.3.4 Service Delivery Framework (SDF) by TeleManagement Forum

To satisfy the dynamic characteristics of the NGN concept, the TeleManagement Forum (TMF) proposed the Service Delivery Framework (SDF) as part of their New Generation Operations Systems and Software (NGOSS) solution framework. The main motivation behind developing SDF is to achieve automation of the whole service delivery and operation process, in particular:

- End-to-end service management in a multiservice provider environment.
- End-to-end service management in a composite, hosted, and/or syndicated service environment.
- Management functions to support a highly distributed service environment, e.g., unified or federated security, user profile management, charging, etc.
- Any other scenario that pertains to a given phase of the service life cycle challenges, such as on-boarding, provisioning, or service creation.

Figure 9.1 illustrates the major SDF components and their interactions during the three main stages, Design, Deployment, and Operation. The SDF defines two basic

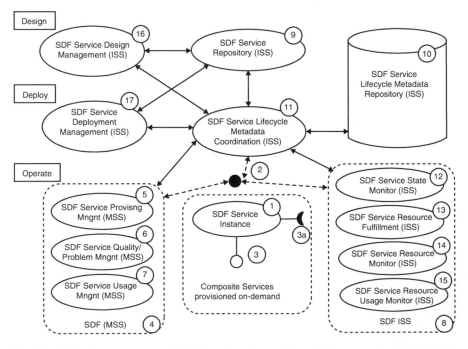

Fig. 9.1 SDF main components and their interaction during design, deployment, and operation stages

Table 9.2 Service delivery framework

Request	Design stage	Deployment stage	Operation stage	Decommission
SLA negotiation	9 – Service repository	10 – Service life cycle metadata repository	5 – Service provisioning management	10 – Service life cycle metadata repository
Provisioning session ID assignment	10 – Service life cycle metadata repository	11 – Service life cycle metadata coordinator	6 – Service quality/ problem management	11 – Service life cycle metadata coordinator
11 – Service life cycle metadata coordinator	16 – Service design management	17 – Service deployment management	7 – Service usage monitor	14 – Service resource monitor
			11 – Service life cycle metadata coordinator	15 – Resource usage monitor
			12 – Service state monitor	
			13 – Service resource fulfillment	
			14 – Service resource monitor	
			15 – Resource usage monitor	

supporting systems: Management Support Service (SDF MSS) and Infrastructure Support Service (SDF ISS). The Service Instance, delivered or provisioned on demand, is presented as containing: (2) Service Management Interface, (3) Service Functional Interface, and (3a) Service Consumer Interface.

The framework specifies the following components involved into the service provisioning at different life cycle stages (Table 9.2). It is important to mention that the key component of the SDF model is the Service/Resource Life cycle Metadata management. This process is designated to ensure the consistency of the service management, and it is in particular important to support consistent security service provisioning and management.

9.3.5 GEYSERS Services Delivery Framework for On-Demand Infrastructure Services Provisioning (SDF-VI)

The GEYSERS Service Delivery Framework is designed to support the novel business and operational models during on-demand infrastructure service provisioning.

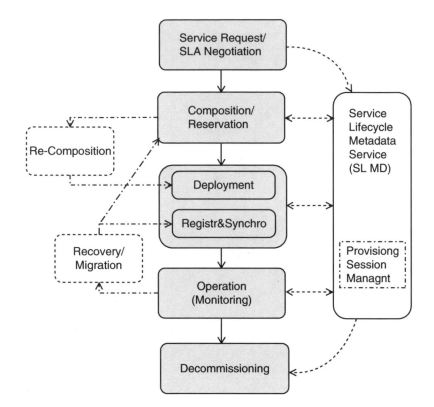

Fig. 9.2 On-demand infrastructure (composable) service provisioning workflow

The on-demand Infrastructure (Composable) Service Provisioning Workflow includes the following stages, as shown in Fig. 9.2. These stages are quite intact with the proposed Complex Resource Provisioned (CRP) model [3], which was used for defining multi-domain authorization infrastructure for on-demand network resource provisioning in the Phosphorus Project.

- Main stages
  - Service Request (including SLA negotiation): The SLA can describe QoS and security requirements of the negotiated infrastructure service along with information that facilitates authentication of service requests from users. This stage also includes generation of the Global Reservation ID (GRI) that will serve as a provisioning session identifier and will bind all other stages and related security context.
  - Composition/Reservation (aka design): Composition/Reservation that also includes Reservation Session Binding with GRI that provides support for complex reservation process in potentially multi-domain, multi-provider environment. This stage may require access control and SLA/policy enforcement.

- Deployment, including Registration/Synchronization: Deployment stage begins after all component resources have been reserved and includes distribution of the common composed service context (including security context) and binding the reserved resources or services to the GRI as a common provisioning session ID. The Registration and Synchronization stage (that, however, can be considered as optional) specifically targets possible scenarios with the provisioned services migration or replanning. In a simple case, the Registration stage binds the local resource or hosting platform runtime process ID to the GRI as a provisioning session ID.
- Operation (including Monitoring): This is the main operational stage of the provisioned on-demand composable services. Monitoring is an important functionality of this stage to ensure service availability and secure operation, including SLA enforcement.
- Decommissioning: Decommissioning stage ensures that all sessions are terminated, data are cleaned up, and session security context is recycled. Decommissioning stage can also provide information to or initiate services usage accounting.

- Additional stages, which can be initiated from the Operation stage and/or based on the running composed service or component services state, such as their availability or failure.

  - Recomposition should address incremental infrastructure changes.
  - Recovery/Migration can use SL-MD to initiate resources re-synchronization but may require recomposition.

The whole workflow should be supported by the Service Life cycle Metadata Service (SLMD).

Defining different life cycle stages allows using different level of service presentation and description at different stages, and addressing different aspects and characteristics of the provisioned services. However, to ensure integrity of the service life cycle management, consistent service context management mechanisms should be defined and used during the whole service life cycle, including the corresponding security mechanisms to protect integrity of the services context. The problem here is that such mechanisms are generically stateful, what imposes problems for a SOA environment, which is defined as generically stateless.

9.4   The Proposed Composable Service Architecture

In the following, we are going to introduce the (Open) Composable Service Architecture (CSA/OCSA) which is an architecture based on SOA and OGSA and aims to provide a framework and a foundation for building composable services and corresponding infrastructures to support on-demand services provisioning in grids and federated systems.

9.4.1 CSA Functional Design

CSA (Fig. 9.3) has been introduced in the GÉANT3 project and provides a general framework for the GEMBus (GÉANT Multidomain Service Bus) development. It is based on the industry adopted Enterprise Service Bus (ESB) [1, 5, 31] extended to support dynamically reconfigurable virtualized services in the GÉANT3 services infrastructure environment and addresses multi-domain issues and distributed services composition and orchestration.

CSA considers the existing grid standards, and specially OGSA, and is used to integrate heterogeneous systems in both ways:

- Integrate OGSA services among them.
- Integrate OGSA infrastructures with additional services.

This is achieved through a set of common services for security, registration, accounting, and composition supporting a service life cycle model for dynamic provisioning.

In what follows, we will describe the overall architecture for Composable Services and provide a framework for defining functionality and operation of all its components.

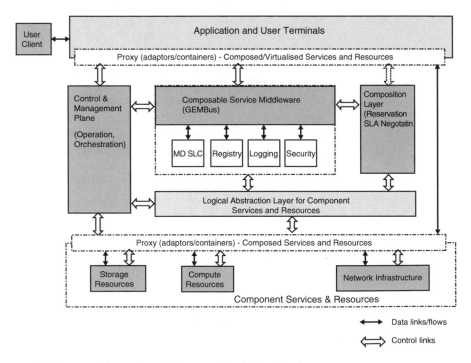

Fig. 9.3 Composable service architecture and main functional components

The proposed CSA provides a framework for the design and operation of the composite/complex services provisioned on-demand. It is based on component services virtualization, which in its own turn is based on the logical abstraction of the component (physical/real) services and their dynamic composition. Composite services may also use the Orchestration service provisioned as a CSA infrastructure service to operate composite service-specific workflows.

One of the important components of the proposed architecture is the CSA middleware that should ensure smooth service operation during all stages of the composable service life cycle.

To be included into CSA infrastructure, component/physical services need to implement a special adaptation layer that is capable of supporting major CSA provisioning stages, in particular, services identification, services metadata including security context, and provisioning session management.

CSA defines and implements also special adaptation layer interfaces providing the necessary functionality to support dynamically provisioned control and management.

Composable Service Middleware (CSA-MW) is an important component of the CSA that provides a common interaction environment for both (physical) component services and composite services (composed of the former). Besides exchanging messages, CSA-MW also contains/provides a set of basic/general infrastructure services required to support reliable and secure (composite) service delivery and operation.

The ongoing GEMBus development will provide a generic/reference CSA middleware implementation. CSA implementation suggestions and details are discussed in the next section.

9.4.2   Architectural Layers

CSA is built on GEMBus [19] which is a multi-domain communication environment that adopts the layering approach defined in WSA [9]. CSA extends WSA with additional lower and upper layers to reflect use cases specific to Internet and telecommunications services.

These include the following layers as shown in Fig. 9.4:

- Networking Layer: This layer provides the possibility to apply technologies typical in distributed enterprise applications, such as VPN.
- Transport Layer: This layer may define functionality specific for service communication such as transport layer security (using TLS/SSL protocols), assigning service (types) to specific ports, etc.
- Messaging Layer: This layer defines functionality related to message handling such as message routing, message format transformation, etc.
- Virtualization Layer: This actually consists of a Logical Abstraction Layer and a Composition and Orchestration layer. This layer provides functionality to compose services and support/drive their interaction, e.g., with workflows, to ensure application interactions.

Fig. 9.4 Composable
service architecture layers

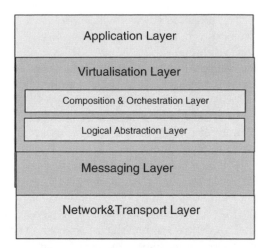

- Application Layer: This layer hosts application-related protocols and represents applications, where the major goal is application-related data handling.

Security services are applied at multiple layers to ensure consistent security. Management functions are also present at all layers and can be seen as the management plane, similar to the NGN reference model.

9.4.3 CSA Implementation

9.4.3.1 CSA Middleware and GEMBus

Figure 9.5 illustrates the planned GEMBus architecture.
The GEMBus infrastructure includes three main groups of functionalities:

- GEMBus Messaging Infrastructure (GMI) that includes, first of all, a messaging backbone and other message handling supporting services such as message routing, configuration services, secure messaging, event handler/interceptors. The GMI is built on and extends the generic Enterprise Service Bus (ESB) functionality to support dynamically configured multi-domain services as defined by GEMBus.
- GEMBus infrastructure services that support reliable and secure composable service operation and the whole service provisioning process. These include such services as Composition, Orchestration, Security, and Life cycle Metadata Service, all provided by the GEMBus environment/framework itself.
- Component services, although typically operated by independent parties, need to implement special GEMBus adaptors or use special plug-in sockets that allow their integration into the GEMBus and CSA infrastructure.

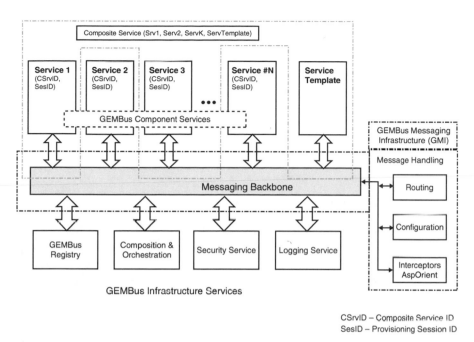

Fig. 9.5 GEMBus infrastructure (including component services, service template, infrastructure services, and core message processing services)

Figure 9.6 illustrates two examples of the composite services that are made of four component services. The difference is that in the second case the composite service contains a special front-end service that is created from the corresponding service template that shall be available for specific kind of applications. Examples of such service templates can be user terminal (or rich user client), or a visualization service. Requiring that the GEMBus framework or toolkit provide a number of typical service templates provides more flexibility in the delivery/provisioning of composite services.

9.4.3.2 General CSA Middleware Requirements

GEMBus as a CSA middleware is committed to provide an open environment for composable service integration and operation. The following are specific features of such an environment:

- GEMBus configuration facility/functionality shall allow service virtualization and dynamic configuration, without (total or partial) GEMBus infrastructure redeployment.
- GEMBus shall support services virtualization by providing configurable logical abstractions of the Composition/Orchestration/Virtualization layer and dynamically configurable message routing.

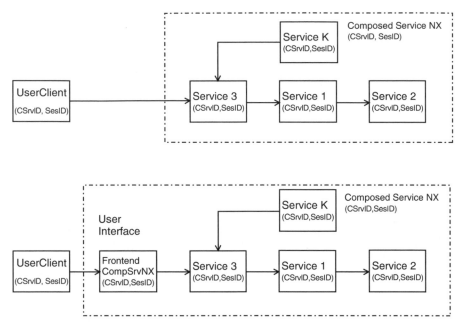

Fig. 9.6 Example of composite service made up of services: Service 1, Service 2, Service 3, Service 4

- GEMBus shall support different stages of the composable services life cycle, in particular, service discovery, composition, operation, and decommissioning. This can be provided via special configuration services and supported by the GEMBus metadata services, providing dynamic services reconfiguration.
- GEMBus shall support event-driven services and allow configurable event recognition, alarming, and recording. This functionality is specifically required for, and targeted to, support service orchestration, workflow management, logging, and accounting.

9.4.4 CSA Security Infrastructure

Security services in the CSA and GEMBus are applied at different layers and can be called from/integrated with different functional components that require, e.g., access control, data protection, or policy-based management.

There are two general areas/domains for which the security measures are defined:

1. Composable security services suitable to be composed with other component services.
2. Security services supporting normal GEMBus operation and service management.

Security services are called from different functional components based on the message properties that are extracted by aspect-based message interceptors. Security services are governed by related security policies. Security services can be designed as pluggable services operating at the messaging layer and can be added as composable services to the other component services. Security services shall support the whole provisioned/composable services life cycle and consequently support session-related security context management.

GSA-Security must implement multilayer security services including transport, messaging, and application/data security, and additionally network layer security for distributed Virtual Private Network (VPN)-based enterprise domains. GSA-Security and GEMBus shall implement basic infrastructure security services to ensure its normal operation such as Requestor identity and message authentication, message content protection including confidentiality and integrity, requestor and request authorization, and others. GSA-Security should support policy-based security services configuration and management and allow policy modification without security services redeployment.

GSA-Security should provide measures for security session context management by securely binding session security context to the session ID. At least three types of session should be considered:

- Message level protocol sequence, e.g., trust/key negotiation, attributes/security tokens exchange, etc.
- Provisioning session that could be identified by the GRI introduced above, which starts from reservation and ends with the service access/use.
- Service resource access, using the same GRI but possibly including multiple/multi-resource access sessions.

9.4.4.1 Security Services Management in CSA

The NIST Special Publication 800-14 Generally Accepted Principles and Practices in Systems Security [29] together with SP 800-27 Engineering Principles for Information Technology Security [28] define a basic set of the generally accepted principles and practices for designing and managing security services. The defined security services life cycle includes the following phases: Initiation, Development/Acquisition, Implementation, Operation/Maintenance, and Disposal. Providing a good basis for security services management, these principles still reflect the traditional approach to services and systems design driven by concepts related to the conceptual and coding phases, omitting service life cycle once they are deployed.

The above-cited NIST special publication 800-14 generally accepted principles and practices in systems security [28] defines security services life cycle in terms of the following typical phases: Initiation, Development/Acquisition, Implementation, Operation/Maintenance, and Disposal.

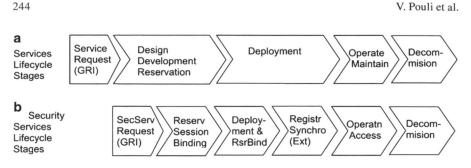

Fig. 9.7 (**b**) The proposed security services life cycle management model and its relation to the general services life cycle management model (**a**)

Figure 9.7b illustrates the proposed Security Service Life cycle Management (SSLM) model that reflects security service operation in a generic distributed multi-domain environment and their binding to the provisioned services and/or infrastructure. The SSLM includes the following stages:

- Service request and generation of the Global Reservation ID (GRI) that will serve as a provisioning session identifier and will bind all other stages and the related security context. The Request stage may also include SLA negotiation which will become a part of the binding agreement to start on-demand service provisioning.
- Design, Development, and Reservation session binding that provides support for complex reservation processes, including the required access control and policy enforcement.
- Deployment stage begins after all component resources have been reserved and includes distribution of the security context and binding the reserved resources or services to the GRI as a common provisioning session identifier.
- Registration and Synchronization stage (that can be considered as optional) that specifically targets possible scenarios after the provisioned services migration or failover. In a simple case, the Registration stage binds the local resource or hosting platform runtime process ID to the GRI as a provisioning session identifier.
- During the Operation stage, the security services provide access control to the provisioned services and maintain the service access or usage session.
- Decommissioning stage ensures that all sessions are terminated, data are cleaned up, and session security context is recycled.

The proposed SSLM model extends the existing SLM frameworks (Fig. 9.7a) and the CRP model earlier proposed by the authors with the new stage Registration and Synchronization that specifically targets such security issues as the provisioned service/resource restoration (in the framework of the active provisioning session), and provide a mechanism for remote data protection by binding them to the session context.

Following, we explain what main processes/actions take place during the different SLM/SSLM stages and what general and security mechanisms are used:

- SLA – used at the stage of the service Request placing and can also include SLA negotiation process.

- Workflow is typically used at the Operation stage as service Orchestration mechanism and can be originated from the design/reservation stage.
- Metadata are created and used during the whole service life cycle and together with security services actually ensure the integrity of the SLM/SSLM.
- Dynamic security associations support the integrity of the provisioned resources and are bound to the security sessions.
- Authorization session context supports integrity of the authorization sessions during Reservation, Deployment, and Operation stages.
- Logging can be actually used at each stage and be essentially important during the last two stages – Operation and Decommissioning.

9.5 Future Research Directions

The CSA specification is considerably based on the GEMBus implementation and will evolve with the GEMBus development. The following issues should be addressed in the ongoing CSA development:

1. Extension to network infrastructure services provisioning allowing also network topology instantiation and control.
2. Provisioning dynamically configurable security services for multi-domain composable services.
3. Applicability for cloud-based infrastructure services provisioning and use of the corresponding open interfaces.
4. CSA compatibility with and positioning with respect to NGN services architecture.

It is also considered that the CSA will be proposed to other GN3 activities and other projects as a common framework for building composed and/or provisioned on-demand infrastructure services. The CSA will be proposed as a contribution to the ISOD-RG (On-demand Infrastructure Services provisioning Research Group) at Open Grid Forum (OGF).

9.6 Conclusions

In this chapter, we have discussed about service-oriented architectures that offer to grid environments a seamless way for communicating services between heterogeneous domains. This kind of architectures is SOA and OGSA, the latter providing additional capabilities and semantics to grid services. Based on these architectures, we have introduced our architecture, CSA, which builds on top of the previous ones and provides additional ways for integrating OGSA and non-OGSA services in a unified way.

We have described the design principles along with the architectural components, the provisioned services life cycle management model, and implementation suggestions and have concluded with the research challenges. We believe that in today's environments where a variety of services is publicly available in various domains, the integration of these services in a unified way using the proposed CSA is of great importance; this can be achieved with the adoption of our architecture.

References

1. Chappell, D.A.: Enterprise Service Bus: Theory in Practice. O'Reilly Media, Sebastopol (2004)
2. Curbera, F., Duftler, M., Khalaf, R., Nagy, W., Mukhi, N., Weerawarana, S.: Unraveling the Web services web: an introduction to SOAP, WSDL, and UDDI. IEEE Internet Comput. **6**(2), 86–93 (March 2002)
3. Demchenko, Y., Cristea, M., De Laat, C., Haleplidis, E.: Authorisation infrastructure for on-demand grid and network resource provisioning. In: Proceedings of the 3rd International ICST Conference on Networks for Grid Applications (GridNets 2009), Greece. ISBN: 978-963-9799-63-9 (2009)
4. Estefan, J., Laskey, K., McCabe, F., Thornton, D.: OASIS Reference Architecture Foundation for service oriented architecture 1.0, Committee Draft 2. http://docs.oasis-open.org/soa-rm/soa-ra/v1.0/soa-ra-cd-02.pdf (2009)
5. Flurry, G., Reinitz, R.: Exploring the Enterprise Service Bus, Part 2: Why the ESB is a fundamental part of SOA. http://www.ibm.com/developerworks/webservices/library/ar-esbpat2 (2007)
6. Foster, I., Kesselman, C.: The Grid 2: Blueprint for a New Computing Infrastructure. Morgan Kauffman Publishers, San Francisco (2004)
7. Foster, I., Kesselman, C., Tuecke, S.: The anatomy of the grid: enabling scalable virtual organizations. Int. J. Supercomput. Appl. **15**(3), 200–222 (2001)
8. Foster, I., Kesselman, C., Nick, J., Tuecke, S.: The physiology of the grid: an open grid services architecture for distributed systems integration. Globus Project. http://www.globus.org/research/papers/ogsa.pdf (2002)
9. Foster, I., Kishimoto, H., Savva, A., Berry, D., Djaoui, A., Grimshaw, A., Horn, B., Maciel, F., Siebenlist, F., Subramaniam, R., Treadwell, J., Von Reich, J.: The open grid services architecture (OGSA), Version 1.5. http://www.gridforum.org/documents/GFD.80.pdf (2006)
10. Fox, G.C., Gannon, D.: Concurrency and computation: practice and experience. Spec. Issue: Workflow Grid Syst.: Editor. **18**(10), 1009–1019 (2006)
11. High, R., Kinder, S., Graham, S.: IBM's SOA Foundation: an architectural introduction and overview. Whitepaper. http://download.boulder.ibm.com/ibmdl/pub/software/dw/webservices/ws-soa-whitepaper.pdf (2005)
12. ITIL: Version 3 Lifecycle Process Model (LPM). http://www.best-management-practice.com/officialsite.asp?DI=597910&trackID=002192 (2010)
13. ITU-T Recommendation Y.2001: General overview of Next Generation Networks (NGN). http://www.itu.int/rec/dologin_pub.asp?lang=e&id=T-REC-Y.2001-200412-I!!PDF-E&type=items (2004)
14. ITU-T Recommendation Y.2011: General principles and general reference model for Next Generation Networks. http://www.itu.int/rec/dologin_pub.asp?lang=e&id=T-REC-Y.2011-200410-I!!PDF-E&type=items (2004)
15. ITU-T Recommendation Y.2234: Open service environment capabilities for NGN. http://www.itu.int/rec/dologin_pub.asp?lang=e&id=T-REC-Y.2234-200809-I!!PDF-E&type=items (2004)
16. ITU-T Recommendation Y.2012: Functional requirements and architecture of the NGN release 1. http://www.itu.int/rec/dologin_pub.asp?lang=e&id=T-REC-Y.2012-200609-S!PDF-F&type=items (2006)
17. ITU-T Recommendation Y.2201: NGN release 1 requirements. http://www.itu.int/rec/dologin_pub.asp?lang=e&id=T-REC-Y.2201-200909-I!!PDF-E&type=items (2006)

18. ITU-T Recommendation Y.2232: NGN convergence service model and scenario using web services. http://www.itu.int/rec/dologin_pub.asp?lang=e&id=T-REC-Y.2232-200801-I!!PDF-E&type=items (Jan 2008)
19. Lopez, D., Thomson, I.: GEANT3 project Deliverable DJ3.3.1: Composable Network Services use cases. http://www.geant.net/Media_Centre/Media_Library/Media%20Library/GN3-09-198-DJ3_3_1_Composable_Network_Services_use_cases.pdf (2010)
20. Merrill, D.: GFD.132 Secure Communication Profile 1.0. Open Grid Forum. http://www.ogf.org/documents/GFD.132.pdf (2008)
21. Microsoft Corporation: Microsoft security development lifecycle – Version 5.0. http://download.microsoft.com/download/F/2/0/F205C451-C59C-4DC7-8377-9535D0A208EC/Microsoft%20SDL_Version%205.0.docx (2010)
22. Open Group: OSIMM: The Open Group Service Integration Maturity Model. https://www.opengroup.org/projects/osimm/uploads/40/17990/OSIMM_v0.3a.pdf (2006)
23. Richardson, L., Ruby, S.: RESTful Web Services. O'Reilly Media, Sebastopol. ISBN-10:0596529260 (2007)
24. Richardson, T., Stafford-Fraser, Q., Wood, K.R., Hopper, A.: Virtual network computing. IEEE Internet Comput. 2(1), 33–38. http://www.computer.org/portal/web/csdl/magazines/internet#4 (1998)
25. Shantenu, J., Merzky, A., Fox, G.: GFD.150 Using clouds to provide grids higher-levels of abstraction and explicit support for usage modes. Version: 1.0. http://www.gridforum.org/documents/GFD.150.pdf (2009)
26. Snelling, D., Kantarjiev, C.: GFD.113 Technical strategy for the Open Grid Forum 2007–2010. Open Grid Forum (2007)
27. Snelling, D., Merrill, D., Savva, A.: GFD.138 "OGSA Basic Security Profile 2.0". Open Grid Forum (2008)
28. Stoneburner, G., Hayden, C., Feringa, A.: NIST Special Publication 800–27 – Engineering principles for information technology security (a baseline for achieving security), National Institute of Standards and Technology. http://csrc.nist.gov/publications/nistpubs/800-27A/SP800-27-RevA.pdf (2001)
29. Swanson, M., Guttman, B.: NIST Special Publication 800–14 – Generally accepted principles and practices for securing information technology systems. National Institute of Standards and Technology. http://csrc.nist.gov/publications/nistpubs/800-14/800-14.pdf (2006)
30. Theilmann, W. et al.: Deliverable D.A1a Framework architecture. European research project SLA@SOI. Empowering the service industry with SLA-aware infrastructures. http://sla-at-soi.eu/wp-content/uploads/2009/07/D.A1a-M12-Framework_Architecture.pdf (2009)
31. Woolf, B.: ESB-oriented architecture: the wrong approach to adopting SOA. http://www.ibm.com/developerworks/webservices/library/ws-soa-esbarch (2007)

Chapter 10
Phoenix: Employing Smart Logic to a New Generation of Semantically Driven Information Systems

Aggelos Liapis, Nasos Mixas, and Nikitas Tsopelas

Abstract The pervasive connectivity of the Internet, coupled with an increasing distribution of organizations, is introducing profound changes in the way enterprises are set up and operated and are intensifying the forces within and across enterprises. To remain competitive under this environment, organizations need to move fast and to quickly adapt to business-induced changes. It must be able to sense the salient information, transform it into meaningful, quality business metrics, respond by driving the execution of business decisions into operational systems; and finally track the results against actions and expectations. In parallel with this trend, there have been interesting developments in the fields of Intelligent Agents (IA) and Distributed Artificial Intelligence (DAI), notably in the concepts, theories, and deployment of intelligent agents as a means of distributing computer-based problem-solving expertise. Intelligent agents are well suited to the emerging character of the adaptive enterprise in which the distributed operations must be orchestrated into a synchronous flow. Despite various efforts in studying object-oriented or agent-oriented adaptive enterprises, there are no working systems being widely used in practice. This is because the state of the art of artificial intelligence has not reached to a stage such that an adaptive system can be operated effectively without human beings involvement. In this chapter, we introduce a prototype semantically driven communication middleware platform (Phoenix), which comprises a set of features, services, and utilities providing RAD capabilities to modern business frameworks and systems. Phoenix has been designed and developed to serve as a

A. Liapis (✉)
Research & Development Department, European Dynamics SA,
209, Kifissias Av. & Arkadiou Str, Maroussi, 151 24, Athens, Greece
e-mail: aggelos.liapis@eurodyn.com

N. Mixas • N. Tsopelas
European Dynamics SA, 209, Kifissias Av. & Arkadiou Str,
Maroussi, 151 24, Athens, Greece

N.P. Preve (ed.), *Grid Computing: Towards a Global Interconnected Infrastructure*,
Computer Communications and Networks, DOI 10.1007/978-0-85729-676-4_10,
© Springer-Verlag London Limited 2011

central hub for building Web-based applications through its supported functionality, and/or for interconnecting them together and with other external Web-based applications.

10.1 Introduction

The distributed application integration has some longstanding problems. For instance, technology and standardization efforts supporting distributed interactions Web services [2], MOM [6], MPI [12], and RPC/RMI [1] have made it possible to implement solutions to the difficult problems of distributed communication; however, a general framework/theory for integration remains elusive. The problem seems to be one of finding the right abstractions [1]. Researchers seem to agree that the problem of communicating autonomous systems is not well understood and yet middleware vendors appear confident that the problem is well understood, at least with respect to their tools [1, 4, 5, 7]. While there are incredibly complex problems yet to be solved in the area of middleware, perhaps those issues and aspects related to coupling/decoupling lie at the very heart of the problem. In their paper about the semantics of blocking and non-blocking send and receive primitives, Cypher and Leu in [4] have stated that: "Unfortunately, the interactions between the different properties of the send and receive primitives can be extremely complex, and as a result, the precise semantics of these primitives are not well understood."

Vendors and standards bodies offer many solutions and ideas within this domain, however each appears to be embroiled in the paradigm it emerged from. For instance, CORBA is founded and based on an RPC paradigm, whereas MOM1 platforms are based on a strongly decoupled paradigm involving a hub architecture, with a MOM service at the center. Despite their different origins, each appears to have technical and conceptual limitations.

Due to the lack of a widely accepted formal theory for communication and the fact that each type of solution is based on a totally different paradigm, models and implementations of middleware-based communication are disparate, and not portable. Rephrased, the models over deployed distributed systems are not portable in the implementation sense, and not even in the conceptual sense. Due to the lack of formality in this domain, solutions and tools for integration are difficult to compare as well.

This chapter describes an advanced open source middleware platform called Phoenix which is based on a multitier dynamic architecture allowing components to be dynamically plugged-in while a system is already up and running. The main characteristics and design of the platform allows third-party developers to use it as a scaffolding or basis for creating larger, more complex applications without having to re-implement commonly needed functionality.

Basic and more advanced features already offered by the different modules of the platform allow its users to focus on the business logic of their particular implementation, leaving the heavyweight lifting of basic functionality such as user management, auditing, logging, security & encryption, etc. being totally handled by Phoenix CM.

Additionally, more advanced services such as document management, forum, calendar, etc. are also offered as out-of-the-box services to be seamlessly amalgamated with new software. In addition to the core services, Phoenix CM comprises of a Jumpstart module, allowing domain experts to quickly integrate Phoenix Core into their own implementation, effectively hiding the communication layer from the end users, providing integrated and developer friendly wrappers.

The front-end part of Phoenix CM is a modern Web 2.0 Web application providing Web-based access to the functionality of Phoenix Core and Phoenix Jumpstart.

10.2   Background

This section provides an overview of background knowledge related to the study of decoupling in communicating middleware. It first defines some essential terms used throughout the paper, and proceeds with an overview of related work.

10.2.1   Definitions

An endpoint is an entity that is able to participate in interactions. It may have the sole capability of sending/receiving messages and defer processing the message to another entity, or it may be able to perform both. An interaction is an action through which two endpoints exchange information [10]. The most basic form of this occurs during a message exchange (elementary interaction).

A channel is an abstraction of a message destination. Middleware solutions such as JMS, WebsphereMQ, and MSMQ use the term "queues" to mean basically the same thing, but the crucial point here is that a channel is a logical address, not a physical one, thus they introduce a space decoupling to traditional point-to-point messaging. Thus, the sender is able to address a message to a symbolic destination, and the receiver may register the intention to listen for messages from the symbolic destination. Interestingly, such a decoupling means that a channel is not necessarily restricted to one message receiver – many endpoints may share one channel, in which case they may either share/compete for each message, depending on whether or not the channel is a publish–subscribe. Channels have been enhanced and extended with many functions, including the preservation of message sequence [4, 5] authentication and nonrepudiation [6].

A message is a block of data that gets transported between communicating endpoints. Depending on the middleware, it could contain header elements such as a message ID, timestamp, and data type definition or it could just contain data. The message may contain a command, a snapshot of state, a request, or an event among other things. It may be transactional, reliable, real-time, or delayed, and it often is transported over a "channel." However, it could just as easily be sent over sockets.

10.2.2 Related Work in Middleware Classification

Cross and Schmidt in [3] have discussed a pattern for standardizing Quality-of-Service (QoS) control for long-lived, distributed real-time and embedded applications. This proposal briefly described a technology that would be of assistance. They outlined the technology as configuration tools that assist system builders in selecting compatible sets of infrastructure components that implement required services. In the context of that paper, no proposals or solutions were made for this; however, the proposals of our paper perhaps provide a fundamental basis for the selection of compatible sets of infrastructure.

Schantz and Schmidt in [11] have described four classes of middleware: Host infrastructure middleware provides a consistent abstraction of an operating system's communication and concurrency mechanisms, for example, sockets. Distribution middleware abstracts the distribution and generally allows communication over heterogenous systems as if they were running in one stand-alone application, for example, CORBA and RMI. Common Middleware Services group together middleware that can provide higher level services such as transactions and security, for example, CORBA and EJB. Domain-Specific Middleware Services classify those that are tailored to the requirements of a specific real-world domain, such as telecom, finance, etc. (e.g., EDI and SWIFT). This classification provides a compelling high-level view on the space of available middleware, but it does not give a precise indication of the subtle differences between alternatives in the light of architectural requirements.

Thompson in [13] has described a technique for selecting middleware based on its communication characteristics. Primary criteria include blocking versus non-blocking transfer [13]. In this work, several categories of middleware are distinguished, ranging from conversational, through request–reply, to messaging, and finally to publish–subscribe. The work, while insightful and relevant, does not attempt to provide a precise definition of the identified categories and fails to recognize subtle differences with respect to non-blocking communication, as discussed later in the chapter. Cypher and Leu in [4] have provided a formal semantics of blocking/non-blocking send/receive which is strongly related to our work. These primitives were defined in a formal manner explicitly connected with the primitives used in MPI [12]. This work does not deal with space decoupling. Our research adopts concepts from this work and applies them to state-of-the-art middleware systems.

10.2.3 Issues, Controversies, and Problems

During the past decade, a substantial amount of R&D effort has focused on developing standards-based middleware, such as Real-time CORBA [8] and QoS-enabled CORBA Component Model (CCM) middleware [14] to address the challenges outlined in the previous paragraph. Middleware is systems software that resides between the applications and the underlying operating systems, network protocol stacks, and hardware and provides the following capabilities:

1. QoS-enabled component middleware is based on the expectation that QoS properties will be developed, configured, monitored, managed, and controlled by a different set of specialists (such as middleware developers, systems engineers, and administrators) than those responsible for programming the application functionality in traditional middleware systems.
2. Standards-based QoS-enabled component middleware defines communication mechanisms that can be implemented over many networks and OS platforms. Component middleware also supports containers that (a) provide a common operating environment to execute a set of related components and (b) shield the components from the underlying networks, operating systems, and even the underlying middleware implementations. By reusing the middleware's communication mechanisms and containers, developers of DRE systems can concentrate on the application-specific aspects of their systems and leave the communication and QoS-related details to middleware developers.
3. QoS-enabled component middleware defines crisp boundaries between components, which can help to reduce dependencies and maintenance costs associated with replacement, integration, and revalidation of components. Likewise, common components (such as event notifiers, resource managers, naming services, and replication managers) can be reused, thereby helping to further reduce development, maintenance, and validation costs.

Despite significant advances in standards-based QoS-enabled component middleware, there remain significant technology gaps that make it hard to support large-scale systems in domains that require simultaneous support for multiple QoS properties [9]. Key technology gaps include the following:

1. Advances in middleware technology and various standardization efforts, as well as market and economical forces, have resulted in a multitude of middleware stacks, such as CORBA, J2EE, SOAP, and .NET. This heterogeneity makes it hard to identify the right middleware for a given application domain. Large-scale systems are therefore built with too much reliance on a particular underlying middleware technology, resulting in maintenance and migration problems over system life cycles.
2. Component middleware enables application developers to develop individual QoS-enabled components that can be composed together into assemblies that form complete systems. Although this approach supports the use of "plug and play" components in large-scale systems, system integrators now face the daunting task of composing the right set of compatible components that will deliver the desired semantics and QoS to applications that execute in large-scale systems.
3. In QoS-enabled component middleware frameworks, application components and the underlying component middleware services can have a large number

of attributes and parameters that can be configured at various stages of the development life cycle, such as:

- During component development, where default values for these attributes could be specified
- During application integration, where component defaults could be overridden with domain-specific defaults
- During application deployment, where domain-specific defaults are overridden based on the actual capabilities of the target system

4. The component assemblies described in bullet 2 above must be deployed in the distributed target environment before applications can start to run. Large-scale system integrators must therefore perform the complex task of mapping the individual components/assemblies onto specific nodes of the target environment. This mapping involves ensuring semantic compatibility between the requirements of the individual components, and the capabilities of the nodes of the target environment.

10.3   The Phoenix Platform

Phoenix Core amalgamates a variety of technologies in a cutting-edge technological stack based on Open Source Software. Phoenix Core is based on a multitier dynamic architecture allowing components to be dynamically plugged-in while a system is already up and running. This section presents the technology stack, the technical architecture as well as the components comprising Phoenix Core in detail. All the components of the Phoenix Core are assorted by detailed Use Cases, thus effectively capturing the requirements of the platform.

10.3.1   Technical Architecture of Phoenix

The Phoenix Core is the heart of all Phoenix-based systems. It is a central integration point allowing functionality to be deployed and later on being accessed by various applications following a Service-Oriented Architecture (SOA) paradigm. In order to allow Phoenix Core to be modular and highly configurable as well as to support runtime deployment/un-deployment of services and external services integration, Phoenix Core can also expose all of its services over Enterprise Service Bus (ESB) architecture (Fig. 10.1)

The ESB refers to a software architecture construct typically implemented by technologies found in a category of middleware infrastructure products, usually based on recognized standards, which provide fundamental services for complex architectures via an event-driven and standards-based messaging engine. An ESB provides an abstraction layer on top of an implementation of an enterprise messaging system, which allows integration architects to exploit the value of messaging

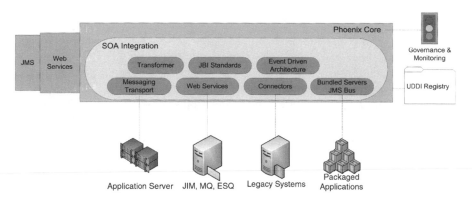

Fig. 10.1 The ESB running on Phoenix Core

without writing code. Contrary to the more classical Enterprise Application Integration (EAI) approach of a monolithic stack in a hub and spoke architecture, the foundation of an ESB is built of base functions broken up into their constituent parts, with distributed deployment where needed, working in harmony as necessary. An ESB does not implement a SOA per se, but provides the features with which one may be implemented.

In Phoenix Core architecture, the ESB is the central piece of software that lies between the business applications and enables communication among them. Phoenix Core is able to replace all direct contact with the applications on the bus, so that all communication takes place via the bus. In order to achieve this objective, Phoenix core encapsulates the functionality offered by its component applications in a meaningful way through the use of an enterprise message model. The message model defines a standard set of messages that the ESB will both transmit and receive. When the ESB receives a message, it routes the message to the appropriate application.

In addition to the actual services/functionality offered by the modules being deployed on Phoenix Core, a set of salient characteristics are also provided by using an ESB:

- Invocation: Support for synchronous and asynchronous transport protocols, service mapping (locating and binding)
- Routing: Addressability, static/deterministic routing, content-based routing, rules-based routing, policy-based routing
- Mediation: Adapters, protocol transformation, service mapping
- Messaging: Message processing, message transformation, and message enhancement
- Process Choreography: Implementation of complex business processes
- Service Orchestration: Coordination of multiple implementation services exposed as a single, aggregate service
- Complex Event Processing: Event interpretation, correlation, pattern matching
- Quality-of-Service (QoS): Security (encryption and signing), reliable delivery, transaction management
- Management: Monitoring, audit, logging, metering, and admin console

10.3.2   Services Life cycle

As mentioned above, the functionality offered by Phoenix Core is following the SOA paradigm. SOA provides methods for systems development and integration where systems package functionality as interoperable services. A SOA infrastructure allows different applications to exchange data with one another and aims at a loose coupling of services with operating systems, programming languages, and other technologies that underlie applications. SOA separates functions into distinct units, or services, which developers make accessible over a network in order that users can combine and reuse them in the production of applications. Figure 10.2 presents a typical example of SOA providing a Document Upload service.

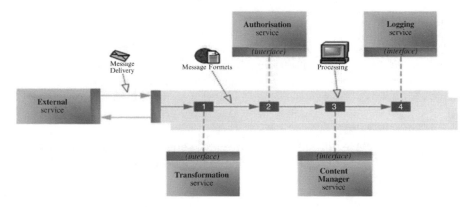

Fig. 10.2 Services life cycle

This represents a combination of existing systems wrapped with a services interface and new services created to enhance the business process. This example illustrates how a document upload command originates from an external system, undergoes a transformation of data elements to support the requirements of the Phoenix Core system, flows through to trigger an authorization check, being processed, and ultimately gets logged as a completed transaction in the Logging Service. Rather than an integrated application, in this case the document upload process is executed as a sequence of heterogeneous process steps, coordinated by the SOA infrastructure. In this example, the Phoenix Core is providing the connectivity with routing between services, the transformation of XML data to allow services with varying interfaces to communicate, and the business process sequencing of services.

10.3.2.1   ESB Services

ESB services may be any of a number of types. Typical ESB services which implement mediation are XML Transformation, Content-Based Routing, User-Defined Mediation, etc. An XML Transformation Service provides data conversion from one XML document to another according to an XSLT specification. A Content-Based Routing Service directs messages to various other service endpoints according to configured routing rules. A User-Defined Mediation Service implements a function such as logging or custom validation which complements the core business logic. A User-Defined ESB Service connects to business services to implement core business logic.

The ESB services are deployed and executed on an ESB, providing the system management interfaces, the management of communication protocols, the capability to have multiple threads executing services for scalability, and the standard capability to execute distributed processes.

10.3.2.2   Connected Business Services

Deployed services implement the business logic for Phoenix Core-based applications. Types of business services include: Content Manager, Cryptography, Calendar, Wiki, Blogs, etc. Each of these types of business services can communicate with each other through the ESB, and with ESB services to perform mediation.

10.3.2.3   Communications and ESB Processes

A service being deployed on Phoenix Core sends and receives messages through references to ESB endpoints and ESB addresses. For example, an ESB service such as the Document Manager server can configure its Exit to refer to the ESB address of another service to receive output messages – in this example that would be the Logging Service. Alternatively, the ESB address can refer to an ESB process.

An ESB process is defined by an ESB Itinerary which contains a sequence of Process Steps. Each process step can invoke one (or multiple) ESB services, other ESB processes, or an external Web service. The ESB itinerary is carried with its associated ESB message providing a completely distributed, and hence reliable, execution environment for the ESB process. There is no central processing engine for the itinerary as each ESB container can process and route the next step in the ESB itinerary. This provides both efficient execution without the need to communicate to a central site and reliability as processing can continue even with some losses of connectivity. It is noteworthy that each ESB service can have its entry and exit endpoints changed without requiring changes to their implementations.

Service Endpoints

The Service Endpoint provides the capability for ESB services to send and receive messages with a specified Quality-of-Service, for example, best-effort, reliable or guaranteed, once-and-only-once, etc. The connection tells what supporting messaging channel is used by an ESB endpoint to connect with an ESB service or a business service. This messaging channel can use an ESB native connection, or for external systems can use Web Service Connection, JMS

Connection or JCA (J2EE Connector Architecture) Adapter, etc. The ESB Connection employs user-configurable asynchronous and synchronous delivery semantics including "publish-and-subscribe," "send-and-forget," and "request–reply." If a business or ESB service needs to change the manner in which it connects, this can be affected without requiring changes to its implementation. When services require differing types of connections, the ESB provides the mediation between the differing protocols.

Industry-standard Web Services Definition Language (WSDL) definitions can be created for ESB services and ESB processes. This allows the use of standard tools and integration with other SOA infrastructure components such as a UDDI Registry. Key benefits of this approach to implementing ESB services, mediation, and connection to business services include:

- Business agility through rich support for mediation services, including XML transformation and built-in support for distributed ESB processes
- Broad reach across many kinds of business services and communications protocols; integration of heterogeneous legacy and new Web service elements
- Distributed process execution, performance, and reliability even in highly distributed deployments

10.3.2.4   Messaging

Communication between Phoenix Core and external application takes place using a messaging infrastructure. Messages can originate from different communication protocols and the ESB makes sure that those messages are converted to a "neutral" form once inside the bus.

Normalized Messages

The ESB used in Phoenix Core uses a neutral message format, a normalized message, consisting of a payload, optional attachments, and metadata for interaction between consumers and providers. Message normalization is the process of mapping context-specific data to a context-neutral abstraction to transport data in a standard format. A normalized message consists of three main parts:

1. The Message content, also referred to as payload, which is an XML document that conforms to an abstract WSDL message type with no protocol encoding or formatting.
2. The Message properties or metadata that hold extra data associated with the message. This metadata can include security information, transaction-context information, component-specific information, etc. Message properties form the first part of what is referred to as the message context.
3. Message attachments referenced by the payload, contained within a data handler used to manipulate the attachment's contents. Attachments can be non-XML data. Attachments form the second part of the message context.

Normalized Messages Router

The message exchange, when Phoenix Core services are deployed on an ESB, depends on a component called Normalized Message Router (NMR) to route message exchange objects between service consumers and providers. The NMR performs such message delivery with varying qualities of service, depending on application needs and the nature of the messages being delivered. An NMR is not embodied by any concrete object. It is abstracted as a set of Application Programming Interfaces (APIs) and Service Provider Interfaces (SPIs) as well as components. The NMR APIs include:

- JBI Message API
- JBI Service API
- JBI Message Exchange Factory API
- Service Description SPI
- Message Exchange Patterns API
- Endpoint Reference API

The principal purpose of the NMR is to route normalized message exchanges from one component to another where messages are delivered in a normalized form. Binding components must convert protocol/transport-specific messages to a normalized form. Binding components and service engines interact with the NMR via a delivery channel, which provides a bidirectional delivery mechanism for messages. An external service consumer sends a service request across a specific protocol and transport to a binding component. The binding component converts the request to a normalized message. The binding component then creates a message packet called a Message Exchange (ME) and sends it across the binding component's delivery channel to the NMR for delivery to a service provider. After receiving a message, the consuming service engine or binding component creates a normalized message, putting it into a new Message Exchange instance, and sends it to the target ServiceEndpoint instance. After accepting the ME, the ServiceEndpoint component de-normalizes the message into protocol and transport format, and sends the message along to the external service provider.

10.3.2.5   Binding Components

Binding Components (BC) are standard JSR 208 components that plug in to NMR and provide transport independence to NMR and Service Engines. The role of BCs is to isolate communication protocols from the underlying container so that Service Engines are completely decoupled from the communication infrastructure. For example, a BPEL Service Engine can receive requests to initiate BPEL process while reading files on the local file system. It can receive these requests from SOAP messages, from a JMS message, or from any of the other binding components installed into JBI container. Figure 10.3 shows how BCs fit into the Phoenix Core architecture.

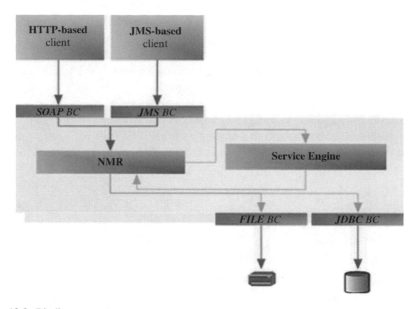

Fig. 10.3 Binding components

As it is depicted on the above figure, BCs act as the entry and exit points of the Phoenix Core services and are capable to understand a variety of different communication protocols. For example, a client application may be using JMS as its communication protocol. Deploying a JMS BC into a Phoenix Core service, allows an application to communicate with the service without having to change its communication protocol stack or having to implement any Phoenix Core-specific intercommunication bridge.

As soon as the message is received by the Phoenix Core JMS BC, it is forwarded to the NMR which converts the incoming message to a "neutral" message (a normalized message) that can be understood by all the other components of the ESB. As long as the processing of the external message remains inside the ESB, the message remains on its normalized form. When processing is done and the message needs to be sent back to the caller application or to another target specified by its routing instructions, the normalized message is forwarded to a new BC capable of understanding how to convert the normalized message to a target-specific format.

In the example of the Figure above, protocol-specific messages are indicated with green arrows whereas protocol-independent messages (normalized messages) are indicated with orange arrows.

Service Engines

A Service Engine (SE) is a JSR 208-compliant JBI runtime component that provides services for executing business logic. SEs are deployed on the ESB similar to the

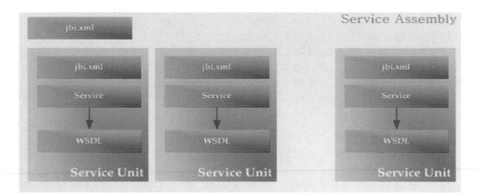

Fig. 10.4 A service assembly deploying multiple service engines

BCs and provide all the custom functionality offered to the third-party applications. In order to deploy a Phoenix Core service as a SE to the ESB, it is necessary to package all of the relevant files into a Service Assembly (SA) file. The SA is essentially an aggregation of one or more Service Units (SUs). Figure 10.4 depicts a typical structure of the SA incorporating multiple SEs.

The SA contains multiple individual units containing a different SE each. The SA package is described by a global jbi.xml file, which describes the contents of the SA being deployed.

Service Orchestration

Orchestration describes the automated arrangement, coordination, and management of complex computer systems, middleware, and services. The standard set of Web service technologies (XML, SOAP, WSDL) provides the means to describe, locate, and invoke a Web service as an entity in its own right. Although a Web service may expose many methods, each Web Service Description Language (WSDL) file describes fairly atomic, low-level functions. What the basic technologies do not give us is the rich behavioral detail that describes the role the service plays as part of a larger, more complex collaboration. When these collaborations are collections of activities designed to accomplish a given business objective, they are known as a business process. The description of the sequence of activities that make up a business process is called an orchestration.

Phoenix Core services, when deployed on an ESB, support an intelligent, fully configurable orchestration engine based on the Business Process Execution Language (BPEL). BPEL is an orchestration language, not a choreography language. The primary difference between orchestration and choreography is executability and control. An orchestration specifies an executable process that involves message exchanges with other systems, such that the message exchange sequences are controlled by the orchestration designer. A choreography specifies a protocol for peer-to-peer (P2P) interactions, defining, for example, the legal sequences of messages exchanged with the purpose of guaranteeing interoperability. Such a protocol is not directly executable, as it allows many different realizations (processes that comply with it). A choreography can be realized by writing an orchestration, for example, in the form of a BPEL process, for each peer involved in it.

In addition to providing facilities to enable sending and receiving messages, the BPEL programming language also supports:

- A property-based message correlation mechanism.
- XML and WSDL typed variables.
- An extensible language plug-in model to allow writing expressions and queries in multiple languages: BPEL supports XPath 1.0 by default.
- Structured programming constructs including if-then-else-if-else, while, sequence (to enable executing commands in order) and flow (to enable executing commands in parallel).
- A scoping system to allow the encapsulation of logic with local variables, fault-handlers, compensation-handlers, and event-handlers.

10.4 Phoenix Components

The following sections present the components comprising the Phoenix Core. For each component, a short description is provided followed by a high-level database schema supported by a front-end snapshot.

10.4.1 User Authentication, Authorization, and Accounting

User Authentication, Authorization, and Accounting (AAA) is a module providing an end-to-end user management functionality. AAA is based on the NIST RBAC model; however, it enhances it in various places to provide additional functionality required in most modern projects.

Authentication refers to the process where one entity verifies another entity's claim to holding a specific digital identity. Commonly, one entity is a client (a user, a client computer, etc.) and the other entity is a server (computer). Authentication is accomplished via the claimant's presentation of an identifier and its corresponding credentials to the verifier. Examples of types of credentials are passwords, one-time tokens, digital certificates, and phone numbers (calling/called).

Authorization refers "to specify access policy," an important security function. The function that the middle "A" in AAA actually refers to is "access control," i.e., the granting or refusing of privileges to an entity for accessing specific services. The access control function uses the access policy specified for an entity to determine whether an access requests from the entity shall be granted or rejected.

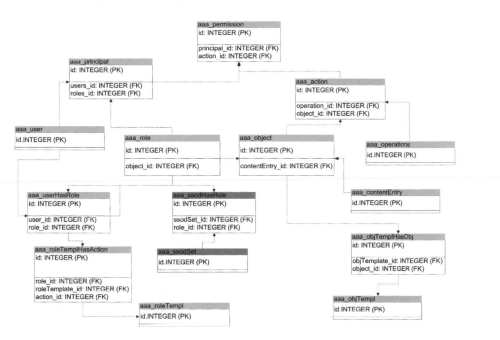

Fig. 10.5 Authentication, authorization, and accounting – high-level database schema

Access control may be based on restrictions, for example, time-of-day restrictions, or physical location restrictions, or restrictions against multiple logins by the same entity or user. Access privileges normally enable an entity to use a specific service. Examples of types of service include, but are not limited to: IP address filtering, address assignment, route assignment, QoS/differential services, bandwidth control/traffic management, compulsory tunneling to a specific endpoint, and encryption.

Accounting refers to the tracking of the consumption of network resources by users. This information may be used for management, planning, billing, or other purposes. Real-time accounting refers to accounting information that is delivered concurrently with the consumption of the resources. Batch accounting refers to accounting information that is saved until it is delivered at a later time. Typical information that is gathered in accounting is the identity of the user, the nature of the service delivered, when the service began, and when it ended (Fig. 10.5).

10.4.2   Cryptography Module

Cryptography is the practice and study of hiding information. In modern times, cryptography is considered a branch of both mathematics and computer science and is affiliated closely with information theory, computer security, and engineering. Cryptography is used in applications present in technologically advanced societies;

examples include the security of ATM cards, computer passwords, and electronic commerce, which all depend on cryptography.

The cryptography module provides users with a set of functionality related to secure message transition, verification, and password management. In order to protect confidential data, users are enabled to use one of various ranges of encryption techniques. Also, developers can use this module to retrieve information about security providers.

10.4.3   Chat/IM Module

Chat/IM module provides a real-time text-based communication between two or more participants. It also supports file graphical emotions, sound effects, text, avatar icons, and more. It is fully http-based, with Ajax interface that performs message exchange without page refreshing. The Chat/IM module can be used to offer full-scale multiuser chat rooms or to provide IM kind of services that end applications can transparently use to provide to their users IM capabilities integrated with them (Fig. 10.6).

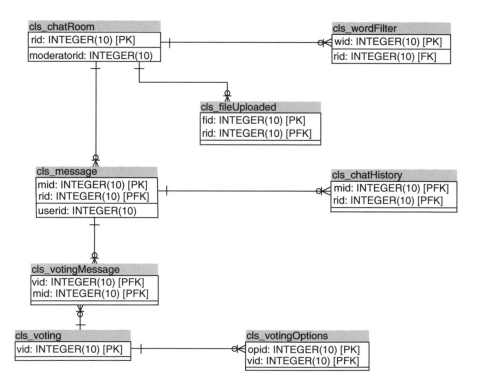

Fig. 10.6 Chat/IM module – high-level database model

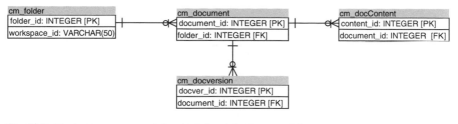

Fig. 10.7 Content manager module – high-level database model

10.4.4 Content Manager Module

The Content Manager module captures, shares, and retains content, enabling users to version document, upload document, download document, view document metadata, view folder, open folder, etc. Users arc given roles for particular actions depending on their access privileges (Fig. 10.7).

10.4.5 Calendar

The Calendar functionality allows users to create calendar events and to arrange meetings (create, modify, submit, and cancel meetings) using e-mail invitations/responses. Two types of Calendar Entries exist: (1) Events, and (2) Meetings. A user that is invited to a meeting/event can accept/decline the invitation. Both calendar entries send e-mail to specified recipients at creation and modification time.

10.4.6 Forum Module

The Forum module enables the users of the platform to interact with each other by exchanging tips and discussing about different topics in threaded discussion groups (fora). This module saves information posted on a particular topic for other people to see at any time, thus creating a dynamic discussion environment (Fig. 10.8).

10.4.7 Scheduler Module

Scheduler implementation is based on Quartz open source software and uses the common database as the repository for its job information. Multiple tasks can be combined under one group and triggered at specific schedule. A set of parameters can be configured to pass to the task at execution time and tasks can be run daily, weekly, monthly, yearly, or scheduled with custom schedules via support of cron-like expressions.

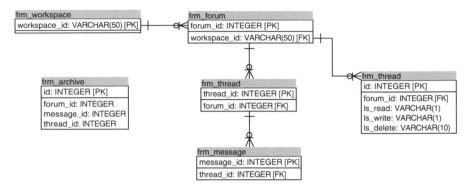

Fig. 10.8 Forum module – high-level database model

The scheduler module can automate many of routine tasks, setting users free from having to wait until some time to run needed applications. It also provides reminders so that user does not forget important things that he/she was planning to get done. It can record all executed tasks to the log file, so that the user stays informed of which task and at what time it was executed.

10.4.8 Lexicon Module

The Lexicon module provides multilingual services to application and Lexicon component allows the manipulation of multilingual elements providing functionality to also manipulate look-up fields. This module can be considered of as a database-driven properties file in which we store key/value pair. These key/value pair pertain to one or more languages defined in the System. This module also has a mini template-processing engine by which user can process template by supplying a template and data to the engine. This also helps to maintain a single source code base for all language versions of product.

10.4.9 Imaging Module

The goal of this module is to provide a Web service that allows developers to provide different image-related functionalities to the end user. Those functionalities may be divided into three separate fields: image manipulation, retrieving information about the image, and OCR (Optical character recognition) . Image manipulation may influence the image dimension, brightness, contrast, color, or any other visible characteristic. The importance of this functionality is the fact that users may use them without extensive knowledge in photography theory.

Users may use this module to retrieve different kind of information about the image: height, weight, creation date, etc. Optical character recognition performs translation of images of handwritten, typewritten, or printed text (usually captured by a scanner) into machine-editable text. In other words, users may submit their image and receive text written at the image as a response.

10.4.10   Mailing

The Mailing component provides fast and reliable service for the management of electronic mails in different forms. It provides process automation by using distribution lists, newsletter templates, and other features. A distribution list is a collection of e-mail addresses. User can use a distribution list to send an e-mail message to multiple people at one time. Phoenix Mailing module provides ways to create, manage, and send newsletter to distribution lists. It also allows users to subscribe to a newsletter as well as allowing easy monitoring of the status of each newsletter, such as e-mails delivered, e-mails pending, etc (Fig. 10.9).

Fig. 10.9 Mailing in Phoenix

10.4.11   Ticket Server Module

Ticket server supports electronic ticket management. Electronic tickets are piece of data that shows that the user is entitled to certain rights. The Ticket server module provides complete support for ticket life cycle.

In the first stage, the user selects the target items and sends the request to the Issuer. Then, the server composes a ticket from the chosen service and hands it over to the client. When the service is being accessed, the ticket would be presented for validation. The ticket information should be read, modified, and updated on the ticket to reflect the current status.

10.4.12   Services Registry Module

The Services Registry allows components to register with the Phoenix Core, so that other components can dynamically find them. The Services Registry is not based on UDDI nor does it envisage replacing UDDI features and registration procedures. End applications incorporating different layers of functionality can, on the runtime, query the Services Registry and according to the existence of a particular service, enable or disable certain features of their functionality.

10.4.13   Clipboard

The Clipboard module can be used by end applications for short-term or long-term data storage and/or data transfers. Applications can dynamically add elements to the clipboard, query the clipboard for the list of the elements previously added, and get items out of the clipboard. The clipboard can be used to transfer information from one place to another as well as a bookmark placeholder.

10.4.14   Dynamic Algorithms Module

The Dynamic Algorithm module provides storage for end applications to deploy script-based algorithms directly into the platform. Currently, algorithms based on BeanShell scripting language are supported. The algorithms deployed into the module can be used either directly by end applications or can be incorporated into components that support integration with the module (such as the User Authentication, Authorization, and Accounting module) to provide dynamic evaluation of results on the server-side.

10.5   Communication Middleware Front End

Further to the above modules, a front-end solution to Phoenix is currently active, providing access to the functionality of Phoenix Core and Phoenix Jumpstart (Fig. 10.10). It is be a Web-based solution using popular and modern Web 2.0 technologies. It focuses mainly on the front-end User Interface components, providing configurations and API for fast development. From technical perspective, it is based on the Strtus 2, a Model View Controller framework, using as a business component framework the Enterprise Java Bean (EJB).

Fig. 10.10 Phoenix front end

10.5.1   Technology Architecture

Figure 10.11 displays the technology architecture of the front-end part of Phoenix CM. It is a modern Web 2.0 Web application providing Web-based access to the functionality of Phoenix Core and Phoenix Jumpstart. It is based on the Struts2 framework and provides a UI using Freemarker template engine.

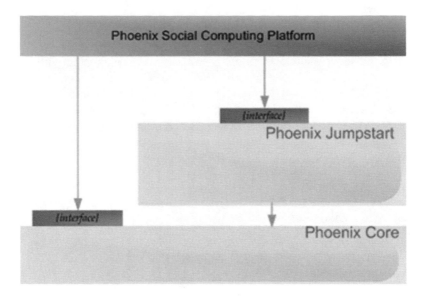

Fig. 10.11 Front-end solution connectivity

The Phoenix component model allows for additional functionality to the application in a controlled and maintainable manner. The developed components make it a breeze to develop transactional Web applications. The object-relational mapping framework (i.e., entity beans) allows us to focus on the abstract data model without having to deal with database-specific SQL statements (Fig. 10.12).

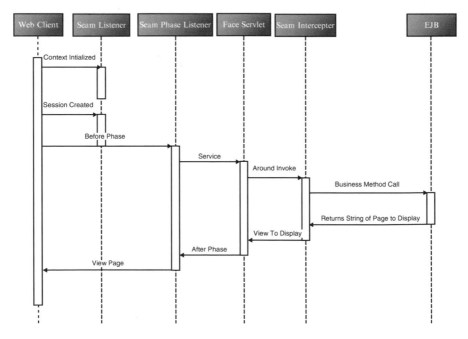

Fig. 10.12 Life cycle of a request

10.6   Future Research Directions

Many claims have been made about the benefits of middleware but, in truth, these claims have not yet been fully substantiated. In practice, experiments have focused on rather narrow and in some ways obvious areas (most notably, mobile computing). While this is beneficial, it is also important for the subject to validate the ideas more generally. Therefore, we are currently investigating the applicability of the middleware approach in a wide range of additional application domains.

The middleware that has so far emerged to support grid applications can be viewed as falling into two generations. The first of these was exemplified by the Globus 2 Toolkit, which provided a loosely coupled set of tools (e.g., for discovering Grid resources, providing security, initiating remote job execution etc.). The second generation then attempted to structure these tools in a more architected way by subsuming them under a Web Services-derived Service-Oriented Architecture.

From the perspective of the broader middleware community, these platforms appear quite primitive. They are extremely limited, in comparison to object-based middleware platforms, in terms of:

1. The provision of generic services (cf. CORBA's fault tolerance, persistent state, automated logging, load-balancing, etc., services).
2. Scalability and performance (cf. EJB and CCM).

Second, they have little or no support for QoS specification and realization as required by sophisticated grid applications. A prime cause of this deficiency is an overreliance by these platforms on SOAP as a communications engine. Although very flexible and general, SOAP clearly shows its limitations when relied on exclusively to support large-volume scientific datasets and its lack of support for interaction types other than messaging and request–reply interactions is also a severe limitation.

Third, current platforms are monolithic; they have zero support for flexible configuration and reconfiguration as found in modern reflective middleware platforms and thus (for example) cannot realistically be deployed on "limited" hardware platforms such as PDAs.

10.7   Conclusion

The Phoenix project targets an ambitious middleware development geared toward social networks and enterprise grids. Phoenix addresses the complexity of the software design through the reuse of many external components (including the CORBA, J2EE, SOAP, and .Net middleware stack) and a sound study of the software architecture. The main challenge here is to meet the expectations of the end users and to foster the adoption of enterprise grids in a community-driven, business environment.

However, technically accessible experience shows that the particular goal is difficult to achieve due to human factors such as security protective measures, data ownership, or legacy systems exploitation. The approach adopted in the design phase of Phoenix was a close interaction with the system end users and the integration of their site-specific constraints. It resulted in heterogeneous site data schemas integration techniques and the definition of a site-centric policy. The Phoenix middleware will thus bridge enterprise grids and local resources to match user desires to control their resources and provide a transitional model toward them.

References

1. Beugnard, A., Fiege, L., Filman. R., Jul, E., Sadou, S.: Communication abstractions for distributed systems. Paper presented at the ECOOP 2003 Workshop Reader, Darmstadt (2004)
2. Chinnici, R., Gudgin, M., Moreau, J., Schlimmer, J., Weerawarana, S.: Web Services Description Language (WSDL) Version 2.0. W3C Recommendation (2004)
3. Cross, J.K., Schmidt, D.C.: Applying the quality connector pattern to optimise distributed real-time and embedded applications. In: Rabhi, F.A., Gorlatch, S. (eds.) Patterns and Skeletons for Parallel and Distributed Computing, pp. 209–235. Springer, London (2003)
4. Cypher, R., Leu, E.: The semantics of blocking and nonblocking send and receive primitives. Paper presented at the Proceedings of 8th International Parallel Processing Symposium (IPPS), Cancún (1994)
5. Eugster, P., Felber, P., Guerraoui, R., Kermarrec, A.: The many faces of publish/subscribe. ACM Computing Surveys 35(2), 114–131 (2003)
6. Hohpe, G., Woolf, B.: Enterprise Integration Patterns: Designing, Building, and Deploying Messaging Solutions. Addison-Wesley, Boston (2003)
7. Kaddour, M., Pautet, L.: Towards an adaptable message oriented middleware for mobile environments. Paper presented at the Proceedings of the IEEE 3rd workshop on Applications and Services in Wireless Networks, Bern (2003)
8. Krishna, A.S., Schmidt, D.C., Klefstad, R., Corsaro, A.: Real time COBRA Middleware. In: Mahmoud, Q. (ed.) Middleware for Communications. Wiley, New York, pp. 413–434 (2004)
9. Liapis, A., Christiaens, S.: Collaboration across the enterprise: an ontology based approach for enterprise interoperability. In: Mentzas, G., Gouvas, P., Bouras, T., Friesen, T. (eds.) Semantic Enterprise Application Integration for Business Processes: Service-Oriented Frameworks. IGI Global, Harrisburg, pp. 1–18 (2009)
10. Quartel, D., Ferreira, L.P., Sinderen, M., Franken, H., Vissers, C.: On the role of basic design concepts in behaviour structuring. Computer Networks and ISDN Systems 29(4), 413–436 (1997)
11. Schantz, R., Schmidt, D.: Middleware for Distributed Systems: Evolving the Common Structure for Network-centric Applications. In: Marciniak J.J. (ed.) Encyclopedia of Software Engineering vol.1. Wiley, New York (2002)
12. Snir, M., Otto, S., Walker, D., Huss-Lederman, S., Dongarra, J.: MPI-The Complete Reference. The MPI Core, vol. 1, 2nd edn. MIT, Cambridge (1998)

13. Thompson, J.: Toolbox: avoiding a middleware muddle. IEEE Software **14**(6), 92–98 (1997)
14. Wang, N., Gill, C.D., Schmidt, D.C., Gokhale, A., Natarajan, B., Loyall, J.P., Schantz, E., Rodrigues, C.: QoS-enabled middleware. In: Mahmoud, Q. (ed.) Middleware for Communications. Wiley, New York, pp. 281–302 (2003)

Part IV
Grid Computing and Scientific Problems

Chapter 11
State-of-Art with PhyloGrid: Grid Computing Phylogenetic Studies on the EELA-2 Project Infrastructure

Raul Isea, Esther Montes, Antonio Juan Rubio-Montero, and Rafael Mayo

Abstract PhyloGrid is an application developed in the framework of the EELA-2 project devoted to the calculation of Phylogenies by means of the MrBayes software, that is, Bayesian statistics. To the moment, it has been used to perform studies on the Human Immunodeficiency Virus (HIV), the Human Papillomavirus (HPV), and the DENgue Virus (DENV). PhyloGrid aims to offer an easy interface for the bioinformatics community, which abstracts the final user from the ICT (Information and Communications Technology) underneath, so only the definition of the parameters for doing the Bayesian calculation should be set, including the model of evolution as well as a multiple alignment of the sequences previously to the final result. This chapter provides a description of the application and some new results related to the aforementioned diseases is also shown.

11.1 Introduction

Nowadays, the determination of the evolution history of different species is one of the more exciting challenges that are currently emerging in the Computational Biology [30]. In this framework, phylogeny is able to determine the relationship among the species and, in this way, to understand the influence between hosts and virus [15]. Even more, this methodology is allowing the opening of new strategies for the resolution of scientific problems such as the determination of the preserved

R. Isea
Fundación IDEA, Caracas, Venezuela

E. Montes • A.J. Rubio-Montero • R. Mayo (✉)
Centro de Investigaciones Energeticas Medioambientales y Tecnologicas (CIEMAT),
Avda. Complutense, 22, 28040 Madrid, Spain
e-mail: rafael.mayo@ciemat.es

N.P. Preve (ed.), *Grid Computing: Towards a Global Interconnected Infrastructure*,
Computer Communications and Networks, DOI 10.1007/978-0-85729-676-4_11,
© Springer-Verlag London Limited 2011

regions from the probabilistic relationship among the phylogenetic profiles of organisms [18]. It is also being used in the calculation which determines the protein–protein interaction [28], so it is important to develop a tool which could integrate the information coming from a research area with no computing limitations for the determination of such a relationship. With respect to the phylogenetic calculus, the main limitation lays on the computational time which demand, the ratio of which raises with the number of sequences, so it is crucial to develop efficient tools for obtaining accurate solutions. Thus, 1,000 taxa generate $2.5 \cdot 10^{1167}$ trees, so among all of them the potential consensus tree is found. To this, the storage requirements must be added since the generated outputs can rise to the range of TB. That is why, it is clear to understand the computational challenge that this work represents.

Because of this, several techniques for estimating phylogenetic trees such as the distance-based method (which generates a dendrogram, i.e., they do not show the evolution, but the changes among the sequences), the maximum parsimony technique, the maximum likelihood method, and the Bayesian analysis (mainly Markov Chain Monte Carlo inference, MCMC) have been developed. The latest is based on probabilistic techniques for evaluating the topology of the phylogenetic trees; so it is important to point out that the Maximum Parsimony methods are not statistically consistent, that is, the consensus tree cannot be found with the higher probability because of the Long Branch attraction effect [3].

During the past few years, MrBayes software [27] has been used inside PhyloGrid for obtaining phylogenetic trees in several biological challenges. It is important to indicate that MrBayes is relatively new in the construction of these trees as the reader can check in the pioneering work of Rannala and Yang in [26]. This methodology works with the Bayesian statistics previously proposed by Felsentein in 1968 as indicated in [11], a technique for maximizing the subsequent probability. The reason for using this kind of approach is that it deals with higher computational speed methods, so the possible values for the generated trees can all be taken into account not being any of them ruling out the others. From the biological point of view, it is important to point out that these trees can lead to a final consensus tree, the value of which could be obtained with this methodology (known as parametric bootstrap percentages or Bayesian posterior probability values) and can give information about the reproducibility of the different part of the trees, but this kind of data does not represent a significant statistical value [9].

Thus, based on MrBayes software, the PhyloGrid application aims to offer to the scientific community an easy interface for calculating phylogenetic trees by means of a workflow with Taverna [21]. In this way, the user is able to define the parameters for doing the Bayesian calculation and to determine the model of evolution. In addition to this, no knowledge from his/her side about the computational procedure is required.

Some scientific results obtained with PhyloGrid are related to the Human Papillomavirus (HPV) [12], the Human Immunodeficiency Virus (HIV) [13], and the Dengue Virus [14].

The main profit that this kind of workflows offers is that they integrate in a common development several modules (tools) connected one to each other. Even more, the deployment of the application with Taverna allows any researcher downloading the complete workflow, making easy in this way their spread in the scientific community. Taverna also allows the user to access biological databases and applications, construct complex analysis workflows from components located on both remote and local machines, and run these workflows on their own data and visualize the results.

There are two approaches for integrating and accessing an application in Taverna: Web services and Taverna plug-ins. We have chosen the first one. The reason, besides Taverna was originally designed to integrate and interoperate with Web services, is that creating a Web service for an application makes this application usable for any Taverna Workbench without requiring any installation. Moreover, using Web services is the standard way of interoperating with grid services, for instance Globus services.

In the following sections, we provide a brief description of the different tools and software which are present inside PhyloGrid and the details about how the Web service connecting Taverna with PhyloGrid has been implemented. In addition, some biological examples are also described.

11.2   PhyloGrid Structure

PhyloGrid is based on several modular tools and software which make up its structure. All of them are open source and can operate with any Linux Operating System, so it aims to be used by any bioinformatics community. In the next subsections, the main characteristics of them can be found, as well as the problems and drawbacks that restrict or make conditional their use.

11.2.1   MrBayes

Bayesian inference is a powerful method which is implemented in the program MrBayes [27] for estimating phylogenetic trees that are based on the posterior probability distribution of the trees.

Currently is included in different scientific software suites for cluster computing. This easiness allows the program to be ported to the grid. On the other hand, its main drawback is that its execution for millions of iterations (generations) requires a large amount of computational time and memory. An example is [4], where 143 angiosperms were determined by means of MrBayes. In that work, four independent Markov Chains were run, each with three heated chains for 100 million generations, the authors sampled the runs every 10,000 generations and used a burning of 70 million steps to generate a majority rule consensus tree that was used to calculate PDC.

Such a methodology is basically the same for other calculations and the number of iterations will depend on the convergence from the chains. In fact, this kind of scientific calculation is extremely complex from a mathematical point of view, but also from the computational one where the phylogenetic estimation for a medium size dataset (50 sequences, 300 nucleotides for each sequence) typically requires a simulation for 250,000 generations, which normally runs for 50 h on a PC with an Intel Pentium 4 2.8 GHz processor.

Even more, Pérez et al. in [24] shows that the study of 626 domains of prokaryotic genomes, due to they are a major class of regulatory proteins in eukaryotes, represents by itself a computational challenge that must be limited to the analysis of the results instead of trying to delimit the number of obtained results by the number of sequences that implies the computational time.

11.2.2   Is the MrBayes Program the Best Option?

With respect to the convergence of Bayesian inferences, the online system for graphical exploration of Markov Chain Monte Carlo (MCMC) AWTY [20] offers two diagnostics and can be very useful since it is geared toward assessing convergence of topologies (the tree itself), rather than convergence of molecular evolutionary parameters. First, the slide command shows the posterior probabilities of clades for nonoverlapping samples of trees in the sample (basically, a sliding window of posterior probabilities). If a coarse scale of analysis shows posterior probabilities that vary widely during the course of a single run, this is strong evidence that runs have not converged. Second, the compare command option, which plots pairwise split frequencies for a series of independent MCMC runs. With this tool, further wrong convergence results can be avoided.

This tool is useful for the Bayesian case as it also allows the analysis of the methods currently used by practicing systematists for evaluating the utilized convergence assessments. Thus, it can be inferred that the examination of stationarity of InL values is commonly not adequate. Besides, analyzing multiple runs can be done by means of checking the standard deviation of split frequencies for independent runs or comparing posterior probabilities for independent runs; it could be a good approach in general, but it could fail if only two independent runs are taken into account (in the case that the trees pace for the dataset could contain, for example, two [rather different] topologies of high and equal probability, so at convergence, the MCMC sampler should visit both of these topologies in proportion to their posterior probability).

Nevertheless, a major problem arises if it takes many generations to move between these topologies. Even for a highly optimized MCMC sampler, it might take many millions of generations to move between "distant" regions of tree space, particularly for large datasets. If this is true, two runs is far from adequate, because there is a 50% chance that two independent runs will find the same high-probability topology first, and if not run for a sufficient number of generations, it will appear as though the runs have converged, based on both similarity of posterior probabilities, standard deviation of split frequencies, etc. This is something of a worst-case scenario, because certain clades would appear to have ~1.00 posterior probability, when in fact the true posterior probability might be closer to 0.5.

Another frequent strategy is to check convergence of molecular evolutionary parameters, either by estimating effective sizes of parameters or by checking the Gelman–Rubin proportional scale reduction factor. The problem here is that a little correspondence between convergence of molecular evolutionary parameters and convergence of topologies could be found if both methods are applied independently.

11.2.3 Taverna: A Tool for the Implementation of Workflows

The workflow is fully built in Taverna [21], whose support for SOAP-based Web services has been enhanced within the last releases. This enhancement, in particular, relates to the support of Web services that require and/or return data encapsulated in XML format and covers both Document/literal and RPC/encoded-based services.

The workflow is structured in a set of connected WSDL processors that are equivalent to the different steps required to submit a gLite job that performs MrBayes execution, check the status of the job, and finally retrieve the job output. This solution makes the calculations of molecular phylogenies very easy to the researcher by not requiring to type any kind of command at all.

The main profit that these kind of workflows offer is that they integrate in a common development several modules (tools) connected one to each other. Even more, the deployment of the application with Taverna allows any researcher to download the complete workflow, making easy in this way their spread in the scientific community.

This is so because Taverna allows the user to construct complex analysis workflows from components located on both remote and local machines, run these workflows on their own data, and visualize the results. To support this core functionality, it also allows various operations on the components themselves such as discovery and description and the selection of personalized libraries of components previously discovered to be useful to a particular application. Finally, we can indicate that Taverna is based on a workbench window where a main section of an Advanced Model Explorer shows a tabular view of the entities within the workflow. This includes all processors, workflow inputs and outputs, data connections, and coordination links. For using Taverna, it is recommended to create a Web service for the required application that will be integrated into the software. Lately, this Web service will perform the real job submission for the MrBayes execution inside the workflow.

11.2.4 The PhyloGrid Workflow

The structure of the Taverna workflow can be seen in Fig. 11.1, the structure of which has been improved since the first works performed with the PhyloGrid application [19]. Once the user has logged, registered a valid proxy, and introduced all the data needed for his/her job, a background process performs the execution of the PhyloGrid workflow with the input provided by the user.

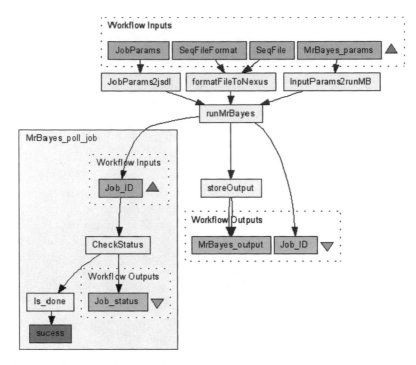

Fig. 11.1 The Taverna workflow used in this work

The workflow receives several inputs: the MrBayes parameters (labeled as MrBayesParams in Fig. 11.1) that define the evolutionary model that will be used in the analysis and the settings for Markov Chain Monte Carlo (MCMC) analysis; the parameters needed to construct the appropriate grid job file (JobParams); the input file with the aligned sequences (Sequences) to analyze; and the format of the file (SeqFormat).

The first three processors of the workflow (JobParams2JDL, inputToNexus, and BuildMrBayesExec) are executed simultaneously and perform some tasks prior to MrBayes execution. Thus, as aforementioned, the processor named JobParams2JDL creates the appropriate file for the job submission to grid; the inputToNexus processor, if necessary, converts the file with the aligned sequences to NEXUS format (not available in the first PhyloGrid release); and the BuildMrBayesExec constructs an executable file with MrBayes commands from the MrBayesParams.

The output of these processors is sent to the core processor of the workflow, that is, submitMrBayes. This processor submits a MrBayes analysis job [12]. Due to the long time that the grid job can take, specially for large data sets, a call to a nested workflow (Check_Workflow) is included to check periodically for job status until the job execution has finished.

The last processor, getResultsMrBayes, retrieves the standard output of the job together with the results obtained from MrBayes execution, previously stored in a

Storage Element. This processor is coordinated from the previous nested workflow. This prevents the final processor running before some condition is true. In this case, the condition is that the job has completed, either with "Done" or "Cancelled" status.

Once the workflow execution ends, the user can retrieve the results of the analysis from the PhyloGrid portal. The PhyloGrid Web service is a WSRF (Web Services Resource Framework) compliant service developed by means of the Open Source Perl implementation of WSRF (WSRF::Lite).

WSRF::Lite is based on SOAP::Lite, the Web services module for Perl, and provides support for most of the Web service specifications (WS-Addressing, WS-Resource Properties, WS-ResourceLifetimes, WS-BaseFaults, WS-ServiceGroups, and WS-Security).

In the tool, several values are previously set such as the number of iterations and the evolution model, so PhyloGrid built the script for running the calculation with no more dependence from the user, making in this way an easy-to-use interface. Inside the tool, the number of iterations is labeled as ITER, the evolution model is defined by the lset variable and the sequences archive must be in nexus format in the current release. An example would be as follows:

```
begin mrbayes;
set autoclose=yes nowarn=yes;
execute file alineado.nex;  # File containing all the
aligned sequences
lset nst=6 rates=gamma; #Definition of the evolution model
mcmc nruns=1 ngen=ITER samplefreq=FREQ file=file-alineado.
nex1;
mcmc file=file-alineado.nex2;
mcmc file=file-alineado.nex3;
end;
```

This is the workflow that must perform its load section by section. Since the first two instructions are always the same for any kind of calculation, the workflow has to begin with the third one (execute...), making a call for aligning the sequences to be studied, and finally the necessary end instruction. As aforementioned, MrBayes uses an evolution model set by the user, which appears in the fourth instruction (i.e., lset...) of the previous example. Here, two options are possible: to allow the researcher to select a specific one or to allow the workflow to do so.

The following instruction (mcmc nruns...) sets the number of executions to be made (ITER, sometime one million iterations) with a concrete frequency (FREQ) and the name of the output files that are going to be generated such as 100 or 500, which will be able to be monitored thanks to the mcmc command. All these options are able to be changed by the final user, who at the beginning of the process has simply defined the name of the output files since MrBayes sets the corresponding extensions for them (the output files are generated with p, t, and mcmc extensions).

Once the workflow has started, MrBayes automatically validates the number of iterations; meanwhile it begins to write the output file and sets the burning value for generating the phylogenetic trees. Once the whole calculation is ended, it can be downloaded by the user for further analysis.

11.2.5 GridWay: A Metascheduler for Improving the Executions on Grid

Even when PhyloGrid is producing reliable scientific results, the improvement of the tool is a key factor for this work team. That is why we are planning to introduce GridWay [10], the standard metascheduler in Globus Toolkit 4, into the whole structure of the application in order to perform the submission of jobs in a more efficient way.

Since GridWay enables large-scale, reliable and efficient sharing of heterogeneous computing resources managed by different LRM systems, it is able to determine in real time the nodes that best fit the characteristics of the submitted jobs. In the case of MrBayes and its parallel mode, this functionality is not only limited to match, in any resource, the adequate tags into the information systems whatever the installed mpich version the node had, but also to select the best resources by means of several statistical methods based on accounting of previous executions. As a consequence, the calculation will be done in the lowest possible time.

At the same time, GridWay can recover the information in case of a canceled job since it creates checkpointers. It also automatically migrates failed jobs to other grid resources. Thus, it performs a reliable and unattended execution of jobs transparently to Taverna that simplifies the workflow development and increases the global performance of PhyloGrid.

11.3   Results

The for developing PhyloGrid is to create an application that offers to the final user a friendly and easy way to obtain accurate biological results by means of a simple interface, so the researcher can block out from the technological grid complexity that lays underneath and focus only on the scientific challenge. This point is extremely important because it prevents the production of "automatic" results that could be flimsy from the biological point of view.

11.3.1   Human Papillomavirus

All of this has been applied to some biological cases; the Human Papillomavirus (HPV) is one of them. With respect to it, it is important to bear in mind that 20% of the female human being are carriers of HPV, which is associated with the development of cervical cancer [17] and is the most transmitted sexual disease around the world. HPV is a member of the Papovaviridae family and is formed by a double DNA circular chain of around 8,000 pair of basis. All of them count on eight genes of early expression (identified as E1–E8) that are involved in virus regulation and replication and on two genes of late expression (L1 and L2) that are responsible for the virus capsid assembly. To date, more than 100 kinds of viruses affecting human beings have been identified and have been classified according to the L1 gene variability, that is, a new type is classified if the similarity with L1 is under 90% with respect to the rest of the known viruses. Because of this, the viruses have been divided into two different categories which correspond to the virus capacity for transforming an infection into a malignant pathology, that is, its oncogenic potential.

We have performed a calculation for determining its evolutionary history in oncogenes that can be seen in Fig. 11.2 by means of the Treeview tool [22]. A similar and independent calculation was also done for obtaining the evolutionary history of HPV with 121 sequences from different Papillomavirus based on the nucleotide sequence of the major capsid gene, the most conserved gene in PV genomes.

The calculations have been performed with the explained PhyloGrid application. The two best-fit models obtained by the jModeltest program [25] for the HPV sequence of the 121 sequences were TIM2+I+G ($-Ln=68335.72$) and GTR+I+G ($-Ln=68328.12$). The latest was chosen because it had a little variation with respect TIM2+I+G.

They show different evolutionary histories derived from the E6 and E7 genes since we have compared L1 with L2 late expressions, L1 with E7, and L2 with E7 too. In these three trees, which have been calculated independently and put in order for its representation, there is a topology similarity score of 85% between L1 and L2, so there is no consistency in the derived topology, that is, the classification based on the variability of the L1 gene is not correct. This result has been able to be deduced because a new evolution history has been performed with a higher number of sequences.

11.3.2   Reevaluating the HIV-1 NEF Protein

Since for the current time, a higher number of sequences can be calculated, some previous results can be checked. PhyloGrid is one of these tools that allow the massive phylogenetics calculation because of the higher computational power and has been used to study the relationship among the species in order to understand the influence between hosts and virus. This is not a new challenge, but the result can validate the developed methodology in a previous calculus and can be extended by using a higher number of input data sets. Thus, the work from Korber et al. [15] has been used as sake of comparison. In addition, an excellent work in this line is the one published by Pennis in [23] who has demonstrated that the oldest HIV/AIDS stumps become from one century ago and not more than 1,930 years, as it has been inferred from a calculation performed in a supercomputer [15]. Moreover, the origin of the oldest stumps in HIV/AIDS, apart from the African one, which was found in Haiti [29], was determined. This evidence is very important if new targets for the development of vaccines are being searched since from now on the testing of vaccines for this disease must include both African and Haitian sequences.

At the same time, AIDS in monkeys is also around 100 years old. Both results have been obtained by means of MyBayes software, which is explained along in this text.

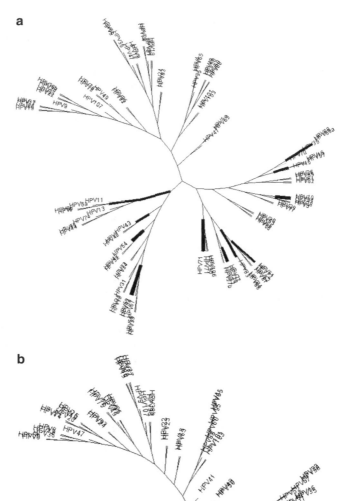

Fig. 11.2 Phylogenetic tree obtained comparing L1 with L2 (**a**) and L2 with E7 (**b**)

Fig. 11.3 Phylogenetic tree
construction using PhyloGrid
of HIV-1 sequences

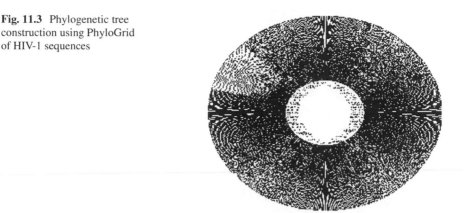

So in this work, the dependence of a successful determination for a biological system with the number of sequences to be aligned is also studied. To do so, the aforementioned HIV case has been selected by using over a thousand different sequences (Fig. 11.3)

In this sense, as can be seen in Fig. 11.4, a calculation where all the sequences of the HIV-1 NEF protein are present is depicted. This protein is one of the rulers of the virus infection. In fact, NEF is the first protein of early stage playing different important roles: the regulation of the CD4 expression in the cell surface [7]; the perturbation in the activity of the T cells and the stimulation of the HIV infection [8]; the induction of the CD4 endocytosis [1]; or a change in its velocity [6]. For performing this result, the evolution model obtained with jModelTest [25] was GTR+G (−Ln=−34634.24).

11.3.3   The Dengue Virus

Dengue virus (DENV) is a pathogen that affects the tropical and subtropical regions all around the world. As a result, 2.5 billion people are at risk from dengue, with an estimate of 50 million dengue infections worldwide every year according to the World Health Organization.

DENV is transmitted among Humans and monkeys by mosquitoes of the genus *Aedes aegypti*, a Flavividae family (genus *Flavivirus*), with a lifetime of around 30 days feeding themselves once every 3 days. To the date, dengue viruses are serologically classified into four antigenically distinct serotypes of mosquito-borne dengue virus identified as DENV-1, DENV-2, DENV-3, and DENV-4 since they are similar from an epidemiologic point of view, but different under a genetic perspective.

In this study, all the available Dengue Virus sequences deposited in GenBank [2] related to the Venezuelan region were used, that is, the four serotypes from the E gene nucleotide envelope sequences of Venezuelan dengue virus of 1,408 bp in

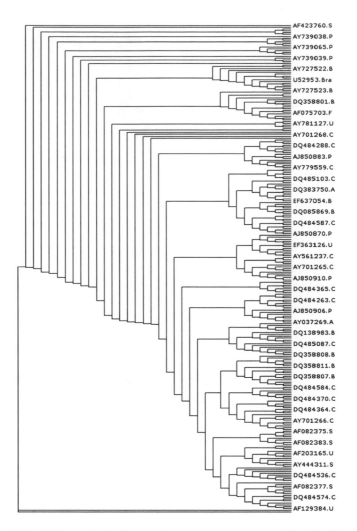

Fig. 11.4 HIV-1 NEF protein phylogeny where some sequences are identified for the reader convenience

length, approximately. Thus, 132 sequences in multi-fasta format were grouped and aligned with the Clustal program [16] using to do so the editor Jalview [5]. The model of nucleotide substitution was obtained with the jModelTest program [25], being the best GTR+I+G (−Ln=68328.13) with a negative log likelihood equal to −Lnl=68328.13.

The calculation demonstrated that all phylogenetic methods resulted in trees that did not differ in their main topology, that is, all specimens were assigned to the same main clades and the relationships between these clades held.

Fig. 11.5 Circular Bayesian phylogenetic tree of the dengue virus E glycoprotein of the Venezuelan isolates with the four serotypes DENV-1, DENV-2, DENV-3, and DENV-4

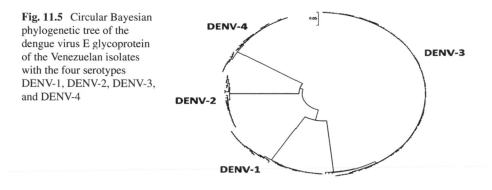

The used computational grid platform has been the same as in previous PhyloGrid works, that is, the ce-eela.ciemat.es site. The calculation lasted for 185 h on 20 cores inside 5 Intel Xeon X5365 (3 GHz, 4 MB L2 cache per 2 cores in the quad-core processor) with 2 GB of memory per core. The output file can be seen in Fig. 11.5 and more details about this work can be found in [14].

11.4   Conclusion

In this work, a brief description of the application and the Web service implemented in the PhyloGrid applications is presented. This Web service is responsible for the communication between MrBayes software and the grid, so it simulates the common MrBayes commands for defining a job as well as the final grid submission and management.

The great advantage of this methodology is that creating a Web service for an application makes this application usable for any Taverna Workbench without requiring any installation.

Some biological results have been also provided. To check if the current categorization really fits the evolution history of the HPV and check out, at the same time, that this methodology is feasible for being used in a more ambitious study focused on the evolution history of HIV-1 is one of them. From the phylogenetic results presented in this work, we can infer that a classification of the HPV based on the variability of the L1 gene is not correct once we have obtained its evolution history with a higher number of sequences. Other works focused on the dengue virus classification were also performed.

Acknowledgments Authors thank in particular the support provided by the EELA-2 Project (E-science grid facility for Europe and Latin America, http://www.eu-eela.org), Grant Agreement No. 223797 of the EU Seventh Research Framework Programme-Research Infrastructures.

References

1. Aiken, C., Konner, J., Landau, N.R., Lenburg, M.E., Trono, D.: Nef induces CD4 endocytosis: requirement for a critical dileucine motif in the membrane-proximal CD4 cytoplasmic domain. Cell 76(5), 853–864 (1994)
2. Benson, D.A., Karsch-Mizrachi, I., Lipman, D.J., Ostell, J., Sayers, E.W.: GenBank. Nucleic Acids Res. 38(suppl1), D46–D51 (2010)
3. Bergsten, J.: A review of long-branch attraction. Cladistics 21(2), 163–193 (2005)
4. Cadotte, M.W., Cardinale, B.J., Oakley, T.H.: Evolutionary history and the effect of biodiversity on plant productivity. PNAS 105(44), 17012–17017 (2008)
5. Clamp, M., Cuff, J., Searle, S.M., Barton, G.J.: The Jalview Java Alignment Editor. Bioinformatics 20(3), 426–427 (2004)
6. Cohen, E., Dehni, G., Sodroski, J.G., Haseltine, W.A.: Human immunodeficiency virus vpr product is a virion-associated regulatory protein. J. Virol. 64(6), 3097–3099 (1990)
7. Cullen, B.R.: HIV-1 Nef protein: an invitation to a kill. Nat. Med. 5(9), 985–986 (1999)
8. García, J.V., Miller, A.D.: Serine phosphorylation-independent downregulation of cell-surface CD4 by nef. Nature 350, 508–511 (1991)
9. Hall, B.G., Salipante, S.J.: Measures of clade confidence do not correlate with accuracy of phylogenetic trees. PLoS Comput. Biol. 3(3), e51 (2007)
10. Huedo, E., Montero, R.S., Llorente, I.M.: The GridWay framework for adaptive scheduling and execution on grids. J. Scalable Comput. Pract. Exp. 6(3), 1–8 (2005)
11. Huelsenbeck, J.P., et al.: Potential applications and pitfalls of Bayesian inference of phylogeny. Syst. Biol. 51, 673–688 (2002)
12. Isea, R., Montes, E., Rubio-Montero, A.J., Mayo, R.: Computational challenges on grid computing for workflows applied to phylogeny. LNCS 5518, 1130–1138 (2009)
13. Isea, R., Montes, E., Rubio-Montero, A.J., Mayo, R.: Challenges and characterization of a Biological system on Grid by means of the PhyloGrid application. In: Proceedings of the 1st EELA-2 Conference, Bogota, pp. 139–146 (2009b)
14. Isea, R., Montes, E., Rubio-Montero, A.J., Rosales, J.D., Rodríguez-Pascual, M.A., Mayo, R.: Characterization of antigenetic serotypes from the dengue virus in Venezuela by means of Grid Computing. In: Solomonides, T., Blanquer, I., Breton, V., Glatard, T., Legré, Y. (eds.) Studies in Health Technology and Informatics 159:234–238 (2010)
15. Korber, B., Muldoon, M., Theiler, J., Gao, F., Gupta, R., Lapedes, A., Hahn, H.B., Wolinsky, S., Bhattacharya, T.: Timing the ancestor of the HIV-1 pandemic strains. Science 288(5472), 1789–1796 (2000)
16. Larkin, M.A., Blackshields, G., Brown, N.P., Chenna, R., McGettigan, P.A., McWilliam, H., Valentin, F., Wallace, I.M., Wilm, A., Lopez, R., Thompson, J.D., Gibson, T.J., Higgins, D.G.: CLUSTAL W and CLUSTALX version 2.0. Bioinformatics 23(21), 2947–2948 (2007)
17. Lowy, D.R., Schiller, J.T.: Prophylactic human papillomavirus vaccines. J. Clin. Investig. 116(5), 1167–1173 (2006)
18. McAuliffe, J.D., Pachter, L., Jordan, M.I.: Multiple-sequence functional annotation and the generalized hidden Markov phylogeny. Bioinformatics 20(12), 1850–1860 (2004)
19. Montes, E., Isea, R., Mayo, R.: PhyloGrid: A development for a workflow in Phylogeny. In: Silva, F. (ed.) Second Iberian Grid Infrastructure Conference Proceedings, pp. 378–387. Netbiblo, Cristina (2008)
20. Nylander, J.A.A., Wilgenbusch, J.C., Warren, D.L., Swofford, D.L.: AWTY: A system for graphical exploration of MCMC convergence in Bayesian phylogenetics. Bioinformatics 24(4), 581–583 (2004)
21. Oinn, T., et al.: Taverna: lessons in creating a workflow environment for the life sciences. Concurrency Comput. Pract. Exp. 18(10), 1067–1100 (2005)
22. Page, R.: Tree View: An application to display phylogenetic trees on personal computers. Bioinformatics 12, 357–358 (1996)

23. Pennisi, E.: Revising HIV's History. ScienceNOW. Retrieved from http://sciencenow. sciencemag.org/cgi/content/full/2008/625/1 (2008)
24. Pérez, J., Castañeda-García, A., Jenke-Kodama, H., Müller, R., Muñoz-Dorado, J.: Eukaryotic-like protein kinases in the prokaryotes and the myxobacterial kinome. PNAS **105**(41), 15950–15955 (2008)
25. Posada, D.: jModelTest: phylogenetic model averaging. Mol. Biol. Evol. **25**, 1253–1256 (2008)
26. Rannala, B., Yang, Z.: Probability distribution of molecular evolutionary trees: a new method of phylogenetic inference. J. Mol. Evol. **43**(3), 304–311 (1996)
27. Ronquist, F., Huelsenbeck, J.P.: MrBayes 3: Bayesian phylogenetic inference under mixed models. Bioinformatics **19**(12), 1572–1574 (2003)
28. Sun, J., Xu, J., Liu, Z., Liu, Q., Zhao, A., Shi, T., Li, Y.: Refined phylogenetic profiles method for predicting protein–protein interactions. Bioinformatics **21**(16), 3409–3415 (2005)
29. Thomas, M., Gilbert, P., Rambaut, A., Wlasiuk, G., Spira, J.T., Pitchenik, E.A., Worobey, M.: The emergence of HIV/AIDS in the Americas and beyond. Proc. Natl. Acad. Sci. U.S.A **104**, 18566–18570 (2007)
30. Woese, C.R.: The universal ancestor. Proc. Natl. Acad. Sci U.S.A **95**, 6854–6859 (1998)

Chapter 12
The Usage of the Grid in the Simulation of the Comet Oort-Cloud Formation

Giuseppe Leto, Ján Astaloš, Marián Jakubík, Luboš Neslušan, and Piotr A. Dybczyński

Abstract The research of the reservoirs of small bodies in the Solar System can help us to refine our theory of the origin and evolution of the whole planetary system we live in. With this chapter, we introduce a numerical simulation of the evolution of an initial proto-planetary disc for 2 Gyr period, in which 10,038 studied test particles, representing the disc, are perturbed by four giant planets in their current orbits and having their current masses. In addition, Galactic-tide and stellar perturbations are considered. The simulation is performed using the grid computing. We explain which circumstances allow us to use the system of independent, online not communicating CPUs. Our simulation describes the probable evolution of the Oort cloud population. In contrast to the previous simulations by other authors, we find an extremely low formation efficiency of this population. The largest number of the bodies (66.4%) was ejected into the interstellar space. Besides other results, we reveal a dominance of high galactic inclinations of comet-cloud orbits.

12.1 Introduction

The Oort cloud (OC) is a comet reservoir at large heliocentric distances. Its origin is related to that of giant planets and trans-Neptunian populations of small bodies. Since the databases of the small bodies observed in the planetary region have largely

G. Leto (✉)
INAF-Osservatorio Astrofisico di Catania, Via Santa Sofia 78, Catania I-95123, Italy
e-mail: gle@oact.inaf.it; gle@astrct.oact.inaf.it

J. Astaloš
Institute of Informatics, Slovak Academy of Sciences, Bratislava, Slovakia

M. Jakubík • L. Neslušan
Astronomical Institute, Slovak Academy of Sciences, Tatranská Lomnica 05960, Slovakia

P.A. Dybczyński
Astronomical Observatory, A. Mickiewicz University, Słoneczna 36, 60-286 Poznań, Poland

N.P. Preve (ed.), *Grid Computing: Towards a Global Interconnected Infrastructure*,
Computer Communications and Networks, DOI 10.1007/978-0-85729-676-4_12,
© Springer-Verlag London Limited 2011

grown during the last decades, we can also improve our knowledge of the distant comet reservoir.

The most reliable and, thus, mostly used method to study the OC-formation scenario is a numerical simulation. The initial population of small bodies, which was formed in the Proto-Planetary Disc (PPD) in the beginning of the Solar System existence, can be represented by a large set of massless Test Particles (TPs). Using a robust computational capacity, the dynamics of these TPs in the gravitational field of the Sun and under perturbations of giant planets, as well as relevant outer perturbers can be followed, via numerical integration, for a reasonable long period.

In this chapter, we describe the simulation of the OC formation using the grid computing. Specifically, a brief summary of the concerning investigations in the past is provided in Sect. 12.2, the initial cosmogonic assumptions are given in Sect. 12.3, the computational procedure and grid usage are described in Sect. 12.4, and important achieved results are presented in Sect. 12.5. The conclusions are presented in the final Sect. 12.6.

12.2 The Past Investigations

The first observationally proved theory of the Oort cloud existence was published by Oort in [14], a Dutch astronomer, in the middle of twentieth century. Having 19 original (before entering the planetary perturbation region) cometary orbits, Oort noticed the clustering of comet aphelia in large heliocentric distances. This fact led him to predict the existence of the cloud of comets surrounding the Solar System. Later, the cloud was named by his name.

In a subsequent period, the formation of the OC was studied by Safronov in [15] and Fernández in [10], who dealt with "cleaning" of the planetary region in an early era of the Solar System and found that the OC was filled in by the perturbations of Neptune and, in a lesser degree, Uranus. Only few per cents of comet nuclei in the cloud could originate in Jupiter and Saturn ejections.

In the first stage of the research, the OC-comet semimajor axes were predicted to exceed ~20,000 AU, as was observed. Hills in [11], however, noticed that this inner border could be an artifact due to the observational selection. In the Zone of Visibility (ZV) of comets, we can, even at the present, observe only the comets in very distant orbits, on which the outer perturbers can largely reduce the comet perihelion distances within a single orbital period. The reduction from the region beyond the Jupiter–Saturn dynamical barrier down to the ZV is demanded in this context. The comets with shorter aphelion distances can also come to the ZV, but the information about the site of their origin is lost before they are observed. Consequently, the inner part of the OC cannot be detected on the basis of original cometary orbits. Hills in [11] predicted that the hypothetical inner OC should be from zero to ~100 times more populated than the "classical" outer cloud.

Although the first investigations had the character of numerical simulations, the algorithms to integrate the orbits of considered bodies were based on the three-body approximation or severe simplifications. A low number of TPs in orbits that represented an already evolved stage were considered. Only the supposed most important part of the TP evolution used to be followed. The first relatively large numerical simulation, with several thousand TPs, was performed by Duncan et al. in [4]. For 4.5 Gyr, they integrated the motion of TPs in the initially low inclined, but already highly eccentric orbits. According them, the number density profile between heliocentric distances, r, 3,000 and 50,000 AU can be described by the power law as $\infty r^{-3.5}$. About 20% of the TPs residing in the OC after 4.5 Gyr were in its outer part. The directional distribution of cloud orbits was completely random after about 1 Gyr of evolution.

Another simulation of the OC and, also, trans-Neptunian scattered-disc formation, via a robust numerical simulation, was performed by Dones et al. [2, 3]. In comparison with Duncan et al. in [4], they assumed more realistic initial orbits, which were not only low inclined, but also low eccentric. For 4 Gyr, they integrated 2000 TPs in so-called cold run and 1,000 TPs in so-called hot run. The initial conditions in the cold run were more adequate to the assumed real conditions. In this run, the authors found a shallower number-density distribution, with the index of slope ≈ -2.8 (≈ -1.9 for the inner and ≈ -3.7 for the outer OC) than Duncan et al. in [4]. It implies the ratio of inner and outer OC populations about 1:1. Another difference in the results by Duncan et al. in [4] and Dones et al. [2, 3] was the OC formation efficiency. While Duncan et al. in [4] found $\approx 25\%$ of initially considered TPs residing in the OC at the end of their simulation, Dones et al. [2, 3] found only 5.2% of such TPs.

The individual authors or author groups have considered some different initial conditions and some different methods in their simulations. To find which conditions and/or methods are then main reasons of the differences in the results, further simulations are needed.

In the published papers on the OC formation, no specification of used computational equipment has been provided. However, all above-mentioned authors considered the massless TPs, which did not influence each other or, reversibly, the Sun and planets. So, we can deduce that a given CPU, computing the orbits of a subset of TPs, did not need to communicate the other CPUs. Or, it needed to communicate only a single CPU computing the orbits of four massive planets. The computation could be performed using a system of independently working CPUs.

12.3   Our Initial Model

We consider 10,038 TPs representing an initial PPD, the part situated in the distances from 4 to 50 AU (AU is the astronomical unit) from the Sun. The TP distribution corresponds to $r^{-3/2}$ surface density profile. The TPs are initially on low-inclination and low-eccentric orbits. As already mentioned in Sect. 12.1, we follow the dynamical evolution of the TPs in the gravitational potential of the Sun via numerical integration taking into account the perturbations by (1) four Jovian planets in their current orbits and having their current masses, (2) Galactic tide characterized by the density of matter in the solar neighborhood equal to 0.1 M pc^{-3} (M the mass of the Sun and pc^3 is cube parsec) and Oort constants $A = -B = 13$ km s^{-1} kpc^{-1}, and (3) passing stars.

In the latter, we consider 13 characteristic spectral types with an individual radius of the sphere of influence for each type having a different mean velocity and mass. The distance at which an incoming star is added as a perturber in the model ranges from 204,000 AU for M5 stars to 1,973,000 AU for B0 stars. We integrate all TPs that remain within the sphere of 100,000 AU radius for the period of 2 Gyr. The TPs approaching the Sun or planet closer than their physical radius (collided TPs) or TPs exceeding the 100,000 AU border (ejected TPs) are discarded from a further integration. No interaction between TPs or action of a TP on a massive body is considered. The initial assumptions of our simulation are described providing more details in [6, 13].

12.4   The Computational Procedure and Grid Usage

There are several well-known numerical integrators to calculate the orbits of pointlike bodies in the celestial mechanics. We use the RA15 subroutine [9], which is the part of the MERCURY software package [1]. The package enables to consider two categories of bodies, with nonzero and zero mass, and additionally defined perturbations. The Sun and four planets (Jupiter, Saturn, Uranus, and Neptune) belong to the first category, while the massless TPs to the second category. The Galactic tide is added to the package as a user-defined subroutine. The stellar perturbations are calculated by the improved impulse approximation [5]. At the moment of the closest approach of a given star to the Sun, the numerical integration of all TP orbits, by the MERCURY, is interrupted and the perturbation impulse to the TPs is added by an extra code. Then the integration goes on using the MERCURY, again.

The whole computation is designed for 240 independent CPUs in the grid computational system. Specifically, we used the CPUs available within the Virtual Organization for Central Europe (VOCE) and two Italian parts of the grid, TriGrid and Consorzio COMETA.

The distribution to a number of mutually independent CPUs is possible because of the character of the computational task. Since the TPs do not influence each other, there is no need of the information exchange about their dynamical state among the various CPUs. About 50,000 interactions of five massive bodies on these $\approx$10,000 TPs can be divided into an arbitrary number of independent subtasks.

A small difficulty occurs due to the mutual interaction among the five massive bodies. Fortunately, there are only 20 such interactions at every few-millisecond computational step, which can be repeated by every used CPU. The Galactic-tide

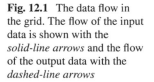

Fig. 12.1 The data flow in the grid. The flow of the input data is shown with the *solid-line arrows* and the flow of the output data with the *dashed-line arrows*

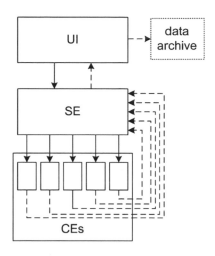

and stellar perturbations are also calculated by every CPU. These are, however, simple and do not represent any significant burden of the CPU.

The grid system does not permit a computation longer than a certain limit. To respect this constraint, the whole computation is divided into a series of subperiods. Each of these subperiods is chosen to last about 2 days.

The distribution of the individual subtasks (on individual CPUs) into the grid is performed in four steps (see Fig. 12.1). The initial data are settled onto the so-called User Interface (UI), i.e., a computer serving as a user terminal. In the second step, the data are copied to so-called Storage Element (SE). In the third step, a management routine is run on the UI. This routine emplaces the individual subtasks from the SE on the individual Computing Elements (CEs) in the grid, initializes starting the computing, and moves the resultant, output data back onto the SE. In the last step, the resultant data from the given subperiod of the computation are moved from the SE on the UI (and further to an archival medium). The second to fourth steps are repeated until the whole computation is completed.

We found that the computation is much faster if we do not allow an emplacement of our subtasks on whatever CPUs in the grid. We constrain our choice to only those CPUs which have the working frequency 1 GHz or higher. And, the CPU must be absolutely free in the moment of starting of our subtask; therefore, this subtask is not forced to wait in a queue.

Testing the calculations using a single 2.8-GHz CPU, we estimated that this CPU would have to continuously work about 21 years to complete the whole task. An ideally running system of the CPUs in grid would need about 3 months to complete the task. In reality, the task was completed within about 5 months, much faster than using a single CPU.

12.5   Results

12.5.1   Inner and Outer Oort Cloud

The division of the OC into its inner and outer parts was already mentioned in
Sect. 12.1. Before describing the achieved results, let us explain the reason for this
division in more detail. The outer perturbers can cause a reduction of comet perihelia down to the ZV. In the case of the comets coming from the outer OC, the reduction is so large that the comets overcome the Jupiter–Saturn dynamical barrier
within a single orbital revolution. Their perihelia are reduced from a value larger
than ≈15 AU to a value corresponding with the occurrence of the comet in the ZV.
The latter is currently situated inside the sphere having the radius ≈6.5 AU. Due to
this favorable circumstance, we are able to trace the comet orbits back, outside of
planetary perturbing zone, and gain the information about the site of comet origin.
The outer OC can therefore be studied on the basis of these comets. On contrary, the
dynamical information on the comets coming to the ZV from the inner OC is lost
before they reach this zone. The inner OC is, therefore, still hypothetical. We regard
a comet as an OC resident, when its semimajor axis, a, is larger than 2,000 AU and
its perihelion is well detached from the planetary region. Specifically, we require the
perihelion distance must be larger than 50 AU. The comet is in the inner OC if its
$a \leq 25,000$ AU, and in the outer OC if $a > 25,000$ AU.

12.5.2   The Evolution of the OC Population

Two snapshots of planetary region in our simulation are shown in Fig. 12.2. Only
two remnants of the initial PPD, the well-known Jupiter Trojans (around the orbit of
the innermost Jovian planet) and the trans-Neptunian belt, survive after 2 Gyr. We

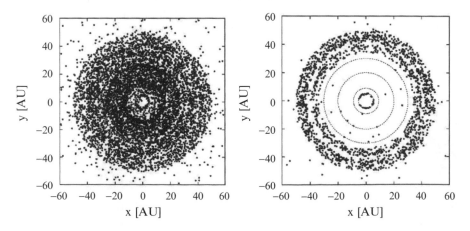

Fig. 12.2 The projection of the TP positions to the invariable plane at 1 Myr (*left*) and 2 Gyr
(*right*). The orbits of Jovian planets are shown with the *dashed-line* ellipses (*almost circles*)

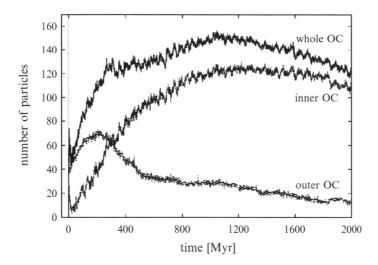

Fig. 12.3 The evolution of the population of the Oort cloud during the first 2 Gyr period of its existence; the evolution of *inner* and *outer* parts of the OC are also shown

further find that 6669 TPs, i.e., 66.4%, were ejected into the interstellar space at that time. A small fraction of TPs was, nevertheless, delivered to the OC. The evolutions of its population as well as subpopulation of the inner and outer OC are shown in Fig. 12.3 for the entire studied period. The outer OC population reaches its maximum at about 210 Myr, while that of the inner OC at about 1,250 Myr.

Our simulation predicts an extremely low efficiency of the OC formation. Only 1.1% (0.14%) of all TPs end in the inner (outer) OC at 2 Gyr. In the simulation by Duncan et al. in [4], 20% (5%) of their TPs ended, at 4.5 Gyr, in the corresponding parts of the OC. According to Dones et al. in [2, 3], 2.5% (their cold run) or 1.7% (their hot run) ended, at 4 Gyr, in the outer OC. In the inner OC, they found 3.5% of cold-run TPs and 1.7% of hot-run TPs.

The most significant reason for the difference seems to originate in a large stochasticity of the problem [7, 12]. In Fig. 12.4, the dispersion of the outer OC population is shown for 750 Myr. This dispersion is estimated dividing the whole set of 10,038 considered TPs into five equal subsets. The initial surface density profile of the subsets is the same, but the individual orbits in each subsets are not identical. The evolutions of the minimum and maximum outer OC populations considering these five subsets are illustrated with down and upper, respectively, dashed curves. The evolution considering the entire set of TPs is shown with the solid curve. The numbers of TPs in each time is divided by five to gauge the behavior to those corresponding with the subsets. The typical dispersion for a simulation with the number of TPs equal to that in a subset, i.e., 2007 or 2008 TPs, is about 25%.

The dispersion for the whole set of 10,038 TPs is expected to be few times lower. From this point of view, our simulation can predict the order-of-magnitude evolution of the outer OC population. This analysis was made on the basis of another simulation for 750 Myr, in which the TPs were followed up to the distance of

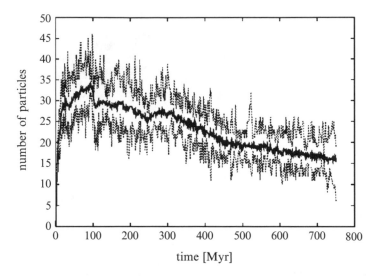

Fig. 12.4 The dispersion of the outer OC population estimated on the basis of five randomly generated subsets from the whole set of TPs considered in our simulation of the OC formation. The uncertainty of the determination of the evolution of outer OC population is indicated by upper and down *dashed curves*. The *solid curve* in the middle shows the evolution of subset averaged outer OC population

400,000 AU. Consequently, the number of TPs in the outer OC is higher than in the first simulation – cf. the population in Fig. 12.2 with that in Fig. 12.4 multiplied by 5.

However, the dispersion considering the subset TPs can, from time to time, exceed such a high value as 60%. An occasional, relatively high increase can also be expected for the larger, 10,000-TP set simulation.

In such case, the result would not be typical. A higher random negative deviation from the typical prediction in our simulation in combination with a lower random positive deviation in the Dones et al. in [2, 3] simulation can perhaps explain the discrepancy between our and their estimates of outer OC population. We hope the future studies considering a larger number of TPs, than we considered, will converge to the quantitatively unique model.

12.5.3 The Radial Distribution and Sites of Origin of Comets in the OC

At 2 Gyr, the OC occurs to be centrally concentrated. The TP distribution in the range $5,000 - 100,000$ AU can be fitted by a power law ($\propto r^s$) with the index of slope $s = -3.529^{+0.031}_{-0.024}$. This value is very similar to $s = -3.5$ found for $3,000 - 50,000$ AU interval by Duncan, Quinn, and Tremaine in [4], but different from $s = -2.9$ found for this interval by Emel'yanenko, Asher, and Bailey in [8] by other method.

The distribution of the semimajor axis at 2 Gyr can also be described by the power law with the index of slope $s = -1.74$ in the 5,000–50,000 AU interval. To reveal the origin of the OC bodies in a more detail, we divide the initial PPD into these regions: Jupiter region extending from 4 to 8 AU from the Sun, Saturn region 8–15 AU, Uranus region 15–24 AU, Neptune region 24–35 AU, and the Edgeworth–Kuiper-belt region 35–50 AU. From these regions, 5, 7, 39, 39, and 20 (2, 1, 3, 3, and 3) TPs of the initial 10038, respectively, reside in the inner (outer) OC at 2 Gyr.

In contrast to the past knowledge, a significant fraction of TPs came to the OC also from the Jupiter–Saturn region. Therefore, the composition of comet C/1999 S4, found to correspond with the origin of this body in this region, is no longer any surprise. As well, another significant fraction came to both inner and outer OC from the Edgeworth–Kuiper-belt region, which was regarded as dynamically inactive, in the past. In process of the dynamical activation of objects, the mean-motion resonances with Neptune seem to be important. The objects being in 8:5, 5:3, and 7:4 resonances were excited to come, finally, to the OC, its outer as well as inner parts. The 3:2 resonance (i.e., Plutinos) contributed with the objects which come to the inner OC.

12.5.4   The Deviations from the Spherical Symmetry

Duncan et al. in [4] and Dones et al. in [2, 3] concluded that the orbits in the comet cloud were randomized after about 1 Gyr of the evolution. This circumstance implies the spherical symmetry of the OC. Our simulation provides a different spatial picture of this reservoir. The difference is mostly transparent in the distribution of the galactic inclination. When speaking about this orbital element on the timescale of 2 Gyr, we must explain our approach. Namely, the Sun moves around the center of the Galaxy and the common galactic coordinate frame is the rotating frame (its x- and y-axes rotate) on the long timescale. To eliminate this problem, we used so-called zero-time galactic coordinate frame. Its axes were identical to the common frame in the beginning of the simulation. During simulation, the orientation of the axes in space was kept stable. So, the zero-time frame is the inertial coordinate frame.

However, when one analyzes the galactic inclination, this orbital element is the same in both zero-time and common galactic coordinate frames, because these frames have identical z-axis and, consequently, the coordinate x-y plane to which the galactic inclination is related. The values of the galactic inclination spans from about 20° to about 160°, whereby the high galactic inclinations dominate among the OC orbits. It is well documented in Fig. 12.5. Such domination can be explained by the action of the dominant outer perturber, Galactic tide. It causes periodic variations of the orbital elements of OC comets. The galactic inclination of orbits, which have their perihelia in the minimum of the periodic libration cycle of this element inside the planetary region, approaches the value of 90° for a relatively long time. Therefore, the probability to find a comet in an orbit with a high galactic inclination is much higher than to find it in a lower galactic inclination. This is reflected in the galactic-inclination distribution.

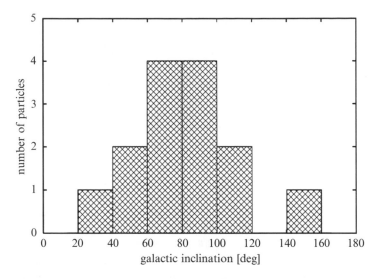

Fig. 12.5 The distribution of the galactic inclination of TPs in the outer OC at 2 Gyr. The modified galactic coordinate system, with x-axis oriented outward from the Galactic center and z-axis oriented toward the South Galactic pole, is used

The orbits in the innermost part of the inner OC have been changed very slowly and, thus, have remained low inclined to the invariable plane (in a similar location as the Ecliptic) of the Solar System during the entire age of the Solar System. This association to the invariable plane can also be documented with the help of final data, for 2 Gyr, from our simulation. We know that the inclination to Ecliptic of the known trans-Neptunian objects does not exceed 40°. The inclination to Ecliptic in our simulation is lower than 45° for the TPs with semimajor axis $a \leq 4{,}000$ AU. Up to $a \approx 8{,}500$ AU, the inclination is within the 0–90° interval.

The interesting phenomenon is the disappearance of TPs with the inclination lower than about 20° for $a \geq 5{,}500$ AU. This phenomenon is likely due to the geometry of initial appearance of bodies in the inner OC and to very long periods of variation of inclination in this part of the OC. The bodies are delivered there along an orbit with a close-to-zero inclination to Ecliptic. This value, which corresponds to the minimum of the inclination within the libration cycle caused by the Galactic tide, is changed relatively quickly. The newly coming bodies move only a short time in orbits with the inclination approaching zero. The nearly zero ecliptical inclination corresponds to ~60° galactic inclination (the inclination of the Galactic Equator to the Ecliptic is 60.2°), which is changed by the tide toward a higher value approaching 90°. When the higher value is reached, the inclination is changed slowly. And, the time of 2 Gyr (or shorter in the case of TP coming into the inner OC later than at the beginning) appears to be too short the libration cycle was completed and a value of ecliptical inclination lower than about 20° was reached again. For $a \geq 10{,}000$ AU, the inclination to the Ecliptic ranges from ~20° to 150°. It does not exceed the value of ~150° even at the outer border of inner OC in 25 000 AU. The absence of orbits with the ecliptical inclination higher than ~150° and lower than ~20°, for $a \geq 5,500$ AU, implies than the inner OC is not spherically symmetric in any part.

12.5.5   The Inner Border of the Inner Oort Cloud

The definition of the OC is not unique. Some authors regarded all comets with semimajor axis exceeding a down limit, several thousands of astronomical units, as the residents of the OC. Another group required a detachment of cometary orbits from the influence of planets, i.e., they also constrained the cometary perihelia by a down limit. From a dynamical point of view, both requirements that (1) the orbits of OC comets must be large enough to be significantly influenced by the outer perturbers and (2) they should no longer be significantly perturbed by planets are reasonable. In this Section, we deal with the determination of the specific value of semimajor axis separating the inner OC from the outer trans-Neptunian population, i.e., from the scattered disc and extended scattered disc.

Bodies close to the planetary region are exclusively perturbed by giant planets, in particular by Neptune. In the context of this partial study, we neglect rare stellar perturbations occurring in the periods of extremely deep passages of stars through the Solar System as well as rare mutual perturbations of bodies at their extremely close approaches. If a planetary perturbation enlarges the aphelion distance of a body, it can become a subject of significant perturbations by the outer perturbers, especially the Galactic tide. We can, therefore, distinguish between the dynamical regime when a body is perturbed only by planets and the regime when it is also significantly perturbed by the outer perturbers. In this Section, we attempt to reveal a border between these regimes. Once an object is perturbed by the Galactic tide, its perihelion distance is earlier or later enlarged and it becomes the resident of the OC.

The planetary perturbations become weak, when a perturbed-body perihelion distance is enlarged far beyond the orbit of the outermost planet, Neptune. Therefore, the perihelion distance cannot exceed a certain upper limit, if the given body is perturbed only by planets. In this situation, the bodies can appear in large heliocentric distances when they move in the orbits with an enlarged semimajor axis, a, but with the perihelion inside or near the planetary region. Consequently, the orbital eccentricity, e, has to increase, approaching unity as the body reaches the OC region. This increase can be seen in Fig. 12.6 (at the left border of the plots), demonstrating the position of all bodies with $a = 3$–50 AU in the eccentricity vs. semimajor axis phase space (also the giant-planet crossers are included).

As it is already mentioned in Sect. 12.5.4, a characteristic consequence of the action of dominant outer perturber and the z-component of the Galactic tide, are periodic variations of orbital elements, with the exception of semimajor axis, which is changed negligibly. The decrease of the eccentricity of some bodies for $a \geq 2,500$ AU in Fig. 12.6 must be an effect of the Galactic tide and, in part, stellar perturbations. This implies that, the border between the trans-Neptunian populations and inner OC is $a_b \leq 2,500$ AU, in terms of the semimajor axis. A more detailed

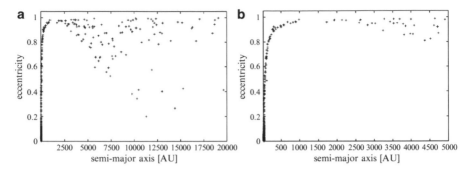

Fig. 12.6 The distribution of the simulated TPs in the eccentricity vs. semimajor axis phase space, in two intervals of the axis. The distribution is constructed for the final time of the simulation at 2 Gyr

analysis reveals that this border can be $a_b \geq 1{,}000$ AU. This uncertainty obviously explains why no more exact specification of the border has been made in the past. Even when we consider ~10,000 TPs and integrate their motion on the Gyr timescale, there is a lack of TPs at the border, therefore it is difficult to diminish the uncertainty.

It is worthy to note that this border is time-dependent, in principle. The Galactic tide also changes the orbits with a very small value of semimajor axis, if there is enough time. Because of practical reasons, it is reasonable to consider only a significant change that can occur during the age of the Solar System. An analysis of the dispersion of eccentricity, perihelion distance, and inclination to Ecliptic as the functions of semimajor axis shows no distinguishable reduction of a_b between 1 and 2 Gyr, however. The dispersion of the orbital elements beyond $\approx 2{,}500$ AU increases with time, but the proper value of the upper limit, a_b, remains practically the same. Consequently, we can expect the upper constraint of a_b to be about 2,500 AU even at 4.5 Gyr. Anyway, the above specification $1{,}000 < a_b < 2{,}500$ AU is too vague.

12.6   Conclusions

The usage of 240 independently working CPUs in the GRID computational system appears to be sufficient to map the formation and further evolution of the distant comet reservoir. To be more specific, the following partial cosmogonic conclusions can be stated on the basis of our simulation:

1. The OC actually formed and its population evolved to survive the entire age of the Solar System. The population of the inner OC reached its maximum about 1,250 Myr after the beginning of the simulation. The population of the outer OC was peaked much sooner, about 210 Myr after the beginning.
2. The formation efficiency in our simulation was extremely low: 1.1% of the considered TPs ended in the inner OC and only 0.14% in the outer OC, at

2 Gyr. These values are lower than the corresponding values found by other authors. The main reason for the discrepancy can be a certain stochasticity of the formation process as well as too a short outer border up to which we followed the motion of the TPs and still too a low number of the TPs (though our number was 5 times higher than the number considered by other authors in the preceding similar simulation).

3. At 2 Gyr, the OC occurs to be centrally concentrated. The TP distribution in the range 5,000–1,00,000 AU, fitted by the power law, has the index of slope equal to −3.53. The distribution of the semimajor axis at 2 Gyr can also be described by the power law. Its index of slope is −1.74 in the 5,000–50,000 AU interval of this orbital element.

4. The cometary nuclei had to come to the OC mainly from the Uranus–Neptune region of the PPD. However, the fractions of bodies, which came from the Jupiter, Saturn, and Edgeworth–Kuiper-belt regions were not negligible as thought in the past. Among these three regions, the latter was, surprisingly, the dominant source. In the past, the region was regarded as absolutely dynamically inactive in respect to the OC formation.

5. In contrast to previous authors, we did not confirm the complete randomization of the OC orbits, even in its outer part, and the consequent cloud's spherical symmetry. The inclination to Ecliptic increased above 45° only for objects in orbits with semimajor axes exceeding ≈4,000 AU and above 90° only for those with semimajor axes larger than ≈8,500 AU. In the inner OC, the inclination of orbits with semimajor above 10,000 AU did not rise above 150°. In the outer OC, the orbits with a high galactic inclination appeared to be dominant.

6. The natural inner border of the OC in terms of semimajor axis is somewhere in the interval between ≈1,000 and ≈2,500 AU. A more exact specification appeared impossible with the considered number of TPs.

Although the performed simulation revealed several specific details of the scenario of the comet-cloud formation, some questions still remain opened or answered poorly. We met especially the problem of the stochasticity of formation process and uncertain inner border of the OC. The stochasticity could be reduced and the border could be determined more precisely, if a larger number of TPs occurred in both OC and in the region between the trans-Neptunian populations and OC. This can be expected if a larger initial number of TPs, at least an order of magnitude, is considered. This requirement implies a usage of the system of at least few thousand CPUs in future simulations.

Acknowledgments G.L. thanks PI2S2 Project managed by the Consorzio COMETA, http://www.pi2s2.it and http://www.consorzio-cometa.it for the computational resources and technical support. M.J. and L.N. thank the project "Enabling Grids for E-sciencE II" (http://www.eu-egee.org/) for the provided computational capacity and support in the development of the computer code, which was necessary for the management of tasks on the GRID. They also acknowledge the partial support of this work by VEGA – the Slovak Grant Agency for Science (grant No. 0011). P.A.D. acknowledges the partial support of this work from Polish Ministry of Science and Higher Education (year 2009, grant No. N N203 302335).

References

1. Chambers, J.E.: A hybrid symplectic integrator that permits close encounters between massive bodies. MNRAS **304**, 793–799 (1999)
2. Dones, L., Weissman, P.R., Levison, H.F., Duncan, M.J.: Oort cloud formation and dynamics. In: Festou, M., Keller, H.U., Weaver, H.A. (eds.) Comets II, pp. 153–174. University of Arizona Press, Tucson (2004)
3. Dones, L., Levison, H.F., Duncan, M.J., Weissman, P.R.: Simulation of the formation of the Oort cloud. I. The Reference Model. Private communication (2005)
4. Duncan, M., Quinn, T., Tremaine, S.: The formation and extent of the solar system comet cloud. Astron. J. **94**, 1330–1338 (1987)
5. Dybczyński, P.A.: Impulse approximation improved. Celestial Mech. Dyn. Astron. **58**(2), 139–150 (1994)
6. Dybczyński, P.A., Leto, G., Jakubìk, M., Paulech, T., Neslušan, L.: The simulation of the outer Oort cloud formation - The first giga-year of the evolution. Astron. Astrophys. **487**(1), 345–355 (2008)
7. Dybczyński, P.A., Leto, G., Jakubìk, M., Neslušan, L.: Notes on the outer-Oort-cloud formation efficiency in the simulation of Oort cloud formation. Astron. Astrophys. **497**(3), 847–850 (2009)
8. Emel'yanenko, V.V., Asher, D.J., Bailey, M.E.: The fundamental role of the Oort cloud in determining the flux of comets through the planetary system. Mon. Notices R. Astron. Soc. **381**(2), 779–789 (2007)
9. Everhart, E.: An efficient integrator that uses Gauss-Radau spacings. In: Carusi, A., Valsecchi, G.B. (eds.) Dynamics of Comets: Their Origin and Evolution, pp. 185–202. Reidel, Dordrecht (1985)
10. Fernández, J.A.: The formation and dynamical survival of the comet cloud. In: Carusi, A., Valsecchi, G.B. (eds.) Dynamics of Comets: Their Origin and Evolution, pp. 45–70. Reidel, Dordrecht (1985)
11. Hills, J.G.: Comet showers and the steady-state infall of comets from the Oort cloud. Astron. J. **86**, 1730–1740 (1981)
12. Kaib, N.A., Quinn, T.: The formation of the Oort cloud in open cluster environments. Icarus **197**, 221–238 (2008)
13. Leto, G., Jakubìk, M., Paulech, T., Neslušan, L., Dybczyński, P.A.: The structure of the inner Oort cloud from the simulation of its formation for 2 Gyr. Mon. Notices R. Astron. Soc. **391**, 1350–1358 (2008)
14. Oort, J.H.: The structure of the cloud of comets surrounding the Solar System and a hypothesis concerning its origin. Bull. Astron. Inst. Neth. **11**, 91–110 (1950)
15. Safronov, V.S., Chebotarev, G.A., Kazimirchak-Polonskaia, E.I., Marsden, B.G.: Ejection of bodies from the solar system in the course of the accumulation of the giant planets and the formation of the cometary cloud. In: The Motion, Evolution of Orbits, and Origin of Comets – Proceedings of the IAU Symposium No. 45, Leningrad, pp. 329–334. Springer, New York/ Berlin (1972)

Index

N.P. Preve (ed.), *Grid Computing: Towards a Global Interconnected Infrastructure*,
Computer Communications and Networks, DOI 10.1007/978-0-85729-676-4,
© Springer-Verlag London Limited 2011